Social Issues and Service at the Middle Level

edited by

Samuel Totten
University of Arkansas–Fayetteville

Jon E. Pedersen
East Carolina University

Allyn and Bacon
Boston • London • Toronto • Sydney • Tokyo • Singapore

Jon E. Pedersen dedicates this volume to his wife Conni M. Pedersen, his best friend, whose love, support, and encouragement has guided and inspired him through the journey of life.

Samuel Totten dedicates this volume to some of the many individuals who have inspired him to think about, wrestle with, and address key social issues that confront humanity today:

Kathleen Barta	*Robert Jay Lifton*	*Charles Rivera*
Israel W. Charny	*Leo Kuper*	*John Anthony Scott*
Maxine Greene	*Sam Natoli*	*Rose Styron*
Robert Hitchcock	*William S. Parsons*	*Michael Price Totten*
Bruce Hoffman	*Jon E. Pedersen*	*Elie Wiesel*

LC
220.5
.S63
1997

Copyright © 1997 by Allyn & Bacon
A Viacom Company
Needham Heights, MA 02194

Library of Congress Cataloging-in-Publication Data

Social issues and service at the middle level / edited by Samuel
    Totten, Jon E. Pedersen.
        p.   cm.
    Includes bibliographical references.
    ISBN 0-205-15093-4
    1. Student volunteers in social service—United States.   2. Middle
schools—United States—Curricula.   I. Totten, Samuel.
II. Pedersen, Jon E.
LC220.5.S63   1996
361.3´7—dc20   96-13392
                                                                                    CIP

Printed in the United States of America
10 9 8 7 6 5 4 3 2 1   00 99 98 97 96

Contents

PART 2   Service

Preface

AUTHORS AND ESSAYS IN THIS BOOK

In order to solicit essays for *Social Issues and Service at the Middle Level,* we sent "author calls" out to colleagues as well as scores of individuals who are noted for their work in the areas of social issues, community service, and/or service learning. We also published close to a dozen "author calls" in various education journals. Finally, we asked those individuals who submitted proposals to encourage their colleagues and friends to submit chapter proposals. Over a two-year period, we received close to 100 proposals.

Each proposal was critiqued and rated according to (1) the significance of the topic, (2) the interest level of the project, and (3) the clarity of the writing. Early on, we also decided that since the essays in the book would focus on the practical aspects of incorporating the study of social issues into the extant curriculum and service through learning, it was vital to include the work, voices, and ideas of as many middle-level school practitioners as possible. In other words, we purposely selected a fair number of proposals submitted by individual middle school teachers, middle school teachers *and* administrators, and middle school teachers *and* professors. What we did not want was a book of essays solely or even mostly written by professors of education who were not in the "trenches" on a daily basis. Although we value the expertise of such professors (indeed, we are professors of education), we especially prize the hard work, unique perspectives, and valuable insights of those folks who work with middle-level students on a daily basis—middle school teachers and administrators.

We also made a sincere effort to include educators from various regions from around the United States. We assumed that educators in different areas of the country would likely be focusing on different issues, partly because their regions would dictate the type of topics and projects that would most engage their students.

In addition, we made a point of seeking pieces from as diverse a group of educators as possible (e.g., women and men, individuals with varied professional experience as well as length of experience, different ethnic backgrounds and races, etc.). In doing so, we sent calls to a wide variety of journals, including those whose readerships reach educators of diverse ethnic and racial backgrounds (e.g., *The Black Educator, The Radical Teacher,* and *Teaching Tolerance*).

Finally, we also tried to include a more or less even number of essays that address the study of social issues and learning through service. Concomitantly, we included as many different social issues (e.g., the plight of the disabled vis-à-vis access to buildings, the homeless, genocide, the environment) and types of projects (e.g., environmental, tutoring, befriending and caring for the elderly) as we possibly could.

We are pleased that we reached most of our goals. That is, we have an excellent mix of contributors: 11 middle-level teachers, 4 middle-level school administrators, 1 state department employee, 9 (outside school) project coordinators, and 8 professors (one of whom was a social studies supervisor in a district office when he and a middle-level teacher initially submitted a chapter proposal). Among the contributors are 20 women and 16 men. Combined, the contributors represent 13 states: Alabama, Colorado, Florida, Illinois, Iowa, Maryland, Massachusetts, Minnesota, New Jersey, New York, Pennsylvania, Washington, and Wisconsin. As hard as we tried, the major downfall is in the lack of inclusion of people from diverse backgrounds. This problem disturbs us, but for a full 2½ years, we made phone calls, wrote letters, and sent "calls for proposals" to various agencies and journals; in the end, however, we came up short.

FORMAT OF THE VOLUME

The book is comprised of two parts—Part One: Social Issues, and Part Two: Service. Originally it was our intent to divide the book into three parts—social issues, service learning, and community service—but the cross-pollination of many of the projects suggested to us that it would be much wiser to place all of the service-oriented projects under the rubric of "service."

We asked all of our contributors to follow several guidelines in writing their essays. Among the key components we asked each of them to include were the following: teacher voices that comment on the unit and student voices that provide a sense of them wrestling with the curriculum as well as addressing their new insights. Over and above that, whenever a teacher or student was mentioned, we asked that the person "come alive." That is, we requested that the contributor provide us with a sense of how the individual looked and spoke, and/or something about his or her personality. Since we wanted to assure student anonymity, we asked the contributors to use pseudonyms or simply first names.

CONCLUSION

When all is said and done, the various voices, perspectives, and programs highlighted in this book provide a powerful and clear picture of some of the many outstanding programs that have been designed and implemented across the nation for the purpose of providing young adolescents with rich, meaningful, and powerful learning activities. We hope that the readers will find the various pieces as engaging as we do.

In closing, we thank the reviewers of this book for their comments and suggestions: Sean Harmon (Buford Middle School, Virginia) and Brian Mulvey (Fallon Memorial Elementary School, Rhode Island). Most importantly, we sincerely thank all of the contributors to this book for the arduous work they put into writing and revising their essays. Over and above that, we greatly appreciate their dedication to providing young adolescents with a relevant and high-quality educational program. It has been a true pleasure working with so many fine and dedicated educators.

Introduction

SAMUEL TOTTEN   JON E. PEDERSEN

These are heady times in education, particularly in the area of middle-level education. Indeed, there is possibly more innovation taking place in the area of middle-level education than at any other level. Teachers, administrators, and many others are developing and implementing a vast array of new curricular and extracurricular projects and programs whose specific purpose is to make learning exciting and relevant to the lives of young adolescents (10- to 15-year-olds). Among the more notable of these are two that comprise the focus of this book: the study of social issues within the middle school curriculum and student involvement in service (e.g., service learning, community service, or a hybrid of the two). Not only is the learning going on exciting but it is also imbued with a sense of social and personal relevance for the student—both of which are key tenets of middle-level education.

TERMINOLOGY

Like many terms used in educational circles, the terms *social issues, service learning,* and *community service* are often defined differently in different circles and thus understood to be different things to different people. The drawback of this is obvious: It hinders, if not prevents, clear communication. Ultimately, if the terminology is not clearly understood, it is quite likely that implementation may take different forms in different places. The latter situation would not necessarily be harmful *if* all of the projects were implemented in a pedagogically sound manner; however, that is often not the case. Consider the following: Most experts in the area of service learning agree that a key component of service learning is structured reflection where students systematically and thoroughly examine the project, the activities in which they are engaged, *and* the outcomes of the project. If teachers and students implement something they refer to as service learning and do not include structured reflection, then a vitally significant component is missing from the experience. Indeed, it is hardly likely that the experience will be as powerful as it could or should be for the students. Finally, such an activity could not legitimately be considered service learning.

In light of the aforementioned confusion, it is not surprising that many of the individuals who submitted chapter proposals (and we received 98 in all) were, themselves, confused by the terms *service learning* and *community service.*

In order to clarify what certain researchers and organizations mean by these terms, we shall provide a brief overview of their definitions. As for the term *social issues,* we stand by the following definition: "Social issues refer to those complex problems/issues faced by society. There may or may not be a consensus as to the cause and/or solution of the problems, and many, in fact, may be controversial" (Totten, 1992, p. 44).

We have come across two definitions of *community service* in the literature that we think are worthy of consideration. In the first definition, Rolzinski (1990) has stated that community service constitutes those programs in which

> *young people engage in service programs that are improving living conditions in their urban, suburban and rural communities. Young people are protecting natural resources, caring for the elderly, tutoring educationally at-risk youngsters, working in homeless shelters and much more. . . . [Community service] is education and can serve as a means of learning life skills as well as serving as a bridge to learning academic coursework. [Community service] programs are most effective when they are organized through collaborative relationships among a broad base of community organizations and agencies and the schools. The development of a [community service] program should integrate the specific needs, traditional and emerging cultural considerations and particularly community politics within each community. (pp. 4–5)*

The second definition is by Boyte (1991):

> *Community service refers mainly to a variety of individual voluntary efforts, from working in food banks and shelters for the homeless to helping in nursing homes to participating in tutoring projects and literacy campaigns. In addition, the phrase sometimes encompasses activism with regard to such issues as homelessness and drug abuse. (p. 766)*

As one will readily note, community service is not necessarily an activity that is *purposely* and/or *intricately* tied to the extant curriculum. Although it may serve as a "bridge to learning academic coursework," that is not an absolute must. Furthermore, such service does not necessarily include a reflective component in which students are encouraged and assisted to examine and ponder their efforts.

As for *service learning,* we have located three definitions of special interest. The first one is used by the National Center for Service Learning in Early Adolescence to explain the focus of its work:

Service learning is a unique form of community service that combines meaningful work, in young people's schools and neighborhoods, with training and regular, on-going reflection. Structured reflection—the process of thinking, talking and writing about situations that arise while serving—enables youth "to learn from experience," and is therefore critical to the depth and quality of a program."

The second definition, used by the National Youth Leadership Council to define the focus of its work, is somewhat different:

Service-learning is the blending of "service and learning goals in such a way that the two reinforce each other and produce a greater impact than either could produce alone" (Barry Fenstermacher). . . . It is not only community service, it is connecting service with traditional classroom instruction and learning.

The third definition is from Gomez and colleagues (1990):

Service learning is student learning and development through active participation in thoughtfully organized service experiences that meet real community needs and that are coordinated in collaboration with the school and community. The service-learning is integrated into the students' academic curriculum and provides structured time for them to talk, write, and think about what they did and saw during the actual service activity. . . . Service-learning is the intentional integration of curricular content with community service activities. . . . At the present time, too few school-aged youth participating in community service do so as part of the school-community connection; that is, as an outgrowth of the curriculum or as part of school-related values education. By designing school-based programs, service can be integrated into the curriculum, building both academic skills and affective understanding. (p. 4)

Service learning, then, involves much more than students simply participating in beautification projects or collecting food for the needy.

Obviously, there are some key similarities and differences in how people and groups define, for example, the term *service learning,* but there are also distinct overlaps (e.g., focus, purpose, language usage to describe the activity) as to how people use *community service* and *service learning.* It is our sense, then, that what technically differentiates community service and service learning is that, at its best, service learning involves students in (1) intentional and thought-provoking application of their classroom learning to meaningful work and service in their schools and community, (2) active and engaging work that somehow connects their school and community; and (3) structured reflection.[1]

In an ideal situation, the students are trained to conduct the service. This is the best way to make sure that they fully understand the purpose of their efforts. It also fully prepares them to conduct the service. These concerns are often over-looked by many schools; and not surprisingly, the lack of attention to training results in numerous problems that could have been avoided had the training taken place. Nothing, of course, precludes incorporating any of these compo-nents/aspects into community service projects; indeed, it seems that if such com-ponents were included, it would strengthen and enhance the value of the project.

In light of the various and different ways in which educators, in general, and the contributors to this book, in particular, have used the terms *community service* and *service learning,* we, the editors of the book, have purposely grouped all of the essays that deal with some form of community service or service learning under the rubric of "service." Originally, we had intended to entitle this book *Social Issues, Service Learning, and Community Service at the Middle Level;* however, upon close examination of the chapters that address service, it became increasingly evident that many authors used the terms interchangeably. In fact, even those projects that are consistently referred to by their authors as "community service projects" include some of the key aspects of an ideal ser-vice learning project. It should be noted that the chapters in Part Two: Service begin with those that most closely approximate the ideal definition of service learning and continue on to those that are more of a hybrid of service learning and community service. It should be understood that we think *all* the chapters in Part Two are extremely interesting, thought provoking, and worthy of attention by educators who are interested in incorporating some type of service into their school program.

RATIONALE FOR INCORPORATING SOCIAL ISSUES AND SERVICE INTO THE EXTANT CURRICULUM

As anyone who works with young adolescents knows, students "caught in the middle" are truly unique (cognitively, socially, emotionally, and physically). In light of that, curricular and instructional programs for young adolescents should include ample opportunity for them to engage in age-appropriate, high-interest, and powerful learning activities. More specifically, such students should be given ample opportunity to engage in critical *and* creative thinking and hands-on en-gagement vis-à-vis ideas, concepts, and concerns that they find personally and socially significant. Concomitantly, the curricular and instructional programs should provide middle-level students with ample experiences to broadly ex-plore their own world, instead of some watered-down high school curriculum (which, in more cases than not, is virtually meaningless to them). Constructed and implemented in a sound manner, such curricular and instructional programs are capable of imbuing the subject matter with a sense of relevancy. They could also provide an opportunity for students to develop problem-solving and deci-sion-making skills that prepare them to function in an increasingly complex democratic society. It is our sense that the study of social issues and/or involve-ment in service projects are ideal ways to accomplish the latter goals (Totten and Pedersen, 1993, p. 26).

Engaging early adolescents in a study of social issues and learning through service is directly in line, of course, with the recommendations made in *Turning Points: Preparing American Youth for the 21st Century,* the highly acclaimed report on middle-level education by the Carnegie Council on Adolescent De-velopment (1989). In his preface to *Turning Points,* David W. Hornbeck, Chair of the Task Force on Education of Young Adolescents, stated that education in our nation's middle schools should eventuate in a situation where our 15-year-olds will

- *Accept responsibility for shaping and not simply being shaped by surrounding events*
- *Demonstrate good citizenship in which the youth is a doer, not just an observer*
- *Understand the way government in the United States func-tions at the local, state, and federal levels and participate in appropriate ways in creating and maintaining a healthy community*
- *Possess a feeling of personal responsibility for and connection to the well-being of an interdependent world community*
- *Not only develop the capacity to think clearly and critically, but act ethically, and*
- *Embrace many virtues such as courage, acceptance of respon-sibility, honesty, integrity, tolerance, appreciation of individual differences, and caring about others. [In doing so,] the young person will demonstrate all these values through sustained ser-vice to others. (p. 16)*

All of these points and their relation to the focus of social issues and learn-ing through service dovetail with most, if not all, of the "seven key develop-mental needs that characterize early adolescence (which are based on extensive research): (1) Positive social interaction with adults and peers; (2) Structure and clear limits; (3) Physical setting; (4) Creative expression; (5) Competence and achievement; (6) Meaningful participation in families, schools, and com-munities; and (7) Opportunities for self-definition" (Scales, 1991, pp. 13–14). Clearly, those educators who are attempting to engage students in a study of social issues and/or provide them with opportunities to engage in learning through service are on to something.

On a related note, in the draft of a position paper entitled "Middle Level Curriculum: A Work in Progress," a National Middle School Association task force delineated what it perceived as key learning experiences for middle-level students. Many of the key points, directly and indirectly, support the involvement of middle-level students in the study of social issues and learning through service. More specifically, the task force stated that it supports learning experiences that

> *Help young adolescents make sense of themselves and the world about them*
>
> *Are highly integrated, so that students see the connectedness of life*
>
> *Address students' own questions and focus upon enduring issues and ideas*
>
> *Open doors to new ideas, evoking curiosity, exploration, and, at times, awe and wonder*
>
> *Actively engage students in problem-solving and a variety of experiential learning opportunities*
>
> *Draw on varied forms of intelligence and multiple modes of expression*
>
> *Nourish the imaginative life, cultivate initiative and responsibility*
>
> *Involve students in meaningful and useful service activities*
>
> *Emphasize collaboration, cooperation, and community*
>
> *Encourage and challenge students to give their best efforts as life-long learners and doers*
>
> *Above all, seek to develop good people, fostering caring for others, democratic values, and moral sensitivity. (NMSA, 1993, p. 2)*

On a different but related note, an issue that all educators who work with middle-level students need to focus on is addressing the students' own questions about key issues. Throughout our work on this book, we have frequently wondered just how many of the projects highlighted herein are predicated on or generated by student interest versus that of teacher interest. The point is: If the study of social issues and participation in service is going to be as powerful as it could be, then teachers need to truly take to heart *and* act upon the notion of student interest.

Finally, in a powerful and thought-provoking essay entitled "A Curriculum to Empower Young Adolescents," Arnold (1993) forcefully and convincingly argued (and then asked): "Given the neglect, ignorance, stereotyping, and impact of societal forces related to early adolescence, it seems clear that middle schoolers need learning experiences which are liberating and empowering. What would such a curriculum entail?" (p. 6). He went on to delineate five interrelated principles, four of which are especially pertinent to the focus of this book:

- *An empowering curriculum will enable young adolescents increasingly to assume control over their own learning, exercising initiative and responsibility.*
- *Such a curriculum will help young adolescents make sense of themselves and their world, frequently dealing with their own questions, not just those posed by texts and teachers. Hence it will be rich in meaning, dealing with issues that are worth knowing; exploring values which are involved; relating these issues to students' lives and extending them into a larger context; and translating all of this into activities geared to their level of understanding.*
- *An empowering curriculum will encourage young adolescents to contribute to the well being of others, at the same time helping youth to feel needed and useful.*
- *An empowering curriculum will help young adolescents understand and counter the forces which are exploiting them and/ or hindering their development. (p. 7)*

Most, if not all, of the projects described within this book address a host of these vital concerns. The educators whose voices are heard in these chapters typify what we consider to be thinking, caring, and proactive teachers. That is, they carefully weigh what they are doing *and* why they are doing it. They care about their students as learners *and* as human beings. They care about what and how their students are learning. They care about whether their students' learning will result in anything worthwhile. They care about the world; and in that regard, they want to prepare students who will also care about the world. Finally, they are proactive in the sense that they do not wait for someone to dictate a new or innovative curriculum; rather, they sense that something could be done better or more powerfully, perceive the need as a challenge and want to overcome it, and then act accordingly by designing and implementing new and innovative projects. We commend such dispositions and actions.

THE ECLECTIC NATURE OF INCORPORATING THE STUDY OF SOCIAL ISSUES AND/OR SERVICE INTO THE MIDDLE-LEVEL CURRICULUM

Moving from a Passive to an Active Learning Situation

As various researchers on schools have repeatedly noted, far too often school work is repetitive, dull, and mindless. It is little wonder that many students are bored, disengaged, and not a little put out that they are "condemned" to 12 years of schooling. In his landmark study of schooling, *A Place Called School*, Goodlad (1984) reported,

The two activities, involving the most students, were being lectured to and working on written assignments (and we have seen that much of this work was in the form of responding to directives in working books or on worksheets). When we add to the time spent in these learning modes the time spent on the routines of preparing or following up instruction, the extraordinary degree of student passivity stands out. The amount of time spent in any other kind of activity (e.g., role playing, small group planning and problem solving, constructing models) was minuscule—and does not add up to a great deal even when the totals for all such deviations are computed. . . . Usually, in the course of a day, students in elementary classrooms encountered up to five different kinds of activities or groupings but with advancement through the grades to secondary schools, they commonly encountered only lecturing and seat assignments.

. . . We do not see in our descriptions, then, much opportunity for students to become engaged with knowledge so as to employ their full range of intellectual abilities. And one wonders about the meaningfulness of whatever is acquired by students who sit listening or performing relatively repetitive exercises, year after year. (pp. 230, 231)

Middle-level pedagogy is predicated on a minds-on, hands-on approach. Put another way, such an approach is totally antithetical to the passivity in classrooms that typify much of what is being passed off as education in many of our nation's classrooms. It is our sense—and certainly the projects highlighted within this book corroborate that sense—that the incorporation of the study of social issues and learning through service are outstanding vehicles that lend themselves to making the middle-level curriculum and instructional programs minds-on, hands-on learning situations.

In *A Place Called School,* Goodlad (1984) went on to say,

Important work of several decades ago, as well as much of what has since been in the forefront of education thought, stresses the importance of teachers' finding ways to make subject matter relevant to students, to involve students in setting their own goals, to vary their ways of learning, to use approaches that employ all of the senses, and to be sure that there are opportunities for relating the knowledge to experiences or actually using it. These things are not easy, and teachers learn some of the rhetoric but rarely practice the techniques in teacher education programs or later. (p. 231)

Even though Goodlad's report was published in 1984, our observations of classrooms suggest that things have not changed all that much over the past decade or so. However, when *structured properly,* we think that the study of social issues and the incorporation of service projects are capable of making learning relevant to students. Due to the unique nature of the projects, they are frequently undertaken in innovative ways that make rich use of the eclectic teaching methods and learning activities to which Goodlad alludes.

That is not to say that just *any* study of social issues or just *any* service project will automatically result in a study imbued with those elements that Goodlad suggests are needed for an exciting and effective learning situation (Goodlad, 1984, p. 231). Indeed, many such projects can be and, unfortunately, often are, as deadly for students as the traditional curriculum often proves to be. Be that as it may, the projects highlighted in this book are, for the most part, projects that purposely set out to engage students in important studies and projects as well as engage them in rich, exciting, and relevant pedagogical ways.

Interdisciplinary Instruction

Another key tenet of middle-level education is that of interdisciplinary instruction. Unfortunately, as Beane (1990) and others have pointed out, although certain middle-level educators have designed and implemented interesting and powerful interdisciplinary lessons and units, there is still a long way to go in regard to developing and implementing an outstanding "general framework for a middle school curriculum" that is truly interdisciplinary in nature (George et al., 1992, p. 88). For an engaging discussion of key concerns along these and others lines vis-à-vis middle-level curriculum, see Beane's chapter in this book as well as his highly acclaimed *A Middle School Curriculum: From Rhetoric to Reality* (1990). *Social Issues and Service at the Middle Level* certainly does not solve this problem, but what it does do is highlight some of the attempts that teachers, alone and/or in conjunction with others, have made in an attempt to move beyond the typical, dry curriculum. Simply put, there is a lot of food for thought here in regard to how teachers can begin to move toward an interdisciplinary approach.

Exploratory Curriculum

Another key component of the middle-level philosophy, and by extension, the middle-level curriculum, is the focus on exploration. Ideally, an exploratory component should be interwoven throughout *all* aspects of the school program and not simply constitute an add on (e.g., a single course that focuses on exploratory topics while the rest of the curriculum is bereft of an integrated exploratory approach). Again, it seems to us that the incorporation of a study of social issues and involvement in service are ideal ways to begin to interweave a meaningful exploratory component throughout the curriculum. Explicitly and implicitly, our authors "speak" of the exploratory nature of their programs.

ENDNOTE

1. It is also worth noting that another term, *community service learning,* is also being used by certain groups. According to the Community Service Learning Center, "Community service learning is a demonstration of the new partnership between the school and the community. Students can learn on-site about community needs and issues—the homeless, the hungry, the elderly, the environment—while working to meet them. Students participate in activities integrated into the curriculum, so that the learning process is focused and organized, and in so doing, they participate in problem-solving and learn about the community and the meaning of participation and citizenship. The service activity becomes the motivator for learning."

REFERENCES

Arnold, John. (1993, Fall). "A Curriculum to Empower Young Adolescents." *Midpoints, 4*(1): 1–11.

Beane, James A. (1990). *A Middle School Curriculum: From Rhetoric to Reality.* Columbus, OH: National Middle School Association.

Boyte, Harry C. (1991, June). "Community Service and Civic Education." *Phi Delta Kappan, 72*(10): 765–767.

Carnegie Council on Adolescent Development. (1989). *Turning Points: Preparing American Youth for the 21st Century.* New York: Carnegie Corporation of New York.

Community Service Learning Center. (no date). Brochure. Springfield, MA: Author.

Conrad, Dan, and Hedin, Diane (1991, June). "School-Based Community Service: What We Know from Research and Theory." *Phi Delta Kappan, 72*(10): 743–749.

George, Paul S.; Stevenson, Chris; Thomason, Julia; and Beane, James. (1992). *The Middle School—And Beyond.* Alexandria, VA: Association for Supervision and Curriculum Development.

Gomez, Barbara; Kielsmeier, James; Kinsley, Carol; McPherson, Kate; and Parsons, Cynthia. (1990, March). "Service-Learning Advances Education Improvement: A Position Paper." Unpublished.

Goodlad, John. (1984). *A Place Called School: Perspectives for the Future.* New York: McGraw-Hill.

National Center for Service Learning in Early Adolescence. (no date). "How Learning Service Works." New York: Author.

National Middle School Association. (1993). *Middle Level Curriculum: A Work in Progress.* A Position Paper.

National Youth Leadership Council. (no date). Brochure. Roseville, MN: Author.

Rolzinski, Catherine A. (1990). *The Adventure of Adolescence: Middle School Students and Community Service.* Washington, DC: Youth Service America.

Scales, Peter. (1991). *A Portrait of Young Adolescents in the 1990s: Implications for Promoting Healthy Growth and Development.* Carrboro, NC: Center for Early Adolescence.

Totten, Samuel. (1992). "Educating for the Development of Social Consciousness and Social Responsibility." In C. Mark Hurlbert and Samuel Totten (Eds.), *Social Issues in the English Classroom* (pp. 9–55). Urbana, IL: National Council of Teachers of English.

Totten, Samuel, and Pedersen, Jon. (1993). "Strengthening Community Service Projects in Schools by Undergirding Them with the Study of Pertinent Social Issues." *Current Issues in Middle Level Education,* 2(1): 16–30.

The Wingspread Journal. (1989, October). "Principles of Good Practice for Combining Service and Learning." *Wingspread Special Report.* Racine, WI: The Johnson Foundation.

► 1

Social Issues in the Middle School Curriculum
Retrospect and Prospect

JAMES A. BEANE

The year is 1910. The country is struggling with the meaning of democracy. Waves of immigrants are arriving to carry out the labor of emerging industrialism. Literary "muckrakers" scream out at deplorable working conditions. Debate over child labor laws is in full swing. A new class of industrial wealth is rapidly emerging. Urban centers teem with cultural diversity. Cultural bias and racism are widespread. And in Berkeley, California, and in Columbus, Ohio, a new kind of school is established. It is called a junior high school.

The lack of fanfare over these new schools is not surprising though they are the culmination of two decades of debate over the education of young adolescents. Many educators had concluded that the final years of the K–8 elementary schools were inappropriate for these young people who were no longer children. Nearly two-thirds dropped out of school by the end of eighth grade. Meanwhile, leaders in higher education, such as Charles Eliot of Harvard University, were concerned over the "advanced" age (roughly age 18) of those entering college. Moreover, growing enrollment in elementary schools was causing severe overcrowding.

So it was that the junior high school was established. Its purposes represented a convergence of the grounds of the debate over what to do with young adolescents in school (Kliebard, 1986). Young adolescents would experience something more sophisticated than the elementary school program designed for children. Those planning to continue their education would have accelerated courses that would introduce them to the high school curriculum at an earlier age. Those who were perceived as potential drop-outs would receive vocational guidance as well as some cultural capital through watered-down versions of "junior" high school subjects. And, of course, overcrowding in the elementary schools would be relieved by simply removing grades 7 and 8 and adjoining them to grade 9. It was, by intention, a junior version of the high school. Its program—the one that has cast a long shadow over middle-level education ever since—was no accident.

In retrospect we can see that the first junior high schools shared many characteristics with today's middle schools. Among these is the fact that they served a time that was ripe with social issues: the relation between economic growth and democracy, growing cultural diversity, inequitable distribution of wealth, continuing bias and racism, the threat of global conflict, unrest in urban areas, and the devaluing of children and youth. Another is that like our own middle schools, the early junior high school offered a curriculum that largely ignored such issues, consisting instead of a collection of academic courses, a bag of character education virtues, and a generally sterilized view of the world.

To understand this version of a curriculum and how it came to be, we must first understand whose interests it presented. The curriculum of the early junior high schools, like that of other schools at the time, was created out of a convergence of three views. The first was what we now call *classical humanism,* the perennialist view of worthwhile knowledge as that which has been passed down over time and which claims justification on the grounds of tradition. It was exactly this view that was presented in the high school curriculum recommendations of the Committee of Ten in its influential 1895 report that was to "trickle down" to the junior high school (Kliebard, 1986). The second was a push for *character education* programs that would improve the moral virtue of immigrants who represented a variety of cultures. It is instructive to note that these were called "Americanization" programs, their intention being precisely to introduce immigrants to the values of the dominant culture of those who reached the country's shores first. The third was the interests of *business and industry,* which were seeking industrious and compliant laborers for construction, manufacturing, and other trades (Spring, 1986; Beane, 1990a). It was this interest that drove the vocational guidance and manual training parts of the junior high school.

In this picture we may see why particular programs were included in the junior high school curriculum, but also why other possibilities were left out. Clearly, there was a dominant culture at work here whose interests were served by the curriculum. Classical humanism sought to preserve the traditional "high-culture," character education sought to impose certain behavioral virtues on all young people, especially immigrants, and vocational guidance and manual training aimed at guiding young people into particular career paths depending, of course, almost entirely on socioeconomic class, race, and ethnic origin. If we include domestic training, later to become home economics, we can complete that picture by adding gender as a factor in tracking young people in the junior high school.

No doubt many long-time proponents of middle-level education wish that they could claim their roots in a prettier picture than this one. To say, for example, that early junior high schools were intended to meet the needs of early adolescents is fine, so long as we understand that those "needs" had nothing to do with perceived needs or interests of early adolescents but rather with those of the same dominant culture that was influencing education in general at the time.

It is exactly in this point, too, that we may finally see why social issues were not a part of the junior high school curriculum in its early days. The public schools of those times were, more than anything else, a site of dominant culture interests. Those who held dominant social, political, and economic positions would hardly want early adolescents or anyone else to engage in study of social issues. Such studies could be seen only as formenting dissatisfaction and resistance or, worse yet, a desire to seek resolution of social issues in ways that might contradict the interests of those in power. So complete was the dominance, incidentally, that the Socialists started their own "Sunday" (weekend) schools to broaden the political and economic education of their children (Teitelbaum, 1987), while W. E. B. DuBois (1902) and other African Americans developed their own line of research to expose racial bias in the curriculum.

This story should, of course, say something to us about our own times. Needless to say, the parallels are dramatic. We are now experiencing the same kind of reactions in, for example, the "English-only" and Eurocentric opposition to cultural diversity, the growing support for a national curriculum based on high-culture subjects, the increasing interest in "tech-prep" vocational programs, and the rebirth of behavioristic character education programs. Meanwhile, issues such as inequitable distribution of wealth and power, the preponderance of low-wage jobs, homelessness, gender inequity, homophobia, racism, crass commercialism, and others continue almost unabated. And, too, these issues continue as an "absent presence" in the curriculum—they are part of the real, lived experience of many young people yet are either completely left out of the curriculum or linger only on its far edges. In times like these, when power has shifted so clearly to the dominant culture, we could hardly expect otherwise (Apple, 1986, 1993).

So far, I have sketched a very dismal picture with regard to the place of social issues in the curriculum or, more accurately, their displacement. But this picture did not go completely unchallenged. In the midst of the Great Depression, for example, a number of progressive educators, such as George Counts and Harold Rugg, following the work of John Dewey (1916), called for the school to pay greater attention to problems of the age and to bring social issues into the curriculum. Among those who took up this call were junior high school educators who sought to place such issues in what came to be called *problem-centered core programs*. Within a few decades, their efforts had contributed to a rich literature on this idea.

William Van Til, a leading junior high school figure, suggested "centers of learning experience" such as Intercultural Education, World Views and Ideologies, Propaganda, and War and Peace (1946, pp. 15–16). Gertrude Noar (1953, pp. 163–169) reported on schools having core programs organized around such themes as Intercultural Tensions, Juvenile Delinquency, Labor Unions, Housing, and Conservation. Moreover, Van Til, Noar, and other progressive educators of those times placed such issues in a classroom context that emphasized democratic living, including the use of teacher-pupil planning to identify aspects of the thematic curriculum they proposed.

Again, it would be a more satisfying story if we could say that such efforts were simply a hidden part of the history of the middle-level curriculum, censored out by those who either ignore or object to the idea of placing social issues in the curriculum. But as Grace Wright reported in 1958, such programs were found in only about 12 percent of junior high schools, a proportion that is hardly overwhelming. The space that I have given them here is, then, symbolic of the space such programs actually occupied in the schools. Juxtaposing the richness of these progressive efforts with their limited popularity leaves one with the accurate impression that the dominant interests of earlier times never really abated, to say nothing of feelings of sadness and frustration. Unfortunately, one may experience those same feelings in looking at middle-level education in our own times.

THE MIDDLE SCHOOL MOVEMENT

By the late 1950s and early 1960s, events once again turned attention to middle-level education. Children of the postwar "baby boom" were moving through the elementary schools and creating severe overcrowding. Rather than building an increasing number of neighborhood elementary schools, school boards began to consider the idea of adding on to the high school, moving ninth grade to that level, and adjoining the sixth grade to seventh and eighth grades. At the same time, mounting evidence regarding a downward shift in the average age for achieving puberty suggested revision of the ages ordinarily associated with early adolescence (Tanner, 1962). The convergence of these two factors offered administrative and developmental justification for a new school that would replace the junior high school. It would be called a *middle school.*

Specialists in middle-level education seized the moment and called for a rethinking of schooling at that level. Such rethinking was to be based on a renewed study of the characteristics of early adolescence and development of new structures and programs that would respond to those characteristics. The need for reform at the middle level was not a notion held by educators alone. Charles Silberman (1970) expressed the sentiments of a far larger number of people when, writing in *Crisis in the Classroom,* he proclaimed that the junior high school, "by almost unanimous agreement, is the wasteland—one is tempted to say the cesspool—of American education" (p. 324).

From the very beginning of the middle school movement, certain reforms were pressed. Improved school climate was to follow from increased sensitivity by middle level educators to the physical and social ambiguities associated with puberty. More persistent personal and social guidance was to be provided for early adolescents as they negotiated those ambiguities, an idea that would eventually evolve into teacher advisory programs. Interdisciplinary teams were to reduce anonymity and alienation through "schools within the school." These teams would also presumably explore the possibilities for making the curriculum more coherent by connecting the traditionally fragmented subjects they taught.

For our purposes, however, we need to ask whether the idea of including social issues in the curriculum was also a part of that early agenda. The answer is that, except for a few holdovers from the progressive camp of the junior high school movement, early leaders in the middle school movement simply did not address that possibility (Beane, 1990b; Wraga, 1992). To understand why, we need only to remember the crucial lesson from the beginnings of the junior high school—namely, that in shaping curriculum, external social and educational issues loom larger than interests internal to the middle level itself.

Overcrowded elementary schools and new data on early adolescents offered propitious timing for the start of middle schools, but these were not the only developments taking place. In the late 1950s, the country in general and progressives in particular were still reeling from the chilling climate of the ultra-conservative McCarthy era. The launching of the Soviet satellite *Sputnik* in 1957 resulted in a cry for a more technical scientific-mathematical emphasis in the curriculum. This and renewed assaults on education by the classical humanists led to massive funding of curriculum development projects focused on the "structure of the disciplines."

Even the voice of Jerome Bruner, whose 1960 book *The Process of Education* served as the grounding for these projects, went unheeded. Ten years later, in reconsidering that earlier work, Bruner (1971) had this to say:

> *I believe I would be quite satisfied to declare, if not a moratorium, then something of a de-emphasis on matters that have to do with the structure of history, the structure of physics, the nature of mathematical consistency, and deal with curriculum rather in the context of the problems that face us. We might better concern ourselves with how those problems can be solved, not just by practical action, but by putting knowledge, wherever we find it and in whatever form we find it, to work in these massive tasks. We might put vocation and intention back into the process of education, much more firmly than we had it there before. (pp. 29–30)*

It is true that the Civil Rights and anti-war movements of the 1960s fomented social unrest and that many educators did turn their attention to social issues. However, we must remember that the middle school movement was borne out of administrative reorganization of grade levels and concern for developmental characteristics of early adolescence. It was, in this sense, tied much more closely to mainstream educational currents than to disaffection with large-scale social conditions. In other words, not only was this not an inviting time to suggest the introduction of social issues into the middle level curriculum, but, moreover, such a suggestion itself was not likely to come from most of those involved in the early days of the middle school movement.

Given this background, then, the unfolding of the middle school movement is not at all surprising. Certainly, major progress in the area of school climate has diminished Silberman's earlier negative claim about middle-level schools; and, in fact, opportunities for teacher collaboration are a standing feature of many of them. But for our purposes here, I want to focus on how the so-called characteristics of early adolescence have entered into curriculum deliberations, especially with regard to social education.

Middle school educators generally take early adolescence to be a fairly distinct and differentiated period in human development characterized by the physical changes associated with puberty and a heightened concern for self-identity and social acceptance. It is this "nature" of early adolescence that has been of most interest to educators as they have sought to understand and respond to what they perceive to be the *bizarre* behavior of these young people. I use the word "bizarre" in quotes here because it is precisely this sense that has given rise to such popular, and, as we shall see, inaccurate metaphors as "hormones with feet," "range of the strange," and "braindead."

This way of characterizing early adolescents has had two unfortunate effects. First, is has led to freezing early adolescents entirely within a socially constructed and narrow stage description that misses the fact that they are also real people living out real lives in a real world. For the past few years, a number of us have been working out ways to empower early adolescents through their participation in classroom curriculum planning (Brodhagen, Weilbacher, and Beane, 1992). We have found that when asked to identify questions about themselves and their world, they persistently raise questions such as the following:

Will there ever be world peace?

Why are there gangs? Why can't people get along?

Will racism ever end? Why do people hate blacks?

Why do people have to be mean to others to feel good about themselves?

Why are there so many poor people? Do rich people sitting around their swimming pools even care about poor people?

Why did we overpopulate the world?

Will starvation ever end?

Why do insane people have rights?

How come you can cross-breed animals and not humans?

Will we destroy the environment? Will there be a world left when we get older?

Will there ever be a president of the United States who is not a white man?

These are not just isolated questions picked up from one or two early adolescents. Instead, they are the kind that come up again and again as we plan with these young people. The same kinds of issues also became a pattern in an open-ended survey conducted in several rural, suburban, and urban middle schools across Wisconsin (Brodhagen, Jochman, and McDonough, 1990). Clearly, these are not the questions and concerns of "hormones with feet" or persons who are "braindead."

The second unfortunate effect of defining early adolescence in this way has been to limit curriculum deliberations simply to discussions of how the existing curriculum might be adapted to these so-called characteristics. Such discussions have led many middle-level educators to avoid depth of meanings and to concentrate on clever methods to get these young people to stay "on task." I do not want to demean such methods as cooperative learning and exciting activities, since they are important and appropriate. However, simply doing them does not necessarily involve asking what it is that cooperative learning and the exciting activities are about. In other words, most of what has been considered curriculum work in the middle school movement has focused on the *how* and avoided discussions of the *what* in curriculum.

Like the earlier junior high school movement, it is this same idea of adapting the high school version of the curriculum for early adolescents that has helped keep the possibility of social issues off the middle school curriculum agenda. This is, of course, partly due to the stranglehold that the separate subject, academic-focused approach, inspired by classical humanism, has had on the curriculum. But neither can we ignore the political trends of the past two decades, particularly the shift toward increasing radical individualism in which even democracy has been appropriated to mean the right of self-interest apart from the common good or interest (Apple, 1988). Since a curriculum that concerns social issues has the latter as an aim, our own times have hardly been hospitable to such an idea.

Nowhere is this more evident in the middle school movement than in the way that *affect* has been treated in the curriculum. Although this dimension of what it means to be human is broadly defined to include self-perceptions, values, morals, and so on (Beane, 1990a), middle schools have focused almost entirely on the part having to do with self-esteem. Building on well-established correlations between self-esteem and a variety of self-destructive behaviors—substance abuse, adolescent pregnancy, crime, and so on—middle schools have implemented efforts to enhance self-esteem (Beane and Lipka, 1987). Often included within teacher-advisory programs, such efforts have typically been based on an "inoculation" metaphor. That is, they aim to enhance self-esteem on an individual basis so that young people might be "immune" to whatever factors threaten their self-esteem.

Lost in all of this is consideration of the threatening factors themselves—namely the conditions under which so many young (and older) people live (conditions such as racism, poverty, sexism, homophobia, etc.). In other words, social issues are still a kind of "absent presence" in the curriculum, always lurking just beneath the surface in a program directed mainly at putting young people in a position to take care of themselves first and worry about others later. In saying this, I do not mean to imply that middle schools have been part of some deliberate conspiracy to purge social aspects of the curriculum or to lay blame on the schoolhouse steps for the social malaise that has characterized the national mood. Rather, it is the case that middle (and other) schools have followed the larger sociopolitical lead and worked in conjunction with it to divert attention from the powerful social issues that we face.

Retracing our steps, then, it is hardly surprising that middle schools have not embraced the possibility of focusing on or emphasizing social issues in the curriculum. The McCarthy-esque mood of the nation and the launching of *Sputnik,* along with the obsession with structure of the disciplines of knowledge, made the earliest days of the middle school movement an unlikely time for introducing this idea as part of the agenda, especially given the mainstream character of most of its advocates. Despite social uprisings in the 1960s, the succeeding decades proved just as unlikely, particularly as the national mood became increasingly conservative and individualistic. As I have said elsewhere (Beane, 1990b), it is possible that if the movement had called for curriculum reform along these lines, it very likely would not have gotten as far as it has. But this is only a hypothetical issue since even in its most glamorized claims of concern for the characteristics of early adolescence, the middle school movement has clung to the "hormones with feet" metaphor and failed to connect its child-centered advocacy to larger social issues that weigh so heavily on the lives of the young.

We have already seen that the earlier junior high school curriculum was challenged by Progressive Era reforms such as the problem-centered core program and we must realize that the story of curriculum malaise I have just told is likewise not the whole story of the more recent middle school movement. For example, I called for a revival of that same core idea in middle schools (Beane, 1975). So, too, in a more extended way, did John Lounsbury and Gordon Vars (1978) recommend a renewal of commitment to the problem-centered core, including reference to Van Til's "centers-of-experience" mentioned earlier. John Arnold (1980) made a scathing attack on the "hormones with feet" metaphor and followed with a set of curriculum suggestions that included attention to social issues.

Certainly, there must have been cases where teachers in middle schools gave space to social issues during these years. But their lack of attention in mainstream middle school literature is probably testimony to the strength of the individualistic "advisory" programs I described earlier as well as euphoria over fledgling attempts to find connections in the existing curriculum through multisubject units with themes like Ancient Greece, Colonial Living, Medieval Times, and Metrics. To find episodes of attention to social issues, one must instead look mostly outside middle school literature at reports such as Schine and Harrington's (1982) regarding early adolescent participation in community service projects and more recently to some of the teacher stories about integrative studies in Vermont schools (Stevenson and Carr, 1993). It is likely, to say nothing of depressing, that the number of middle schools that have positioned social issues seriously in the curriculum is no larger than the number Wright (1958) found having problem-centered core programs nearly 50 years ago.

PLACING SOCIAL ISSUES IN THE CURRICULUM

There are, of course, many ways in which social issues might be brought into the curriculum. For example, issues such as conflict, cultures, or environment might serve as themes for units. Or, one might take a social perspective on concepts in the existing curriculum, such as a mathematics class exploring what *average* means when applied to people, debating the ethics of technology in science class, or intentionally focusing on cultural diversity in art or music class. Such efforts are relatively rare but not entirely unusual in the curriculum. I certainly do not want to underestimate the importance of such work, but these approaches have a tendency to obscure rather than accentuate social issues and to make them seem like momentary diversions in the curriculum.

I want to spend the rest of the space I have imagining (or re-imagining) what the curriculum might look like if social issues were placed at its very core, as one of the major sources of the curriculum. To do so, I will briefly restate the proposal made in 1990 for a "new" middle school curriculum, but emphasize here particularly the place of social issues in that proposal. As shown in Figure 1–1, the two major sources of the curriculum are personal concerns emerging in the present lives of early adolescents and larger social concerns that affect all persons, young and old, living in the society (regardless of their awareness of the issues). Themes around which the curriculum is organized are found at the intersection of those two sources where it is apparent that self-concerns or interests intersect with social concerns or interests. Table 1–1 illustrates such intersections as, for example, the overlap of personal identity questions with those involved in the issue of cultural identities, of personal wellness and environmental health, of conflict in the peer group and conflict at larger levels, and so on.

Returning to Figure 1–1, personal, social, and technical skills (communication, computation, researching, problem solving, critical inquiry, etc.) are repositioned from separate subjects into the context of personal-social themes where they have meaning, relevance, and application. Moreover, the fundamental concepts of democracy, human dignity, and cultural diversity are seen as permeating the entire curriculum, running through whatever themes are used and/or serving as themes themselves. In the original proposal (Beane, 1990a) and elsewhere (e.g., Brodhagen, Weilbacher, and Beane, 1992), I have offered examples of how this curriculum design might look in actual practice.

It is important to note, however, that my intention from the start was that the actual implementation of the design be planned collaboratively by teachers and early adolescents in classrooms, since the issues that emerge as themes are

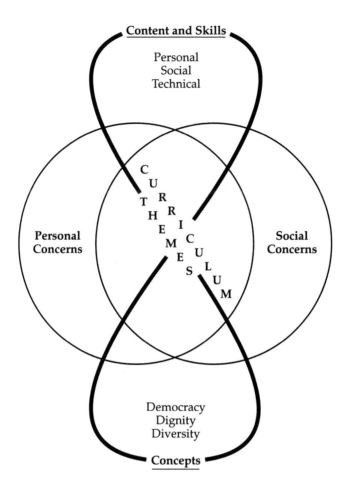

FIGURE 1–1　A Middle School Curriculum

to be of compelling significance to the particular young people who will explore them. The exception to this idea would occur if a particular group of young people might not be aware of some significant issue such as cultural diversity or global conflict. In these cases, teachers have a moral obligation to bring such issues to light as part of their professional responsibility to bring the larger world to young people.

With that brief description I now want to suggest how that curriculum design converges with the idea of placing social issues at the core of the curriculum. First, social issues are considered to be one of the two primary sources of the curriculum. Their importance, however, is not derived simply from the fact that they are "out there," but because they impinge on all of our lives whether

TABLE 1–1   Intersections of Personal and Social Concerns

Early Adolescent Concern	Theme	Social Concern
Understanding personal changes	TRANSITIONS	Living in a changing world
Developing a personal identity	IDENTITIES	Cultural diversity
Finding a place in the group	INTERDEPENDENCE	Global interdependence
Personal fitness	WELLNESS	Environmental protection
Social status (e.g., among peers)	SOCIAL STRUCTURES	Class systems (age, economics)
Dealing with adults	INDEPENDENCE	Human rights
Peer conflict and gangs	CONFLICT RESOLUTION	Global conflict
Commercial pressures	COMMERCIALISM	Effects of media
Questioning authority	JUSTICE	Laws and social customs
Personal friendships	CARING	Social welfare
Living in the school	INSTITUTIONS	Social institutions

we want to think so or not. They are, in a sense, a kind of common glue that binds us and are, therefore, crucial to the kind of general, common education that middle schools are intended to offer.

Second, as we have found in planning with young people, social issues are very much on the minds of early adolescents. Earlier, I sketched out some of the kinds of questions and concerns that early adolescents have raised about themselves and the world. The fact is that those present a virtual litany of social issues and are clearly not the kind of superficial or whimsical concerns that one would expect if the "hormones with feet" metaphor were accurate. It is more than apparent that if we want to offer an education that is perceived as worth having by early adolescents themselves, then social issues must be at its very core.

Third, this curriculum design offers a context in which social issues are approached democratically. The collaborative identification of issues is in itself a democratic act, but just as important, the issues become the direction in which the curriculum is aimed. Moreover, social issues are not something to be taken on later, after the accumulation of various information and skills, but rather a part of the real life in which the young are already engaged. Finally, I have more recently pointed out the intention of making democratic uses of knowledge through application to social problems, creating personal meanings rather than simply accepting those of others, and critically examining the sources and veracity of "facts" or other knowledge brought into the classroom from external sources (Beane, 1993).

Fourth, this kind of curriculum, rooted in personal and social issues, offers a life-like and meaningful context in which to place knowledge and skill. Although this is partly a methodological issue, it also touches on the politics of curriculum and the question of Whose knowledge is of worth? The classical humanism approach is built on the idea that knowledge is external to human experience and is an end rather than a means. For this reason, knowledge is organized in abstract disciplines or subjects that are then presented to people. Progressive approaches like the one I am describing view knowledge as growing out of human experience and as an instrumental means to its clarification. In this way, personal and social issues—the very substance of human experience and attention—are the most important context in which knowledge is used.

Fifth, this curriculum offers meaningful opportunities for community service as social action. Again, social issues are not simply "things out there." Rather, they are problematic concerns that permeate the lives of people. Their presence at the core of the curriculum thus suggests that real learning eventually involves attempts to take action toward their resolution. I do not want to demean charitable acts that are encouraged as an activity in the school program. But the kind of community service this curriculum engages is an integrated part of the everyday, core learning that the school promotes. It is not merely an act of benevolent charity set apart from the rest of life, but an attempt to help young people develop a sense of personal and collective efficacy with regard to social problems.

Finally, the kind of curriculum I have proposed has as its central theme the search for self and social meaning. It is a curriculum that means to help young people in their pursuit of deeper and broader understanding of themselves and their world. What kind of curriculum could be more valuable, more worthwhile? What kind of curriculum could be more nearly centered in the flow of authentic human experience? It is hard to imagine any worthwhile curriculum that is not so centered.

Promise and Resistance

By now, it should be clear that placing social issues at the core of the curriculum is not merely a methodological device. To the extent that it is, surely we might well expect that it would more likely engage the attention of young people than the abstract, subject-centered curriculum we have had for too long. However, the emphasis on social issues and action in the curriculum has much larger purposes as well. One is to be certain that such issues are brought to the attention of the young and treated with the seriousness they deserve. Another is to encourage young people to become "critical readers of their society," to see that nothing should be taken for granted and, moreover, that social issues are not without causes that must be uncovered. Still another purpose is to help the young learn the ways of democracy by having the democratic experience of confronting those social issues that complicate and threaten our lives and in this way to achieve a sense of personal and collective efficacy.

While those purposes are frequently cited, I have saved for last one that is less often discussed yet increasingly significant. In my critique of the middle school movement, I mentioned the issue of individualistic self-interest and its ascendance over a sense of the common interest or good. Then, in describing my curriculum proposal, I spoke to the idea of finding themes at the intersection of self and social concerns. Neither of these was an accidental moment, since they point to a social issue and a social learning that cries out for our attention.

Jason, one of my sons, is a college student majoring in architecture. For that reason, he is required to spend long hours in the studio, often working very late at night. He lives with two housemates in an apartment in a very dangerous neighborhood about a mile from where the studio is located. Jason and I have talked at length about how he might get from the studio to his apartment without being accosted or outright attacked. Could he walk with other students? Could he ride a bike at high speed? Could his housemates meet him? Could he simply move to a safer place? I have worried a lot about this.

But it occurs to me that we might have spent just as much time talking and worrying about the conditions of his neighborhood and how those help to create the lives of his potential attackers. After all, they are victims, too—victims of the social problems that are realities of their neighborhood. It is here that I understand that the fate of my own son, a child of privilege, is inextricably tied to the fate of those who are nonprivileged, those whom the social issues of our times have treated more harshly than Jason. In the end, it is the very conditions under which they live that ultimately threaten Jason—conditions that need our attention at least as much as exploring the routes of safety the privileged might follow.

In this vignette, we may find yet one more crucial purpose for taking on social issues and action in the curriculum. It is that such a curriculum offers hope that young people will do a better job than we have of "seeing their stake in others." We talk a great deal of interdependence and of getting along with others, but we seem too often to be seeking a kind of peaceful coexistence rather than an integrated vision of common interest and the common good. It is here that I would place my greatest hope for the idea of locating social issues at the core of the curriculum. Given these possibilities, it would seem reasonable to expect that the idea would have considerable support. Yet, the long history of omitting social issues is no accident. As we have seen, proposals for their inclusion have not been lacking. And neither have critics of those proposals.

One source of criticism is the classical humanism position and those who cling to it. The argument here is that what is worth knowing is revealed by the "wisdom of the ages," and mainly through the great books and other classical sources. Such knowledge presumably offers whatever guidance one would need when confronting contemporary issues. Therefore, schooling ought to concentrate on lessons from the past so that they may be applied when young people are adults.

Another source of criticism and resistance are those of the dominant, privileged culture whose position is partially defined by their distance from the degrading conditions that plague the lives of the nonprivileged. While typically born into privilege, those of the dominant culture often somehow imagine that they have "earned" their positions on a level playing ground and that others should simply do the same. In this way, accusations of laziness aimed at nonprivileged people are used to cover up root problems such as conditions of poverty and homelessness. Clearly, it is convenient to forget that the socioeconomic playing field is not level and simply argue that paying attention to social issues in the curriculum is a waste of time. At this point, these critics find appeal in the classical humanism position which, by definition, presents the view of the dominant culture.

When the dominant culture position is tied to economics, another kind of criticism emerges. Social issues tend to arise from the contradictions created by narrow self-interests. That is, in order for the interests of some to be served, the interests of others may suffer. When social issues are explored, there is the ever-present possibility that such contradictions will be revealed and subjected to moral scrutiny—a daunting possibility when faced with the clear-cut sense of justice often demonstrated by early adolescents. Given this, it is little wonder that many businesses and industries are reluctant to support school-sponsored study of environmental problems or working conditions.

Yet another source of criticism arises from the beliefs of fundamentalist religious groups. Here, the argument is that all human experience and conditions result from the design or intention of a "Supreme Being." Therefore, social issues are viewed as outside the influence and authority of people and, in fact, should be left up to the Supreme Being who alone has the power and right to maintain or change those conditions. From this position, the claim of those who advocate for social issues in the curriculum and the application of human effort to resolve them is not only seen as irrelevant but wrong.

Akin to this position is one taken by contemporary advocates of "character education," a version of values education that maintains the school ought to exhort young people to behave themselves based on so-called universal values such as honesty, perseverance, loyalty, and industriousness. Here, the argument is that the public schools ought to limit social education to those virtues and avoid issues on which there are differences of opinion in the larger society. Since contemporary social issues are the subject of widespread debate, they would, in this sense, be off limits for the public schools.

Although I have described these objections in fairly discreet categories, their reality is far more complex. The fact is that over the past decade, the positions I have described have converged to create the New Right (Apple, 1988,

1993), an agglomeration of conservative interests that wield considerable power in politics in general and schools in particular. While this scenario may well discourage those who advocate for social issues in the curriculum, I believe that there is a kind of restlessness in the profession and elsewhere to which this kind of curriculum may well appeal. I am speaking here of a growing sense among many people that the effects of social issues are nearing the breaking point, that the degrading conditions faced by many people have become intolerable, and that those conditions are in need of immediate attention. This possibility must be tested with renewed claims for placing social issues in the curriculum. Despite the certainty of resistance, now is not the time for a failure of nerve.

There is one other objection to social issues in the curriculum that needs our attention, especially since it comes from a source that otherwise might seem sympathetic to the idea. There are those who believe that childhood ought to be a happy experience; therefore, they argue against including social issues in the curriculum on grounds that they tend to be depressing when revealed. Along these same lines, it is sometimes argued that young people are simply too "young" to understand the meaning and contradictions in social issues, that such issues are too complex for young people. Ironically, this position is often held by those who claim to have a child-centered sense of sensitivity and caring.

I say "ironically" here because, despite claims of sensitivity, such people are clearly ignorant of the fact that altogether too many young people understand social issues from firsthand experience. When we consider, for example, that fully one-fifth to one-quarter of U.S. children live in poverty, it is hard to imagine that they are unaware of their plight and happy in their fate. As we saw in the kinds of questions about self and world raised by early adolescents, the young people who attend our middle schools are acutely aware of the social issues we face. To deny this and thus to avoid these issues in the curriculum can only make us seem foolish and irrelevant.

Finally, we should be clear that in speaking about resistance to the idea of including social issues in the curriculum, we are not speaking only of those outside the school. Indeed, among those who hold to any of the positions I have described are people inside the profession itself. So it is that we might well expect that arguments against claims for a social issues curriculum are as likely to arise inside the school as outside. On the other hand, there are just as likely to be many who agree that social issues should loom larger in the curriculum than they do now. And it is to these latter colleagues, who are sometimes reluctant to take a public position, that we must make our first appeal.

At the same time, however, we must challenge the child-centered rhetoric of the middle school movement. Those who claim a place in the forefront of the movement because they "love" young people must be helped to see that truly caring about early adolescents means wanting a curriculum that takes on all aspects of the world, including the difficult social issues of our times. To deprive early adolescents of this opportunity is to leave them to their own devices and the vagaries of society to answer the compelling questions they have about themselves and their world. Worse yet, they would be left with an incomplete educational experience, lacking in critical democratic inquiry and empty of social meaning. It is hard to believe that we want such an education for our early adolescents.

REFERENCES

Apple, M. (1979). *Ideology and Curriculum.* Boston: Routledge and Kegan Paul.

Apple, M. (1986). *Teachers and Texts: A Political Economy of Class and Gender Relations in Education.* New York: Routledge and Kegan Paul.

Apple, M. (1988). "Redefining Equality: Authoritarian Populism and the Conservative Restoration." *Teachers College Record* (Winter): 167–184.

Apple, M. (1993). *Official Knowledge: Democratic Education in a Conservative Age.* New York: Routledge.

Arnold, J. (1980). "Needed: A Realistic Perception of the Early Adolescent Learner." *Clearinghouse, 54* (Winter): 4.

Arnold, J. (1985). "A Responsive Curriculum for Emerging Adolescents." *Middle School Journal, 16*(3): 3 ff.

Beane, J. (1975). "The Case for Core in the Middle School." *Middle School Journal, 6* (Summer): 33–34.

Beane, J. (1990a). *Affect in the Curriculum: Toward Democracy, Dignity, and Diversity.* New York: Teachers College Press.

Beane, J. (1990b). *A Middle School Curriculum: From Rhetoric to Reality.* Columbus, OH: National Middle School Association.

Beane, J. (1993). *A Middle School Curriculum: From Rhetoric to Reality,* 2nd ed. Columbus, OH: National Middle School.

Beane, J., and Lipka, R. (1987). *When the Kids Come First: Enhancing Self-Esteem.* Columbus, OH: National Middle School Association.

Brodhagen, B., Jochman, K., and McDonough, L. (1990). *The Responsive Middle Level Curriculum.* Unpublished paper.

Brodhagen, B., Weilbacher, G., and Beane, J. (1992). "Living in the Future: An Experiment with an Integrative Curriculum." *Dissemination Services on the Middle Grades, 23,* 1–7.

Bruner, J. (1971). "The Process of Education Reconsidered." In R. Leeper (Ed.), *Dare to Care/Dare to Act: Racism in Education* (pp. 19–30). Washington, DC: Association for Supervision and Curriculum Development.

Dewey, J. (1916). *Democracy and Education.* New York: Macmillan

Du Bois, W. E. B. (1902). *The Negro Artisan.* Atlanta, GA: Atlanta University Press.

Kliebard, H. (1986). *The Struggle for the American Curriculum: 1893–1958.* Boston: Routledge and Kegan Paul.

Lounsbury, J., and Vars, G. (1978). *A Curriculum for the Middle School Years.* New York: Harper & Row.

Noar, G. (1953). *The Junior High School.* New York: Prentice-Hall.

Schine, J., and Harrington, D. (1982). *Youth Participation for Early Adolescents: Learning and Serving in the Community* (Fastback 174). Bloomington, IN: Phi Delta Kappa Foundation.

Silberman, C. (1970). *Crisis in the Classroom.* New York: Random House.

Spring, J. (1986). *The American School: 1642–1985.* New York: Longman.

Stevenson, C., and Carr, J. (1993). *Integrative Studies in the Middle Grades: Dancing through Walls.* New York: Teachers College Press.

Tanner. J. (1962). *Growth in Adolescence.* Oxford: Blackwell Scientific Publications.

Teitelbaum, K. (1987). "Outside the Selective Tradition: Socialist Curriculum for Children in the United States, 1900–1920." In T. Popkewitz (Ed.), *The Formation of School Subjects* (pp. 238–267). New York: Falmer.

Van Til, W. (1946). "Exploring Educational Frontiers." *In Leadership through Su-pervision* (pp. 1–16). Washington, DC: Association for Supervision and Curriculum Development.

Wraga, W. (1992). "The Core Curriculum in the Middle School: Retrospect and Prospect." *Middle School Journal, 23*(3): 16–23.

Wright, G. (1958). *Block-Time Classes and the Core Program.* Washington, DC: U.S. Government Printing Office.

2

Challenging Barriers

A Unit in Developing an Awareness and Appreciation for Differences in Individuals with Physical and Mental Challenges

PAULINE S. CHANDLER

What inspired me to think that we should do a unit with the middle schoolers on attitudes toward disabilities? Perhaps inspiration came from being named after my great aunt who was a paraplegic. Or perhaps I became aware of the need for an increased understanding toward disabilities when both my mother and cousin had to adapt their lives to physical impairments. In assisting and accompanying these family members, I have dealt with the stares, the condescending offers of help, and the unrealistic, uninformed expectations. For example, my cousin, who is a quadriplegic, has been asked to stand up out of her wheelchair and move over. I have also listened to people make comments, behind my back, that my mother must be drunk because of the way she is walking. Although I am sure these types of experiences shaped my desire to write a curriculum on attitudes toward individuals with disabilities, there was a higher call, and that was helping my students to recognize, accept, and celebrate differences in all individuals.

As the science teacher for 175 students, ages 3 to 13, I have a tremendous opportunity to introduce a variety of topics. There are many challenges and joys in teaching all the students of Media-Providence Friends School, a small Quaker school in an urban suburb of Philadelphia. One of my greatest joys is the freedom and support to develop and try new units and topics. Spending eight weeks immersed in an interdisciplinary study on different types of disabilities was one of those great joys and challenges. Not many schools have the luxury or accept the challenge of spending that amount of time immersed in a topic. But it was the time and commitment that made the difference between a surface change and a genuine evolution of attitudinal change.

EXAMINING DIFFERENCES

Our middle schoolers are no different than most adolescents. They are striving to be like everyone else. In fact, they can often say insensitive things about anyone that exhibits the slightest bit of difference. Their words may not match their inner sympathies but in order to stand with the crowd, they can be heard making comments that lack sensitivity or seen pointing and staring. As more and more schools mainstream children, it seems essential that these types of behaviors be challenged so that every individual has equal opportunity. Establishing this unit for challenging attitudes of individuals without disabilities proved to be a valuable personal and community experience.

The first part of the unit had such basic curricular components as research on disabilities, discussion of disability issues, simulations, and lab work. We covered the anatomy of the nervous, muscular, and skeletal system as well as genetics and inherited diseases. Students researched specific disabilities and taught their classmates what they had learned. At this point, it was a very standard sequence of curricular events. Even though students had participated in 15-minute simulations where they role-played being hearing impaired by wearing ear plugs or being learning disabled by attempting to write and copy notes through mirrors, the subject of disabilities did not really come alive. We had laid a safe, comfortable groundwork for understanding disabilities but we were not getting any closer to challenging attitudes. We continued to study the biological, physiological, and psychological aspects of physical and mental disabilities throughout the unit so as to add depth to the content of our study. At this point, it was still merely school work. However, this all changed the day Alex came to visit.

Alex was the first of many visitors. He is an author, a telephone operator, and an advocate for individuals with disabilities, and he has multiple sclerosis (MS). The class gathered for the speaker about MS with their usual middle school attitude. They were slumped back in their chairs, talking with each other, relieved not to have their regular classes but not very interested in learning about MS.

As Alex rolled his wheelchair in and set up his computer, the interest level changed. Students perked up in their chairs and began to take notice of Alex. He had arrived on his own, had set up his computer independently, and was attaching a variety of telecommunication equipment. As Alex turned on his computer, the unit on disabilities began to come alive.

Alex began to talk about the challenge he has confronted with MS. The students and he began to engage in a dialogue that was open and respectful. The questions started coming: How do you get around? Do you cook? How do you get to the store? What do you do with your free time?

Alex also demonstrated how his computer can be used as an interpreter for individuals that are hearing impaired. He told about some of the books he had written and about his job as a telephone operator. Slowly, as the comfort level between the students and Alex increased, the questions evolved to a deeper level: What was the hardest thing about being in a wheelchair? How did he deal with it at first? Do friends and family treat him differently? Alex answered their questions and slowly the attitudes of judging differences were brought to the surface. Alex told stories of people staring at him and avoiding him at restaurants and stores. He told of going shopping with friends and having store clerks communicating through his friends rather than directly speaking to him. Very subtly, the students' attitudes were being challenged. They were being forced to evaluate themselves on a level that was not very comfortable. Nevertheless, the students were seeing themselves in some of the comments about staring, judging, and not offering to assist a person in need.

As the questions came to a close, Alex packed up his belongings and the class went off to lunch. However, about five students stayed behind to talk with Alex to learn about his job and to see his computer. These were the first students to start really knocking down their attitudinal barriers. They had connected with Alex on a level of not mere curiosity but possible friendship. Some students did leave the room uninterested and complaining about having to listen to Alex. It was going to be a challenge to reach these students and to bring about changes in their attitudes. In their journals that afternoon, the students reflected on the experience they had that morning. Their comments were insightful. Nyhima, an eighth-grade girl with a great deal of sensitivity to the needs of her family and friends wrote, "I learned that a person with MS should not be hard on his or herself or it will be more of a burden. I also learned about the courage and strength a person with MS has."

When I asked how they might approach, treat, or talk to someone in a wheelchair differently now that they had met Alex, Tremayne, a sixth-grader wrote, "I wouldn't treat a person with a disability any different than I treat my friends."

Were these the same students that weeks before had yelled cutting comments across the playground about athletic abilities and appearance and even at times cruelly imitated individuals with mental or physical disabilities? The first bricks of the attitudinal wall had come tumbling down and foundations of acceptance and respect had been laid.

A GROWING APPRECIATION

As the weeks progressed, the students interacted with more individuals with disabilities and also with individuals who work to support people with both physical and mental challenges. A brain surgeon showed a series of slides that demonstrated a host of disabilities, some from injury, others inherited. A fifth-grader brought in her puppy that she was raising to eventually become a seeing eye dog. Another student, a fourth-grader, shared his challenges and joys as an individual born with a severe hearing impairment.

Each week, we had one or two visitors. There were disruptions to the class schedules and the core curriculum but most teachers felt the speakers were worthwhile interruptions. Initially, the visitors would share their medical history. This was interesting to the students but the real interest was when the personal challenges and stories were shared. For example, Rob, a young man who had lost his sight at the age of 22 came to visit. As with most of the visitors, the students began by asking details about his medical story. Rob had diabetes. Next, the class would explore the person's life through a series of questions on life skills and adaptations. The students asked Rob: How does your dog know what to do? How do you pick what to wear so the colors match? How do you cook? At last, as the comfort level increased, the questions asked by the class began to probe more deeply: How did you feel when you lost your sight? Do your friends and family treat you differently? This evolution of questioning was not planned but was repeated time and time again with the different visitors.

The students kept a journal of their thoughts about each visitor. Dylan, a seventh grader who is a very sensitive young man but has built up a tough, noncaring exterior, wrote, " At first I wondered how Rob would know I had my hand up; I think he has handled becoming disabled very well. I would probably have gone nuts. I learned it is still possible to participate in life." Eyra wrote, "I felt kind of guilty for having my sight. I learned from Rob how to forgive and forget and move on."

All our visitors were willing to come and share their experiences. They wanted not only to tell their stories but also to meet the students and help them break down their attitudinal barriers. Some of our other speakers included the following people: a woman who is paraplegic from a car accident, an interpreter for individuals who are hearing impaired, a woman who designs technology for individuals with hearing impairments, a neurosurgeon who specializes in brain disabilities, a doctor who specializes in epilepsy research, a group of cheerleaders from the Philadelphia School for the Deaf, a wheelchair basketball team from Temple University, and a representative from a local disabilities advocacy group known as Barrier Awareness. Each individual and/or group had valuable insights to share with the students and, most importantly, all of them were willing to be honest and frank with our students.

After interacting with speakers associated with the deaf culture, Rebecca, a very sensitive eighth-grader wrote, "The thing I found that was most interesting was that the deaf culture likes to do things on their own. I never thought about it before. I always thought that people with disabilities would want all the help they could get. Now that I think about it, I realize that if I had a disability I would want to do whatever I could to lead a normal life."

After all our guests had visited and the students were trying to gather their thoughts into how their attitudes had been challenged and/or changed, Erica wrote, "Sometimes I think we are the ones with the disability, we never notice how lucky we are. This can be the worst form of blindness."

In this short sentence, this young sixth-grader had captured the essence of six weeks of work. She had confronted her own attitudes, accepted the feelings, and come to a point where she could move forward and open her heart and mind to the issues faced by individuals with physical and mental challenges.

BARRIER AWARENESS

By this point, the students had become more and more accepting of the various people's differences. Their language, vocabulary, and interactions had become more mature, respectful, and even more open minded. In the beginning, their conversations ended the minute the visitors left and journal entries were short and belabored; however, as we progressed, the students began to discuss the situations of different individuals through the lunch hour and recess. The writing began to include more detail. In many classes, we discussed adaptations for life skills: different occupations, strategies for shopping and getting around town, and various types of assistance and support groups available. Students also wanted to discuss and write about the insights of different individuals: their attitudes toward their disabilities and their acceptance of their lives. Despite this growth, our students' greatest challenge still lay ahead of them. It was my feeling that only by really being "disabled" would our students truly appreciate the barriers.

We began by devoting four hours of a school day to a schoolwide simulation. As students filed into my room, they pulled out of a hat a piece of paper with a disability written on it. We then transformed each student into an individual with that physical disability. At first, the novelty kept everyone excited and enthusiastic about the challenge.

Students left my classroom to begin a regular school day with blindfolds, earplugs, frosted and dark glasses, limbs tied down, and in braces. Two students were in wheelchairs. It was Thursday morning and, as usual, the first event of the day was Meeting for Worship. As the students filed into the meeting room for 15 minutes of silent worship, the excitement slowly disappeared and the realization that they were going to have to spend the day physically challenged cast an ominous shadow over everyone.

The energy was very different after they filed out of the meeting room door. There was a seriousness about the activity that had not existed before. There was also a commitment to supporting each other. Those students who were blind were all of a sudden being offered help. The students in the wheelchairs, who before had only been able to get into the meeting room because of teacher help, were now assisted by fellow students. It was interesting to observe the students taking on a more responsible role.

As the day progressed and the uniqueness of the simulations continued to wear off, the energy and attitudes of the students changed. Tempers began to flare as teacher and student communications were challenged and progress in classes was disrupted. Those students who were acting more helpless or dependent than they needed to were slowly being forced to take on more responsibility as their friends had grown tired of helping them. Thom, the math teacher, noticed that students who were usually very outgoing were more quiet and into themselves, especially the students who were "hearing impaired." By lunch time, students came to me asking for permission to end the simulation:

- Can't I please take this brace off?
- I want to have recess and I can't play basketball with this!
- You expect me to eat with this on?

The novelty had worn off and the reality of what it was like to have to adjust to a disability was sinking in. The students who rolled happily away in wheelchairs at 8:00 A.M. with shouts of "This is cool" were now tired of rolling across the campus, running into barriers and not being able to physically interact the way they used to.

Recess was spent resolving conflicts between frustrated students. Students who wanted to play basketball, even with a brace on, were suddenly pushed aside by the more "able" students. The gymnasium was filled with shouting, fighting, and then withdrawing. As the students vented their frustrations, I spoke with the teachers. They had also endured an equal dose of frustration while trying to teach their classes.

The teachers had not anticipated the impact the disabilities would have on their routines and schedules. They had no idea as to the variety of disruptions and challenges the disabilities would present. I interviewed each teacher about his or her day and also asked each to fill out an evaluation form. Thom wrote, "This reveals a lot about your particular style of teaching, communicating, levels of patience and the kinds of things you have a tolerance for."

The teachers were amazed at how difficult it was to teach. One gave up after the first hour and just stopped teaching her designated lessons completely and focused on discussions about the challenges the students were facing. Marguerite, the French teacher, wrote the following in response to my question about the types of frustrations encountered:

> *There isn't enough room on the paper to list them all. Time was a major factor in dealing with the individual and collective disabilities. I had to first take "inventory" to see which students I could pair up to compensate for their problems. It was almost as if I was attempting to take the "parts" and make a "whole". . . . I felt inadequate in terms of educational preparedness to deal with the physical and psychological difficulties.*

She also saw that the greatest value in this activity was to allow the students to interact, figure out how to deal with their disabilities, and become sensitive to the needs of other.

The Spanish teacher, Jeannie, wrote, "After twenty-five minutes of shifting and compensating, I began to feel frustrated realizing that I wasn't going to be able to give the quiz I'd scheduled. The students' problems were time-consuming and required patience from all, MOSTLY ME!" The four-hour disabilities simulation challenged many teachers to analyze the issue of mainstreaming, despite our limited exposure to it due to an independent school's selective admissions process. Teachers were forced to look at their own attitudes and approaches to individuals with disabilities. Many teachers felt they could handle one or two such students in a class, but all of them felt completely overwhelmed by a classroom of diverse disabilities.

At 12:45, the simulation ended. Students stepped out of wheelchairs, took off braces, and removed glasses that had caused varying degrees of visual impairment. Once they stepped out of the role of an individual with a disability, they resumed their normal schedules. After an hour, we pulled the entire middle school together for a meeting in order to share our experiences.

As the group gathered to discuss the day, I encouraged the teachers to share their experiences and feelings with the students. Teachers and students together expressed their feelings, frustrations, and experiences. The honest dialogue that took place was impressive, revealing, and more educational than any book or article about attitudes toward individuals with disabilities.

One feeling expressed by many was best stated by Erica. She had worn lab glasses that had been painted black so absolutely no light could get in. Of the experience, she wrote, "After having my feet run over by Ray and Jodi, I think that people who are blind or in a wheelchair have extreme courage. Since I was visually impaired for only 3 hours, I felt badly because you look at a person who is really visually impaired and they can't take off a pair of glasses to see like me."

Thomas, a seventh-grader who had spent the day with his right arm immobilized, reiterated this sentiment by stating, "I learned being disabled is hard to live with for a couple of hours. It must be real hard for the rest of your life."

The most telling stories were ones that demonstrated interactions with others. Trisha wrote, "When I went in the gym, Mike grabbed my arm and started running. It was scary. I guess I know what Rob [our visually impaired guest speaker] was talking about when he said to always ask [permission of] someone who is visually impaired before helping them out."

As the stories came to an end, the students began reflecting on what they had learned. Bharat, a seventh-grader who wore a brace for the day, commented, "I think now, more than ever, I will offer help to a disabled person. There were many times today where I needed help but could not get it." Another level of understanding was reached when Rebecca, an insightful and very intellectual eighth-grader, spoke up and said, "The greatest value in this activity is learning to respect the disabled as much as you would anyone else. You also realize that you take your own abilities for granted."

There were many other insights, but Nyhima, a very articulate student who has faced several racial and socioeconomic challenges in her community, summed it up best for the class when she shared her thoughts: "I learned that although it can be hard and frustrating at times, you need to get past the frustrating part then start to take life one day, one step at a time. I also learned you may be blind, you may be in a wheelchair, but inside you are really a loving person and I came to find that out with almost everyone I interacted with."

THE AMERICAN DISABILITIES ACT (ADA)

The students' experiences at school introduced them to the true meaning of *barrier.* Eventually, every student experienced at least one barrier. To further this awareness of barriers, the students were challenged to evaluate the school based on their experiences and on some basic codes established by the American Disabilities Act (ADA). Students quickly discovered doors were not wide enough, drinking fountains were too high, sinks were inaccessible, and so on. Several students volunteered to write letters to the board and headmaster of the school to request that changes be made to the buildings on the campus. The students' requests were addressed by the headmaster and requests were made for making the school more accessible. However, finances, as the students would come to learn, played a very big role in the implementation of the changes.

Understanding the American Disabilities Act proved difficult for this group of students that usually interpreted laws as nonnegotiable entities. Unfortunately, the expense involved in making buildings barrier free, the lack of enforcement, and the wording of the ADA have allowed for different interpretations and implementations of the law. The standardized codes and the actual outcomes result in two very different scenarios.

To further the students' understanding of the actual barriers and issues, we took the classes to evaluate a public building. The students had been introduced to the ADA by the president of Barrier Awareness, a local advocacy group for individuals with disabilities. She had shown them how to measure doors, ramps, entrances, and so on in order to ascertain if the physical features of a building were truly accessible. In order to assist the students with their projects, teachers designed a checklist to be used to evaluate the major components of the act: hallways, doors, bathrooms, telephones, parking spaces, ramps, entrance ways, and drinking fountains. The students set out with measuring sticks, checklists, and an understanding of how to evaluate the accessibility of a building.

Unfortunately, there are not very many buildings that meet the current code requirements of the ADA, and building managers are not very eager to have 30 students coming to evaluate their sites. A local mall refused our request to come, even though we insisted that the only result of this exercise might be a letter of recommendation written by a student. The issue of accessibility is difficult. It forces public places to spend money on adapting their physical plant, and many privately owned facilities have avoided the construction modifications because the ADA is not aggressively enforced. I was finally able to obtain permission to bring the students to a local community college, but even that required several phone calls.

We arrived at the college with meter sticks in hand, ready to evaluate the campus. The students took on a detective mode and were eager to find places where the ADA was not being enforced. As I walked the halls, the middle school students began interacting with the college students. They explained their project and made comments on the areas that were not accessible, all based on the ADA regulations. The college students were intrigued by the middle level students' findings and left the small groups saying things like, "We never did meaningful stuff like that when I was in school."

We spent two hours on the campus measuring, talking with the building managers, and interacting with the professors and college students. Everyone we approached was helpful and curious. Many times, college students reached out to assist in some of the measuring. The excitement and energy grew as the time progressed and the middle schoolers began to put the ADA puzzle together.

They began to see how the ADA was misinterpreted or unaddressed, and how disabilities and accessibility issues were misunderstood. As they continued to measure, students would periodically approach me and make such comments as, "The doors are wide enough to get into the building but look at the entrance way! They have a long paved ramp that ends on a cobblestone/brick patio area. How is someone in a wheelchair suppose to get over all those bumps?"

As I walked into the women's bathroom, a group of girls were just finishing the evaluation of the stalls and the height of toilet seats. One girl shouted, "Can you believe this? The entire bathroom meets all the ADA requirements, everything is wide enough and high enough for a wheelchair—BUT the door from the hallway coming into the bathroom isn't wide enough for a wheelchair to get through. They can't even get in here to use this bathroom!"

Students began to see that just because there is a law, it does not mean that all barriers had been overcome. As we exited the building, it was pouring rain and we had to run across the entire campus to our parking spot. As one student jumped across a huge puddle, he shouted, "What is someone in a wheelchair suppose to do in the rain? They'd be soaked by the time they got to their parking spot. Doesn't anybody care?" It was becoming readily apparent that the students were beginning to understand and internalize the issues.

A CHALLENGE IN ATTITUDINAL AND PHYSICAL BARRIERS

After eight weeks, we finally arrived at the culminating day of our unit. The students were now ready to tackle one final challenge that many later referred to as "a day I will never forget." From the first day of the study, the students had heard that I was going to be taking them to the mall for the afternoon of the final day of the unit. They had returned permission slips and were ready to spend school time at their favorite hangout. The mood was immediately transformed when we arrived at the mall and they realized that they were going to spend the afternoon in wheelchairs.

When we arrived at the mall, each student was paired with a friend and an adult supervisor. We entered the mall and found the 18 wheelchairs that I had reserved from a local rental company that was graciously letting us borrow the chairs for the next three hours. Each student would take an one-hour turn in the wheelchair. An adult and another student were to follow a distance behind the wheelchair user and record observations regarding interactions with people in the mall, treatment by store clerks, and physical barriers encountered.

The student in the wheelchair had a specific list of tasks. Among them were the following: Go into your favorite clothing store and try on a shirt or sweater; find your favorite book in the bookstore; find a CD you like in the music store; find the mall bathrooms and drinking fountains; and, optionally, purchase a drink and snack. All of the tasks were focused on things teens would usually do when at the mall, but this time they were not allowed to get out of their wheelchairs.

As I walked the mall with my group of students, it became very obvious that we had become quite an issue of discussion. Store clerks began asking what was going on, mall patrons stared and whispered, and, at one point, the mall security officer decided he was uncomfortable with it all and asked us to leave. After explaining the project and discussing the value of the experience, he agreed to let us stay and continue.

What began with a horserace-like atmosphere and students bolting away in their wheelchairs ended in a more subdued and reflective mood. Students returned to our meeting place with tired arms, heavy spirits, and a sense of how truly difficult it is to be in a wheelchair. As we returned to the school, the comments in the van revealed not only their host of experiences but a definite change in attitude. The stares and comments of the day had definitely impacted their mood. All the way back to school, I heard stories, such as Joanna's: "I went into the bookstore and said: 'Excuse me' to this older couple and they acted like they didn't want to move or that I even existed." Amber was insulted that "the store clerks didn't really even know I was there; they ignored me. People and children stared a lot; they were so rude. Some people helped me out but a lot of people got really mad because I was in their way." Jamie, a seventh-grader, was still infuriated by an experience at the Electronic Boutique where a clerk had been conversing and asking questions to Jamie through his friend rather than speaking directly to Jamie. Jamie, the wheelchair-bound student, was so angry that he shouted at the clerk, "Yes, I'm in a wheelchair but I can still talk!" A few other students commented how, after experiencing lack of respect in a store, they had stood up from their wheelchairs and left; leaving the rude clerk silent in embarrassment.

After we got back to school, all of the students were asked to answer a series of questions regarding their experiences of being (1) an individual in a wheelchair and

(2) an observer. The questions focused on both physical and attitudinal barriers encountered. The questions guided students to summarize their frustrations and to recognize and identify acts of kindness and/or disrespect. They were also asked to identify the value and lessons learned in this experience.

The students sat and wrote diligently. They had obviously encountered a myriad of experiences and were feeling a host of emotions. The examples of frustrations were predictable: not enough space in aisles, doors too heavy to open, shelving too high to reach items, dressing rooms too narrow to enter, and inaccessible bathrooms. There was not one student who did not encounter some physical barrier that either made it either extremely difficult or impossible to accomplish a task. Lack of accessibility, and therefore inequities of opportunity for entrance to a store, were experienced by all.

The real emotions—the writing that really revealed the impact of the day— were the answers to those questions that challenged attitudinal barriers. The encounters the students had with clerks' stares, disrespect, avoidance, anger and mistrust were disturbing and disheartening to all of them.

- "No one really went out of their way to help me. Only one lady offered to help me and that was when I was getting into the elevator and it seemed to me she did it because she thought it would be faster for her to get downstairs if she did help."
- "I had to speak louder for people to take notice of me and hear me."
- "Everybody treated you differently, nobody helped me. It seemed everyone was staring and talking behind my back."
- "Everyone was whispering about me."
- "I found I didn't really talk to anyone and say 'Hi' like I usually would."

The students' comments were painful to read, as they had truly encountered a host of emotional and attitudinal barriers.

The final question asked of the students was: How, in any way, have your attitudes changed since we began this unit? Students wrote some of their most heartfelt writing of the year in these sections. They wrote of how they would no longer stare or make fun of individuals with disabilities; they would treat individuals with disabilities with respect; and they would offer help and assistance if they thought someone needed it. The comments showed a change in attitude, but Jamie summed up the experience and change of attitude especially well when he wrote,

> *My attitude has changed dramatically during this unit. I have noticed so much more from being disabled. . . . In the mall, I came upon another man in a wheelchair like myself, and eventually we started talking. He showed me how to get around. I understood then that he is just like me, he has thoughts, feelings and friends too.*

The unit was an experience that none of us at Media-Providence Friends School will ever forget. We were a community of learners in the truest sense of the expression. We learned together about attitudes and barriers. We shared ideas and experiences with a host of individuals with disabilities who were willing to share openly their life experiences and challenges. We saw the weaknesses in a law that is needed but is often poorly implemented and enforced. We felt empowered to get the law enforced, but were discouraged by our attempts at conversation and letters to building managers requesting changes to facilities with structural barriers. We felt the stares and heard the hurtful comments as we moved through our society that has all too often avoided or pushed aside the issues and needs of individuals with disabilities. We also felt the warmth and compassion from those who are willing to work, help, and defend the rights of people with disabilities.

As a community of learners, we had achieved the ultimate goal. We had challenged and changed our attitudes; opened our minds and hearts to the uniqueness of each individual; acknowledged the need to celebrate differences, and, most importantly, recognized the similarities of all people.

APPENDIX: OUTLINE FOR IMPLEMENTATION

Sequence of Unit

1. How are people alike and how are they different?
   (*Example:* Compare thumbprints. List characteristics of yourself and then have others try to figure out who wrote what list. Chart and graph similarities.)
2. Discuss the power of words. Develop a working vocabulary that respects differences—especially vocabulary used to identify individuals with physical and mental disabilities.
   (*Example:* Discuss epithets. How and why are they used? How do you feel when they are used on you? On others? List common disabilities and evaluate the term—is it respectful or judging? Evaluate the use of words (such as: He is a cripple versus Jon has an orthopedic disability).
3. Get the facts.
   a. Discuss Anatomy (*Example:* Study the ear, eye, nervous system, brain, muscular and skeletal system. Learn about genetics.)
   b. Student Research Projects (*Example:* Write research papers on specific disabilities. Share and teach each other.)
4. Simulate different types of disabilities.
   a. Learning and Communication Skills (*Example:* Trace shapes and words reflected in a mirror. Write with a nondominant hand. Decipher writings by students with spelling and reversal challenges. Listen to someone reading with a stutter.)

    b. Hearing Impairment (*Example:* Conduct class with students wearing earplugs. Watch a video with the sound off. Practice using sign language and lip reading.)

    c. Visual Impairment (*Example:* Wear glasses smeared with Vaseline. Walk with a blindfold. Feel Braille books.)

    d. Physical Challenge (*Example:* Wear rubber gloves for class. Immobilize different limbs.)

5. Implement barrier awareness.

    a. Study the American Disabilities Act (ADA). What are the standards that are expected for public access? Invite someone to speak about the law—its implementation, enforcement, strengths, and weaknesses.

    b. Create a checklist of measurement standards for door widths, ramps, railings, bathroom fixtures, and so on. Use the list to evaluate your own school and another public building.

    c. Write letters to building managers regarding suggestions for ways to better meet the ADA standards.

6. Invite visitors to school.

    a. Contact local organizations that support individuals with disabilities. Often, they will be able to recommend individuals who would be good speakers. Suggestions include individuals who are blind, deaf, or physically impaired with multiple sclerosis, cerebral palsy, paraplegia, and so on.

    b. Invite individuals who support and help people with disabilities, such as doctors, home health-care providers, and spokespeople for national organizations (e.g., United Cerebral Palsy, Muscular Dystrophy, etc.)

    c. Visit care facilities and schools for individuals with physical and mental disabilities. Work on service projects that support the individuals at these facilities.

    d. Invite performances and competitions by individuals with disabilities, such as Theater of the Deaf and Wheelchair Basketball Teams (many universities have teams).

    e. Volunteer to help with the Special Olympics.

7. Experience a disability.

    a. Spend a school day with a disability (visual impairment, hearing impairment, limb immobilization, wheelchair, brace, etc.). Simulate the disability by using simple materials, such as lab glasses smeared with Vaseline or painted black, earplugs, pieces of cloth to tie down limbs, and so on.

    b. Hospitals, drugstores, and rental agencies are often willing to loan out wheelchairs and braces for a few hours for a minimal fee or even free.

    c. Discuss frustrations, challenges, feelings, and so on.

8. Practice barrier awareness and attitude awareness.

    a. Get wheelchairs for students.

    b. Create a checklist of tasks to accomplish while in a wheelchair in a public place.

  c. Organize teams of wheelchair users (a student in a wheelchair, a student observer, and an adult).

  d. Visit a mall or other public place large enough to absorb the group and not make the exercise too obvious.

  e. Keep track of experiences; observer should keep notes on barriers.

  f. Discuss barriers and attitudes.

9. Share experiences with others.

  a. Write newspaper articles describing the unit.

  b. Keep a photo journal throughout the unit. Publish a short book with student quotes and comments.

  c. Write a play or puppet show to teach younger children about accepting differences.

  d. Plan and implement a fund-raiser for an organization that supports individuals with disabilities.

▶ 3

Implementing an Interdisciplinary Unit on the Holocaust

REGINA TOWNSEND   WILLIAM G. WRAGA

"I think I am much less inclined to be prejudiced or anti-Semitic because I know now the prices that many have had to pay and I don't want to cause any trouble by thinking people are bad just because they are different." This was one seventh-grade student's evaluation of an interdisciplinary[1] study of the Holocaust in which he had just participated.

What is the reality of implementing an interdisciplinary unit in a school where the discipline-centered curriculum organization enjoys a long and abiding tradition? During the 1990–1991, 1991–1992, 1992–1993, and 1993–1994 school years, members of the seventh-grade team at William Annin Middle School in Basking Ridge, New Jersey, developed and taught three interdisciplinary units. Each unit examined a curriculum topic through the focus of a central theme. The connection of a theme to a topic prevented the mere presentation of subject facts relating to the topic and instead encouraged the application of information to developing greater understanding not only of the timely topic but also of a timeless theme. Classroom activities in each subject area were correlated to relate to the theme/topic and were coordinated to occur at about the same time.

What follows is an account of the origins and development of a unit on the Holocaust. For most students, this unit served as their initial exposure to the Holocaust. The unit's aim was not only to develop student understanding of the causes, events, and ramifications of the Holocaust but also to engage students personally with these realities through an examination of the impact of the experience on individual lives. Through a study of the topic of the Holocaust, it was hoped that students would begin to form attitudes that reject racism and prejudice and that respect the dignity of the individual. The following account includes a summary of the evolution of the unit; a description of classroom activities students experienced in their social studies, mathematics, science, and English classes; and a discussion of issues that may hold implications for other efforts to implement interdisciplinary units in a predominantly disciplinary curriculum organization.

ORIGINS AND DEVELOPMENT OF THE UNIT

William Annin Middle School serves an affluent suburban community, enrolling about 525 students in grades 6 through 8. Teachers are organized both in grade-level teams (comprised of teachers who teach different subjects at the same grade level) and subject departments (comprised of teachers who teach the same subject at different grade levels). This section chronologically recounts the origins and development of the unit.

1990–1991 Academic Year

During the 1990–1991 school year, a social studies teacher (one of the authors) began a unit on World War II and the Holocaust in her seventh-grade world geography course. She saw this as an opportunity to integrate an examination of human values into the curriculum in a meaningful way. Classroom examination of the Holocaust was complemented by a student field trip to a Holocaust conference entitled "Holocaust and Genocide: Learning through Experience," held at the local community college that included presentations on racism and antisemitism. Looking back on the conference, social studies teachers who attended were dissatisfied with the impersonal nature of the large conference that, ironically, addressed a topic that was usually personally riveting. "A survivor was telling her story to an assembled group. Behind our seating there was a great deal of noise," one teacher recounted. "Other groups had not been sensitized and revealed their lack of understanding with the senseless questions asked." Another teacher observed that "large numbers of students [at the conference] were unprepared. They did not understand the seriousness of the subject matter and acted in an undisciplined manner, even during the survivor's lecture." It was decided that during the next year a Holocaust survivor would be invited to visit the school to provide a more intimate experience for students than the large conference could manage.

The social studies teacher (who also taught English) was aware that just as the Holocaust was studied in social studies, English classes also read Goodrich and Hackett's (1991) dramatic version of Anne Frank's *Diary of a Young Girl* (entitled *The Diary of Anne Frank*). In fact, for many years, Anne Frank's diary had been taught at the seventh grade. During a language arts program revision a few years earlier, however, a reevaluation of literature anthologies resulted in the selection of a series that placed the book in the eighth-grade anthology. Seventh- and eighth-grade teachers decided to leave Anne Frank's diary in the seventh-grade curriculum in order to establish favorable conditions for correlation between English and social studies. This meant that for a few weeks, seventh-grade students would have to use the eighth-grade literature anthology to read *The Diary of Anne Frank.* Yet, due largely to the logistical inconvenience of sharing anthologies, neither teachers nor students in either subject so far had been making explicit connections between the two topics.

1991–1992 Academic Year

During the 1991–1992 school year, the social studies teacher approached the English teachers about correlating the study of the Holocaust in social studies with the reading of *The Diary of Anne Frank* in English. The English teachers welcomed the idea but expressed the concern that they were less familiar with the history of the Holocaust than their counterparts in social studies. "They had a general knowledge of the Holocaust, but lacked any detailed knowledge of its historical inception and of the process through which the [Nazi] government facilitated the 'final solution,'" the team leader observed. The same was true, of course, about the social studies teachers' familiarity with *The Diary of Anne Frank.* They agreed, therefore, that in social studies classes, students would examine the historical context and the events of the Holocaust in order to complement their work in English classes, where they would read, discuss, and write about the dramatic version of Anne Frank's diary. Subsequently, teachers in the two subjects timed their schedules so that the two topics would be taught simultaneously in the separate courses.

1992–1993 Academic Year

Much of the discussion and planning for the correlation of these topics occurred in seventh-grade team meetings with the end result that teachers in other subjects learned of the project. During the 1992–1993 school year, math teachers expressed an interest in addressing the topic through their classes but expressed bewilderment as to exactly how they could contribute constructively to students' understanding of the Holocaust. Again, this was largely due to their lack of familiarity with a topic typically considered outside their field as well as with materials on the Holocaust that were suitable for classroom use. Statistical data about the Holocaust, though, turned out to be an effective vehicle for the math teachers' involvement. Around these data they developed an activity that applied mathematical competencies to understanding the Holocaust. More specifically, in mathematics classes, students calculated the relationship between the number of Holocaust victims and the current population of New Jersey. (This will be discussed in more detail later in the chapter.)

A science teacher was also anxious to have her subject contribute to students' understanding of the Holocaust, but was initially reluctant to commit to the project due to the pseudo-scientific and horrific nature of some of the notorious events of the Holocaust. It turned out, though, that many students in one English class had read, as part of an optional reading assignment, Lois Lowry's

(1989) *Number the Stars,* an account of the nobility of the Danes in their effort to rescue people fleeing Nazi persecution, and this presented (as will be discussed in detail later) the science teacher with a unique entry into the subject matter.

With the four major subject areas now involved during the 1992–1993 academic year, the unit was organized as follows:

1. Background through social studies classes (about one week)
2. Full-day examination of the Holocaust through questionnaire, video, guest speaker, and discussion
3. Related lessons in science and mathematics classes (one period each) within the same week of the full-day of Holocaust-related activities
4. Beginning of a major language arts unit on *The Diary of Anne Frank* within the same week of the full-day of Holocaust-related activities and the related science and mathematics lessons

During the 1993–1994 academic year, these activities were extended with the viewing of a film version of Anne Frank's diary entitled *The Diary of Anne Frank* (1959) and a dramatic presentation called *Through the Eyes of a Friend* about the experiences of Anne Frank and her friends. (Student feedback suggested that between the book, the film, and the presentation, Anne Frank's story was probably "overdone.")

Clearly, this unit was not planned, organized, and implemented in a linear fashion. Rather, the endeavor was prompted by one teacher's interest and unfolded as others saw opportunities to make connections between and among the separate subject areas. Significantly, as discussed earlier, members of the seventh- and eighth-grade teams had previously put in place several favorable conditions for correlating social studies and English. Gradually, over a three-year period the unit grew to incorporate activities, knowledge, and perspectives from the four major academic subjects. Indeed, at the time of this writing, not all members of the team had been involved with the unit and revised activities were in the planning stage for the following year—both indications of the continuing emergent nature of this project. Implementation issues are discussed in greater detail later in this chapter. Let us first turn to the substance of the activities in which students participated in each subject area.

CLASSROOM ACTIVITIES

The aim of the unit was to develop attitudes that respect the dignity of the individual and reject racism and prejudice. While the Holocaust was the topic of the unit, racism was the overriding theme of the unit. What follows are descriptions of the social studies, math, science, and English activities that took place during the second and third years of the unit's implementation.

The Holocaust in the Social Studies Classroom

During the 1991–1993 school year, the second year the unit was conducted, most of the activities in which students participated were based in the social studies, but they were scheduled for a full day with the cooperation of the whole seventh-grade team. During periods one and two, students completed a questionnaire about the Holocaust that was designed to engage them personally in the issue and to familiarize them with important facts of the Holocaust. The questionnaire was part of the support materials for a video instructional kit called *The Holocaust: A Teenager's Experience* (1991). The questionnaire confronted students with 10 scenarios that were faced by Holocaust victims and asked students how they would respond if they were actually in these situations. These scenarios paralleled the events of the accompanying video, asking students how they would respond to the following: newly imposed harsh regulations restricting speech; temporary deportation of you and your family due to your religious beliefs; neighbors who failed to protest your family being escorted off under armed guard; conditions of crowded cattle cars, including the breakup of families; and life-threatening situations in work and extermination camps. Students were also asked to speculate as to why they were one of the few survivors later to be liberated and how they would react years later to allegations that the events they experienced never happened.

Student reactions to these situations were what one would expect from early adolescents who had little, if any, prior knowledge about the Holocaust. For example, one student, finding himself in a situation in which he was guarded by soldiers with automatic weapons during an eight-mile march to and from work, commented that he would handle this dilemma in the following way: "If the guards weren't watching, I would try to steal their guns." (Student comments are edited for spelling.) Upon being passed over to be sent to an extermination camp and thus remaining in a work camp, this same student attributed this turn of events to the fact that "My hard work had paid off and the person in charge thinks that I would be a lot of help in the work camps."

In addition to the questionnaire, the packet conveyed essential facts about the Holocaust to students through a glossary and a body of information set out in question and answer format. Information summarized included the number of people murdered during the Holocaust (including the number that were children) and how the murders took place. Glossary terms included *anti-Semitism, crematorium, displaced persons, extermination camps, genocide, ghetto, Nuremburg Race Laws, persecution, pogrom,* and *scapegoat.* The basic facts were essential to establishing a foundation upon which to build students' understanding of the Holocaust. However, this information by itself was insufficient to convey to students the dimensions of the catastrophe and the gravity of the tragedy, as the naiveté of the above student responses attests. The final activity in this packet had students complete a family tree.

When the questionnaire was completed, students viewed the video in the kit *(The Holocaust: A Teenager's Experience).* The video depicted a factual account of the experiences of a teenager named David Bergman who survived the Holocaust. Students easily identified with Bergman's experience given his proximity at that time to their age. In the video, Bergman's personal narration of his experiences as a 12-year-old was complemented by Nazi and Allied film footage from the National Archives and by photographs and drawings from Bergman's personal collection. While the narrative and visual images presented the grim reality of Bergman's experience as a prisoner at Auschwitz and other camps, the film maintained a desired degree of personal objectivity and historical integrity. This was achieved through Bergman's narrative, which included mention of numerous groups (Jews, Poles, Gypsies, Hungarians, Russians) who were persecuted by the Nazis, an anecdote of the relative humanity of a Nazi guard who spared Bergman a beating upon learning his age, and accounts of how prisoners turned against each other in their desperate attempts to survive.

After lunch and physical education, which allowed students the time to assimilate the materials they encountered during the morning activities, students attended an assembly at which a survivor of the Holocaust spoke with them about his or her childhood experiences in Nazi Germany and answered student questions. (Over three years, two survivors visited the school, one speaking twice.) The survivor who visited the school during the spring of 1994 spoke to students about being declared an enemy of the state and a criminal at age 11, and about his experiences as a prisoner at several labor camps between 1939 and 1945. Many of his experiences were consistent with those depicted in the video that the students had earlier viewed. He described, for example, how the first camp in which he was held contained only Jewish prisoners, whereas the second held a range of political prisoners, including Jews, Gypsies, homosexuals, and prisoners from Denmark and Norway. He also spoke of the occasional humanity of some Nazi guards (including one who gave him extra food) and the different ways prisoners coped with their circumstances (ranging from looking out for fellow prisoners to collaborating with their Nazi keepers). He concluded his remarks by advising students that "racism and prejudice are serious diseases that affect the mind and the heart" and that "those who practice racism are not only unjust, but just plain stupid." He warned students that racism and prejudice are still exploited by some political leaders.

During a question and answer session, students asked a variety of questions, ranging from the simplistic ("Could you bring a pet with you to the camp?" A: "Oh, no. This was not allowed. If you brought one, it would have been eaten. Sorry.") to the profound ("Have you thought about the people who died [while] you were freed?" A: "Yes. But not anymore during the day. Just at night in dreams."). Several of the more sophisticated student questions follow:

Q: How do you feel when people say the Holocaust never happened?

A: At first, I was outraged. Since then, I have learned that people say things for their own personal political reasons. I still think it is incredible that people will deny history. The evidence in archives is overwhelming. They are nuts.

Q: Do you think that the Holocaust can happen again?

A: Hitler came to power during bad political and economic conditions in Germany. Similar conditions exist today. It can happen anywhere. There are even close calls here, too. [Joseph] McCarthy. [David] Duke who ran for governor in Louisiana. But the voting system kept Duke out.

Q: Do you think you were forced to grow up fast?

A: I don't think you grew up faster. Just learned facts about life earlier, perhaps too early.

Q: After the war, did you feel a need for justice because of the loss of your mother and sister?

A: Yes—a sense of outrage. I had to control myself not to jump on Germans. But in time, I learned that not all Germans were Nazis. There were courageous Germans. I realized I couldn't spend the rest of my life hating. It is very bad for your health.

Q: Has talking to students helped you deal with it?

A: After 40 years it has become easier. It's amazing—time is a great healer.

From the students' perspective, the survivors' presentations were the most influential and engaging aspect of the unit. A sampling of student comments from thank you letters written to their guests follows:

> Your story presented the horrors of the Holocaust in a way no book or movie could tell it.

> I didn't know that there were people left from the days of the Holocaust.

> I already knew some about the Holocaust from Hebrew School but, even there it doesn't sound as bad. . . . Even though it was sad to hear, I'm glad you came to speak with us.

> That you, then such a young child, could survive the ordeal is incredible; that you are willing to share the bitter memories, and teach others about the horrors of the Holocaust is simply amazing. One comment of yours touched me more than all your others: "I had no childhood." That one simple sentence seems to sum up some of the worst things the Holocaust caused. It stole a part of people, robbed them of an age, as in your case, a happy childhood. This message conveyed by your talk will stick with me forever.

Many students expressed their hope that the survivors would continue to tell their stories to students in other schools. One student took from the experience more than an informed opinion about the Holocaust: "I myself would like to tell people things like you have been doing, but I have not had an experience that teaches others a lesson." He continued, "So, I've decided to become a writer, of science-fantasy novels, [in order to] tell people what might happen in the future if they don't stop air pollution, toxic waste dumping, creating nuclear weapons, and using too many natural resources when we could recycle. I will also teach them not to start dumping our garbage into space, though I don't think that is a problem yet."

Students spent the last period of the day reviewing their initial responses to the questionnaire, now drawing on their new knowledge of the experiences of two people who actually had lived through the Holocaust, as well as from what they learned from the video and accompanying activities. Many students modified their initial responses which they now saw were uninformed and sometimes flip. Finally, in an effort to graphically depict a particularly saddening aspect of Bergman's experience, students were asked to cross out the names on the family trees they had prepared earlier, until only their own name remained. According to the teachers who led this exercise, students were stunned as they eliminated friends and relatives from their family tree with a stroke of their pen. As one teacher put it, "Their initial reaction was total silence. An atmosphere of awe pervaded the room. One student said, 'I am all that could be left.'" Another teacher observed, "Some kids got angry. They had internalized the experience. It is now personal." Clearly, in this instance, the aim of personalizing the Holocaust experience had been met.

During the 1992–1993 and 1993–1994 school years, this series of social studies activities was complemented by correlated activities in English, mathematics, and science classes over a week-long multifaceted examination of the Holocaust.

The Holocaust in the Mathematics Classroom

"I was shocked at the number of people that died at first but then it was even more scary when you illustrate it on a map. I just couldn't believe that could happen to so many people." Such was the reaction of one student after completing an activity in mathematics class that compared the number of deaths in the Holocaust to the current population of New Jersey. Students were given a table summarizing "Deaths by Country" (Raul Hilberg, *The Destruction of the European Jews,* Volume 3 [New York: Holmes and Meier, 1985, Table B-2, page 1220]) and were asked to look up the population of each New Jersey county in an almanac. After combining country death totals during the Holocaust to approximate New Jersey county population totals, students then shaded in counties on a map. In order to achieve the greatest visual impact, they began with the geographically larger counties . Using basic mathematical competencies of computation, approximation, and graphing, students produced an astonishing effect (see Figure 3–1).

Judging from student responses, this activity achieved both the mathematical and moral lessons it aimed for. "From this activity, I have learned that a

Name: _____ 7th-Grade Math

The following activity will allow you to visualize and better understand the extremely tragic results of the Holocaust.

Directions:

1. Using your almanac, look up the New Jersey population by county.
2. Once located, compare these county populations to your table entitled, "Deaths by Country."
3. Using your New Jersey county map and colored pencils, color code, by grouping the countries, and shade the individual counties. You will, obviously, have to approximate. Please provide a key with your map. *Note: Shade in the larger counties first. This will produce a greater visual impact.*
4. What have you learned from the activity? Using another sheet of paper, please give your reaction(s).

FIGURE 3–1 Mathematics Activity Instructions Handout

visual impact is much greater than the impact you get from a bunch of large numbers," wrote one student. Another student commented, "I can't believe that half of New Jersey's population was killed in Poland! (sic). It was a great shock! This activity had a great impact on me."

The Holocaust in the Science Classroom

As noted earlier, the science teacher involved was initially apprehensive about the possible contributions that science could make to her students' study of the Holocaust. She feared that the grizzly medical experiments conducted by Nazi physicians during the Holocaust that leave adults aghast would be found by young adolescents to be grossly unbelievable and therefore perversely engaging rather than morally outrageous. As the teacher delicately put it, "I suspected that kids would find the medical experiments innately fascinating, at least some of them, but it is not something I would feel comfortable handling in class." When an English teacher brought to her attention the technique to desensitize guard dogs' smelling ability that the Danish resistance used in their efforts to hide Jews from the Nazis, the science teacher saw an opportunity for a substantive science lesson and demonstration lab relating to the Holocaust.

She began the lesson by leading students in a discussion about the issue of good and bad uses of science, contrasting the Nazi's horrific experiments that used prisoners as subjects with the Danes' efforts to desensitize guard dogs' smell to hinder Nazi detection of Jews they were attempting to rescue. In this discussion, students typically asked how the Danes came up with the idea of desensitizing the dogs' smelling ability and commented on the bravery of the Danes' actions. In one class, students raised the issue of whether it is horrific to use animals in scientific research. In order to prepare students for a closer look at the scientific dimension of the Danes' efforts, the teacher then read aloud a passage from *Number the Stars* (Lowry, 1989).

By the time students arrived in science class, some were familiar with the passage in Lois Lowry's Newbery Medal–winning novel, *Number the Stars* (1989) in which the character Annemarie is stopped by Nazi sentries to search her lunch basket. The soldiers suspect—by their guard dogs' reactions—that she is carrying meat in her basket (a scarce wartime ration they desired for themselves), but a humiliating search reveals only bread, cheese, an apple, and a folded white cloth. Although she is allowed to pass, Annemarie is disappointed that some of the lunch was vandalized by the guards. Later, although her parents praise her for completing her part of the plan to save several Jews, she is perplexed as to exactly what she did. Her father explains to her that the handkerchief has been treated with a special concoction designed to ruin the dogs' sense of smell so they could not detect people being smuggled to Sweden in hidden compartments in Danish fishing boats. In an Afterword to the novel, Lowry explains that Swedish doctors devised a simple solution of dried rabbit's blood and cocaine to attract and then temporarily deaden the dogs' sense of smell.

In science class, the teacher explained to students how the sense of smell works through a diagram of the nose and a demonstration activity. In short, molecules of gas released from substances in the environment stimulate receptor cells inside the nose. From the receptor cells, olfactory nerves carry impulses to the brain which then identifies particular odors. In the episode recounted in *Number the Stars,* cocaine numbed the dogs' sense of smell completely, disabling them from detecting the human scent they had been trained to isolate for a short time. Since an exact replication of these conditions clearly was not feasible in a classroom setting, the teacher opted to demonstrate a related physiological effect using a common theory about how smells are differentiated. This theory purports that certain odor molecules stimulate the same receptor cells in the nose. When receptors are activated by one smell in a particular odor family, for a period of time those receptors, already engaged, will not be activated by related smells in the same family.

For the lab demonstration, the teacher provided students with several smells in the same odor family and assigned them to work in pairs quizzing each other on identifying them. Students discovered that after they had breathed a heavy whiff of peppermint, they were unable for a short time to identify the normally distinctive aroma of cedar. In this way, students came to understand and experience the scientific principle involved in the Danish resistance's treatment of the Nazi guard dogs. The teacher was satisfied with this contribution to students' understanding of the Holocaust because, as she commented, it "showed what people can do with some knowledge to help other people." Additionally, this activity not only contributed to students' understanding of the Holocaust but it also complemented two objectives in the local seventh-grade science curriculum: "Students will list ways in which the ears, nose, tongue, and skin are necessary to the body's ability to detect changes in the environment" and "Students will describe how messages travel throughout the nervous system and react with other body systems."

The Holocaust in the Language Arts Classroom

As noted earlier, students in seventh-grade English classes read Goodrich and Hackett's dramatic version of Anne Frank's *Diary of a Young Girl* entitled *The Diary of Anne Frank*. As they had with the narrator of the video, students easily identified with teenager Anne Frank. While instruction focused on analysis of the text, the connections with their social studies classes enabled students to view the text in its social and historical context. As a result, in addition to standard language arts activities such as summarizing the events of each act of the play, visualizing the set from the stage directions, explaining cause-effect relationships in the plot, and examining the use of stylistic techniques such as flashback and foreshadowing, students discussed the use of the journal as a tool for chronicling historic events and for identifying critical issues. They also analyzed the various support systems, both physical and emotional, that people need and depend on in times of crisis. During the 1993–1994 school year, students also viewed a movie version of Anne Frank's experience that complemented their reading of the play.

An essay served as the culminating activity for the study of *The Diary of Anne Frank* (see Figure 3–2). Students chose and wrote about one of four essay topics. One of these topics directed students to "Imagine that it's the anniversary of Anne Frank's death. Write a letter to the editor of your local paper in which you explain why you feel it's good that the play based on her diary is read and performed regularly today. . . . Explain what the theme of the play is and why it is still considered an important message today." Here is an excerpt from one student's essay:

> Besides being a record of the past, the *Diary of Anne Frank* has an anti-racist theme. It reveals the cruelties of anti-Semitism. Through Anne's entries, we can see how people are the same inside, and that no one is inferior. The effects of racism are shown by Anne's record of losing her possessions, freedoms, and finally, her home. But there is a lesson in the story, as Anne Frank, in her annex, still believes that everyone is still good at heart.

As one can see, students in their language arts classes moved beyond a technical analysis of literature texts to consider the impact of racism on individuals and its ramifications for humankind.

Such was the status of the unit by the end of the 1993–1994 school year. True to the reality that curriculum development is never finished, refinements

Name: _____

ESSAY: *The Diary of Anne Frank*

Directions: Choose one of the following essay questions and write a complete essay. Include an introduction, a body, and a conclusion. Use blue or black ink on white composition paper for your final copy.

1. Explain, in a complete essay, Anne's relationship to her mother, her father, and Peter. Be detailed and use specific events from the book. Use the following as your topic sentence: "Anne had very different relationships with her mother, her father, and Peter." Be sure to revise and edit your rough draft for clear understanding of ideas.
2. Imagine that it is the anniversary of Anne Frank's death. Write a letter to the editor of your local paper in which you explain why you feel it is good that the play based on her diary is read and performed regularly today. First, make an outline of at least three points you want to include. Then, explain what the theme of the play is and why it is still considered an important message today. Be sure to revise, edit, and use the correct format for a business letter.
3. Think about Anne's statement, "I still believe, in spite of everything, that people are really good at heart." In a complete essay, explain the importance of these words to the whole play. Choose at least three examples from the play to support this statement, and then explain why it is still important to consider Anne's point of view today. Be sure to revise and edit your rough draft for clear understanding of ideas.

FIGURE 3–2   Culminating Language Arts Activity Handout

of these activities are being planned for 1994–1995. Specifically, student feedback that Anne Frank's diary was "overdone" (noted earlier) gave rise to the teachers' decision to show only excerpts from the movie version of her experience. We cannot emphasize enough that this unit is an ongoing, evolving project that intrigues both teachers and students alike.

IMPLEMENTATION ISSUES

Efforts to enact interdisciplinary units and programs at the middle level described in the educational literature typically face several persistent implementation issues. Among these are issues pertaining to preservice preparation of teachers, departmentalization, planning and instructional time, materials, curriculum correlation, teacher adjustment, and administrative leadership (Wright, 1952; Vars, 1987; Wraga, 1992). We will briefly discuss these issues as they were encountered by the teachers who participated in the unit.

Departmentalization, Preparation, and Correlation

As noted at the outset, the curriculum at William Annin Middle School is organized in a traditional disciplinary fashion: formal curriculum is developed and
revised by subject area; teachers from all three grade levels (6–8) meet as departments on a monthly basis (those who teach more than one subject alternate
between department meetings); and students move from one subject class to
another over the course of the school day. At the same time, teachers at each
grade level meet as a team usually three times a week. Significantly, the coexistence of subject departments (comprised of teachers who teach the same
subject at different grade levels) and grade-level teams (comprised of teachers
who teach different subjects at the same grade level) is not uncommon in middle
schools in the United States (Epstein and MacIver, 1990).

The prevailing departmental mindset was an obstacle to implementing the
interdisciplinary unit on the Holocaust. "Some were so concerned about meeting their own curriculum mandates that they couldn't contemplate giving up
time," one teacher explained. While teachers in both the seventh and eighth
grades clearly considered such an experience a valuable one for students (as
demonstrated, for example, by their decision to keep *The Diary of Anne Frank*
in the seventh-grade language arts curriculum because of its potential for correlating English and social studies), their exclusive experience in their specialty
subjects made drawing connections between and among subjects a novelty and
something of a challenge. The disciplinary basis of their college studies and
their professional preparation contributed to this way of working and thinking,
as well. But the idea of connecting the subjects for students made sense, so they
endeavored to discover ways to make it come alive in their classrooms. As one
teacher put it, "The world is interconnected and school is a microcosm of the
world. The interdisciplinary approach is a better model." Another team member
observed, "The complex problems that students are going to be confronted with
require a variety of approaches to solve. Interdisciplinary studies force them to
think more critically and comprehensively." Like other middle-level educators
involved with interdisciplinary studies, then, the efforts of the seventh-grade
teachers at William Annin Middle School were challenged by issues of departmentalization, preservice preparation, and lack of familiarity with making connections between and among the traditional subjects.

Planning and Instructional Time

The team organization ultimately served as a great advantage in meeting the
challenges to interdisciplinary studies presented by departmentalization,
preservice preparation, and lack of familiarity with making connections between and among the traditional subjects. Traditionally, team meetings were
devoted almost exclusively to student guidance concerns. Over this two-year

period, teachers became increasingly interested in curriculum matters and began devoting a portion of team meeting time to discussion of such issues. As a result, the interdisciplinary units were planned during team meetings. Teachers found the team meeting time invaluable for planning activities across departmental boundaries. A math teacher commented, "It is where the connections take place." The public nature of the planning and coordination of the activities served to inform other members of the seventh-grade team and resulted in the desire of several to contribute to the unit. "As you see the possibilities, interest increases, insecurity decreases," one teacher said of the benefit of collegial interaction about interdisciplinary curriculum matters. Reflecting on the project, the team leader noted, "It is important that the team leader be an advocate because the scheduling and arrangements will probably be his or her responsibility."

Adequate planning time was generated by borrowing from team meeting time, but the necessary instructional time was a more sensitive issue for these teachers. Despite an ongoing concern about numerous classroom interruptions (e.g., assemblies, testing, pull-out programs for the gifted and talented), which required a constant reexamination of the pace and depth of instruction, teachers felt that the relatively modest amount of time required for these activities was justified by the potential educational return for both students and staff. Indeed, the social studies and English content in this unit was part of the regular subject curriculum, and the science and math activities, which complemented local curriculum objectives, each took little more than a class period to complete.

Materials

Once appropriate curriculum correlations were identified, teachers who participated in this unit needed to obtain appropriate materials. Interestingly, this proved to be of least concern to the teachers. The resources accumulated by experienced teachers, the generous collections of the library/media center and the cooperation of the media specialist, and the relatively limited amount of supplementary materials actually needed for this unit made the availability of materials virtually a nonissue for those involved.

Adjustment

Throughout this account, we have alluded to the reality that not all seventh-grade teachers (and therefore students) participated in the planned activities. From the standpoint of the disciplines, subjects such as foreign languages and art, for example, could make important contributions to students' understanding of the Holocaust. Further, not all teachers from the major academic subjects were able to participate in the unit.

Significantly, this unit was developed in a grass-roots fashion, and participation by any team member was completely voluntary. Initially, some teachers were discouraged with the prospect of additional work being added to an already hectic school day. The fact that some teachers taught on more than one grade level and therefore alternatively attended different team meetings made the communication necessary for coordinating activities difficult in some instances. That is, teachers assigned to two grade levels who were unable to attend team meetings did not have ample opportunity to become involved in the planning and implementation of the unit. The most important factor in the teachers' decisions to become involved in the unit was their perception of the pertinence of the unit to their subject. Some teachers initially were unsure as to how their subjects could contribute to what were usually considered social studies topics. Nor did they have information relating to such topics. The latter problem was overcome by teachers simply sharing relevant information with one another. In one instance, statistics included in social studies instructional materials were found to be useful to math teachers; and in another, a passage in a novel read in language arts class held a correlation opportunity for science teachers. After the first unit was completed, teachers and students exhibited enormous enthusiasm for the experience. This enthusiasm, in turn, led to greater willingness to participate in subsequent units.

Leadership

As noted earlier, the development and implementation of this unit was initiated and carried out by teachers on the seventh-grade team. Administrators played essentially a hands-off role in the unit; that is, they provided teachers the autonomy to plan and enact the activities they deemed worthwhile, and contributed directly only by providing encouragement and moral support as well as by assisting with logistical arrangements (such as field trips and assemblies) only as requested by the participating teachers. This indirect approach to leadership on the part of building administrators was vital to the success of the unit.

CONCLUSION

The teachers who participated in this unit are planning to improve activities for the next school year. An important result of the unit was that students *and* teachers found the experience rewarding. Asked to evaluate their experience in this unit, students offered remarks such as the following:

> Since we were studying the Holocaust in every subject, I felt more "into it." . . . Actually seeing a survivor of this terrible tragedy changed my thoughts in such ways that I couldn't get a great feel for what went on without him. Now I have a stronger feeling about being against racism.

I saw it from different angles, and thus could understand it better. The teachers successfully mixed the cold facts (social studies) with the feelings of the people (English).

This learning experience changed my views and I learned more than I would have with a short lesson from a book. Now I am less, much less, inclined to be anti-Semitic. Having this experience, the speakers, movies and all, I have such a broader view and it helped me understand so much more.

If we had just learned about it in social studies everyone would have probably forgotten about this period of history and just treated it as a regular everyday thing that they have learned, instead of really feeling about the ways the Jews felt and how terrible this period really was.

Reflecting on the past year's experience, one teacher commented that he "really enjoyed the cooperation of other teachers" and that he had "gained a great sense of personal satisfaction" from the effort "to end reasons for intolerance and racial prejudice in the minds of my students." Another thought that the unit "forced both [teachers and students] to assimilate and apply information in much more depth and breadth than would have been the case in a traditional approach." This teacher captured what he thought was the essence of the unit when he remarked, "Students and teachers shared an emotional, personal experience which made them more aware of their own humanity." By working collaboratively across traditional disciplinary boundaries, teachers and students were able to establish for themselves what they thought was a more sophisticated understanding of a historic event that continues to hold urgency in a world that seems increasingly torn by racial, ethnic and religious tensions.

Note: The success of this unit depended on the following teachers who participated in it at various points in its four-year development: Debbie Black, Judy Brown, Val Brzdek, Lisa Cerullo, Brian Chinni, Larry Hamil, Sandy Hyde, Ken LeCour, and Regina Townsend.

ENDNOTE

1. In this chapter we define the term *interdisciplinary* as "any curriculum that deliberately links content and modes of inquiry normally associated with more than one of the scholarly disciplines" (National Association for Core Curriculum [NACC], n.d.). The unit described here attempted to correlate (i.e., adjust "the sequences in two or more subject areas . . . so that students deal with the same theme, topic, issue, or problem, in several different courses at about the same time" [NACC]) learnings in social studies, mathematics, science, and English. Such a curriculum arrangement is also called *parallel disciplines, sequenced, shared,* and *multidisciplinary* studies. For an overview of various forms of interdisciplinary curricular organizations, see Wraga (1993).

REFERENCES

Epstein, J. L., and MacIver, D. J. (1990). National practices and trends in the middle grades. *Middle School Journal, 22*(2): 36–40.

Furman, Harry (Ed.). (1993). *The Holocaust and Genocide: A Search for Conscience.* Anti-Defamation League.

Goodrich, F., and Hackett, A. (1991). *The Diary of Anne Frank. In Prentice Hall Literature: Silver* (pp. 300–369) Englewood Cliffs, NJ: Prentice Hall.

The Holocaust: A Teenager's Experience. (1991). Niles, IL: United Learning.

Lowry, L. (1989). *Number the Stars.* Boston: Houghton Mifflin.

National Association for Core Curriculum. (no date). *Interdisciplinary Curriculum Terminology.* Kent, OH: Author.

Vars, G. F. (1987). *Interdisciplinary Teaching in the Middle Grades.* Columbus, OH: National Middle School Association.

Wraga, W. G. (1992). "The Core Curriculum in the Middle School: Retrospect and Prospect." *Middle School Journal, 23*(3): 16–23.

Wraga, W. G. (1993). "The Interdisciplinary Imperative for Citizenship Education." *Theory and Research in Social Education, 21*(3): 201–231.

Wright, G. S. (1952). *Core Curriculum Development: Problems and Practices.* Bulletin 1952, No. 5, Office of Education. Washington, DC: U.S. Government Printing Office.

4

The Homeless

An Issue-Based Interdisciplinary Unit in an Eighth-Grade Class

BELINDA Y. LOUIE   **DOUGLAS H. LOUIE**

MARGARET HERAS

Mrs. Mancuso has been teaching eighth-grade English for four years in Evergreen Middle School. She is a collector of comic books and loves listening to rock music. Her easy-going manner and casual outfits relax people around her.

Evergreen Middle School (Tacoma, Washington) is located between an inner city and an upper middle-class neighborhood, enrolling 800 teenagers in grades 6 through 8. Young people of color comprise one-third of the student body: 20 percent are African American, 10 percent are Asian American, and 4 percent are Hispanic. The centralized location of Evergreen Middle School is the reason for its ethnic diversity. It is the school that serves the predominantly ethnic population in the inner city. At the same time, it also serves the upper middle-class neighborhood at the north end of the city. The school places a strong emphasis on racial harmony, ethnic pride, and the war against drugs. Parents and staff are active and alert, constantly looking for opportunities to unite the student body.

Mrs. Mancuso enjoys teaching middle school students who, she comments, are filled with energy and imagination. They laugh at her jokes and share her excitement for comics and cartoon characters. They argue with her with emergent self-assurance and logical reasoning. However, she finds the standard curriculum fails to capture the curiosity and sparkle in the teenagers' lives. The challenge is not there. There is little connection between the school curriculum and the outside world. Something, she thinks, has to be done to address this!

A call in the professional journals for building participatory citizenship among young people excites Mrs. Mancuso. She wonders, though, how she can modify the curriculum to achieve this goal. How can she guide teenagers from focusing on their social lives to the social issues in the community? How can students learn to analyze issues and take action accordingly? To accomplish her goals, Mrs. Mancuso realizes that certain factors must be in place. Students must have input into the topics chosen in order to channel their concern. The information or reading materials must engage students' minds. The activities must be challenging enough to capture young people's attention. At the same time, instruction must be at a level that will involve students of various abilities.

Her eight o'clock English class is the first group that she wants to initiate the change. There are 26 students in this group: 15 European Americans, 6 African Americans, 4 Asian Americans, and 1 Hispanic. Sandy and Karen, two European Americans, and Jane, who is African American, are students who work hard no matter what the assignment. The giggling trio whisper to each other frequently in class. They love to initiate projects for their little group in class. How can she direct their bubbling energy to issues outside the classroom? Next to the chalkboard are Aaron and Peter, two European Americans, Eugene and Jason, two African Americans. They read comics and draw cartoons in between assignments or even when the teacher is talking. How can Mrs. Mancuso broaden their interest beyond Batman? There is also Con, the Laotian student who works hard to adjust; Ricardo, the 15-year-old Hispanic youth who has been the head of the household since the death of his father last year; Lisa, the alcoholic; and Billy, the special education student who feels totally out of place. Mrs. Mancuso is committed to helping all of them analyze social issues critically; and as a result of that, she decides to start a four-week unit in this eighth-grade English class.

THE METHODOLOGY

Identifying an Issue

When Mrs. Mancuso asks her students what issues they care for most, they suggest dating, driving and drinking at an earlier age, attire worn at school, and cafeteria food. The young people seem to be so engulfed in their own world that they hardly pay attention to the community around them. Mrs. Mancuso feels they need to acquire a broader perspective; and to accomplish this, she initiates an inquiry by asking each student to take a new role:

> You are the newly elected mayor of our city. Taking a tour of different neighborhoods, including the downtown area, right after your inauguration, what do you observe? Based on your observation, write down 10 things that you want the city to work on in the next 4 years.

After each student has responded in writing, groups of three are formed so they can share their ideas. Each member explains, discusses, prioritizes, and negotiates as the trio works to select the two most significant issues for them. The group then draws a web for each issue, providing four to six reasons as to why the two issues are their highest priority (see Figure 4–1). Students store

We want to help all the homeless people because they need a warm place to stay.

We want to help all the homeless people because they need our help in order to survive.

Help All the Homeless People

We need to give the homeless what we have because they are people, too, and they need to live like humans, not dogs.

We should help the homeless have a second chance in life.

FIGURE 4–1   Example of a Group's Web on an Important Social Issue

their individual work in their own portfolios, which represent collections of their rough drafts and polished pieces. They continue to add to this collection as they undertake their study of a social issue.

Jane, Ricardo, and Billy try to finalize the social issue of their choice.

Billy: I really want to talk about the age that teenagers are allowed to get a driver's license. I will turn 15 next month. If I don't need to ask for a ride all the time, I can do much more.

Jane: How is that a social issue of top priority? There are more urgent things in this city than lowering the age so that you can get your driver's license.

Ricardo: Yeah, priority. We need to have more police in our neighborhood. Not just more police, but police with better weapons. A well-equipped police force is a social issue. It affects everybody in the community.

Jane: I want to study about the homeless. Last night on TV, I watched the police taking down the shelter of some homeless people who camped out under the bridge. I wonder whether the police would treat the homeless differently if they understood them better.

Billy: I saw it, too. I wondered where those homeless people would go. It was so cold last night. I kind of felt bad for them.

Ricardo: Why don't we go for this topic? If we can reduce the size of the homeless community, we may not even need to increase the police force.

Afterwards, each group shares and discusses its issues and the reasons for selecting these topics with the whole class. Interestingly, the common issue of most concern ends up being *homelessness.*

> We want the city to do more for people like the homeless. We shouldn't just spend money on building court houses and museums. People are more important. The homeless need food and housing.

> Our group wants to study about the homeless because it is a severe problem in the city. The problem will not go away even if we ignore it. We don't think that the homeless people can rebuild their lives without our help. If they could, they would have done it already.

> If we want the city to grow, we need to clean up the downtown area to attract more business. Nowadays people don't even want to go there because so many homeless people are roaming around. And it is not right for us to allow others to suffer so much. We must help the homeless.

Thus, the class members decide that they will study homelessness in their community.

Sandy, Karen, and Jane are very excited about the topic. They suggest that the class should visit the homeless people in the shelter. Their voices are immediately drowned by a round of protest.

Aaron: I do not want to talk to the homeless people. They are weirdos.

Sylvia: Yeah. They are alcoholic bums. I never know what would happen to me if I talked to them.

Michael: No, some of them are normal people with family and kids.

Peter: Not those that I've seen in the streets. They trot around downtown muttering to themselves.

Many of the student exchanges reveal some of their misconceptions about the homeless. Mrs. Mancuso grasps this moment of tension by asking the students to describe their images of a homeless person during 10 minutes of free writing. Among some of the images they come up with are the following:

- The homeless people are people with no money.
- The homeless people are dirty, depressed, hungry, and on drugs.
- The homeless mug each other to get money, clothing, and alcohol.
- Homeless people live on the streets. They get their food from the mission and garbage cans and dumpsters (sic). Some of them are Vientinam (sic) vets. They sleep and live under bridges, doorways, cardboard boxes and

shelters. When some of them try to get jobs they [employers] won't take them because they are dirty and smelly.

• Homeless people don't have any money. Well they might have a little. Homeless mug each other to get their money, clothing, and alchol (sic). They are people who needs (sic) to have warmth. Sometimes they purposely put themselves in jail just to keep warm. They don't have much clothing, so they search in dumpsters. Many homeless teenagers and children are runaways. A lot of teenagers have babies at a young age. In some cases when the parents are homeless the children are homeless too.

Generating Focal Questions

Some of the comments generated by the students reflect their lack of knowledge about the diverse background of the homeless. Taking a step to break the stereotypes, Mrs. Mancuso reads aloud Eve Bunting's *Fly Away Home* (Clarion, 1991) to the class. The story is about a little boy Andrew and his father who make the airport their home. The father only has a weekend job. Both father and son are waiting for the day that they have enough money to rent their own apartment. Initially, some students sneer at the notion that they are going to listen to "a kid's book."

"My dad and I live in an airport. That's because we don't have a home and the airport is better than the streets." Thus, the story begins. One by one, students focus their attention on Andrew's life. As the students discover, it takes careful planning for a father and son to live anonymously in a large airport terminal. They need to walk around constantly between four and six o'clock in the morning when the airport is quiet. They can sleep for stretches of only two to three hours in order to avoid attention.

Suddenly, there is no more giggling. There is no more joking. Even the students engrossed in their comic books listen to the story. At the end of the story, a voice emerges from a pool of silence, "It brings tears to my eyes," Ricardo says as he quickly dabs his tears. He is embarrassed by his spontaneous remark. Mrs. Mancuso is amazed how these teenagers' defenses can be removed when their hearts are touched by a moving story.

It is very unusual for Mrs. Mancuso to see such solemn expressions on the students' faces. Grabbing the opportunity, Mrs. Mancuso encourages students to express their feelings about the book.

Shirley, a quiet girl who seldom participates in discussion because students like to ridicule her for her large frame, says, "They appear to be nice people. I wonder why Andrew and his father lost their home." Eugene, who has a hard time understanding homelessness because of his well-to-do family, asks, "Why didn't their relatives help them? My family and relatives will never allow me to be homeless."

The unusual setting of the book and the emotional impact of the story stimulate the students to learn even more about the homeless.

Jason: Andrew and his father look like normal people to me. They are not dirty and alcoholic. Andrew's father even has a weekend job. I wonder how many part-time workers are homeless.

Pauline: The father feels bad because they do not have a permanent address so that Andrew can go to school. It must be really hard for him that he cannot even support a 6-year-old son. I hate to think that young children can be homeless too. My brother is 6. I cannot imagine him wandering around without a home. What do homeless parents do with their children when they look for jobs?

Albert: I have never thought about the airport as a homeless shelter. What other public places can the homeless go?

Jane: I have seen some of them in the mall and in the public library.

Initially, each person is asked to generate a personal list of questions that he or she has about the homeless. Next, Mrs. Mancuso records students' questions on butcher paper and posts them on the wall. Students are encouraged to revisit both their own as well as others' questions throughout the unit on the homeless. Among the types of questions that the students wrote are the following:

- How do people become homeless?
- What is it like to live in the street?
- How do homeless people survive bad weather?
- How long do homeless people stay homeless?
- Have homeless people tried looking for jobs?
- Do homeless people have pets?

Formulating Hypotheses

Moving to another step of inquiry, Mrs. Mancuso asks the class to hypothesize answers for the questions (see Figure 4–2). By doing so, she *helps* students articulate their assumptions and understanding of the topic studied. Later, they assess how much they have changed in attitude and increased in knowledge by comparing the hypotheses at various stages of the unit.

Gathering Information

After listening to *Fly Away Home*, students are surprised to discover that clean and so-called normal people often lead a homeless life outside downtown shelters. Mrs. Mancuso asks for suggestions on ways to learn about the homeless community. Within a few minutes, students generate several information sources:

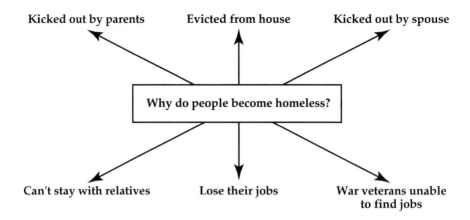

FIGURE 4–2   Example of Students' Hypotheses for a Question

newspapers, magazines, a speaker from a homeless shelter, a homeless person, and books about the homeless.

Mrs. Mancuso is very happy to hear that students wanted to read more literature on the topic (see Figure 4–3). Television, newspapers, and magazines have provided much information, but such knowledge does not seem to work on the hearts of teenagers—at least not those in her class. Mrs. Mancuso believes that young adult literature will help them develop empathy with the homeless.

As for those interested in learning more from newspapers and magazines, several students volunteer to go to the public libraries to find newspaper and magazine articles. Mrs. Mancuso explains that the librarians can teach them how to conduct their search using the *Reader's Guide to Periodical Literature* or the InfoTrac CD-ROM databases. InfoTrac is an automated reference system that provides easy and fast computer-aided retrieval of bibliographic references to more than 4,000 magazines, journals, and newspapers. It is updated and cumulated monthly.

Mrs. Mancuso organizes students to do the search in small groups. She also tells them that once they identify a good article, they can give it to her to make copies for everyone to read.

Contacting speakers is Mrs. Mancuso's job. She calls a family shelter to ask the director to talk to the class, and the director accepts the invitation. In addition, Mrs. Mancuso contacts a teacher she met in an education class at the university who had once been homeless. This teacher accepts the invitation to speak because he wants to use personal sharing to enhance students' understanding of the homeless.

Ackerman, K. (1991). *The Leaves in October.* New York: Atheneum.
Berek, J. (1992). *No Place To Be: Voices of Homeless Children.* Boston: Houghton Mifflin.
Buck, P. (1966). *Matthew, Mark, Luke, and John.* New York: John Day.
Bunting, E. (1991). *Fly Away Home.* New York: Clarion.
Carlson, N. S. (1958). *The Family Under the Bridge.* New York: HarperCollins.
Corcoran, B. (1991). *Stay Tuned.* New York: Atheneum.
Fox, P. (1991). *Monkey Island.* New York: Orchard.
Grove, V. (1990). *The Fastest Friend in the West.* New York: Putnam.
Hahn, M. D. (1988). *December Stillness.* New York: Clarion.
Hamilton, V. (1971). *The Planet of Junior Brown.* New York: Macmillan.
Harris, M. (1989). *Come the Morning.* New York: Bradbury.
Holman, F. (1974). *Slake's Limbo.* New York: Aladdin.
Hubbard, J. (1992). *Shooting Back: A Photographic View of Life by Homeless Children.* San Francisco: Chronicle Books.
Hughes, D. (1989). *Family Pose.* New York: Atheneum.
Hyde, M. (1989). *The Homeless: Profiling the Problem.* New York: Enslow.
Paulson, G. (1987). *The Crossing.* New York: Dell.
Pinkwater, J. (1991). *Tails of the Bronx.* New York: Macmillan.
Spinelli, J. (1990). *Maniac Magee.* New York: HarperCollins.
Tolan, S. (1992). *Sophie and the Sidewalk Man.* New York: Four Winds.
Wojciechowski, S. (1989). *Patty Dillman of Hot Dog Fame.* New York: Knopf.

FIGURE 4–3 **A Booklist on Homeless People**

THE USE OF KEY RESOURCES

Young Adult Literature

With the help of the public library staff, Mrs. Mancuso receives duplicate copies of literature titles for students to read. She then has the students select their own books. The reading levels of the books vary from fourth to eighth grade. In addition to 10 minutes of sustained silent reading during class, students are asked to take books home to read as their homework assignment. Students are not assigned a specific number of pages to read each night, which enables them to read at their own pace. They keep a reading log (a journal in which students write down their thoughts when reading a book) for the purpose of recording book-related reflection and questions. In addition, they are told to work in groups of three or four to write a paper based on materials they read on their own. They are given time in class to share—in pairs, small groups, and as a whole group— their reflections about what they have read and written.

As all teachers readily know, students read at different paces. A good number often do not enjoy the act of reading. However, Mrs. Mancuso's daily reading from a book called *No Place To Be: Voices of Homeless Children* by J. Berek (Houghton Mifflin, 1992) prompts students to compare their fictional characters with the real ones. "Our pride supports us and helps us endure. Your pity not needed, but your understanding, yes" are the words of a teenager recorded by the author. Robert tells the class that this is exactly how the homeless characters in *Monkey Island* feel. He refers to several episodes in the book when the homeless characters' dignity enables them to face physical attack and insult. Other students constantly affirm that the fictional characters have the same feelings as the real ones. "They all feel like they are scum of the world." "The banging on doors, the screams in the night, even shooting on ground floors. That's what the children in *Stayed Tuned* face in the motel." This ongoing reading and discussion helps students continue with their books. A few students devour the books as though they are the best books that they have read. Lisa is one of them.

Lisa is not a very serious student. She giggles, jokes around, and talks to her friends all the time. There is an obvious change in her mood since the beginning of the homeless unit. She has become very sober. Instead of her normal rowdy behavior, she spends much of her time in class reading young adult literature on the homeless and writing in her journal. However, she does not participate in the ongoing discussion. She is quiet even in small groups.

It takes Lisa only one day to finish her first book, *Monkey Island* by P. Fox (Orchard, 1991). During recess, she approaches Mrs. Mancuso and asks if she will go to the school library to look for books with her. She wants to read more books with teenage characters in homeless situations. Quietly, she mentions that she has run away from home five times already. Although she has not slept in the street, she has wandered around and has spent nights at friends' houses. Mrs. Mancuso is not surprised to hear this because Lisa has come to class drunk before. It is gratifying to know that Lisa has found identification and support from young adult literature in which adolescents experiencing similar problems are an integral part of the story.

Homeless characters in literature touch the hearts of many teenagers in class, and writing in their journals provides the students with opportunities to gather their thoughts about the homeless. While reading B. Corcoran's *Stay Tuned* (Atheneum, 1991), Aaron wrote,

> I feel sorry for the kids whose parents die or leave them, especially when they live in a drug infested rundown hotel. I felt happy when the father got a job but felt sad because he had to leave his daughter and send her to their uncle's house. My feelings swayed as the fortune of the family changed.

Jane responded to *Tails of the Bronx* in this way:

> It is a very sad story. It tells me that the government does not care about what goes on in the Bronx. It hurts to hear things like that when most people want to think that it is the homeless people's fault or that it does not go on in their city. I think that those who think this way are ignorant

people. And others who say bad and horrible things about the homeless are ignorant as well.

Reflecting on the books she read, Carol wrote,

It is hard for me to understand how the homeless people can make it through the night. I feel sorry for them because they have no food to eat, no bed to sleep in, no place to call home. People who are homeless must be very strong and courageous. Sometimes people look at homeless people and think, "Gosh, what scum! " But little do they know that they could be homeless themselves later on in life.

Jason reveals that *Family Pose* makes him think. He wrote,

I can understand why homeless people don't want to be noticed. I can also understand why people feel so sorry and helpless for homeless people. It's like seeing a starving, dirty, sick child and not being able to help because of fear. The fear of not knowing how people will react or what they'll say.

Dan found the book *December Stillness* thought-provoking:

By reading it, I'm starting to realize that teenagers can be really cruel to the homeless and the people who try to help them. I also think that no matter how much the homeless emphasize the fact that they don't need anyone, they all need friends.

Karen jotted down these lines while reading K. Ackerman's *The Leaves in October* (Atheneum, 1991):

I gained perspective by reading the story. Not all the homeless people are bums. Some have a job. They are clean. They try to do things for their family. They are not dumb or alcoholics who spent their days in the street. It is very difficult for the kids. They do not know what is happening to them. I think the homeless situation is also very difficult for the parents. They feel guilty that they cannot provide for their children, something as simple as food, clothing, and shelter.

A few students occasionally wrote poems responding to Mrs. Mancuso's reading of *No Place to Be: Voices of Homeless Children*. Anthony drafted this poem:

Some homeless people starve,
Some homeless people live in cars,
Then there are the people who live in the street,

Other people have hurt feet.
I know one who collects cans,
One man has scarred up hands.
Some people want to move.
Most people have nothing to lose.
Homelessness is a way of life.
Some homeless men have homeless wives.
There are homeless youth.
There are also homeless children.
Homelessness is a very big topic.
Now all us have to deal with it.

As students read, write, reflect, and share their thoughts, Mrs. Mancuso is amazed at how literature has changed their attitudes toward the homeless. They grasp the urgency of the issue and realize that people are out there in the street waiting to be helped, that the homeless community cannot and should not be ignored, that they are hurting, and that they are crying out for help.

Mrs. Mancuso asks students to visit their portfolios to compare their opinions of the homeless with their opinions now. Eugene writes, "I really feel sorry because I have not done anything to help the homeless. Now I hate people who are mean to the homeless, calling them names and refusing to help."

Justin believes that "I have learned that 85 percent of the homeless children become prostitutes. We have to help! We can send them items they need or can use like food, clothing, and utensils. We can also call the missions and see what they need too. We have to do something." Although Justin is eager to help the homeless, he only thinks about help in terms of daily sustenance. He does not realize that the homeless issues are very complex. There are many social problems, such as prostitution, which will not be cured simply by providing food and shelter.

Newspaper and Magazine Articles

Using the database InfoTrac at the public library, students found some interesting and useful articles from major national newspapers and magazines. A very controversial feature, "Playing House: Troubled Teenagers Created a Fragile Family Beneath a Busy Street," reported in the *Wall Street Journal* was selected by Aaron and used for a discussion piece with the whole class. The report is about a charismatic ex-convict, Pops who creates a community called "Trolls" for troubled street youth. He provides shelter for homeless teenagers "in a dark, fetid cavern under a busy roadway" and asks them to support him by panhandling, prostitution, and mugging. The class discussion after reading the article is highly explosive:

Mike: Pops was giving drugs and alcohol to the teenagers. He is sending them out as prostitutes. He is taking advantage of them. He is not helping them.

Susan: But at least there is a person who listens to you. Most of the time people simply don't care. It is difficult to find a person who will listen.

Peter: Yeah. He listens but he is sending people out to be prostitutes. Prostitution is hardly a favor to those people involved. I cannot see how he is helping the teenager by (sic) drugs, alcohol, and prostitution. Maybe you don't care. [Maybe] you don't mind being a prostitute if you can find a person talking to you.

Sandy: (turning toward Susan) That's prostitution. I don't like that at all. How can it be good?

Jeremy: But there are two sides of the story. What would happen to these teenagers if Pops was not here?

It seems that everybody has an opinion about Pops. Mrs. Mancuso seizes the opportunity to hold a class discussion. She provides the students with time in class to express their feelings about the article by responding to the following questions:

1. If you have a chance to talk to Pops, what will you say to him?
2. If a friend of yours asks for advice about joining the Trolls, what will you tell him or her?

Many students commend Pops for his support for the teenagers; yet, they advise him to reconsider his demands on the Trolls. Here are examples of students' written responses:

> What you have done to the kids is bad. You seem to stand by their side, but it does not justify the many bad things you have taught them like drinking and drugs. Being sweet to them and sending them out as prostitutes are just what pimps do. You'd better think about what could happen to you and the Trolls in the future.

> I would tell him that what he's doing is very wrong. The newspaper says that at least he keeps the kids out of trouble. I don't know what types of trouble he is keeping them away from. The kids are prostitutes. They take drugs. They fight with outsiders. They are deep in troubles.

Students also bring in other articles on the plight of homeless families, including but not limited to cooperation among homeless families who combine their resources to rebuild their lives, the plea of homeless advocates urging government to increase low-income housing, community efforts in renovating inner-city houses for the homeless, food drives, coat drives, blanket drives, and the overnight transformation of an established community into a homeless community of individuals because of natural disasters such as hurricanes and floods. It is the first time that these students pay serious attention to the homeless people in the nation and in the local community. Aaron's response sums up the students' reaction to the news articles: "Gee, I know that homeless (sic) is a national issue, but I did not realize that there were homeless people all over the States. They are all in need. We cannot only ask the government to do something with them. We need to do something for them too." By reading newspaper and magazine articles, students are exposed to the struggle of the homeless and the effort in helping them.

Speakers

Two speakers are invited to Mrs. Mancuso's class. The first one is a teacher, Mr. O'Neil who had been homeless in the past. This provides the students with firsthand information about the life of a homeless person as well as the opportunity to evaluate their own images of the homeless. "How can a teacher become homeless?" is the first question they ask. The teacher relates to them that during the first year of college, his part-time job was insufficient to support him.

> After tuition, there was some money for food, but there was not enough money for a room or an apartment. Therefore, I slept in my car. It was not very comfortable but at least I had some shelter. I had my meals in the campus cafeteria. After work, I spent all my time in the library because [there was] heat and [a] restroom. The main library closed at midnight. It was a great help to me! In the morning, I went to the gymnasium to take a shower. When the campus was closed during quarter break, I usually went to visit my parents or friends.

Students ask him why he did not get help from people that he knew. They are puzzled when he tells them that it is a matter of integrity that he did not stay with friends or relatives. "We cannot burden people all the time." It is a difficult concept for the teenagers to learn. At various points in their literature journal, they have stated that they will never become homeless. Their families, relatives, and friends will never let them live in the streets. Up to this point, the students had hardly contemplated the issue of personal integrity and their own responsibility not to burden people with their own needs. In addition, the students are confronted with the fact that not all the homeless people are dirty and alcoholic.

The other speaker is Ms. Kalton, the director of a local family shelter. She explains to students the homeless situation in the local community, including the fact that many homeless families have young children. She tells them that providing shelter and schooling are the priorities of her center. She also describes the National Network of Runaway and Youth Services, emphasizing the effort of her staff on placing students in public schools, including this one. Students can hardly believe that there are homeless youth among them. And to their surprise, they cannot readily identify the individuals.

The most poignant part of Ms. Kalton's talk was the journal that she read aloud to the class.

DEAR TEACHER

2/7/91   I know you were very mad at me today when I fell asleep during school. I'm sorry but I was just so sleep (sic). You see, my mom, my three brothers and my new baby sister all share one room at the motel where we live. There are only two beds in the room. Most times, I sleep in the bed with my mom and baby sister. That isn't too bad. But on the nights when my mom's boyfriend stays over, I have to sleep in the bed with my three brothers and my baby sister. On these nights, I never sleep because the bed is so crowded that my baby sister cries all night. My mom's boyfriend always gets drunk and I've even seen him and my mom sniff cocaine. They make so much noise and laugh all night long. I promise I will try to stay awake from now on.

2/16/91   You must be really, really mad at me now because I haven't been in school for a few days. I had to stay home and baby-sit my three brothers and my baby sister so my mom could go do laundry. My mom said she would only be gone for an hour but she didn't come back until late at night. My baby sister cried the whole time because she was so hungry. There was no food in the room. My mom never did do the laundry and I couldn't come to school yesterday or the day before because all of my clothes were really dirty. I am sorry and will try to come to school every day from now on.

2/26/91   I am sorry that you caught me eating that candy bar in school today. It was just that I was so hungry. We ran out of food stamps a couple of days ago and we didn't have any food. Please don't tell anyone but I took five candy bars and some baby food from the store today. I know that stealing is very wrong but my three brothers, my baby sister and my mom are very hungry.

3/1/91   I know that you must be really, really mad at me for losing my report card but yesterday we had to move from the motel into a shelter. My mom had to throw all of our things into garbage bags and I can't find anything. I am scared being at this shelter. There are so many strangers.

Students feel the hurt of the homeless teenager. There is a period of silence before they start talking.

Kathy: I thought things like this only happened in movies. Not any more. I am trying to imagine how difficult it is for a person my age to be in such a rough situation. This girl's journal was just like the writing in Mrs. Mancuso's book, *No Place to Be.* These are voices of real people. It hurts.

Peter: What is her name? Amanda? Why doesn't she just take off and let her mother take care of the kids?

Eugene: It is easy for you to say. Where can she go? She does not like to be among strangers in shelters. If she is alone, it is even more scary.

Jerry: I feel sorry for Amanda and I am mad at her mother. Those are her kids, not Amanda's. Why doesn't she do some more instead of dumping the responsibility on a teenager?

Lisa: I don't know whether she can even if she wants to. She must be very depressed, so many kids, no home, no food. In *Monkey Island,* a book that I read, the mother just quit, disappeared. She needs support, not blame.

The students ask Ms. Kalton what happen to the children and youth who are turned away from shelter programs and where they can go. Ms. Kalton says that about 60,000 children and youth were turned away last year in the state of Washington. Some with families keep on trying various programs; some are forced to stay in the street; in fact, nobody knows what really happens to them. This question has haunted the agency for a long time.

Students also want to know how people can help to enroll the homeless youth in school and to assure their attendance so that they will have an opportunity to break the cycle of homelessness and poverty.

Ms. Kalton: The job is very difficult. Do you have any suggestions?

Sandy: I think the homeless teenagers feel out of place at school. Very often we talk about shopping and complain about allowances. They must feel very uncomfortable about this kind of talk. We should be more sensitive to them.

Michael: I don't know who they are. How do I know when I should talk differently? I don't think they want us to dream up new topics to talk about just because of them. Yes, we should help them feel at home, but not by changing the way we talk.

Eugene: But there is a lot to change in how we talk. I have said so many bad things about the homeless before this unit. It must be awful for them to hear what I said. Now, I think about the homeless as courageous people instead of alcoholics and scum.

DEVISING SOLUTIONS

After reading, writing, and discussing various aspects of the homeless issue, Mrs. Mancuso directs students to evaluate their initial impression of the homeless people recorded in their portfolios. By the conclusion of the unit, many students began to see the plight of the homeless in a different light:

> Homeless people are not what they seem. I used to think that they were all dirty, old, mean, and I always used to think the bad and negative about them but I guess I was wrong. I really learned a lot about the

homeless in this unit. I'm glad it was to be taught to us. It really did change my behavior and attitude. I became more positive about the homeless. [Otherwise,] I would never have [had] empathy for them. I guess I really never realized how bad they live and how much they have to suffer to keep alive.

This unit has changed me a lot. When we first started the homeless unit, I have to admit I was a little prejudiced. I thought that those who were homeless deserved to be homeless. Now I realize that it is sometimes not that person's fault for being homeless. After all, it might not be their fault that they couldn't earn enough money. And it takes a lot to survive out on the streets.

A few students went to the downtown Union Gospel Mission on their own. Together, they interviewed a volunteer who was a former homeless person and wrote the following report:

Rusty was an intelligent girl who did well in school, but then her father died and her mother suffered from clinical depression. At first Rusty tried to do all the housework and her schoolwork too. But soon she felt lonely. She wished she had more time to play with her friend. Soon she grew close to Sam, a boy in her class, and that closeness developed into a sexual relationship. Although she didn't like it, she did not want to lose Sam.

When Rusty was thirteen, her first baby was born. Rusty's mom scolded her about it, but she enjoyed having the baby around and it lifted her depression. This did not solve Rusty's problems, though, and she wondered if her baby would be growing up loving her grandmother more than her mother. When the baby was six months old, Rusty felt the situation was hopeless. So instead of taking the bus to school, she took one to the city.

Soon Rusty met two girls who were friendly to her. When they heard about her situation they invited her to live with them in an abandoned building. Although the lack of food was partially solved by dumpsters, it was very dirty. But what could Rusty do? She had no where else to go.

Rusty's friends spent part of the night soliciting on the streets. They were young prostitutes, they didn't like what they were doing, but it made good money. Rusty's friend told her that most of the money was going to their pimp, a "charming man" who protected them, and they asked Rusty to join them. They didn't mention that he beat them when they did not earn enough money. So she said yes; after all, she did need the money.

Rusty's experiences as a prostitute made her own home look wonderful. She often wondered how her mother and baby were doing. One day she saw a poster for the National Runaway Switchboard and called without telling her friends or pimp. Rusty's message was sent to her mother. A couple of days later a message returned saying COME HOME.

Rusty was lucky. She managed to escape from the pimp. But many are unable to get away from their pimps—men who beat them and torture them for even trying to leave. There are many who still get caught in these situations. The National Runaway Switchboard estimates that it reaches one in six of the children who run away from home each year.

All the students agree that they have learned a great deal about the homeless community. To further their understanding of the homeless perspectives, Mrs. Mancuso gives students a written hypothetical scenario in which they form new identities to discuss and to formulate solutions.

There is a mobile home park off the highway where many of the migrant workers can live during harvest seasons, for reasonably low rent. The mobile homes are pretty run down due to the many different families and people that come in and live for short periods of time. Because of the lack of the upkeep of the park, some people are complaining that it is an eyesore and want the development torn down. A very wealthy developer wants to come in and build a coliseum to attract more people to town, helping out local businesses. However, if the mobile home park is torn down the migrant workers will have no place to live during harvest. You are a person who lives in this development on occasion. Pick a name, decide how old you are, create a personality for yourself, and describe what you do. How do you feel about the current situation? What can you do for the community?

Students are asked to form family units. They may be groups of single adults, grandparents with children, or single parents with small children. Every person will be the head of a household in the mobile park community. Using construction paper to construct an identification tag, each student creates a character with a name, age, personality, and occupation. A town meeting is held for community members to express their concern about the situation and brainstorm strategies to ameliorate it. Students approach the issue from the perspective of their characters, experiencing their frustration and constraints.

Mrs. Mancuso is the facilitator in the town meeting. She copies all the possible solutions that have been written on the chalkboard: Fix up the houses, riot, petition to the governor, get help from gangs, talk to the mayor, organize a sit-in, take the case to court, or find another mobile park to live. Next is a process of elimination; students cross out items that are either ineffective or not probable. No matter whether an item is retained or removed, students need to discuss the pros and cons of the suggestion. For example:

Joel: (taking the role of a 45-year-old worker with six children) I like the idea of a sit-in. Police can come and arrest me. It will delay the process and generate publicity for our cause. It is far better than getting the gangs involved. I don't want to jeopardize my safety because the gangs are pretty violent. By the way, I already have a very hard time keeping my kids away from them.

Jennifer: (taking the role of a 30-year-old single mother with two young children) I am not sure. I don't know how long do I need to sit here (sic). If I do not work, they will replace me. I need the money to feed my kids.

Peter: (taking the role of a single man of age 25) None of us likes the idea of not working. But we cannot go to work and ignore the situation at home. We will only survive as a group. The developer wants us to be divided so that he can get rid of us one at a time. This is the only place that I can stay. I checked around. Other places are too expensive for me.

Justin: (taking the role of an 8-year-old boy) I am scared. I don't want people to take away our homes again. It seems that no matter where we go, people try to move us to other places. We have to tell people that this is our home now. And we like to stay.

Michelle: (taking the role of a 15-year-old Hispanic girl who is learning English) I really think that we need to tell the developers to stop. My English is not good. They won't listen to me. If we sit outside government buildings, other people can understand our lives more and they can be our voices.

(*Note:* In the script, this event involves only the homeless community because students need to understand the perspectives of the homeless. The climax is the town meeting in which the homeless community brainstorms to solve the problem.)

After a lengthy meeting, community members decide to organize a sit-in as soon as possible in government buildings to attract public attention. They will all seek help from some civic groups to send a petition to the mayor and the governor.

Throughout the process, students are very involved in developing their characters. They care about how the characters look and what kind of life they live. When they talk, it is their character talking. Students assume the role of heads of households, taking care of the well-being of family members. They have to be responsible for their dependents. Nobody can take a passive role, as many of them have done in real life, expecting other people to solve the problem. As Mrs. Mancuso assesses this learning experience, she decides to include more characters in the future—for example, the nonhomeless, the builders, and the speculators.

ORGANIZING FOR ACTION

After an emotional time as residents of the mobile park, students are called back to reality to think about what they can do for the local homeless communities. Some students suggest that they want to go beyond a clothing and food drive to do something more personal for the children in the homeless shelter. Sandy and Jennifer, tired of waiting for the class to act, have already started volunteering to serve food in a soup kitchen sponsored by a church. They share with the class that there are many children who are hungry. Some of them come to eat without their parents. Other people just come to eat and leave without saying much. The soup kitchen clients are not the cleanest, yet they are not the dirty bums that the class envisioned. The two teenagers learn to appreciate what they have in life. Sandy reports, "Those homeless people do not look very different from us. I wonder what misfortune has happened to them to make them lose their homes. I am just thankful for what I have. If there are things that I can do to help them, I'll try to do it. I wonder why it took me so long to do something for them."

There emerges a prevailing belief among the eighth-grade students that the homeless community needs to feel loved and cared for by other people. In addition to donating clothing and food, students want to instill a sense of hope in the homeless—especially among the children in the shelter. Recalling the request of Ms. Kalton, the class works together to make a big banner with a colorful rainbow, flowers, birds, yard toys, and encouraging phrases. They get a big piece of fabric and use fabric crayons to create the design. Mrs. Kalton wants to hang the banner in the main room to cheer up the families. When it is dirty, she can wash it; and, after a year, she can take it down and make a quilt for a child.

In addition, students work in small groups on various other projects. Volunteers go to home-decorating centers and request old wallpaper samples. These samples become beautiful covers for the blank books that they are going to make and give to the children in the shelter for their writing and drawing. A separate group works on a blackline drawing for pages in a coloring book. Another group works on homemade games, designing game boards, making tokens, and creating game rules. Others work on cut-and-paste puzzles and word puzzles for children. Looking at the pile of gifts that they have assembled, students are filled with a sense of pride and satisfaction for what they have done for the community.

Students also want to spend time with children in the family shelter. They can get permission from their parents and the school to provide seasonal parties for the children. Parents can help to prepare party snacks; students can decorate the center and organize games. The biggest impact for the students is their visit to the family shelter. Students' interaction with the homeless families confirm their growing understanding that the homeless can be normal people. The homeless children love to play games just like children of their age.

Ms. Kalton has shared with the class that a local high school has a team that comes from their school every Tuesday afternoon by school bus. The high schoolers play ball, sing songs, read books, and do a variety of activities with the homeless children. Mrs. Mancuso's students are really inspired by such action. They would like to organize after-school tutoring groups to play and to help children in the shelters do their homework. Mrs. Mancuso meets with the principal in order to discuss the possibility of giving community service credits to the students who want to participate in the project. Ultimately, parental permission is obtained for those students who start working in Ms. Kalton's center after school. Parents are also encouraged to visit the center with their children to support their outreach effort.

At the end of the unit, Mrs. Mancuso asks the students to visit their portfolios again in order to assess how much they have learned. Sylvia responds as follows:

> During the homeless unit I learned a lot. I used to think all homeless people were bums. Lots of homeless are children. That surprized (sic) me. I think the homeless programs are great. They get people back on their feet again. It makes the homeless not be so dependent anymore. After the unit I could see how they were trying to survive. Not just asking for money all the time. Now that I've read about them and went to the shelter I don't feel prejudice against them anymore. Sometimes its (sic) not their fault they're homeless. Now that I know [what] the shelters want I can give all year round. Not just Christmas and Thanksgiving.

After four weeks of exploration about the homeless community, Mrs. Mancuso is intrigued by how the study of social issues leads to voluntary community service among the eighth-grade students. She is ready for the next issue, and so are the students. Going back to the original brainstormed list, the class selects *gun control* as its next issue. The mind-opening experience starts all over again!

▶ 5

Making Plays, Making Meaning, Making Change

KATHY GREELEY

It is opening night. The school cafeteria has been transformed. Strips of tar paper seamed together with duct tape hide the institutional checkerboard floor. Suspended from the ceiling on window poles, large sheets of cotton muslin peopled with black silhouettes conceal the juice machine and cinderblock walls. I smile as I recognize Paul's high-top haircut and Marie's stocky figure posed in relief. Three trees of stage lights make the transformation complete. When the power is switched on, their rosy glare dictates the limits of another world.

The audience streams in noisily. Cast members are flitting about anxiously. We are trying to herd them "backstage" into the music room. I know I look calm, cheerful, and confident, but inside, my stomach is churning and my armpits are extra sweaty. I go over in my head what I want to say to them. I've never had to do this alone before. In years past, there was Diana or Steve— experts, seasoned veterans, professionals who knew just how to focus 34 young and very nervous performers. But this time I am on my own.

We begin with warm-ups, relying on routine to calm and center us. Next, we do a simple clapping game. I stand in the middle of a circle and begin to clap my hands over my head. Like Simon Says, they join in and catch the rhythm. The trick is to pay attention to when I don't clap. The first time I pause, there is a wide sprinkling of claps as those not focused continue in the rhythm. Giggles. The second time a handful of clapping bandits. A groan. The third pause is marked with a unified silence, and then a cheer.

"You are a remarkable group," I tell them. "Together, you have created more than a play; you have created a piece of art. Our play is about courage. You have all shown real courage by taking the risk to speak from your hearts. Because of that, your work will reach into the hearts of others. I have never seen a group of people work so well together. This was collaboration in the truest sense of the word. Be proud. And don't forget"—on this they all join in— "be loud, clear, and slow."

The cast files out silently to get into their positions. I take my seat, clutching the script. The lights dim to total blackness. The audience hushes. The music begins. And I watch magic unfold.

As I look back on that moment, I ask myself, How did we ever do that? How did we build that trust, that willingness to take risks, that commitment to let go of our own personal little investments and do what's best for the whole? How did we get 34 preadolescents to focus, to work together, to give voice to some of their deepest thoughts? It seems like magic.

I do believe in magic, but I don't believe magic just happens. Magic is made. Sorcerers know the steps. Certain potions must be mixed together; the ingredients have to be right. And, like the Sorcerer's Apprentice discovered, you can't just open a book and follow the recipe. It takes time, support, experimentation, and guidance.

I am not a drama teacher. I teach seventh- and eighth-grade humanities, an integration of language arts and social studies, at the Graham and Parks School in Cambridge, Massachusetts. A K–8 alternative public school, Graham and Parks is located in a racially and economically diverse neighborhood, although students come from all parts of the city. There is also a large Haitian population, as the school houses the city's Haitian bilingual program. By the seventh and eighth grades, many bilingual students have joined mainstream, English-speaking classes. Unlike the lower gradess the seventh and eighth grades are partially departmentalized. I teach two different humanities sections, and because of the integration of language arts and social studies, I have a large block of time (100 minutes) with each group. This move toward integrated curriculum and a longer teaching time was a critical prerequisite in being able to do activities and projects like the play.

I have always had a passion for history—a fascination with learning about and understanding people's lives in other times. Unfortunately, all my students did not share this view. They saw history as a string of events irrelevant to their own lives. I began to think that maybe if they could "try on" these other lives through theater, they would begin to see themselves as threads in a larger weave. Performance would not allow passivity or apathy. They would have to get engaged.

The problem was I knew nothing about theater. My biggest dramatic experience had been playing Blackbeard in a fifth-grade production of *Treasure Island.* I had three lines. I don't remember the lines, but I will never forget the exhilaration of performing them, or my pride in the cardboard waves we had laboriously painted. *Treasure Island* was one of the highlights of my entire school career.

Not knowing where to begin, I looked up an old friend, Steve Seidel, who had taught theater for years. Coincidentally, his son was going to be in my class that coming year. "Let's start with why you want to do a play," he said. "What are your goals? What do you hope to accomplish?" I thought for a minute, and replied, "Well, it's quite simple really. My goal is to do something with these students that they will never forget. When they are 50 years old, I want them to say, 'I remember this great play I did when I was in the eighth grade.' That's all." He smiled and said, "Sounds like a good goal to me."

That year, in 1990, we produced *On the Line* by Carol Korty, a play about a 14-year-old immigrant mill worker in Lawrence, Massachusetts, during the famous Bread and Roses Strike of 1912. The play brought together themes we had been studying all year in regard to immigration, the Industrial Revolution, and the growth of the labor movement. By the time of the play, we had visited the cities of Lowell and Lawrence, studied writings of the mill girls, and researched the experiences of immigrants. Students knew what a mill looked like, what a power loom sounded like, what living conditions were like, what mill girls ate for lunch, how much they earned in a week, and how much that could buy them.

What we didn't know was how to produce a play. So I drew on every possible resource I could find. Steve agreed to work with us a couple of days each week. A talented graduate student from Emerson College seeking an internship, Diana Moller, joined our production team. From the beginning, we shared a vision of a different kind of student theater production.

Traditionally, adults are the experts and they tell students what to do. But my classroom operated more by consensus. Although students knew that I was ultimately in charge, I emphasized the value of listening to and learning from each other, not just expert adults. My students were used to voicing their opinions and having a say in decision making, so I knew that having an outsider come in and dictate things would not work with these kids. My goal was one of ownership. I didn't just want my students to perform a play; I wanted them to shape it. The real work had to be done by the students themselves. So we formed committees and everyone was invited to sign up for what interested them: directing, set design, costuming, music, or publicity. There was one requirement: Everyone had to act, even if it meant walking on stage and saying one line.

The student directors loved the idea of directing their own scenes, but they quickly realized that they didn't know where to begin. The set designers were anxious to build an elaborate set, but they couldn't agree on a design. Rather than entering the kind of power struggle with adults that can happen at this early adolescent stage, my students recognized the need to get advice. So we turned to our community to draw on the resources and expertise around us. A professional set designer from the Boston University theater met with the design committee one morning to discuss theme, color, and design. An artist came in a few weeks later to help them implement their design. A local actor/director shared his directing stories with the directors' committee one evening over pizza. A local musician friend agreed to meet with our "minstrels" once a week. Parents also joined the crew, helping with costumes, supervising set construction, and rehearsing lines with actors.

We made many mistakes and things did not always (in fact, often) did not go smoothly. A week before the performance, a student playing a major character was suspended from school for 10 days. The rented lights were dropped off at the school with no instructions, the night before the show. During our final desperate rehearsal, two cast members got in a fist fight, sending one to the hospital and the other banned from the performance.

But, in spite of these crises, or perhaps because of them, I watched a remarkable feeling grow among the members of the class. I saw them pull together, support each other, push each other, and demand of each other and of themselves their very best. A transformation had taken place. It was no longer the "smart" kids versus the "dumb" kids exchanging put-downs and competing for attention. If we were going to succeed, we needed everybody. We had become a real community.

Far from simply making history come alive, I discovered that this process of making theater made kids come alive. And even though this was probably one of the most exhausting experiences of my teaching career, it made me come alive. As we were striking the set at 11:00 P.M. on a Friday night, I was already thinking about what our next play would be. I was hooked.

The year after *On the Line,* Diana returned to guide us in a spirited production of Bertold Brecht's *The Caucasian Chalk Circle.* (My first thought was, Junior high students doing Brecht?) The following year, Diana and I decided to make the leap into original scripting. It was the year of the Columbus Quincentennial and we were exploring the question What makes America, America? in the curriculum. Working from the richness of students' own family histories, we began to explore, to imagine, to improvise on the threads of stories that made the fabric of the American experience. Looking for America became an exploration of the myths and realities of the American Dream, both past and present.

Three years later, a tradition of quality theater had been established. In 1994, as my new students filed into the classroom in September, the questions started up before the kids had even sat down. "Are we going to get to do a play this year?" "What play are we going to do?" "Can we write our own play this year?" "When are we going to do the play so I can tell my parents?" I knew they were hooked. I smiled at them confidently. But inside I was asking myself the same questions.

For the past three years, finding the right play to do had been fairly easy. But this year, I was really stumped. Our curriculum theme for the year was Change: How do societies change? How do people make change in their society? How are we changing? Luckily, I have a lot of freedom to develop and choose curriculum. Although some curriculum areas are recommended, there are not rigid requirements. I planned to begin the year with the Facing History and Ourselves curriculum. I had started teaching this curriculum in 1988 and had always been drawn to the way it helped adolescents reflect critically on key social issues and their own choices in life.

By using the rise of the Nazi Party in Germany in the 1930s and the resulting Holocaust as an historical case study of human behavior, the Facing History curriculum challenges students to reflect on the causes and consequences of present-day intolerance, violence, racism, and passivity. The course begins by asking students to consider key questions about individual identity and social behavior. It then moves on to the historical roots of anti-semitism, and then a rigorous study of German history from 1914 to 1945. Students examine the social, political, and economic factors that led to the rise of the Nazi Party and the steps Hitler took to consolidate his power to create a dictatorship, including the roles of propaganda, racial theories, as well as the victims, victimizers, and bystanders during this period. Throughout the curriculum, students are encouraged to identify parallels between this history and current events and to make connections to social responsibility, the importance of thinking for oneself, standing up for one's beliefs, and building a community committed to justice.

Completing that curriculum, I then planned to shift to a study of the Civil Rights movement in the United States. I figured that after having examined a society that institutionalized racism and carried it out to its most extreme end and having raised questions about resistance, social change, justice, and hope, it was important to explore our own American version of this history. We would try to place common events (our school was named after Rosa Parks and every child in it knows the story of the Montgomery bus boycott) within the complex framework that gave rise to those events. We would also look at how ordinary people, through remarkable acts of courage, were able to change history. The theme of change would tie together these different units.

As I spoke to friends and colleagues about ideas for a play, people would say "Hey, there are lots of good plays for kids to do." But that wasn't the point. I was not looking for a good play to do. I was not interested in just putting on a play. There had to be an organic connection to the curriculum. The point of making theater was to reach inside ourselves, to reach out to our community, and to make sense of what we were learning. The material we were dealing with was both deeply disturbing and extremely inspirational. And the issues of justice, power, and courage were richly compelling ones for my students. It was clear to me that we had to do an original production again. But how? Where would the stories come from?

There is a wealth of stories in these histories. But, unlike the year before with Looking for America, they weren't our stories. I couldn't envision us doing a play of Holocaust vignettes or trying to reenact the Civil Rights movement or anti-war protests on stage. I worried that the scale of those stories of life and death could too easily be trivialized. Our play had to be built from a place that the kids could feel. When students would ask me, "What is our play going to be about?" I'd just smile and say "I don't know yet. We need to figure it out." During Open House in September, a parent asked expectantly, "Are you doing a play this year?"

"Of course," I answered.

"What is it going to be about?" another parent inquired.

"We don't know yet, but we'll keep you posted." I acted nonchalant, but inside I was panicked.

I started to obsess about what the play would be about. Diana, who was now living in Connecticut with a new baby, reassured me over the phone.

"Don't worry. It will come," she said.

"Right." I replied flatly. "

Diana answered, "Trust me. It worked last year."

"But last year, we had the family tree stories. They were hanging up all over the room. The stories were right there." I was really getting worked up.

"The stories are there," she said calmly, with Eliza cooing in the background. "You just haven't found them yet. Trust me."

So we began the year not knowing—a very scary thing for a teacher, I think. But I was keeping my ears open—listening, waiting, trying to trust, and trying to keep my anxieties in check.

Rather than leaping into pre-World War II Germany, as I mentioned, Facing History and Ourselves begins with an exploration of some of the fundamental themes raised in the curriculum. We began the course by reading a newspaper article about the Kitty Genovese murder in Brooklyn, New York, in 1965, in which 38 people watched as a young woman was repeatedly stabbed. The police were called only after the victim was dead and her assailant had fled. Students, shocked by the story, struggled to understand. "Why didn't they do something?" "Why did people let this happen?" We began to brainstorm possible reasons for their lack of response. Was it fear? Apathy? Paralysis? "Maybe they thought someone else had already called the police." "Maybe they were afraid the killer would come after them." "Maybe they didn't know what to do." As we talked, the lines between right and wrong seemed very clear. Someone should have intervened.

"But, what if, during recess, you hear someone call someone else a nigger or a stupid Haitian? What would you do?" I ask. "That's different," they reply. "That's not murder."

"It's really none of my business," says Sarah Jane. "Kids do stuff like that all the time. You can't stop that."

"But how can you stop a murder if you can't even stop a 'dis'?" I persist. "Being able to get involved, to do the right thing, to stand up for what you believe takes practice. If we can't act on the small things, how can we ever imagine we will act when the big ones happen?"

As we got deeper into our study of the Holocaust, these questions emerged over and over. Why did people let this happen? Why didn't somebody do something to stop it when it could have been stopped? When must we act and where do we find the courage to do so? Why do some people just go along while others will stand up for what they believe in? Why did some people choose to perpetrate violence and hatred? How did others become targeted as the victim? And what about the majority of people who were simply bystanders?

In October, we started experimenting with theater games once every week or two. All the games pushed us to get out of our heads and into our bodies more, to stop thinking and just do. The process reminded me of freewriting or "writing to think." When you let go of your mind, amazing things would come out.

After each game, we would sit in a circle and talk about what we had learned from it and how it felt. One day, we played a familiar observation game. Students got in pairs and Diana asked them to turn around and change three things about themselves. Rings came off, shoes were untied, earrings disappeared. After a minute or two, they turned around and tried to guess what had changed about each person. "Okay," she said. "Now turn around again and change eight more things." Students groaned, but turned around. Sweatshirts came off, shoes were put on opposite feet, facial expressions changed. "Good," Diana said. "Now try changing fifteen more things." Before the protests could get very far, she interjected. "Just try it." Now things got really active. They took books from the bookshelf. They swapped clothing. They borrowed glasses and pencils from their neighbor. Postures changed. Different hands were leaned on.

"You see, you could do it!" Diana congratulated them. "That's Lesson Number One. Never say you can't do something. What else did you learn? How did you solve your problem? What did you draw on?"

"Well, first we changed things on ourselves," said Anna.

"Then what?" Diana coaxed.

"Then we started using each other," ventured Emilio.

"Excellent. And finally? Where else did you turn?"

"To things—like books and pencils and stuff just lying around," Ariful responded.

"Exactly!" Diana exclaimed. "So that's the other lesson. When you run into a problem that you are trying to solve, there are three places to turn to for answers: look inside yourselves, turn to each other, and use your environment."

We would also talk about what we needed from each other to make the process really work. We needed to be willing to take risks, to try new things. We didn't want to be laughed at for looking silly or making mistakes. We needed to focus and concentrate. We had to keep an open mind and not dismiss ideas with which we didn't agree. We needed to trust each other and feel safe. We kept this list posted in the classroom as a reminder and added to it as we needed.

In November, we were fortunate to have a guest speaker. Gregory Alan Williams is an African-American actor who lives in Los Angeles. During the Los Angeles riots of 1993, Mr. Williams saved the life of a Japanese-American man who was being brutally beaten by a mob at the infamous corner of Florence and Normandy Streets. He had written a book called *A Gathering of Heroes: Reflections on Rage and Responsibility* to describe his experiences that day and the events in his own life that motivated him to act as a rescuer.

Mr. Williams is a large man and has a commanding presence. With dramatic flair, he began to tell his story. He told about the rescue, but he also described having chosen to not help someone else in danger earlier that same day because "they were not my people." He told about being the victim of racial violence, but he also described being part of a group that severely beat a young man for the crime of being different. He spoke about standing against the mob *and* also going along with the crowd. He challenged us to think about what a hero really is. Yes, someone who rushes into a burning building and saves a life is a hero. But what about a single mother who works day and night for years to support and sustain her children? Maybe that takes even more courage.

"But how can we make a difference," the kids asked. "We're just kids." Mr. Williams replied, "If not you, then who? And if not now, when? You can't sit and wait for the 'right' moment. And you can't necessarily do it alone either. But if you are willing to speak out, to take a stand, then maybe another will be inspired to join you. And then another, and another. That's the 'power of we.' With the 'power of we,' you can make a difference."

When we got back to the classroom, the class was buzzing with energy. A deep chord had been struck. I grabbed a piece of newsprint and taped it up on the board. "What makes a hero?" I asked. "What is courage?" And the ideas flowed. Taking a stand for what you believe. Being willing to take a risk. Trying to live life by your principles. Giving other people hope. Admitting to having done wrong. Being honest with yourself. Taking responsibility for your actions and for others. Dedicating your life to something bigger than yourself. And the list went on. We had just a few minutes left when Emily raised her hand. "I think this is what our play should be about." The consensus was immediately apparent in all the nodding heads.

So we started to explore this idea of heroes. We made webs and students interviewed young children about who their heroes were and why. For several children, their heroes were in their own family: an older sister or brother, or a parent. One 6-year-old girl said, "My daddy is my hero because he is friendly and nice. And he listens to me." Another 8-year-old admired her dad because he "helps me with my homework, cooks good dinners, and kills spiders." An 8-year old named her stepmother "because she is nice, she teaches me manners, and she helps me." For several children aged 7 and younger, the Power Rangers were their heroes. The Power Rangers were "cool and strong." They "saved people," "could do flips," and "had special powers."

Students also interviewed their peers and we mapped out all the data we collected. Different heroes emerged. For many, especially boys, sports figures were big: Michael Jordan, Troy Aikman, Larry Bird, Julius Erving. They admired these athletes' determination, discipline, and talent. For others, political or civil rights activists stood out: Malcolm X, Martin Luther King, Gandhi. These people had sacrificed themselves to fight for the rights of oppressed peoples, people without power or privilege. And there were some more personal choices. One 14-year-old girl said she admired people who had a terminal illness who fought to live. A 14-year-old boy admired a friend who was in a music band because "he is so good at what he does at such a young age."

In the Facing History curriculum, we had also studied heroes. Each student had read and written about a resister or rescuer during the Holocaust. There was Mordechai Anilewitz, a young man who led the Warsaw Ghetto Resistance, and there was Irene Harand, an Austrian gentile who used stamps to counteract anti-semitic Nazi propaganda. There also was Janusz Korczack, a Polish physician who ran a Jewish orphanage, who chose to go the gas chamber with his charges rather than abandon the children who had come to depend on him. There was Andre and Magda Trocme, a husband and wife, who organized the village of Le Chambon in France to hide 5,000 Jewish children. And, of course, there was also the now famous Oskar Schindler.

I asked students think about what motivated each of these people to risk his or her life by resisting to Nazi control. Why did these particular individuals act when others did not? Ariful wrote about Mordechai Anilewitz: "I think anger motivated Mordechai to fight back. At one point, he realized that they were all going to be killed. So he decided to go down fighting. Even though he knew he was going to die, he still wanted to live. He didn't want to just save himself because he cared about his fellow Jews."

When Adam wrote about the village of Le Chambon, he recognized the value of their own historical experience as a people. "The town was very religious. . . . Their religion told them to love every human just as much as the next, so they didn't see how they could help to kill the Jews. More importantly, they were Huguenots, and had been persecuted and almost exterminated earlier in their history so they could identify with the Jews. . . . [This gave] them a lot of support in knowing what they were doing was right."

"Were they heroes?" I asked. "Yes," answered Laska. She wrote, "Januscz Korczak could have saved his own life, but he sacrificed it for the comfort of 'his children.' They died, but there was nothing he could do about it, except to keep them happy, make them feel protected, and let them know he would always be there for them. . . . Although he didn't save lives, he kept their spirits alive as long as possible."

"I think that Chana Senesh [a young Israeli woman who parachuted behind Nazi lines on a suicide mission] was a hero because she risked her life to save others," wrote Jash. "She was very courageous when she didn't give the radio code even when they tortured her and when they threatened to kill her mother. When the hangman killed her, she refused to put on the blindfold. She did all of this because she wanted other people to have the chance to taste freedom. This is why I think that she was a hero."

Students shared their profiles through brief dramatic presentations. Working in small groups, they had to think about the essence of each hero's action and portray that moment. It could be the moment that Mordechai decided to take his own life rather than turn himself into the Gestapo, or the point when Januscz Korczack entered the gas chamber with his charges rather than abandon the children who had come to depend on him. But students had to choose that essential moment, imagine the characters that would be involved, and set the scene in a physical space and time.

As we discussed courage, we also talked about fear. Did heroes feel no fear? Or was real courage overcoming our fears? We wrote "Five Sense" poems about fear. The poem emerges from a series of questions: What color is it? What does it smell like? What does it sound like? What does it taste like? What does it feel like to the touch? How does it make you feel? Carrie wrote the following:

Fear is dark blue and brown
musty and sweaty, sticky and rotten,
a drum beating, pounding
a salty taste.

I can't swallow it
because it is a knot
tied deep inside of me.

We also made body sculptures. Students worked in pairs where one was the "clay" and the other the "sculptor." The "sculptor" shaped the "clay" into his or her interpretation of fear. Bodies twisted, hands were raised, heads turned away. The pairs switched and we then tried sculpting courage. Arms reached out, backs straightened, heads were raised. And we talked. What is it young adolescents most fear? "Getting shot," said Troy, an eighth-grade African-American boy. Troy is usually one of the jokesters of the class. But this time he wasn't laughing. "What other people think of you," said Leana, a tall willowy girl, a dancer. Others nodded. We added to the list: looking different, being left out, secrets becoming public, wearing the right clothes, getting picked on by bigger kids, gangs, and war. There were a lot of things to be afraid of.

The year was moving along. We had finished the Facing History curriculum in January and began working on the roots of the Civil Rights movement. Using the model of our Holocaust study, we started looking for key elements of when and where the seeds were planted. What were the social, political, and economic conditions that gave rise to a movement for justice, equality, and change? We went back to the Civil War, the Reconstruction Era, the beginning of Jim Crow and the key rulings of the Supreme Court. Students picked a topic that interested them (the origins and growth of the Ku Klux Klan, African Americans in the military, the Harlem Renaissance, the founding and development of the NAACP). They researched it, wrote about it, and presented it, as an expert, to the class. Students were beginning to see that, once again, history was complex, events and people influenced each other, and significant periods of change didn't just happen.

It was now February and we still didn't have a script. We didn't even have a story yet. But we had been gathering material, collecting pieces of ideas and experiences, and generating building blocks of writing, research, techniques, and process. The kids kept asking when we would start working on the play.

"We are working on the play," I'd answer.

"Yeah, but when are we *really* going to work on the play? You know, write the script, cast the parts, rehearse, make the set?"

"Soon, trust me," I'd say, trying to keep my own anxieties under control and my mind open.

Also that month, we were lucky to have another visit from Gregory Alan Williams. This time, he came as a playwright consultant. "So, what's your play about?" he asked.

"It's about heroes and courage and change and . . . well, we don't know everything yet. We don't have a script yet." Embarrassed giggles. A few of them glare accusingly at me.

"That's okay. What is it you want to say to your audience? What is your message?" he pushes.

"Well, uh—we kind of want to talk about perpetrators, victims, and bystanders and . . ." Embarrassed giggles.

"That's a good place to start. Have any of you ever been a victim, a perpetrator, or a bystander?" Embarrassed silence. He persists. "Has anyone ever made fun of you or put you down? How about you?" He is looking at Brady, a gangly seventh grader whose long hair usually dangles down to his chin, hiding his eyes. Brady rises to the occasion.

"Yeah, I guess. Sometimes other kids make fun of me because I like to wear my hair long. Usually it doesn't bother me, but every once in a while it does."

Mr. Williams nods sympathetically and says softly, "Brady, can you show us how it feels—those times when it really gets to you? Show us with your body?" Brady stands up awkwardly. I am watching intently. So is the rest of the class. This is a boy who barely speaks in class. He strikes a pose. His head is down, his knees are slightly bent, his hands are holding an invisible burden over his back, like a wretched Santa Claus. There is silence and Brady continues to hold his position. "Thank you, Brady," Williams says quietly. "That was terrific." The class bursts into applause.

He asks for another volunteer, this time to share an experience as a perpetrator. Troy stands up, points his finger at an invisible target, half covers a smirking smile with his hand, and cocks his head. Williams silently motions Brady into Troy's line of vision. A picture is coming into focus. "How about a bystander?" Anna, a very bright but somewhat withdrawn seventh-grader, stands up, circling the two boys for a minute and then stops, just outside their sphere. She turns her body away, puts her hands up to shield her eyes, but is surreptitiously watching. The triangle is complete.

Looking at the tableau, we recognized that each of us had been, at least once in our lives, in each point of that triangle. We all knew the powerlessness of the victim. We knew the inflated self-importance of the perpetrator. But, most deeply resonant was the distance of the bystander. How many times had we heard a remark that made us uncomfortable, yet we said nothing? How many times had we witnessed an incident we wanted to interrupt or intervene in, but didn't know how? How many times had we gone along with the crowd, afraid of being singled out? As one German citizen reflecting back on the Nazi era said, "Suddenly it all comes down, all at once. You see what you are, what you have done, or more accurately, what you haven't done. For that was all that was required of most of us: that we do nothing" (Strom and Parsons, 1982, p. 105).

As the class looked at the tableau, we realized that we had found our focus. Like a string in sugar water, this tableau became the anchor around which ideas crystallized. Our play would be about this relationship: the victim, the perpetrator, and, primarily, the bystander.

The time had come to begin constructing the play. Diana came back to help us shape, mold, and fashion all the pieces into a cohesive whole. To remind ourselves what we had to work with, we wrote on newsprint a list of all the activities and exercises we had conducted: fear poems, body sculptures, resister and rescuer skits and profiles, hero webs and interviews, superhero and other improvisations, folktales of courage, mirroring exercises, "sound" theater, and student writing about changing, witnessing prejudice, and being afraid.

Then Diana asked, "What is someone called who writes plays?"

"A playwright," a number of students called out.

"Spell it for me," she said.

"P-L-A-Y-W-R-I-G-H-T."

"Great," she said. "Can anyone tell me why it isn't spelled P-L-A-Y-W-R-I-T-E?" I was stumped. Not only did I not know why, but I had never even wondered why. "Can you think of any other jobs people do who are called 'Something-wright?'"

"A shipwright?"

"Yes! And what does a shipwright do?"

"They build ships."

"Yes, and playwrights build plays. As you begin to work on actually writing your play, think of it as building something together. You will mold and shape it. A basic form will emerge, you will make many changes before it is finished. Now, what kind of play do you want to build?"

We started brainstorming all our hopes for this production. It should be mainly about kids, but there could also be adult characters. It should take place partly in the present, but should incorporate the lessons of the histories we had been learning. It had to be funny, but also deal with serious issues. It shouldn't paint things as good versus bad; life is more complex than that. The students didn't want to offer pat answers; they wanted to ask questions ("We don't want it to be like an after-school special"). They wanted the audience to leave thinking.

After this meeting, Diana and I started drafting a storyline. This was a major leap. After months of soliciting ideas, inviting feedback, turning ownership over to the students, I worried that there would be a reaction to our taking such a unilateral step. Would there be a power struggle? Would they feel the adults had taken over the process?

Our first draft was rejected—but it was not rejected for any of the reasons I had worried about. On the contrary, the kids welcomed the structure. As adults know, it is usually much easier to work from something concrete and make changes than expect something to emerge from a large group. The story just wasn't saying what they felt they wanted to say.

Back to the drawing board. I kept trying to pull from that visual image of our tableau. Someone becomes a bystander when they witness an incident, an act, and fail to get involved. It seemed like our play had to start with some kind of incident. I thought back to an incident that had actually occurred during the beginning weeks of school in September. A group of kids, several of whom were in my classes, had started chasing another seventh-grade boy—in fun, they said. But it had turned ugly. Once they cornered him, a crowd had gathered that egged the kids on to beat him up. These were not "bad" kids. They had intended no harm. But something had happened to them that they could not explain, or even understand at the time.

I started running ideas by as many people as would listen to me. One Sunday morning, sitting in a cafe with a friend, jotting notes on a small paper napkin, the pieces began to fall together. I rushed home to bang out Draft Number Two and presented it the next day to my classes.

"Okay, listen to this." I started reading my notes. "There is an explosion of activity on stage. A group of kids are chasing another kid. They catch him and beat him up. The audience gets the idea of a violent act with a victim and a group of perpetrators, but no faces are seen. In the next scene, lights come up on a school cafeteria. The kids are buzzing with excitement. We focus in on three kids who are talking ("Did you hear what happened yesterday?"). As they talk, they reveal what they know about "the incident" from a certain perspective. At least one of them was witness to the incident. They think the victim got what he deserved. We shift to another location (recess, hallway) and we hear the story again from other kids—this group is more sympathetic to the victim. A few of these kids were also witnesses. Do we have a third scene? We then shift to the teachers' room to hear a few teachers talking about the same incident—this time in simplistic terms ("Those kids are such bullies.").

"Of all the kids who were witnesses (bystanders), there are two or three who begin to wonder if they have done the right thing by saying and doing nothing. Each one turns to her or his hero to ask advice about what to do. Each kid's hero takes the kid on a journey to a place where, in spite of the risks, a person has decided to "do the right thing." One scene visits the Holocaust and a resister, one scene visits the Civil Rights movement, and maybe one takes a present day person's story. In the next series of scenes, we need to see these kids back in their own environment, but somehow they have to change or act differently, though in small ways. Somehow the kids should come together, but I don't know how."

As I was reading the outline to the class, I glanced up to see heads nodding in approval. "That's much better than the last one." "Yeah, that's good." But then came the questions: "What is the incident going to be?" "What are the kids who go to 'heroland' like?" "Who are the heroes?" "What stories do the bystanders visit?" "How is it going to end?"

"I don't know the answers to those questions. We are going to have to figure them out together," I responded. At least we now had a rough draft—a real place to start, a skeleton to flesh out—and we had consensus. We were headed in the right direction.

It seemed that we should be building from the guts of the play rather than starting at the beginning. And the guts of the play were the "heroland" stories about courage that were rooted in our historical study. We had to make sure that the lessons each bystander learned from his or her journey would have meaning for that character and for the incident. Because we were dealing with real stories, we had to choose carefully the story that demonstrated an important message.

We decided to look first at the Holocaust stories of resisters and rescuers. We got out all the profiles students had written in the fall, spread them out on a table, and started reading them over again. Once students had a chance to refresh their memories, they broke into groups of four and had to choose the story they felt had the best message for the play. They had to identify the elements of courage embodied in the story and then develop a skit that illustrated these elements. I reminded them that they needed to be thinking about what best served the play and not necessarily the story they found most interesting or thrilling. For example, some students really liked the story of Joseph Gani, a young Hungarian Jew who joined a desperate rebellion in one of the concentration camps. The kids admired his refusal to be a victim and his decision to fight back even when there was no hope of winning. But the group decided the hopelessness of his situation was not what we wanted to communicate to our audience.

Two stories emerged as our final candidates. The first was the story of Oskar Schindler. We had read about Schindler and some students had seen Spielberg's movie, *Schindler's List*. They were intrigued with the way Schindler had changed from being purely out for himself to risking his privilege, his fortune, and ultimately his life to be a rescuer. They also admired how he stood up for others and used his position of power to help. His story fit our themes of change and courage well. The second candidate was the story of Andre and Magda Trocme. In full view of the Vichy government and Nazi SS, the Trocmes led the people of their village, Le Chambon in southern France, to save thousands of Jewish children and adults from certain death. The Trocmes, and most of the village, were Huguenots and had known persecution in Catholic France. They drew strength from their own oppression to fight against the oppression of others. The story of Le Chambon also embodied the "power of we" that Gregory Alan Williams had spoken about. There was not one hero that saved the day, but rather a whole group of people who, inspired by the courage and commitment of the Trocmes, agreed to work together to do what they could to oppose violence and destruction.

We discussed at length which story would work best in our play. In the end, the students chose the Trocmes and the village of Le Chambon. They liked the message that by coming together people can make a difference in the lives of others, even when the odds are so overwhelming. We also found the Trocme improvisations worked better. Students had had a hard time capturing the importance of Schindler's story in just one scene. It had taken Spielberg a whole movie to do it; how could we do it better? Finally, we decided it was important to have a story that was less known to people. We wanted people to know there were many unsung heroes.

Now that we had a story, we began to build the scene. We went back to the original improvisations the small groups had done. Two groups had worked on the Trocme story. One scene took place in the Trocme kitchen with Andre and Magda talking about the problems and dangers they had encountered that day. The second scene showed Andre taking two Jewish children door to door through the village until he found a family who could take them in. Which one did we like better? Both scenes conveyed important information about the story to the audience. The kitchen scene gave the characters an opportunity to share the inner thoughts of these two people. The night visit scene dramatized the involvement of the whole village. Why not blend them together, we decided.

Previously, when any improvisations or scenes were shared, my mantra had been, "What works?" We rarely discussed what hadn't worked. That was usually fairly obvious. By focusing primarily on the strengths of an improvisation, we achieved two important goals. First, students overcame their fears of performing, of being judged or laughed at. A sense of trust and confidence grew in the classroom that encouraged everyone to take risks. Second, we gradually built an awareness of what makes good theater. "I liked how you really stayed in character the whole time." "Your facial expressions were great. We really knew what you were thinking without you saying a word." "I loved how you had the characters flash back to an earlier time right in the middle of the scene."

As we began to mold the scenes for the play, I was struck by how good my students were at giving each other supportive, insightful feedback. I realized that they were simply transferring a skill we had been working on all year to making theater. In the beginning of school, we had analyzed a wide range of student-written stories to identify the elements of good writing. We had introduced response groups for the writing process. We had strict rules about being respectful and considerate, focusing on the positive first, and giving concrete, constructive feedback. Students had used this format to critique projects as well as writing. Whenever we did projects, we would discuss criteria for excellence. How do we know we have done quality work? What are the elements to be striving for?

Something different was happening. I had always been committed to writing as a process and response as a critical part of that process. But it did not always come easily with kids. Many were afraid at first to share their work. Some students were comfortable with giving others feedback, but some rarely contributed. Others had to be continually reminded of the rules. There were days when one or another response group worked really well, but I was always wondering just how deep the process had sunk in. But as we worked together on scenes for the play, a new feeling emerged. It was like taking the training wheels off a bike and riding freely. The supports, the reminders, the attention to the structure just melted away as we all became engrossed in the product. Finally, the process was working—really working.

I have wondered why this transformation happened. Was it because the groundwork had been laid in the fall and it finally kicked in? Or was it easier to critique unwritten work? Did it have to do with a group presenting work as opposed to an individual? Was it a matter of ownership? Or was it the nature of the work itself? This play was our creation. It expressed our inner thoughts and emotions. Other people were going to see it. The stakes were high. I imagine that all these factors entered in. My gut sense was that the authenticity, the trueness, the deep meaning of the work was the real catalyst. We were committed to high quality work. The kids understood that getting response, shaping, and reworking was the way to reach the standard we set for ourselves.

Having decided to blend the two scenes, we referred the scene to a committee of writers. A small group of students (including two who had originally researched the Trocmes) went off to further develop the scene and to write a first draft of the script. Through discussion, they decided the danger the Trocmes had lived with on a daily basis had to be demonstrated in the scene. New characters were thus added—two Gestapo agents who barge into the Trocme home. They engaged the characters in various improvisational dialogues. What would Magda say when Andre returns an hour late one evening? How would she be feeling? What would the children feel when they first met these two strangers? What is the relationship between them? How do they react when Nazis appear suddenly at the door?

While the Trocme scene was growing, the rest of the class turned its attention to the preceding scene. In this scene, we would meet one of the bystanders who had witnessed the incident and was disturbed by his own failure to act. Who would this person be? Why would he be questioning his own behavior? What is his relationship to the victim? To the perpetrators? What hero visits him? How will he change? Because the Huguenots of Le Chambon had been motivated to act as rescuers due to their own persecution, we decided this character would similarly be motivated by his own experience of being a victim. As we look back over our charts of superheroes, we decide to have the character meet the Pink Power Ranger, a popular superhero of the younger set. Two volunteers jump up to try improvising.

"Where will this scene take place?" I ask. "What makes sense?"

"Adam should be coming home from school."

"Okay, let's help him out a bit. How is Adam feeling when he gets home?"

"Frustrated."

"Angry."

"Upset."

"Okay. Think frustrated, angry, upset, Adam. Now, what can he be doing? What is the first thing you do when you get home?"

"Get something to eat."

"Okay. Let's see what happens." Adam walks onto the "set." "How did you get in?" I ask. "Can we see you coming through the door?" He starts again. "Pretend you can't find your key," someone calls out. He looks for his key to open the door. He can't find the key. He rummages through his pockets, his bookbag, his pockets again. His frustration is mounting. He pounds on the "door." The class is cracking up. He calls, "Mom? Mom?! Anybody home?" He pounds again. Someone calls out, "Look under the mat!" He looks under the "doormat," finds the key finally, and stumbles into the house. He drops his bag in the "kitchen" and mimes going into the refrigerator. "Okay, who drank all the $@*%# Pepsi?" he mutters. He gets out a milk carton, pours a glass, takes a long drink—and gags. "This milk is disgusting!" he cries. Then he goes to make a sandwich. The jelly jar is stuck closed. The peanut butter jar is empty. He explodes in frustration. The class explodes in hysterics. Another scene is coming to life.

Recently, as I was trying to write about the making of this scene, I went back to Adam. "Was this how it happened, how this scene came together?" I asked. "Yeah, sort of," Adam responded. "I remember someone telling me to check under the doormat. But I don't think that I did all those things right away. I kept doing it over and over again. Each time we added something else in. People kept giving suggestions and it kept building. I didn't think all those things up on my own."

Another group started working on the second "heroland" visit. This scene would take place during the Civil Rights movement. We chose the story of Mose Wright, the uncle of a 14-year-old black boy named Emmett Till who was brutally murdered one night by a group of white men in Mississippi in 1955. Young Till made the mistake of saying, "Bye, baby," to a white woman in a store. Mose Wright, under the threat of losing his life, stood up in court to point out the murderers. Students were inspired by this story. Through our studies of the roots of the Civil Rights movement and reading *To Kill a Mockingbird; Roll of Thunder, Hear My Cry;* and *I Know Why the Caged Bird Sings,* they began to understand the depth of this old man's courage.

This time, the whole class worked on ideas for the scene. Students divided into three groups and each one developed a scene that focused on the essential message of the story. We then presented each one and discussed what worked well. While all the scenes had similar elements, each one introduced an interesting twist. One scene started with the accused white men meeting with their lawyer who confidently assured them that they had nothing to worry about. Another scene used a court clerk to establish time and place. A third interjected a flashback of Till being forced out of Wright's house in the middle of the night. All these ideas were eventually incorporated into the final scene.

As students experimented with improvisations, I took copious notes on each character created, every good line, every suggestion that worked, and as many stage directions as I could remember. For some scenes, students went off in pairs or small groups (like in the Trocme scene) and developed a draft of the script. Other scenes I would draft from the improvisation and bring the script back the next day for critique. I worried, again, that students might resent the loss of control over the process. But students nearly always felt that I had been able to capture their words, their characterizations, their intentions on paper. And that was fine. The lines between student and teacher were beginning to disappear, at least in terms of whose play this was. It wasn't their play or my play. We were a real team with the goal of making the best product we could.

By the end of two weeks, we had a script. A story with seven scenes and 27 characters. The play opens on an empty stage. As the lights come up, a slow-walking boy named Robert is being hailed: "Hey, Robert! . . . We just wanna to talk to you!" Robert runs, but cannot escape. Five kids close in on him. In slow motion, they begin beating him down. Other characters quietly file in behind, watching. The attackers fade away, leaving the victim crumpled in the center of the stage. The bystanders, one by one, turn their backs.

The next day, the school is abuzz with rumors. We begin to hear, from various points of view, about "the incident." Some feel the victim got what he deserved for "talking trash" about another student, claiming she was being beaten by her father. Others are more sympathetic. A few are neutral. Two characters,

Janessa and Marcus, leave the scene feeling bothered by what they had witnessed. They turn to superheroes for answers. Marcus, at home alone in his kitchen, begins talking to his younger sister's Pink Power Ranger doll. Janessa, shooting hoops with her nerf ball in her bedroom, tells herself that Michael Jordan would know what to do. Both heroes magically appear and try to offer solace. But the Pink Power Ranger can't give any advice. TV heroes are not like real heroes, she explains. The scriptwriters tell her what to do, good always wins out over evil, and everyone lives happily ever after. Michael Jordan sees solutions through his endorsement products. "Maybe you should get some Nikes and run away fast."

Failing to provide answers, each superhero takes his new friend on a journey through time. Marcus and the Pink Power Ranger visit the Trocme house and witness how they provide shelter to Jews escaping the Nazis. Janessa and Michael Jordan go to Money, Mississippi, in 1955 to see the trial where Mose Wright testified. In the conclusion of the story, Janessa and Marcus, back at school, are challenged to put their lessons of courage and real heroism into practice. As Robert enters the cafeteria alone, Marcus's friends begin to mock him and call him a "faggot." Marcus objects to their language and tells them to leave the poor kid alone. Janessa, watching Marcus with his friends, simply gets up from her table and goes and sits defiantly with Robert. While neither is ready to take on the world, they both are willing to take small steps.

There were some rough spots and we were still missing our final scene, but we now had a real script to work from. We knew how many characters we had, who they were, and where and when the scenes took place. We knew enough to move to the next step: production.

We formed five different committees: assistant directors, set design and construction, costumes, music, and publicity. As in every other year, everyone would act. Students could request a large part or a smaller part, but everyone had to walk on stage and say at least one line. Students were invited to sign up for the committee that interested them. The next day, we met in our committee groups. The set design crew went to investigate our performance space (the school cafeteria), the costume committee went to the library to get books on World War II to see how people dressed then, the publicity crew started brainstorming ideas and designs for the poster, and the assistant directors gathered together to make up a list of the characters they needed to cast.

Casting our plays has always been done democratically. Each student is given a list of characters and is asked to rank the ones he or she is interested in playing. We then make a grid with every character on one axis and every member of the class on the other and we fill in the chart according to each student's request. The assistant directors work as a group to cast the parts. I instruct them to use two guidelines in their casting decisions. First, they should think about who can play which part best. We do not audition for roles. Because we have been doing improvisations and role-plays for months and because the students have created and experimented with the characters, the assistant directors have a good sense of each student's talents. Second, they should try to honor people's requests for particular parts. But ultimately they need to make decisions in the best interest of the play as a whole.

I maintain the right of final veto or ultimate decision making, but I have never used it. In our first play, *On the Line,* the students cast a Haitian girl who had just been mainstreamed into an English-speaking classroom in a major role. Although they had rarely heard her speak, they thought her personality really fit the character. They also cast a boy with a serious speech disability as a union organizer who had a one-and-a-half-page monologue. In each case, they recognized the risks, but felt that with support and practice, Jodelle and Chris would be great in the parts. They were right. Jodelle never dropped a line, and Chris delivered his speech from a soap box without falter. Later, when asked how he felt about doing the play, Chris wrote, "I felt like a knight in shining armor and I could do anything!" I was convinced that our process worked.

This year, we ran into a different problem with casting. There were two boys and two girls who had chosen to be assistant directors. The two girls had both requested one of the lead acting roles. Usually, I would not encourage directors to take on leading parts, but this time they were the only two girls in the class who wanted the role. The two boys had also requested a part, along with two other students in the class. I wondered how this situation would resolve itself. Would they use their power to cast themselves in the roles they wanted? Or would they try to think about what was best for the class, and the play, as a whole?

They made their grid and I suggested they start with the easy decisions and work their way up to the hard ones. Finally, they had cast all the roles but the ones they had asked for. They talked about who was best for what part. They talked about what role they could give people who didn't get the part they wanted. They were very concerned that people feel satisfied with their final assignment. They didn't want to waste any talent and they didn't want to hurt anyone's feelings. They were stuck.

"Tell us what to do," they said.

"I can't," I replied. "Directors get faced with tough decisions sometimes. You can't just back off when the going gets tough. Anyway, I don't know what the right decision is either. You have to find a way to make a decision. We can't go on with the play until this is resolved."

We decided to take the dilemma to the rest of the class. Who did they think should play the part? Should we take a vote? Should we audition this time? How can we decide? The class responded, "You are the directors. You should decide, not us. We trust that you'll make the best decision for the play." The students caucused again and still could not decide. Finally, I suggested they divide up. The girls should choose the part for the boys and the boys should choose the part for the girls. They agreed. After about 10 minutes of agonizing, each group finally made a decision. There was great excitement for those who got the parts they wanted; there was tremendous disappointment for those who didn't. But having been part of the process, the students were able to put their personal desires aside for what was best for the whole. The decision had been made and we moved on.

I was continually struck throughout this play at how committed students were to the big picture. Often, kids (and adults) can get very invested in their particular contribution and have a harder time seeing what's best for the whole. I had struggled with this myself. I'd had certain ideas about staging or set design that the kids either resisted or sometimes flat out rejected. When I tried to force it, I saw it as just that—a force fit. The kids' instincts were right; I too needed to stay open to our collective wisdom.

Another major example of this commitment to the whole was when we were developing the ending scenes of the play. We wanted to show how Marcus's journey to the Trocme household had changed him. We wanted to give him an opportunity to move beyond his role as a bystander and take a stand for what he knew was right. One group had come up with a good idea. On his way home from school, Marcus runs into a few of his buddies outside a video store. They invite him to go in the store with them. He realizes that they are planning to steal a tape. He refuses to join them and tells them they are wrong to do it. They call him a goody-goody and go in anyway.

The class really liked the scene. It was realistic, and it didn't have a happy ending in that Marcus was not able to convince others to do the right thing. But still, he had made a stand at the risk of being seen as a wimp. It was a good scene. But, as we put it together with the rest of the scenes, we realized it was unnecessary. It was taking the message that had been suggested in the scene before and making it totally explicit for the audience. Did we want to hit the audience over the head with our message? Or did we want to leave them pondering? We went back to our original goals to remind ourselves that we had wanted the audience to leave thinking. We did not want to neatly wrap up our story like an afternoon TV special. After much discussion and debate, the class agreed to drop the scene. It was not easy to do, but we knew the play would be better without it.

One day, as we began to prepare for actual rehearsals, the assistant directors came to me. They were worried. None of them had ever directed before and they were anxious that their peers might not listen to them. Their fears were legitimate. In other plays, there had been problems with actors refusing direction from their student directors. We had also had the reverse problem of student directors getting a bit intoxicated with power over their peers. At least a couple of our directors this year had dictatorial tendencies and throughout the year had not been particularly supportive or constructive in their feedback to others. I agreed it would be wise to deal with the actor/director relationship before it became a crisis.

We called a class meeting and the directors shared their concerns with the class. We then put up two pieces of newsprint: What do directors need from actors? and What do actors need from directors? We began to discuss the relationship and identified key elements that would make it work. Directors needed actors to focus, to cooperate, to be prepared, to be willing to try something risky, to keep an open mind, to trust the director's judgment. Actors needed from directors patience, suggestions rather than orders, constructive criticism, willingness to listen, support for building self-confidence, agreement to not abuse their position of authority. The bottom line for both groups was to feel respected.

This 20-minute discussion changed the tenor of rehearsals. Although we had our difficult moments and our frustrations, there was an underlying sense of trust that we were all in this together. I watched kids really push each other—to articulate lines more clearly, to slow down, to use silence, to let go of self-consciousness, to take tremendous risks. When tensions arose or relationships were strained, we would go back to our lists (which we kept posted in the classroom). We were all trying to make the play work. With the commitment to process, we were able to keep our eyes on the prize.

Opening night was a week away and Scene Eight, the final scene of the play, had still not been written. In this scene, students wanted to speak directly to the audience about their own experiences, their own learning. They wanted to leave the audience, thinking hard about their own choices and actions in life. But we had not figured out just how to do this. Several ideas had been made, but nothing felt quite right.

"What do we do about Scene Eight?" I asked the kids.

"We should ask the audience questions," said Emily, an outspoken eighth-grader.

"What kinds of questions?" I responded.

"Well, like, what would they do in those situations? Or maybe we should talk about the real-life things that happen to us all the time. Or maybe—oh, I don't know."

"Okay," I said. "Just try this. For homework tonight, write down how you think we should end the play. Or write down questions you would like to ask the audience. Or write down an incident that happened to you or a friend. Just write down some thoughts about the ending and we'll see what we get."

The next day, a jumble of responses came in. Some kids had written down simple questions such as "What would you do if you were Janessa or Marcus?" Others had staging ideas "Each person should stand in front of someone in the audience and look right at him or her." Some had written about their own experiences as bystanders and how they hoped they would now act differently. How could we put this all together in a way that made any sense?

As I leafed through the papers they had turned in, I started to jot down questions or phrases that stood out to me. I started remembering lines from poems we had read, stories told by witnesses, reflections of survivors, excuses people had offered for inaction, excerpts from the students' writing from earlier in the year. Beginning with the famous quote from Reverend Neimoller, "First they came for the Communists, but I wasn't a Communist so I said nothing," I started weaving these strands together, interspersing lines such as "Mind your own business," "We wear the mask," and "I don't want to get involved," with the kids' own experiences: "One time I was out trick or treating. We were about a block from my house. When this group of bigger kids started saying things like, 'Oh, I remember him. He's that fat faggot.' They came by me and grabbed my bag. I resisted, but they took it anyway. Nobody helped me."

I also reached back into the Facing History curriculum to draw on the lessons of the past. A university professor tried to explain his failure to take a stand against the Nazi regime: "Each act, each occasion was worse than the last. But only a little worse. You wait for the next, and the next. You wait for one great shocking occasion, thinking that others, when such a shock comes, will join with you in resisting." And I took lines from their own wishes, dreams, hopes, and fears : "Will anyone remember the poems I wrote? Or will they be burned in a bonfire in the back of their minds?" and "What's that you say? Another child blown away in the crossfire of gang warfare?" and "I don't want to be another statistic or a number without a name." A scene began to take shape.

The next day, I brought in my draft. I was nervous about how the kids would respond. Was I conveying their message, or mine? They listened intently as I read it aloud. With the final lines, "Then they came for me, and there was no one left to speak for me," the class broke into applause. That night, Nierika wrote in her journal, "Today we worked on Scene 8. I love [underlined four times] that scene. It'll bring the audience to tears! It is a great way of 'wrapping it all up.' It ties all the themes of the play together so that it'll move the audience and they'll be thinking about it for a while!"

As rehearsals progressed and the set came together and costumes and props piled up in the room, I felt a strange sense of calm. Usually, the week before the show panic sets in. You are always wishing you had just one more week to prepare. You can't imagine that the set is going to be finished. You don't know where the music for the last scene is going to come from. You realize how one scene really hasn't received the attention it needs. It would be false to say that I was not anxious. But there was a calm that came from another place. Whether or not the play worked (and I was praying that it would), I knew the process had worked. I had witnessed deep thinking and honest struggle around tough issues of standing up for what you believe, for acting on your convictions, for not going along with the crowd. Not only did the kids understand the history but they were also responding to it every day in how they worked together. We had built a strong community in our classroom. I saw students supporting each other, encouraging each other to take risks, giving each other positive feedback, honest critique, and encouragement. I saw that they saw they could trust each other and count on each other. I saw that kids had not just learned about history, but had come to own it for themselves. I was calm because I knew we had already been victorious.

As the lights dimmed on the final lines of Scene Eight, there was a hush in the cafeteria and then the audience burst into applause. I looked around to see people wiping tears from their eyes, just as Nierika had predicted. I saw cast members hugging each other, parents hugging kids, kids from the audience hugging the actors. We had just witnessed a powerful piece of magic.

The days after the play glowed. The kids basked in their success. They felt good about themselves and good about each other. They recognized what they had achieved. But I wondered, What had they learned? What lessons would stay with them beyond the excitement of the play? How deep did the learning go?

Two months later, in June, I asked students to reflect on their experiences over the year and to think about what important lessons they had learned. I was deeply moved by their responses. Nierika wrote, "The most valuable experience that I have had all year was definitely the play. I had never done anything like it before, so everything was new to me. I enjoyed directing a lot and I think I did a good job at it. I also liked acting and writing parts of the play. But my favorite part of the whole experience was the feeling I got after one of our performances. I felt proud. I felt more pride than I'd felt for almost anything in my whole life. I was proud of myself, I was proud of you, but most of all I was proud of the class as a whole. It was amazing to realize what a great thing we could create by working together."

Carrie, who played Janessa, wrote, "When I think about risks I think about important things that happened to me. I think about the play, I think about class discussions we had, I think about the opinions that I defended, but most of all I think about what I learned about taking risks, and how hard it is to fight for what you believe in, but how important it is to take those risks."

Emilio wrote, "I know that I can now try to help other people and try to solve problems in my life a little better. I am learning not to be a bystander, but I haven't been able to show this. I have never done anything to stop a fight before—but I have grown to the point where I want to do something."

Perhaps the most eloquent response came from Emily, a quiet seventh-grader who had struggled all year with being sure of herself:

> I only hope that everyone learned as much as I did from *The Incident* and that they took it back in their heads or hearts, because although you don't always think with your head, your heart is always in what you say.
>
> I say all this because today at lunch I was sitting with a kid who was in the play and he said, "He's gay" and I do not mean in the sense that yes, he was homosexual or yes, he is happy, but I mean in the insult form. I jumped on him (verbally). "Do you remember anything from the play?" I sat back as two others (one who had been in the play and one who had seen it) also made angry remarks about his bad choice of words. I don't remember his exact response, but it was something like, "Yeah, you're right. Sorry." This is true! The names are withheld to protect the guilty, who apologized. I was freaked out that someone (especially someone who was in the play) would say that, but I was glad, ecstatic almost, that at least three people objected to his actions and he did apologize and realize what he had done.
>
> I realize while typing these words that I myself am a perpetrator, we all are. At least once in some point in everyone's life you will hurt someone. . . . But now that I know that, I can work to not hurt anyone in the future.
>
> I hate being labeled. I shall not label others.
>
> I hate being teased. I shall not tease others.

I hate it when people joke about my shortness which I cannot change.
I shall not joke about others' physical features they cannot change.
I hate being judged unfairly. I shall not unfairly judge others.
And I shall never ever steal from others their pride, dignity, or happiness.

As I look back over this year, I realize that there were two important forces at work in creating this powerful learning experience for both my students and myself. The first was a rich and deep curriculum that tapped into critical issues in young people's lives: justice, courage, freedom, and personal responsibility. Facing History helped students to confront the complexities of history in ways that promoted critical and creative thinking.

But the content alone was not what moved Emily to a place where she could act to interrupt intolerance. Through the process of creating a play, students were able to make their own meaning from the lessons of history. They were able to put this meaning into practice. Not only did students learn about people who had taken risks in the past but they also learned how to take risks themselves. They read about people who had asked questions and looked critically at personal choices, and they looked deeply into themselves. As they learned about people who had worked together for a better world, they worked together to experience the "power of we" for themselves. The curriculum gave them the examples from the past and inspired a hope for the future. The play provided a forum in which they could demonstrate to themselves, and to others, the power they have to make change.

REFERENCE

Strom, Margot Stern, and Parsons, William S. (1982). *Facing History and Ourselves: Holocaust and Human Behavior.* Watertown, MA: Intentional Educations, Inc.

NOTE

Individuals who are interested in obtaining a copy of the script (for educational purposes) are welcome to contact Kathy Greeley, c/o Graham and Park School, 15 Upton Street, Cambridge, MA 02139. (617) 349-6612.

▶ 6

Teleconversing about Community Concerns and Social Issues

JUDITH H. VESEL

> *"This program* [the National Geographical Society (NGS) Kids Network] *with all the schools is cool because we get to talk to people we can't see!"—Dustin Carter (7th-grade student) and Logan Wade (7th-grade student), Craigmont Junior High School, Memphis, Tennessee*

WHAT IS THE NGS KIDS NETWORK?

The National Geographic Society (NGS) Kids Network is a telecommunications-based science curriculum for students in middle grades. It was developed by TERC (formerly Technical Education Research Centers, Inc.) with funding from the National Science Foundation (NSF) and the National Geographic Society (NGS). The title of each of the units in the series—What Is Our Soil Good For?, How Do Our Bodies Get the Oxygen They Need?, How Loud Is Too Loud?, and How Can We Protect Our Water?—provides a central question and an ongoing focus for exploration and discussion. Each of the units is shaped by the following principles:

- Students address topics that enable them to think in depth about aspects of the natural world and to apply their ideas to related important environmental and social concerns.
- Students engage in activities similar to those undertaken by professional scientists. Learning is connected to collecting, recording, and analyzing data; in turn, the data are used to make predictions and ask questions, to explain phenomena, to develop scientific ideas, and to ask further questions.
- Students use a computer network to exchange their findings, ideas, and questions with students in other classrooms. Collaboration with other stu-

dent scientists helps them to understand their own data in the context of broader scientific issues and to participate in a larger scientific community.

NGS Works, a powerful integrated software tool, supplies the technology necessary to support the curriculum. It has features for telecommunications, word processing, data display and manipulation, graphing, and mapping. What Stories Do the Data Tell?, a fifth unit funded by NSF and NGS, accompanies the software. It focuses on the role of data in the research process.

Each Kids Network unit consists of 24 sessions comprising eight weeks of class work. Every unit is divided into four parts, each of which emphasizes a different aspect of scientific research. By developing ideas that build on one another, students deepen their understanding and generate new ideas. In Part I, students conduct investigations yielding qualitative data—what they can learn by observing. In Part II, students conduct investigations resulting in quantitative data—what they can learn by measuring. In Part III, students exchange data on the network and analyze the larger data set. In Part IV, students return to a question raised by their studies and design their own investigation to answer that question.

Who Are the People Dustin and Logan Cannot See?

Students doing an NGS Kids Network unit work collaboratively to investigate a topic. The work begins as a class, then extends to a group of classes called a research team. Later on the work involves all the classes doing the unit.

In 1993, 35 classes in grades 6 through 9 took part in a field test of How Do Our Bodies Get the Oxygen They Need? Dustin's and Logan's class, located in Memphis, Tennessee, was one of the field-test sites. Their class belonged to a research team of 17 classes called the *Arms*. The members of the Arms team and their locations are listed in the Table 6–1.

Throughout the unit, students wrote letters and short notes to members of their entire research team or to selected members of their team, and transmitted them on a computer network. These electronic communications, referred to from this point on as *teleconversations*, gave students the opportunity to exchange their ideas, findings, and questions with other student researchers, simulating the routine collaboration that often occurs among a community of professional scientists. Later in the unit, all 35 classes exchanged data on the network and analyzed the larger data set looking for patterns and trends to help them deepen their classroom understandings.

How Are Teleconversations Useful for Studying Community Concerns and Social Issues?

Teleconversations build on the natural curiosity that students have about other students. They provide opportunities for sharing ideas and questions. They are

TABLE 6–1   Members of the Arms Team and Their Locations

Row	Team	Location
1	Arms	Alexandria, VA
2	Arms	Ann Arbor, MI
3	Arms	Fresno, CA
4	Arms	Horsham, PA
5	Arms	Kokomo, IN
6	Arms	Madison, WI
7	Arms	Memphis, TN
8	Arms	Fort Bragg, CA
9	Arms	N. Easton, MA
10	Arms	N. Easton, MA
11	Arms	Norfolk, VA
12	Arms	Orlando, FL
13	Arms	Spokane, WA
14	Arms	Appleton, ME
15	Arms	W. Bloomfield, MI
16	Arms	Windsor Locks, CT
17	Arms	Winfield, WV

a way to solicit additional information to further classroom studies and can motivate students to research new topics. Teleconversations also serve to extend and reinforce classroom understandings about community concerns and related social issues.

What Ideas and Questions Do Students Share in Initial Teleconversations?

In Part I of How Do Our Bodies Get the Oxygen They Need?, students first determine how the lungs, heart, and blood vessels work together to supply the body with oxygen and to remove carbon dioxide. Next, they expand their classroom studies by conducting research in their community into risk factors that affect the respiratory and circulatory systems. The research can be a review of articles from local newspapers about risk factors of concern to the community; or an analysis of survey data collected from questionnaires distributed to parents, neighbors, and others in the community; or discussions with professionals at local branches of the American Heart Association, the American Cancer Society, the Department of Public Health, the Environmental Protection Agency, or a community-action organization. Doctors and nurses associated with a local hospital or medical center or scientists working at a local college or university can also be valuable sources of data. Then the class groups its research findings into one of three risk-factor categories: hereditary (received from one or both biological parents), environmental (determined by exposure to potentially harmful materials in the surroundings), or behavioral (associated with habits). The students count the entries in each category and use the information to decide which risk-factor category is the most prevalent in their community.

At the conclusion of Part I, students summarize the findings from their investigations, write a class letter, and transmit it on the network to their research teammates. The initial teleconversation begins scientific collaboration with other members of the research team by giving students an opportunity to ask their colleagues for assistance with their research. The questions students ask in these initial teleconversations often motivate them to extend their own studies to topics that go beyond the prescribed curriculum (Refer to How Do Subsequent Teleconversations Extend Classroom Understandings? and How Do Teleconversations Stimulate Individual Research? later in this chapter.)

The initial teleconversation is a collaborative process that involves each student in the class. The steps of this process are as follows. First, the teacher divides the class into five groups and assigns one focus question (from the following list) to each group:

- What would we like our research teammates to know about us, our school, and the community we live in?
- What can we tell our teammates about our respiratory system?
- What can we tell our teammates about our circulatory system?
- What can we tell our teammates about risk factors of concern to our community?
- What questions do we have about the respiratory and circulatory systems? How can our teammates help us answer the questions?

Next, members of the group write down on a sheet of paper their ideas for answering the question assigned to them. Then they discuss their individual ideas with other members of the group and draft a final answer to the question they were assigned. Next, they write their answer on chart paper and prepare to read the sentences the group wrote to the class. As students share their sentences, members from each group attach their chart paper to the chalkboard. After all the groups have finished, the class determines the order of the sentences and the final wording of the letter. For homework, students type the letter using NGS Works. Before they send it to their teammates over the network, they have the final wording checked by an adult. Typing and sending the teleconversation does not always happen in a science class. It sometimes takes place before or after school, during lunch, or in a computer or language arts class, as evidenced in the first teleconversation written by seventh-grade student researchers from the Abbott Middle School: "We stayed after school to type this and the late bus will be here soon so we are gone. We are outta here! Bye!"

Each class participating in the field test of How Do Our Bodies Get the Oxygen They Need? had its own interesting findings as they investigated the respiratory and circulatory systems. However, a series of teleconversations be-tween students in Orlando, Florida, and students in Ann Arbor, Michigan, West Bloomfield, Michigan, Memphis, Tennessee, and Spokane, Washington, stood out. In the words of one of the teachers whose class participated in the ongoing exchanges between the five schools, "They exemplify the real potential [for learning] that is possible with Kids Network" (Robert Kopicko, Abbott Middle School, West Bloomfield, Michigan). The excerpts that follow will identify the initial ideas and questions about community concerns and social issues these five sites shared with their teammates in their first teleconversation. Subse-quent excerpts will demonstrate how these areas of interest evolved into re-search that went beyond the confines of the prescribed curriculum.

January 25, 1994
From: Orlando, Florida (Southwest Middle School, Eighth Grade)
To: The Arms Team

Dear Research Teammates,

Orlando is a city of opportunity and entertainment. We have a sneak-ing suspicion that our school is better than yours; but you are probably out of school because it is snowing. Lucky you! We don't even get days off when there is a hurricane, since we're in the middle of the state. Even so, Southwest is a good school. It is three years old, and has over 1,800 students. Unfortunately, the school was designed to hold 1,200. We have all the latest technology and really nice teachers.

Our school has had problems with keeping our classrooms clean of bacteria and fungi. With our humid air, we believe our air conditioning is not capable of eliminating the moisture that encourages the growth of fungi.

Diseases are always a community concern and Orlando is no ex-ception. Orlando has problems with heart disease, hypertension, and respiratory diseases such as lung cancer. Florida is ranked number one with West Virginia in cases of lung cancer. This may be the result of all of the retirees moving down to Florida, bringing with them not only their polyester pant suits but also their diseases.

Another problem in Orlando is smoking. The restaurants have no-smoking areas, but several students found that in many cases, the non-smoking area is right next to the smoking area. People are being ex-posed to secondhand smoke even when they think they are safe. Teen-age smokers are a large local concern. We feel that more action needs to be taken with [our teenagers].

Some local businesses and restaurants have taken action. Local res-taurants are adding new low fat meals to their menus. Businesses are taking away the smoking privilege for their employees while at work.

Through our research, we have come up with a few questions. We would greatly appreciate it you would help us answer them.

1. What makes schools have unhealthy air and what can we do about it?
2. How long do you have to smoke before your lungs are affected?
3. Why does your heart beat rapidly when you are scared?

Sincerely,

Southwest Middle School
Orlando, Florida

January 26, 1994
From: Ann Arbor, Michigan (Scarlett Middle School, Seventh Grade)

Dear Research Teammates,

Hello. We are your Scarlett Middle School teammates. We live in Ann Arbor, Michigan. It is special because it has lots of fun things to do. We have colleges in the Ann Arbor area, like the University of Michigan and Eastern Michigan that are a very big part of our lives. Last year the University of Michigan "Wolverines" won the Rosebowl. Ann Arbor is mostly residential. It does not have big factories, but it is close to two cities that do, Ypsilanti and Detroit. Just outside our city boundary lines, there are farms, country land, and some wooded areas. Our crime rate is nothing compared to other cities in Michigan.

We have looked into the health concerns of our Ann Arbor community and some of the actions that are being taken to improve health. We gathered information by surveying our parents and other adults (total of 135 people) about clean air, healthy foods, and exercising. We also interviewed people over the phone. Here is some of the information we got from interviews with local health "experts."

The director of our county American Heart Association says that smoking affects everyone, not just people that smoke. He talked to us about better publicity about (sic) the hazards of smoking. We have groups in our community that promote better health and cleaner air. Another of our "experts" sent us a Smoking Pollution Control Ordinance that is being presented to our city council. If this law is passed, smoking will be prohibited in these places:

- Schools and school grounds
- Elevators
- Buses, taxicabs, and other public transit
- Restrooms
- Service lines
- Retail stores

- All business and nonprofit entities patronized by the public
- Restaurants

Mrs. Scott's Science Classes
Scarlett Middle School
Ann Arbor, Michigan

January 25, 1994
From: West Bloomfield, Michigan (Abbott Middle School, Seventh
    Grade)

Dear Teammates,

We are seventh-grade students at Abbott Middle School in West
Bloomfield, Michigan. Our school is located about 30 miles northwest
of Detroit. There is no industry in our community, just houses, condos,
apartments, restaurants, and small businesses. Our township has 25 lakes
in it and our school is between two of the biggest ones.

Our community seems pretty normal. We are concerned about smoking and how it hurts our health. Our school is a smoke-free school. All
of our restaurants have no-smoking sections. Some of our restaurants
have "heart smart" choices on the menu. Most of us are very active in
sports. Most of us think smoking is really the biggest problem. Our
community is concerned about the Sick Building Syndrome (where
workers suffer eye irritations, headaches, and other problems from the
benzene and formaldehyde fumes in carpeting, plywood, and other
things) and about the use of lawn care pesticides. We are going to find
out more about this [pesticides].

We have some questions we are going to try to answer. How harmful is second-hand smoke? What happens in your body when you inhale polluted air? Why are people cutting down forests when they supply oxygen to the world? What happens if you only smoke one cigarette?

We stayed after school to type this and the late bus will be here
soon so we are gone. We are outta here! Bye!

Student Researchers
Abbott Middle School
West Bloomfield, Michigan

January 16, 1994
From: Memphis, Tennessee (Craigmont Middle School, Seventh Grade)

Dear Teammates,

Hey! We're here at Craigmont Middle School, located in Memphis, Tennessee. Memphis, is home of the blues, the King (Elvis Presley), the Pyramid, and the Civil rights Museum; not to mention Anfernee "Penny" Hardaway, who now plays for "The Magic."

Craigmont is a great school. We have over 2,000 students in grades 7–12. Craigmont is an optional school for international studies. We all take at least one foreign language. We have our own planetarium, radio station, greenhouse, and auto shop.

Even though Memphis is a wonderful place to live, all of us are worried about what our future will bring. Our reports about the concerns of our community show that we are most concerned about pollution due to smog and secondhand smoke. We are also worried about diseases that go hand in hand with pollution, such as heart disease, lung cancer, emphysema and even allergies.

We're waiting for your letters, so for now, "Nice talkin' to ya."

Your Craigmont Friends

January 27, 1994
From: Spokane, Washington (Sacajawea Middle School, Seventh Grade)

Dear Teammates,

Hi. We go to Sacajawea Middle School. It is located in Spokane in the northwest corner of the USA. Spokane sits in a valley surrounded by mountains on the East and the Palouse (a rich wheat growing area) on the West. We get prevailing winds from the Southwest, which brought us ash from Mount St. Helens when it erupted in 1980.

In our class, we decided on three main community concerns. One is the Hanford Nuclear Site built in 1943 and one of the first places to help make atomic bombs. Today, people are concerned that Hanford gases and other harmful chemicals have been released into the air. These can cause thyroid and lung cancer. Another concern is our air pollution. Our air is considered one of the worst in the nation. We live in a valley with little rain and lots of "inversion" days that trap the dust and smoke from burning wheat and grass fields, from the local trash incinerators, and from cars and factories. The third concern is the deadly Hantivirus. It is carried by some animals including deer mice. At first the symptoms are just like the flu, but then you die all of a sudden. There is no cure and no treatment. It was detected in Idaho, only a few miles from where we live.

We have many questions. Here are just a few of them:

1. How does the body make blood?
2. What causes blood clots and strokes?
3. Why doesn't blood collect in your legs?

We look forward to hearing from you!

TELECONVERSATIONS AND CLASSROOM UNDERSTANDING

How Do Subsequent Teleconversations Extend Classroom Understandings?

In Part II of the unit, students collect numerical data about vital capacity (the maximum volume of air a person can exhale in one breath after inhaling as deeply as possible), pulse-recovery time (the number of minutes it takes for the pulse to return to the resting rate after performing a standard aerobic activity), and exposure to secondhand smoke (tobacco smoke inhaled from the environment). The analysis of these data enable students to consider their community's concerns and related social issues in more depth.

As an integral part of their ongoing research into the respiratory and circulatory systems, students try to answer questions raised in the initial teleconversations. They first select a question from the teleconversations. The question the students select is usually one that they find puzzling or that intrigues them in some (often indescribable) way. Then they apply their classroom understandings from Part I and Part II about the respiratory and circulatory systems and their understandings about the research process to the task of collecting data to answer the question. Next, they communicate their findings in a second teleconversation to their teammates. Therefore, the questions posed in the initial teleconversations extend classroom understandings of community concerns and related social issues beyond the confines of the curriculum by stimulating students to extend their research into many related areas. The following is an excerpt from a second teleconversation sent by students at the Scarlett Middle School in Ann Arbor.

February 23, 1994
From: Ann Arbor, Michigan (Scarlett Middle School, Seventh Grade)

Dear Arms Team,

After researching [the questions in your letters from January 1994], we think we can help answer some of them.

1. "What makes school air unhealthy?" (Orlando, Florida). We have discussed these possibilities
   - Smoking by staff or students
   - Radon, a naturally occurring gas that seeps into buildings from the ground surrounding it and can cause lung cancer
   - Toxic fumes used for cleaning that can harm the respiratory system
   - Asbestos, an insulation material used in older buildings that can cause lung cancer

We discussed these solutions:
   - Encourage people not to smoke through education and advertisements and by passing laws against tobacco use on school grounds.
   - Test for radon by hiring a company to put radon detectors in each classroom for two days and then follow the recommendations made by the experts [after the data are analyzed].
   - Encourage the use of nontoxic cleaners in your school.
   - Find out if your school insulation is made of asbestos and, if it is asbestos, replace it with safer materials.

2. "Why does your heart beat more rapidly when you are scared?" (Orlando, Florida). We learned that there is a special gland that releases a hormone called adrenaline into the blood. That makes the heart beat faster. It also makes people do amazing things. For example, a person can pick up a car if a child is trapped under it or people can fight [off attackers] when they surprise them.

3. "How does your body make blood?" (Spokane, Washington) We found that the blood replaces itself in the bone marrow. Red blood cells are very fragile and only live 120 days. So new blood needs to be made all the time.

Each of our small class teams will be researching a particular question. As a whole class, we still hope to find out answers to some of the following questions:
1. Can a person get addicted to secondhand smoke?
2. How much smoke has to get in your lungs before they are damaged?
3. How long does it take for the lungs to repair themselves after a person stops smoking?
4. Do lions, bears, and other animals have heart attacks if they [are in the zoo and] do not exercise regularly?

If you have information about any of these questions, please don't hesitate to send us a message.

Sincerely,
Mrs. Scott's Science Class
Scarlett Middle School

Without teleconversations, the students in Ann Arbor might never have extended their investigations of community concerns and social issues to include these topics. And without their fellow researchers who provided an audience, the ways in which they extended their classroom understandings might never have been shared with other researchers. Conversely, the other researchers may never have had an opportunity to benefit from their research.

How Do Teleconversations Reinforce Classroom Understandings?

In Part III of How Do Our Bodies Get the Oxygen They Need?, students analyze data (transmitted on the network) by their teammates. Before they analyze the network data, they use information from earlier teleconversations and ideas from the unit to predict what they will find. Then they use their findings from the analysis of the network data to verify or refute their predictions. Discrepancies between students' expectations and their findings or between the majority of the data and a single data point often raise "burning" questions. Teleconversations provide an opportunity for researchers to obtain answers to these questions. The scenario described here recounts how a "burning" question stimulated a series of teleconversations, and how the ideas conveyed and, in turn, reinforced classroom understandings of community concerns and related social issues.

First, each class in the field test recorded data collected from the class investigations related to the circulatory and respiratory systems and transmitted them on the network. The Arms teammates transmitted their class's data about the following characteristics:

Location (Site, such as Orlando, Florida, where the data were collected)

Pulse Recovery Time (The mean number of minutes for the class based on pulse recovery time as the time it takes for the pulse to return to the resting rate after performing a standard aerobic activity)

Vital Capacity (The mean volume in milliliters for the class based on vital capacity as the maximum volume of air a person can exhale in one breath after inhaling as deeply as possible)

Predominant Risk Factor (Described as "hereditary," "environmental," or "behavioral" based on the class's findings from the community research in Part I of the unit)

Smoking Opinion (Described as "ban" or "allow" based on the majority opinion of the class about whether smoking in public places should be banned or allowed)

Cigarette Equivalents (The percentage of students in the class who were exposed during the five day test period to environmental-tobacco smoke equivalent to one or more cigarettes)

Before they examined the data, the members of the Arms team made predictions about the patterns they would find in the data for the "Environmental Risk Factor" column and for the "Smoking Ban" column. They knew from the detailed information in the letters that the Memphis community was concerned about air pollution. They knew that people in the Spokane area were worried about radioactive contamination from the Hanford Nuclear Site and the poor quality of their air. Whereas they knew that communities in Orlando, Ann Arbor, and West Bloomfield were concerned about smoking, healthy eating, and exercise, they also knew that their teammates in each of these five sites were concerned about the effects of cigarette smoke on the circulatory and respiratory systems. Therefore, logical predictions from the available data are that their teammates in Memphis and Spokane would transmit "environmental" as the risk factor of greatest concern; their teammates in Orlando, Ann Arbor, and West Bloomfield would transmit "behavioral"; and all five sites would vote to ban smoking in public places. The network data that the members of the Arms team used to verify their predictions are listed in the Table 6–2.

When the student researchers analyzed the data in the "Environmental Risk Factor" column, it must have verified their expectations because the analysis did not stimulate any teleconversations. Whereas the data in the "Smoking Opinion" column defied expectations and the researchers in Spokane, Washington, posed a "burning" question to the researchers in West Bloomfield, Michigan, that resulted in a sincere exchange of ideas that reinforced classroom understandings about community concerns and social issues.

TABLE 6–2   **Network Data Used by the Members of the Arms Team to Verify Their Predictions**

Row	Location	Risk Factor	Smoking Opinion
1	Alexandria, VA	Hereditary	Ban
2	Ann Arbor, MI	Behavioral	Ban
3	Fresno, CA	*********	***
4	Horsham, PA	Environmental	Ban
5	Kokomo, IN	*********	***
6	Madison, WI	Behavioral	Ban
7	Memphis, TN	Environmental	Ban
8	Fort Bragg, CA	Environmental	Ban
9	N. Easton, MA	Environmental	Ban
10	N. Easton, MA	Environmental	Ban
11	Norfolk, VA	*********	***
12	Orlando, FL	Behavioral	Ban
13	Spokane, WA	Environmental	Ban
14	Appleton, ME	Environmental	Ban
15	W. Bloomfield, MI	Behavioral	Allow
16	Windsor Locks, CT	Environmental	Ban
17	Winfield, WV	Behavioral	Ban

1. The "Burning" Question

To: West Bloomfield, MI (Abbott Middle School, Seventh Grade)
From: Ledgerwood, Spokane, Washington (Sacajewea Middle School, Seventh Grade)

We were wondering why you were the only school that chose to allow smoking in public places? Will you please share with us the reasons. Thanks.

2. Teleconversations from Teammates in Support of the Vote

February 21, 1994
From: West Bloomfield, Michigan (Abbott Middle School, Seventh Grade)

Dear Teammates,

I agree with the majority of students in my class who voted to allow smoking in public places. America is the land of the free and that means people can do what they want to do. I'm not saying that I would like it if everyone in the world smoked because that would be horrible. But I am saying that the people who want to smoke can and the people who don't want to should just avoid it somehow.

Kelli Edwards,
Student Researcher

February 21, 1994
From: West Bloomfield, Michigan (Abbott Middle School, Seventh Grade)

Dear Teammates,

I agree with the majority of students in my class who voted not to support the ban on smoking in public places. I believe this because people who smoke should not be excluded from our society. It is not fair to cater only to nonsmokers. I think people who are worried about secondhand smoke should stay in the nonsmoking sections and be quiet.

Bryan Miller,
Student Researcher

February 22, 1994

From: West Bloomfield, Michigan (Abbott Middle School, Seventh
    Grade)

Dear Teammates,

I agree with the majority of students in my class who voted not to
support the ban on smoking in public places. I believe that a person
should smoke when or where he or she likes-except if a person is for-
bidden to smoke. Otherwise people could smoke at any time. Right
now I think the smoking and non-smoking areas are just fine.

> Danielle Spigno,
> Student Researcher

3. Teleconversations from Teammates in Opposition to the Vote

February 21, 1994

From: West Bloomfield, Michigan (Abbott Middle School, Seventh
    Grade)

Dear Teammates,

I disagree with the majority of students in my class who voted not
to support the ban on smoking in public places. I think smoking is unat-
tractive. People who smoke end up talking raspy and their teeth turn
yellow.

On the other hand, it also ruins your lungs! The tar that you breathe
in from cigarettes coats your lungs and makes it difficult for you to
breathe. Also, not only could it kill you, but the smoke from cigarettes
travels to people around you [when you smoke]. They breathe it and it
affects their health too!

> Beth Snyder,
> Student Researcher

February 21, 1994

From: West Bloomfield, Michigan (Abbott Middle School, Seventh
    Grade)

I disagree with the majority of students in my class who voted not
to support the ban on smoking in public places. I hate smoke. I'm aller-
gic to it. I heard that secondary smoke is almost worse than smoking

yourself. That's why I disagree with some of the students. There are millions of older people dying who chose not to smoke but [were exposed to secondary smoke] in public places where people were blowing smoke everywhere [and are dying from it].

Steven Sadoway,
Student Researcher

February 28, 1994
From: West Bloomfield, Michigan (Abbott Middle School, Seventh Grade)

Dear Teammates,

I disagree with the majority of students in my class who voted not to support the ban on smoking in public places. I think that smokers are not only harming their own health, but they are harming mine as well. When I wore the Smoke-Check Badge [used to measure exposure to passive smoke in cigarette equivalents], it was a scary thought to find out that I got exposed to two cigarettes without even smoking. I hope somebody will do something about allowing smoking in public places soon.

Jennifer Bone,
Student Researcher

4. A Teleconversation from the Teacher Providing Additional Information

February 28. 1994
From: West Bloomfield, Michigan (Abbott Middle School, Seventh-Grade Teacher)

Dear Ms. Ledgerwood and Class,

You might be interested to know that our class discussions were always very serious and my students spoke clearly to both sides of the issue. I was impressed with their willingness to listen to each other and to keep focused on the discussion. I never attempted to sway their opinion in either direction. The vote was a secret written ballot under the most serious and controlled voting conditions. You would also be interested to know that it was not a close vote—approximately 66% voted to ALLOW smoking in public places.

I thought that most classes would discuss the grim findings of recent reports on the consequences of smoking. I thought that the amazing statistics surrounding the issue would influence the vote to ban smoking in public places. Yet the vote in my class perhaps represents a very sad but realistic picture: Every day in this country 3,000 kids add to the 46,000,000 people who smoke 495,000,000,000 cigarettes annually for $50,000,000,000 in annual sales.

I don't really know exactly why my students voted to ALLOW smoking in public places. I do know the discussions centered more on issues of individual rights rather than on the adverse health consequences of cigarette smoke. In that light, I think my students saw the question as more of a rights issue than a health issue. The opinions expressed by the six students who responded to your question represent the opinions of the two views of our class.

Best regards,
Robert Kopicko, Teacher

5. A Teleconversation in Support of the West Bloomfield Decision

March 2, 1994
From: Memphis, Tennessee (Craigmont Middle School, Seventh Grade)

Dear Bryan Miller,

I agree with you that the smokers should be part of our society. The nonsmokers, such as myself, should not care what the smokers do. I believe that we should all be free to do what we choose.

Sincerely,
Crystal Byrd,
Student Researcher

6. Teleconversations in Opposition to the West Bloomfield Vote

March 2, 1994
From: Memphis, Tennessee (Craigmont Middle School, Seventh Grade)

Dear Beth Snyder,

We agree with you all the way on banning smoking in public places. There were only a few people who voted to allow smoking in public places in our class. We found that smoking leads to lung cancer. Lung cancer starts early with only one cancer cell, and that cell takes over your other cells. Before you know it, you've got lung cancer.

We think smoking is very harmful, and some people just don't know exactly what all it can do. There are seventh and eighth graders here at Craigmont who smoke, and since they're so young they are really harming their bodies!

Sincerely,
Shelley LeBlanc and
Heather Odiorne,
Student Researchers

February 25, 1994
From: Orlando, Florida (Southwest Middle School, Eighth Grade)

Dear Beth Snyder,

I totally agree with you.

Did you know that cigarette smoking causes 87% of lung cancer deaths? It also causes cancer of the mouth, larynx (voice box), and esophagus (swallowing tube). It's amazing that people still smoke knowing how harmful it is. The reason I think we should ban smoking in public places is because when we inhale smoke from other smokers, the smoke gives off even larger amounts of cancer-causing substances! Also children whose parents smoke are more likely to suffer from pneumonia or bronchitis than in households where no one smokes. When I realized all that can happen to people who inhale secondhand smoke, I realized how important it is to ban smoking in public places.

It's my choice not to smoke, and I don't think it's fair that I should have to risk my health every time I go out. Let those who choose to smoke should (sic) do it in private and not make all of us who choose not to smoke suffer from their mistake.

Natalie Nickerson,
Student Researcher

This exchange shows how teleconversations produce a wave that reinforces classroom understandings of community concerns and social issues as it travels through the research community. A simple question asked about the reasoning behind a puzzling data point was the disturbance that started the wave. As researchers in one location explained and defended their position, other student researchers were motivated to respond to the position taken by their colleagues. As the question and its answers traveled through the research community, classroom data and resulting ideas were revisited and, as a consequence, classroom understandings were reinforced.

How Do Teleconversations Stimulate Individual Research?

One of the principles that shape NGS Kids Network units is that students will apply their understanding about the natural world to related environmental and social issues. In Part IV of How Do Our Bodies Get the Oxygen They Need?, students design and conduct investigations in which they probe their own questions.

A review of the teleconversations written by the eighth-grade students from the Southwest Middle School in Orlando, Florida, the seventh-grade students at the Sacajawea Middle School in Spokane, Washington, and the eighth-grade students at Craigmont Middle School in Memphis, Tennessee, provide evidence that teleconversations contributed to the questions students chose to investigate in Part IV and to the way these students applied their new knowledge to an environmental concern of importance to them. In their initial teleconversation, eighth-grade students at the Southwest Middle School in Orlando, Florida wrote: "Restaurants [in Orlando] have no-smoking areas, but in many cases, the non-smoking area is right next to the smoking area. People are being exposed to second-hand smoke even when they think they are safe." These observations, written at the end of Part I, culminated in an individual investigation in Part IV in which a group of student researchers tried to answer the question: Are non-smoking sections in restaurants really smoke free?

Based on ideas developed from the unit, the student researchers predicted that people who eat in nonsmoking sections of restaurants are exposed to secondhand smoke. The students devised a procedure to test their prediction.

Procedure for Measuring Tobacco Smoke in Nonsmoking Areas

1. Gather the materials.
   - Four Smoke-Check Badges
   - Paper
   - Poster board for diagramming the layout of each restaurant
   - Tape
   - Floppy disk
   - Computer
2. Find four restaurants that are willing to help us conduct the experiment.
3. Place a Smoke-Check Badge in a spot in the nonsmoking section of each restaurant where the manager and we agree that it will not distract or upset customers. (*Note:* Smoke-Check Badges use a standard scale located below an exposure strip to measure exposure to secondhand tobacco smoke in cigarette equivalents. Students used the badges in Part II of How Do Our Bodies Get the Oxygen They Need? to determine their individual exposure to secondhand tobacco smoke in cigarette equivalents. They transmitted on the network the percentage of students in the class who were exposed during the five-day test period to environmental-tobacco smoke equivalent to one or more cigarettes.)

4. Wait five days and then pick up the badge and place it in a plastic bag.

5. Record and analyze the data.

Next, the students conducted their investigation and recorded the data. These data are recorded in Table 6–3.

Finally, the student researchers used the data to evaluate their prediction and presented their findings to the class. They concluded:

> Nonsmoking areas in Ponderosa, Denny's, Sizzler, and Ming Court are not smoke free. We learned in How Do Our Bodies Get the Oxygen They Need? that every time we breathe in smoke from someone else's cigarettes, we breathe in the same harmful cancer-causing chemicals inhaled by smokers. The Environmental Protection Agency estimates that 146,000 lung cancer deaths happen every year and that 3% of the annual death toll is from people breathing in other people's cigarette smoke. We think that nonsmoking sections should be required to test for secondhand smoke and put up a sign stating that the area is not smoke free.—Eighth-grade student researchers from the Southwest Middle School

In their initial teleconversation, seventh-grade students at the Sacajawea Middle School in Spokane, Washington wrote:

> One [concern in their community] is the Hanford Nuclear Site built in 1943 just 100 miles from our homes and one of the first places to make atomic bombs. Today, people worry that Hanford gases and other harmful chemicals have been released into the air. These can cause thyroid and lung cancer.

These observations precipitated an in-depth study at the end of the unit in which the whole class studied Hanford for a four-week period.

Virginia Ledgerwood, seventh-grade teacher at Southwest Middle School writes:

TABLE 6–3   Results of Student Investigation

Restaurant	Cigarette Equivalents (in five days)
Ponderosa	1.0
Denny's	1.0
Sizzler	0.5
Ming Court	0.5

This whole study came about after we researched environmental concerns about breathing and the blood and shared our research with our teammates. My students did not understand radiation, Three Mile Island, or Chernobyl. They wanted to find out more about the impact of these things on themselves and about their total impact on the world.

Students began their individual research about Hanford by interviewing their parents or a neighbor to find out what had gone on there in the past. Next, they shared their findings with the class. Then each student decided on a question to investigate. Some of the questions students tried to answer are the following:

- How does radiation affect the human body and the bodies of other animals?
- How does radiation affect cells and what about mutations?
- Why did they dump all that waste knowing that it could hurt people?
- How is radiation stored?
- How can we get power from nuclear reactors?
- How can we protect the environment from bad effects of places like Hanford?
- Hanford hurt people my parents' age but can it still hurt me?
- I have heard that radiation is not all bad and is used in medicine. How do doctors use it and what do they use it for?

Unlike the eighth-graders at the Southwest Middle School in Orlando, the students in Spokane, Washington, used materials from the library and survey data to answer their questions. They presented their findings to the class and shared their research with their parents. Nathan Swinton, one of the seventh-grade students at the Sacajawea Middle School wrote, "It [our research into Hanford] gave us a lot to talk and think about."

In their initial teleconversation, seventh-grade students at the Craigmont Middle School in Memphis, Tennessee, wrote, "Even though Memphis is a wonderful place to live, all of us are worried about what our future will bring. Our reports about the concerns of our community show that we are most concerned about pollution due to smog and secondhand smoke." These observations culminated in an individual investigation in Part IV in which a group of student researchers tried to answer the question: What affects peoples' opinions about smoking in public places?

The student researchers in Memphis created a questionnaire, which they administered to 100 people over age 16. The questions students asked and the data the students collected are listed here:

Questions

1. Do you smoke?
2. Have you ever smoked?

3. Do you live with someone who smokes?
4. Would you visit a public place if smoking were allowed (nonsmoker)?
5. Would you visit a public place if smoking were banned (smoker)?

Collected Data

1. 10% of the individuals who smoke thought smoking should be banned in public places and 90% thought it should be allowed.
2. 15% of the individuals who once smoked thought smoking should be banned in public places and 85% thought it should be allowed.
3. 18% of the people who lived with someone who smoked thought smoking should be banned in public places and 82% thought it should be allowed.
4. 35% of nonsmokers would visit a public place if smoking were allowed and 65% would not.
5. 21% of smokers would visit a public place if smoking were banned and 79% would not.

From the analysis of the collected data, the student researchers concluded that peoples' opinions about whether smoking should be banned in public places are related to their personal habits.

Each of the three individual investigations cited employed very different methods. The student researchers in Orlando, Florida, conducted a modified laboratory investigation, whereas the students in Spokane, Washington, investigated topics of personal interest using data collected from the library and from personal interviews. In contrast, students in Memphis, Tennessee, used survey data to answer their question. Despite the differences in research methods, each investigation in which "students immersed themselves in an issue surrounding current and compelling issues developed and grew out of ideas shared in teleconversations" (Robert Kopicko, Teacher, Abbott Middle School, West Bloomfield, Michigan).

CONCLUDING THOUGHTS

Teleconversations provide opportunities for student researchers to deepen their understanding in several ways. They enable students to learn about the concerns of students in other geographic areas. They motivate students to extend their research into new and different areas. They provide a mechanism for sharing information on an ongoing basis. And they give students an opportunity to express their own opinions about concerns and issues that are important to them and to take exception to the opinions of others. In short, NGS Kids Network would not be NGS Kids Network without teleconversations.

Note: Those educators who would like to become a part of the NGS Kids Network should write or call: The National Geographic Society, Educational Services, PO Box 98018, Washington, DC 20090-8018. Phone: 1-800-368-2728, weekdays, 8 A.M. to 5:30 P.M. Eastern time. For NGS Kids Network outside the United States: 1-301-921-1322, 8 A.M. to 5:30 P.M. Eastern time.

▶ 7

Using Telecommunications to Nurture the Global Village

DELL SALZA

> Thank you so much for helping us with our well and pump. Now that I
> don't have to walk four kilometers every day to get water, I can go to
> school.

This letter from a 13-year old girl in a rural village in Nicaragua helped
spur students in five states of the United States and Barcelona, Spain, into action that resulted in numerous rural Nicaraguan villages gaining access to clean
water for the first time. Using e-mail and other forms of telecommunication,
students collectively raised over $10,000. In the process, these students learned
math, language arts, and social studies; expanded their world view; experienced
their own communities in new ways; and understood that their actions can make
the world a better place.

The International Education and Resource Network (I*EARN), founded
and funded by the Copen Family Fund since 1990, provides access to the international educational community while the Association for Progressive Communications (APC) provides the technological framework for this project.
I*EARN includes over 200 schools in 23 countries around the world. Five
I*EARN Centers (or clusters of schools with a coordinator) in the United States
have piloted this effort: New York, Massachusetts, Washington, Minnesota, and
New Mexico. There are also Centers in Spain, Russia, China, the Netherlands,
Australia, Argentina, and Canada. Computers and modems in these schools are
linked through the APC computer network for the purpose of enabling students
to work together with their peers in other countries on projects that contribute to
the health and welfare of the planet and its people. I*EARN chose to use the
APC networks because they are nonprofit and they are used by numerous
environmental and social change organizations, thus providing a wealth of

information for the kinds of projects this unique network of schools hopes to encourage.

A few middle-level teachers have been among the courageous who have dared to go out on a limb to experiment not only with using this exciting technology but also with involving early adolescents in service learning projects that help them experience their own power to make change. This chapter will focus on the efforts of the latter individuals.

The I*EARNetwork has established an innovative convenient structure for engaging students in projects. Students and teachers post project ideas on an electronic conference called <iearn.ideas>. Any student or teacher in the network can then respond. Once individuals or classes interested in working on that project are identified, the project is moved to its own conference where topics relevant to that effort can be developed and discussed. Figure 7–1 is a sample index for the <iearn.ideas> conference. The column farthest to the left is the date the entry was posted. The next column has the number of the project followed by a code indicating subject area (ENVironmental = science and math,

FIGURE 7–1   I*EARN Educational Project Ideas

3/03/92	1 Purpose of Conference	4 ed 1
	2 Procedures & Project Process	1 ed 1
	3 Project Idea Outline Format	ed 1
	4 Sample Project Idea Outline	2 ed 1
9/18/92	5******READ ME FIRST!!! ******	walkabout
10/09/92	6 Soc/S. Global News Magazine	4 coldspring
	7 Arts/S. Global Literary Magazine	2 coldspring
	8 Env/S. Environmental Newsletter	1 coldspring
12/12/92	9***PROJECTS IN PROGRESS INDEX**	1 walkabout
12/16/92	10 I*EARN IDEAS ARCHIVED PROJECTS	1 walkabout
12/24/92	11 Env/M,S. The Global UVB Watch	4 peg:bcoppinger
1/18/93	12 Soc/M,S. Solidarity w/Croatian Sch	18 gn:nvives
2/04/93	13 Env/M,S. AquaData: Water Quality Mo	7 ed 1
4/01/93	14 Int/S. VideoLetter Exchange	8 gn:pbaak
5/04/93	15 Int/E,M,S. iearn.planet conference	walkabout
5/07/93	16 Int/E,M,S. First Peoples IYIP'93	2 peg:broadfordsc
	17 Soc/M. World Tour By E-Mail	3 cortlandtms
5/14/93	18 Int/E,M,S. Save the Children	28 somers
5/31/93	19 Env/E,M,S. Ribbons of Blue Austral	2 peg:mansfield
6/08/93	20 Int/M,S. 3 Projects from Europe	3 gn:pbaak
6/12/93	21 Env/M. Columbia River Watershed	4 covington
8/08/93	22 Arts/M,S. Children's Ecol Art Exch	20 aalm@econews.igc.apc.org
8/19/93	23 Int/E,M,S. No Child W/Out Smiles	43 doversherhs
8/27/93	24 Env: Elementary/Middle School News	11 cortlandtms
8/30/93	25 Soc/S. Man and Urban Pop Growth	10 cpem
9/14/93	26 Env/E,M,S. Rainforest Project	1 dschroeter
9/17/93	27 Int/E,M,S. Random Acts of Kindness	8 apsits

(Continued)

FIGURE 7–1   *(Continued)*

10/12/93	28 Int/M,S. Holocaust/Genocide Projec	coldspring
10/18/93	29 Soc/Lang/S: Current World Events	elnal
10/24/93	30 Soc/M,S. Violence and Youth	4 gates
10/27/93	31 Int/S: Women in the World	14 brighton
	32 Soc/S: Protect Human Rights!	coldspring
	33 Lang/S,M: French Environmental Studies	albuquerque
10/31/93	34***Soc/S IYIP 93 Teleconference***	peg: broadfordsc
11/10/93	35 Int/S. Inside View Magazin	2 erasmus
11/11/93	36 Env/S. Local Environmental Issues	1 web:weldona
11/18/93	37 Int/M. Trabajoy Paz	9 edl
12/07/93	38 Int/E,M,S. Clean Water for Nicar	elnal
	39 Arts/M,S. Music Around the World	2 aces
12/11/93	40 Soc/M,S. Impac to dela Nuclear En	2 dreyes
12/22/93	41 Environmental Projects-Exchange w	2 web:weldona
12/25/93	42 Soc/M,S. Investigate Small Politic	5 elahav
1/10/94	43 Arts/S. Women in Literature	5 coldspring
1/17/94	44 Int/M,S. Impact of Nuclear on Socie	3 dreyes
1/19/94	45 Soc/M,S. Dialogue for TC	coldspring
	46 Soc/M,S. Interviews for TC	coldspring
	47 Env/S. Polar Project	8 aces
2/07/94	48 Sci/S. Programming (mathproject)	6 ortmaalot
2/08/94	49 Soc/E,M. Mystery Boxes	3 fiske
2/11/94	50 Int/Soc. Dialogue on Croatia	1 styves
2/19/94	51 Int/Soc/M,S. Dialogue: Croatia	ryp@baraka.UUCP
	52 Int/Soc/M,S. Dialogue: Russia Sch	ryp@baraka.UUCP
3/01/94	54 Int/S+:iearn.recovery project	7 aces
3/02/94	55 Soc/Int/M,S. Japan Study Project	3 sbhs
	56 Int/M,S. International Cookbook	sbhs

**** End of Topics ****

ARTS = literature, art, music; LANG = language based; SOC= social studies; and INTerdisciplinary) and approximate grade level (elementary, middle, secondary). These codes are followed by a brief title, a number indicating the number of responses that have been made to that particular topic, and the username of the person who posted the project idea.

Upon typing in the number of the topic in which one is interested, a description of the project can be found, including the target age group, when the project will take place, what outcomes or products are expected, and how the project will contribute to the health and welfare of the planet. Some find that last aspect restrictive; others see it as what makes this network unique, vital, and powerful. The entry for the Clean Water for Nicaragua project (#38) follows:

1. *Description:* Participants in this project can help rural Nicaraguans install rope pumps and dig wells to provide clean water for their villages. Interdis-

ciplinary lessons can be developed about Nicaraguan life, history, and culture, about water-borne diseases and parasites, Spanish language activities and more. Responses will be received from Nicaraguans working on this project.

2. *Grade/Age Level:* Elementary through high school.
3. *Curricular or Extracurricular:* This project can be done as part of a class or as an extracurricular group or school project. Students can do fundraising projects along with conducting research and educating their communities.
4. *Project Starting Date:* The project began in October 1991.
5. *Project Ending Date:* This project is an ongoing project of I*EARN. Schools can begin and end at any time.
6. *Expected Outcomes/Products:* We hope to provide the raw materials for Nicaraguans who will provide the labor to install rope pumps (and dig wells, if necessary) to provide access to clean water in their villages. In the process, we can educate ourselves and our communities about conditions there with help from communications we receive from the Nicaraguans.
7. *Impact on Health and Welfare of Planet:* These efforts will make it possible for people living in rural villages to have access to clean water and perhaps cut down on diseases resulting from drinking contaminated water. This will be a significant step in raising the standard of living in those villages. In addition, this project raises the level of awareness about access to the resources of this planet. It provides an opportunity for communication and goodwill between cultures.
8. *Number of Participants:* Unlimited.
9. *Project Coordinator:* Dell Salza, Program Coordinator
   The ELNA Global Age Project
   29 Hart Street
   Beverly, MA 01915
   USA
10. *Username:* elna1

Along with this posting on the <iearn.ideas> conference, the following message was sent out to schools that might be interested and did not have access to the conference. The <iearn.pump> conference was created for those who wished to communicate with each other about the project or to receive information about what other schools were doing, letters from Nicaraguans, updates from El Porvenir, and so on. The following was posted as an introduction:

The Rope Pump Project for Nicaragua

Water is easily accessible to most of us, and it is hard for us to imagine what it would be like to spend a good part of our day struggling to get it, making do with one or two bucketfuls a day. We would have a hard time drinking water that was not clean, that we knew would make us sick, and it is hard to imagine not having a choice.

Several schools in the I*EARNetwork are working on a project to raise money to buy rope pumps for rural villages in Nicaragua that do not have access to clean water. The pumps are made with wheels similar to bicycle wheels and rope. They cost about $100 to build and install if the village already has a well. If there is not already a well, the cost is greater depending on how deep they have to dig for the water. The problem is that the water in the well gets contaminated from people throwing their dirty buckets down into the well all the time. Installing the pump involves capping the well.

We are very excited about this project because we think we can make a significant difference in the lives of people in these villages by helping to protect them from the myriad water-borne diseases and parasites that plague them.

We also feel that this effort can be a meaningful learning experience for students, teachers, and communities. It has tremendous possibilities for interdisciplinary intercultural lessons. In science, for example, students could study water-borne diseases and malnutrition. They could learn about how the pump works. We have directions so students can actually build a pump to see how it works! The directions are in Spanish, so Spanish classes or Spanish-speaking members of the community could be enlisted to translate. The history of Nicaragua, the ways that it is tied in with our own history, and what that all means for the future are important areas to be studied along with the literature, art and music of this rich culture. Students' work in these areas could be presented to the community to expand their awareness and understanding.

Students in Massachusetts, New York, Oregon, Texas, Washington, and Barcelona, Spain, have worked on this project so far. It should be noted that the following statements were "posted" during the I*EARNetwork conference. That being the case, one will note that a number of high school teachers and students took part in the conference. Even though the focus of this essay is on the middle level, it is hoped that the inculsion of elementary, middle-level, and secondary voices will provide ideas that might be useful to middle-level educators.

- One middle school teacher in Wenham, Massachusetts, incorporated it into a "Water Awareness Unit" and students in the school's environmental club raised money doing bake sales at all school events. They also held a very successful T-shirt sale.
- A high school group in Dover, Massachusetts, organized a bike-a-thon. They called it "Pump It Up!," described the problem and solution in their brochure, and invited their town to participate in the event.
- Students in a high school in New York put together a slide show about Nicaragua; did research on living conditions, history, and

water contamination issues; and made presentations to all the elementary schools in their district.

- Students in an elementary school in Newton, Massachusetts, learned in their classrooms about the problem and decided to do chores, collect the money they earned, and send it to El Porvenir. They earned enough to fund three pumps and part of the digging of a well.
- Students in an elementary school in Wayland, Massachusetts, are planning a walk-a-thon. They will walk several laps around their school yard up to 3 miles. They will have a few bucket*s of water and see if, between them all, they can carry the water three miles.*

To do this project, we are working with an organization called El Porvenir. El Porvenir means "the future." It is a small nonprofit organization dedicated to basic development projects in poor communities in Nicaragua. Its priority is small water projects. Sometimes the members of the organization work with Habitat for Humanity. Habitat volunteers build the houses and El Porvenir works on providing access to clean water in that community. El Porvenir works with a very small staff, and all the work of digging the well and installing the pump is done by the people living in the village. Checks for funds raised for this project should be made out to El Porvenir and mailed to:

Dell Salza
The ELNA Global Age Project
29 Hart Street
Beverly, MA 01915

For a packet of materials—including a photograph of the pump, directions for building the pump, an order form for an excellent curriculum on Nicaragua, a description of El Porvenir (the organization through which we are working), and a "map" for incorporating a community service project into the curriculum—send your mailing address to Dell Salza, <elna1 on PeaceNet>.

The following materials are available on e-mail from Dell:

1. Interviews conducted by high school students about the project
2. An excerpt from *Gaia: An Atlas of Planet Management* on "Water That Kills"
3. Descriptions of villages in Nicaragua needing pumps and wells
4. Letters from Nicaraguan children (with translations)
5. Dell's account of her visit to Nicaragua in July 1991

We have received letters and photos back from the villages in Nicaragua. . . . We believe we are doing important work and that everyone involved benefits. We invite you, wherever in the world you are, to join us in this effort. Gracias, amigos!

Students from grades 3 through 12 Massachusetts, New York, Oregon, New Mexico, Texas, and Spain shared information on the network and then worked independently in their schools. Middle-level students responded to the project with energy and enthusiasm. The following exchange took place between the facilitator of the project in Boston and sixth graders in Texas:

> From chris@tenet.edu Tue Apr 6 10:25:17 1993
> Date: Tue, 6 Apr 1993 12:04:31 -0500 (CDT)
> From: Chris Rowan <chris@tenet.edu>
> Sender: Chris Rowan <chris@tenet.edu>
> Reply-To: Chris Rowan <chris@tenet.edu>
> Subject: Money for El Riego
> To: elna1@igc.apc.org
> Mime-Version: 1.0

Hello! My name is Pamela Castillo. I'm in the 6th grade, with the Nicaragua project. We have been trying really hard to raise some money. Our group had a bake sale, and we raised $39.25 cents. Mr. Rowan decided that it would be best to send the money. After all, the people in El Riego are not going to wait forever. The group THANKS you for all the things you have done for us!! The money will be sent off today. Our group is from Morningside Elementary, Brownsville TX.

> Sincerely,
> Pamela Castillo &
> The Nicaragua group

Dear Pamela and the Nicaragua group,

What a nice surprise to get your letter! I am really happy that you were able to raise $39.25 for Nicaragua. The money that students are raising to help with this project is making a big difference in the lives of people who live in rural villages in Nicaragua. They are doing a lot of hard work to put those wells and pumps in, so I think they feel very good when we can help them out a little.

Did you learn some things about Nicaragua while you were working on this project? I hope so. I have some new pictures that just came from Nicaragua. Would you like me to send copies of them to you? If so, please send me your mailing address.

If you would like to continue to work on this project in the future, that would be terrific.

Many thanks for all your hard work. You've done something good and I hope you all feel great! I look forward to hearing from you again.

> Sincerely,
> Dell Salza

From chris@tenet.edu Mon Apr 12 10:48:09 1993
Date: Mon, 12 Apr 1993 12:19:10 -0500 (CDT)
From: Chris Rowan <chris@tenet.edu>
Subject: Thank you notice !!!!
To: Dell Salza <elna1@igc.apc.org>
Mime-Version: 1.0

Dear Dell Salza,

Thank you for making us feel that we're making a difference in this world. We did learn a lot from the projects, things that we never would have learned about Nicaragua. THANK YOU for YOUR hard work on the pictures you gathered for us and on the Nicaragua project. You have been a great help on the project. We hope to keep in touch with you, so write back soon!!!!!!!!!!!

Your Friends,
The Nicaragua Group
Pam Castillo
Esme Campos

Elaine Messias is a fifth-grade teacher at the Mitchell School in Needham, Massachusetts, a fairly affluent and homogeneous suburb of Boston. She is a confident, creative, and experienced teacher, short and slightly hunched over with a crop of graying curls on top of her head and bright inquiring, responsive blue eyes. Her students respond well to her continuous challenges to think and learn and to her obvious caring about each child and about the world.

Along with their I*EARN partner class at the Sunset School in West Linn, Oregon, just outside of Portland, Elaine's class was studying the importance of clean water. Her students tested the pH of local bodies of water to see what species could be living in water with that pH and what species were threatened by the increasing acidity of the water due to acid rain. They wanted the Oregon class to test the Willamette River so that they could compare the results with their tests of the Charles River and make predictions for the survival of species in both places.

In discussing local issues concerning water, Elaine made the connection with issues of water contamination in Nicaragua. She showed students slides of conditions there and told them there was something they could do to help. They eagerly became involved in the rope pump project and shared what they were doing with the Portland class. One student sent a message describing their activities succinctly:

We have heard you want to know how we raised some money for Nicaragua rope pumps. This is how we did it. Each fifth-grader did a small job at home and were paid. Then we brought $2.00 of the money to school.

Willy Snook, the partner teacher in Portland, picked up on the idea with enthusiasm. He noted:

> What particularly interested me was the community service piece. . . .
> [In our school], we came very close to actually having certain stages—rites of passage if you will—to get out of the fifth grade into the sixth grade, to get out of the eighth grade into high school. . . . Anyway, that was a big piece of it—community service has always been of great importance to the West Linn School District and definitely in the hearts of the people who I work with here at Sunset.
>
> We want to expose kids to what we believe are the elements of being good people, and obviously one is a clear understanding of themselves, but there's another piece—the piece outside of themselves of giving and affecting the world around them. First, they learn about themselves early on in their school career. They learn about sharing and reaching out a little bit further; and by the time they get to fifth grade, they're very very ready—kind of like concentric circles, I've described it that way—they're very ready at that point to touch someone outside of their school and that community. That was a real exciting piece for this particular project. That's what was a real draw for us.
>
> One other thing, too, that was of interest to me in this project and to the people who helped me pull this together was the cultural aspect of it—getting outside of ourselves, making the world just a little bit smaller, not just for kids but for all of us. It brought a real passion back to us about what we do. . . .

Soon after hearing about what Elaine's class had done, Willy wrote:

From sunset Wed Apr 21 09:03:40 1993
Date: Wed, 21 Apr 93 09:03:39 PDT
From: Sunset School <sunset>
To: needham
Subject: Rope pump project
Cc: elna1

Dear Elaine and Class,

I am very pleased to tell you that our entire school has decided to raise money for rope pumps for the people of Nicaragua. We are having an all-school walk-jog-run-athon in mid May, with a target goal of $500.00. With this fundraiser, one of our leadership groups (the "issues" group) will present the educational piece of all this to every class in our school of 550 students.

We are excited and deeply commited to this task and this cause. I was deeply moved by the strong endorsement and passion given by our teachers this morning at our staff meeting. I'll be sure to keep you up on how things go!

Your Friend,
Willy Snook

Situated on a hill among well cared for homes in a comfortable Pacific Northwest suburban neighborhood, the Sunset School has the utilitarian rectangular architecture of most American schools, but the front doors feel wide and more welcoming than most. There is a semi-circular driveway for the buses to drop their 5 to 12-year-old passengers right at the door. A well-lighted wide hallway adorned with children's work goes past the library on the right, an intersecting hallway on the left, and then around to the right and up half a flight of stairs to the office—a busy place with people running in and out, purposeful and smiling. The staff seem to be predominantly in their late 20s to mid-40s, energetic, and friendly. Camaraderie among them is evident, as is a keen interest in new and challenging educational ideas. The principal is an approachable, principled, well-loved man wearing jeans and a shirt that is open at the neck. The school is clearly a place of nurturance and creativity for children.

Willy Snook is a trim, vigorous man with thick, dark brown hair, a classically handsome face, and infectious enthusiasm. Willy and his fifth-grade leaders engaged the whole school and many members of the community in the effort to provide wells and pumps for rural villages in Nicaragua as part of the leadership program for the fifth grade. First, they invited Dell Salza, who helped start the Rope Pump Project, to come to their school to show slides about the living conditions and the critical lack of access to clean water that makes many Nicaraguan *campesinos* so susceptible to disease and early death. As a volunteer for Habitat for Humanity, Dell had worked in Nicaragua for two weeks in the summer of 1991 along with her husband and daughters, ages 15 and 13. Through her work with Habitat, Dell came in contact with El Porvenir. She and Pat Baker, a long-term volunteer for Habitat Nicaragua, were able to arrange for a staff person at El Porvenir to send letters from and photographs of children in the Nicaraguan villages where the work that I*EARN students funded went on. After seeing the slides, Willy's students wrote back to Elaine's about their plans:

> You probably know about the water in Nicaragua. To help we are going to get people to sponsor us. We're going to run around the track and people will say something like, "We'll give you a dollar for every ten minutes you run." The money our school earns will be used to buy pumps to keep the water in the wells clean. Many people are dying there so we are going to help them. A lady from Boston named Dell Salza came and showed us slides about the people. It was really sad.— Brittany, age 10

We're doing a project for the people in Nicaragua. What it is really is trying to do a jog-a-thon and get pledges from friends and family. How we are helping them is by getting enough money to pay for wells so they can have fresh water rather than contaminated water. Dell Salza told us that their water was usually brown and while she was down there a man got a cut on his hand. He washed it in the water and the cut got badly infected. He almost died. Is your school working on the project?—April, age 11

Our school is going to have a Jog-a-Thon to raise money for Rope Pumps that will go to a place in South America called Nicaragua because of the gross water they have to use. The new well will have a top on it so it doesn't get contaminated.—Tim's telepal, age 10

We're raising money for a South American country whose water is poisoned with disease. The money is to buy pumps that will keep the water clean. You're probably imagining what I look like, unless you get our class picture! Anyway, stop imagining, you probably make me out to be this computer nerd kind of guy, well your right, NOT. . . . By the way, you might know we are going to have a jog-a-thon and get pledges from friends and family. We hope to install as many rope pumps as possible for $100 each.—Kamarie, age 10

We're going to have a walk-a-thon to try and raise money for Nicaragua. You probably know about their situation. They don't have much money for food, clothes, houses, cars, etc. Most important they don't have money for a running water system so they use wells. The only problem with that is the wells are open and exposed to dirt bugs ECT. Also the buckets are on the ground and get stuff you don't even want to talk about on them, then they use them to get drinking water and whole well is contaminated.—No name, age 10

I hope you got the letter that I sent you. In Leadership, we are doing a Rope Pump Project for the people of Nicaragua. We saw a slide show today of the villages where we are putting the pumps in. They are very poor villages where the water is contaminated and they get parasites in them, and get very sick. We are getting money for how long we can stay moving. Lots of other places that are doing this project also are: Texas, New Mexico, New York, and Barcelona, Spain. Hope you have a great summer!—Matt's telepal, age 10

One thing I don't get—when the person gets the water it will be clean because they get it out of a clean bucket but as soon as they pour the water into one of their own buckets the water now has the diseases, but we can't help them with that. We are just giving them the money to give them the well.—No name, age 11

Fifth-grade students at Sunset went around to all the classrooms, explaining the project and answering questions. Faculty and parents were drawn in, so that the entire community played an active role in the project. Support from outside the classroom was a key element in the accomplishments of those schools that were successful. Willy Snook notes,

> This was an all-school thing, not just a fifth-grade thing. A lot of money was involved and a lot of heartfelt support. There were contributions from local businesses as well. We had sponsorship from the whole school really—not just monetarily but the complete emotional buy-in as well. That includes my principal and administration. They were involved not only in the endorsement, though; they were involved in helping coordinate the activity. We had the jog-a-thon. We had the whole school out in different shifts. Parents were at different corners making sure the kids were safe. They helped do some phone calling to remind kids to bring in pledges and they helped type out notices of the particular events. Again, it couldn't have happened without them—it wouldn't have happened without them.

Snook adds,

> There was a coming together of the community. They understood, they learned, they became educated about the particular situation there. It was a coming together for a common goal. That whole sense of community is something that the Sunset School community has always very much gotten behind, so this was a natural thing, but it was a first as well. That's what was exciting, because we were really stepping out of the traditional ways in which we've joined together as a community to help others. This was more global; there was more of an educational piece than in some of the other opportunities that we've seized. It was unique and very, very valuable. Kids were moved and affected by it, and community members were as well—the whole Sunset community was.

At Sunset and at other schools, there was a small group of people who felt that students should be working on problems closer to home rather than on a global scale. Willy Snook replies,

> There was some sentiment from a very very small minority questioning why we were putting our energy into this. Once they received the education and saw the commitment level of the kids—not just at fifth grade, but throughout the building—there was complete buy-in. How did we overcome them? A lot of communication and eye-to-eye contact. "I understand you have some feelings about this. How can I help you? Is there something that you need so you feel more comfortable being involved in this project? " I did a lot of that myself, and I enjoy doing

that. There wasn't much of it to do in all actuality, but getting past those barriers was an initial challenge and actually a real breakthrough because in fact it got everybody involved in a more genuine way.

Although support from the administration at her school was lukewarm, Elaine Messias experienced no opposition from parents. "In fact," she says, "one parent went on to start it as a project in her church and they raised over $300 for the project."

Believing that "strong community involvement and support here at school is vital to the success of how we teach kids," Willy worked on getting administrators to play an active role on the kids-parents-teachers-administrators team. He says,

> [The administrators in the West Linn School District] are big thinking, big feeling people who have world views and understanding about truly what is the best for kids and educating children. . . . The administrator in my particular building, Thayne Balzer, is a remarkable person. . . . Thayne is a very supportive person. He believes that it's important for kids to experience the kinds of things that are consistent with the ELNA mission [emphasizing the teaching of social responsibility], so he's right there, as is our instructional coordinator. He's an ambassador for our building in that way. He believes in community service and community outreach. So he was just a peach about everything and right there with his sleeves up ready to help out and again this very likely would not have come off—or at least not nearly to the successful end it did—had he not been involved. . . . One of the ways in which he provided that, besides the emotional and ambassadorship kind of support, was in publications. We have a weekly bulletin that goes out to parents. He created the themes for a number of weeks around the kinds of things we were doing and the value of that kind of giving and the need, etc. He helped them focus because all of the Sunset community, parents and staff, reads those bulletins and his messages are not just, "Hey, in Mr. Snook's room, they're doing this and in Mrs. Drake's room, they're doing that." They're big-picture kinds of things and he really seized the opportunity and combined it with what we were doing to have a real impact.

The project enhanced the curriculum in numerous ways. In some cases, it was connected in a broad context of teaching global understanding and caring. Narcis Vives, eighth-grade teacher in Barcelona, Spain, states,

> The project helped to improve students' communication skills and use of a foreign language. They practiced skills of cooperative learning and also linguistic abilities when they tried to persuade people to con-

tribute. Mostly, it interested me to have a humanitarian project that utilizes electronic mail for bringing us a little nearer to the reality of Nicaragua. The project invites youth to action. My objective was to give my students knowledge of a difficult situation that moves them to help people in far-away rural places like Nicaragua.

Along with their study of water in science, Elaine, like Narcis, related this project to the curriculum in the area of language acquisition, both in English and in Spanish. Her students were able to practice description skills in the letters they wrote to students in Nicaragua.

My name is Meredith Hutcheson and I'm ten years old. I have blonde hair and blue eyes. Now I go to a school called Mitchell, but next year, in the sixth grade, I will go to a school called Pollard. I live in the town of Needham in the state of Massachusetts. My family consists of my mother, father, and sister, whose name is Amanda. Also, we have a dog named Austin. My father was in an organization called "Amigos de las Americas," and he went to Nicaragua to give vaccinations and things like that. I want to become a member.

Write soon!

I'm ten years old and in the fifth grade. There are four people in my family—me, my parents, and my brother. I have blue eyes and blonde hair and my hair goes down my back.

I like to play soccer with my friends and to sing, but I don't play very well. I also like to act in plays. A little while ago, I was in the play of "Aladdin." In school, I like to read and write.

I live in the town of Needham, which is near Boston. I've lived in the state of Massachusetts all my life.

How old are you? How many brothers and sisters do you have? Are you the oldest in your family? Please write to me soon.

Love,
Julie Keefe

It should be understood that at this point the primary concern of the teacher was not to have her students discuss the relevant issues, but to provide an opportunity for her students to get to know one another and to practice descriptive writing.

My name is Matt and I'm ten years old. In case you don't know the name, Matt, I am a boy. My height is 4 feet, 6 1/2 inches. I live in Needham, Massachusetts, USA. My hair is brown like my eyes. I have a brother, a stepsister, mother, father, and stepmother.

I'm in fifth grade and I like to draw. I hope to be a cartoonist some day. I love to read, too. I just read a book that had 314 pages. It's called *The Voyages of Doctor Dolittle.* It's a great book. My favorite foods are Italian, American, and other places. What are your favorites? What books do you like? Are you a good artist? Please write. I want to get to know you better.

Sincerely,

Matt

When students received letters from children in Nicaragua (in Spanish), Elaine asked them to guess at the meaning of some of the words in the letters. "What do you think they might say to you in an introductory letter? " she asked. "They might say how they look, what color their hair is, how old they are," students responded. Studying the words in context, they came up with a list of 30 Spanish words they thought they understood. Then they sent the letters to the high school Spanish class to be translated. After they received the translations, they wrote back and sent their letters to the high school to be translated into Spanish. They typed their own letters in Spanish into the computer to be sent via e-mail. In the process, they were able to pull out more words whose meaning they understood to add to their dictionaries.

Willy used the project to teach math as well as language arts:

In math, we did a lot of measuring and calculating distances based on the story about a particular child having to walk a certain distance every day to and fro to get water. A lot of calculating that way, a lot of writing in language arts, projecting, putting themselves in other people's places, persuasive writing—convincing others of the need for this particular project and endorsing them for their pledges, etc. And then the oral presentations, educating other classrooms as to what we were working on. They had to do a lot of research as well to find out about it before they could do their presentations.

In addition to incorporating it into the formal curriculum, Willy had the flexibility to let learning flow in the direction of student interests. While not beginning with the purpose of studying particular social issues, he responded to and promoted discussion of whatever issues arose. In regard to that, Willy says,

We talked about socioeconomic status and situations and world economics, the haves, the have-nots, power, money, health. We talked about water quality, which is a big project for us this year. We have a grant;

we received money as part of our leadership program to pursue water quality type projects and to learn about water in our area. . . . We dealt with social justice issues a lot, which came up naturally from talking about the haves and the have-nots, but it wasn't particularly a focus initially. It just kind of arose from that, but we spent quite a bit of time talking about it after it came up. Lots of spin-offs came from this project, and not all of them were just particularly about the situation in Nicaragua but health. We were doing a jog-a-thon, so the whole notion of bodily health and taking care of the machine, so to speak, and your system and what you have to do to keep it healthy. . . . Public health was a social issue that came up. What we're going to do about health and health care. A lot of questions.

The letters students received from children in Nicaragua had a tremendous impact. Nicaraguan children wrote:

My name is Migglena Juarez Ruiz. I am 13 years old. My town is called Los Cocos. My father's name is Cristino Juarez Juarez. My mother's name is Juana Ruiz Torrez. My school is small and has no doors.

We carry the water from the ravine and make a hole in the side of the ravine. My mother works at home and gets us ready for school. My father works on a farm. We drink water from a well and we drink contaminated water.

I have 10 brothers and sisters and some work as bricklayers. My town is small and has 35 houses. There is a very dangerous illness close to our town called cholera.

My name is Carmen Delia Ruiz Mendoza and I am 12 years old. I have 6 sisters and 7 brothers. I like to help my mother with her work. I sweep the house, wash the dishes, and help take care of my little brothers and sisters. I am in the fifth grade at the primary school in Regadillo. My favorite things to do in school are play, sing, laugh, and sweep the patio.

My name is Alejandro Torres Vega and I am 15 years old. I have 7 brothers and 3 sisters. My mother had 3 other children but they are no longer alive. I do not remember how they died because they died when I was very young. When I am older, I want to get married because family is very important.

I farm beans, corn, and trigo with my father and brothers and we have chickens and pigs, too. My family is very poor and we do not always have enough food to eat. Two of my sisters had eye infections and we could not afford medicine. Now their vision is very bad and they need glasses. We do not have money for eyelasses either. I want to have a job that pays money but there is no work in Nicaragua.

My family uses a well which is 2 kilometers from our house. This well does not have a pump. I want our well to have a pump because I know that with a pump our water would be cleaner and easier to obtain.

My name is Elizabeth Vega Tremino and I am 15 years old. I finished school after the sixth grade and now I stay home with my mother and work in the house. I make the beds, sweep, wash clothes and dishes, make tortillas, and make cuijada. Cuijada is a white cheese that many people eat in Nicaragua. I cook food for my family over a fire. The smoke is very strong and makes me cry. I know that the smoke is unhealthy for my eyes.

My father sells clothes in Ciudad Dario. He makes 16 dollars a week. My father also farms with help from my brothers. They grow corn, beans, yukka, and trigo. When my family needs other food, we buy it from the market in Dario with the money that my father makes.

I carry water every day from a well to my house. Fifteen other families share this well. The well is very important to all of us because the water is clean and it is our drinking source.

"What can we learn from these letters and photographs?" Elaine asked her class.

"It seems like all the people in the village have the same name."

"The girls have to stay home."

"They do way more chores than we do, and they have to take care of the younger kids in the family."

"They don't have as much stuff as we do. Their houses are really small and bare. They don't even have bikes or anything."

Elaine made the following observations about what and how students learned:

There was an element of discovery in it. Kids have an appreciation for that. They examined the letters and the photographs, and they could see the pump, the buckets, the contamination. It was really helpful to have the pictures and the letters made it much more real. The kids appreciated that they were finding out what's happening in the world. They realized that they can do jobs and earn money to help. They can go beyond themselves.

Linda Cole's seventh-grade social studies class at Pollard Middle School in Needham, Massachusetts, saw the slide presentation and discussed some of the issues but did not actually work on the project. The day after they saw the slide show and heard about the project, Linda asked her students, "When you think about yesterday's presentation, what images come to mind?" Two students responded:

Skinny, little children
Dirty Dirty, undrinkable water
Malnutrition
Skinny dogs
Bricks
The kids don't have toys
Parasites
Wells, brooks
Buckets (dirty)
Rope pump
Scorpions (check shoes)
Dark
Candles
Holes in floor
Gross toilets!!
Lizards
Cots
Good graffiti
Not a lot of $

Starving animals
Male-dominated society
Some villages don't have enough
   kids for a school so they don't
   have one
Cement (windows and walls)

The lists of two other students were as follows:

Poor
No toys
No money
No running water
No electricity
Diseases
Depend on family crops
Hardly any education
Not any industrial jobs or
   companies or even products
Malnutrition

Very poor houses
Malnourished children and animals
No electricity
No floors in the houses
Poor water supply
Dirty toxic cans used to hold water
   for family
No toys for the children
No school in most places
Lots of open land

Linda then asked, "What surprised you the most? What is our role, if any, as Americans?" Students replied:

I was surprised because they don't even have children's toys! Or even electricity for that matter! About the only thing store bought was their clothes which were probably from community shelters. The clothes other people don't want. I think we should be helping just because we are able to.

I was semi-surprised. My mom has friends there and told me a little bit about it. Mom's friend is wealthy so I was surprised about the horrible conditions. Not just because we're Americans, but everyone should help people in need. We should sponsor organizations that help people.

[What surprised me was] the skinny dog and cow. Because you see most animals having a lot of meat on them, especially cows, because if you raise one you use it for meat after you've fed it well. They didn't have anything to feed it, so they used it for milk, which probably wasn't that good. If we got something in turn maybe [we should help], but I think it's good to have families like Mrs. Salza's,that go and help. Our federal goverment doesn't have the commitment to help without our tax dollars, but it's good to help them with money raised from people who want to help.

Finally, Linda asked them how they felt about what they saw. Students wrote:

I felt bad! Because I think how we get food and doctors (our dogs, too!) and they don't get anything! It's all dirty and they can get sick so easily!

I've seen other presentations on South America so it didn't really make me feel or think that much. During it I was, but after I didn't really think about it.

It made me feel disgusted that people in the world are living like that and people [here] are riding around in Mercedes Benzes. I told my mom I think I might try to go down and help Habitat for Humanity.

I didn't think about it much, probably because I was avoiding it. I do not like to think of these things because it's so sad.

While the students' answers reflect attempts to connect on both cognitive and emotional levels, an experiential connection might have made it possible for them to move from despair or denial to confidence in their own ability and responsibility to make a difference.

In another school that worked on the project, faculty and staff wanted to promote concern for others but were not prepared to make action part of the curriculum. Instead, the action component was part of an extracurricular project. Students in the classes of sixth- and seventh-grade science teacher Margaret Nolan at the Buker Middle School in Wenham, Massachusetts, learned about water contamination and the effects of pollution. They were told that if they would like to do something about the problem, they could join the extracurricular group STAT (Students Taking Action for Tomorrow). One student observed, "Ms. Nolan started the club because students were interested in trying to help out." They conducted bake sales at every event in school, explaining the project to students, faculty, and parents, and raising enough money to enable Nicaraguans in several villages to have access to clean water for the first time. Students described clear educational benefits from taking action on a problem:

> It put confidence in my mind that I was helping, so I wanted to help more. If I helped more, I'd learn more. When we learned about water in science, I could relate to it.—Christine Lovelace, age 12

> I learned more about things I can do, because I am interested in going into this field when I'm older. It showed me more about how things get done—the process. It also got me interested in environmental issues. The awareness and interest that sprung from this was like a spark to learn more classroom-type stuff.—Mandy Cooper, age 14

These same students were disturbed that more was not done in their school.

> There should be more education about what's going on. We have times where we study pollution and AIDS but we should have more because more people would feel like they should do something. If it's really part of school—not after-school—then we can do more because there'd be more people to do it. Some people get bored just reading books. If you're doing things, people are getting a more positive attitude about it and then they'll want to learn and do more.—Christine Lovelace, age 12

> We should have more emphasis on the environmental aspects of things—the problems that are out there and current. It's important to have this in school because when we get older, we're going to have these problems. The courses were set up before people were concerned. If we don't deal with them now, we'll never understand what's happening. Community service is nice with an environmental component. Things like that aren't happening. There's a lack of interest. If schools were teaching more and putting more academic emphasis on these issues, there would be more interest among kids—not all of them, but more. Now it's about zero. If, in classes, we were taught that this is a problem and some teachers, as adults, if they think something can be done, kids will think so and try to do something.—Mandy Cooper, age 14

In most of the schools that worked on this project, technology was used primarily to find out about the project and to receive updates and encouragement. There was little planning together or reporting back to each other. Some of them communicated on a small scale—as one student said, "A couple of us wrote messages about what we were doing so other kids would know and maybe start something like we had"—but it was done without forming the long-term connections and dialogue that were part of other I*EARN projects. Often, teachers were just establishing their own e-mail skills and were not yet ready to give students access, which made some students impatient.

> We would have liked to share ideas with other students about what they've done that's successful, but the librarian did all the e-mail. Teachers have to make this stuff known to kids.—Mandy Cooper

Another difficulty within the area of technology was in trying to communicate with schools that do not have pencils, paper, and electricity, let alone computers. In this case, students sent letters via the modem in the Habitat office in Managua. The El Porvenir staff person would download the letters and take them out to the villages in the countryside the next time she went out.

> We sent letters to Nicaragua to tell them we were raising money for them. We read the conference to get the news about the project. It was scary to feel like they didn't have any clean water.—Timmy Ho, fifth grade, age 10

An intern in Managua typed the letters of the Nicaraguan children into the computer and sent them off. Although not as efficient as e-mail contact in more developed countries, it was superior to "snail mail" in a country without a postal system in rural areas.

Along with using e-mail, students also used the Lumaphone, a telephone that transmits and receives a small still black and white picture of the person who is talking. The phone can be hooked up to a television monitor to enlarge the picture so that the whole class can see. It also has a speaker phone so that everyone can hear. The ideal thing would have been to connect American students with Nicaraguan students, but due to lack of electricity and phone lines in rural Nicaragua, that was impossible. The Lumaphone was used, however, in communication between schools in the United States and Spain to share ideas about working on the project. At a student conference in which there was a workshop called "Telecommunications for a World of Difference," eighth-graders in Spain spoke with students at the conference describing the work they were doing in Barcelona for "solidarity" with the people of Nicaragua. One student wrote, "It was great to see Spain and the United States in live interaction. It demonstrated that we can and do have similar goals to make our world a better place."

In a separate effort unrelated to the Rope Pump Project, Timmy Ho, a Chinese-American fifth-grader from Newton, Massachusetts, reflected on a Lumaphone call he did with China. The call was made in the early evening because of the time difference. Since many students could not attend, the call was videotaped. Timmy was accompanied by his parents, who volunteered to translate and by his teacher and principal. He described its impact on him.

Something freaked me out. My face going to a satellite and bounced back to China. You can see their faces, so you *know* who you're communicating with. Even if they describe themselves in a letter, they're still kind of a mystery.

In a time of growing global interdependence, values that allow people to work together, and attitudes that help to overcome cultural barriers become increasingly critical. Fifth-grader Timmy Ho said,

If we use computers in the future, they shouldn't be too advanced because then everybody can't understand them. They should be used for helping people that are in need of help—not just to waste electricity and money.

The Rope Pump Project effectively promoted such values and attitudes among some students:

It taught me a lot about the responsibilities we have. Because it's achievable, we should be doing these things. It taught me a lot about Third World countries and how doing just a little here can make big changes there. It raised questions and increased my awareness a lot.—Mandy Cooper

Students became aware that they can do things that are worthwhile, even save the lives of other people through their own efforts. This project gave my students knowledge of a difficult situation that moved them to help people in far-away rural places of Nicaragua. Students discovered the importance of solidarity.—Narcis Vives

Along with the project's motivational impact for learning, it had a notable impact on self-esteem, an area so critical for this age group. With a pained expression turning into a smile, fifth grader Nikki Roberts said, "I learned how hard it must be for them. I felt bad for them. I felt proud that we were sending money to them and earning it."

Willy Snook observed:

Clearly, students learned about themselves. They got a sense of themselves in the large landscape of humanity—that we were different but we were very similar in many ways to the people we were trying to help and that in fact we *can* help. The kids felt that they *had* power, that there *is* a way that they could truly contribute to make a difference. Once they sensed and got in touch with that empowerment, they were different right away. They learned that they *could* make a change. They learned about their community as well—that their community was just one large voice that could really be heard if they were organized and committed. Everybody was kind of working together to try and make this thing special, and kids learned that there's power there as long as it's organized and clear in its vision. . . .

There is an immediate compassion that kids have, particularly at this age but not specific just to this age. They were compassionate to the facts that they'd seen—the need out there. They want to help. Another motivating factor was just that sense of empowerment, that feeling of strength they got from their involvement—everybody being on the same team working toward something *so* wonderful. I believe that was very motivating to kids. Also, the whole team approach of being part of that big picture—not just with other students but with the administration, teachers, parents, and community members. That was real big. They felt real important.

In a simple, instructive, and powerful statement, sixth-grader Christine Lovelace observed, "It makes you feel special that you're helping and not just learning about helping."

Kristi Kraus, a fifth-grader at Sunset, described her experience in this way:

Bike Rope Pump Project

This whole project started with a slide show presentation given to us by Dell Salza. She visited our school and told us about her trip with her family to Nicaragua. She explained to us how desperately rural Nicaraguan villages need a bike rope pump. The pumps are going to provide families to with clean water, instead of dirty, infected water. When Dell was explaining this, I became very interested. I thought about what might happen if these families didn't get the clean water that their families so badly needed to live. Her slide show was very interesting and very inspiring. Kids from one of our fifth-grade leadership groups organized brief presentations for all the classes about the jog a-thon that our whole school was going to do. They also told us information about conditions in Nicaragua and the great need for these pumps. We got pledge sheets and began signing up people to pay us money for jogging for rope pumps. Everywhere we went in the school, we saw pictures and posters on the walls. Then I knew that this was truly a schoolwide team effort. The pumps cost $100.00 each, and I wished we could earn a lot, because I felt really badly for the people in Nicaragua and I wanted to help.

The jog-a-thon was a big success, with each grade jogging for an hour around the school. Throughout the day during the jog-a-thon, we had a water shuttle where kids had to carry buckets of water 50 meters. Every student, from kindergarten to fifth grade, carried water at least once for 50 meters. Every 40th trip of 50 meters, down and back, we rang a bell to announce we had reached four kilometers. That's the distance that one girl from Nicaragua had had to walk to get water every morning. When the bike rope pump was installed in her village, she wrote a thank-you letter saying that since the pump had been installed, she didn't have to walk four kilometers every morning and could now go to school. Our teacher, Mr. Snook, collected all the money for a week or so, then sent a big check to El Porvenir in care of Dell Salza. The Jog-a-thon raised $2,143.00—that's 21 pumps! I was so excited! I couldn't believe that our school had bought 21 pumps! This is the best thing that our school has ever done! I hope other schools will do this, too. Thank you Dell Salza for presenting this to us!

Social action and service learning projects using the tools of modern technology are steps in a new direction, occasionally making teachers feel that they are "out on the skinny branches." They are not quite sure what will happen next as they struggle to incorporate meaningful action into the curriculum and to give students opportunities and practice with technologies that are rapidly changing the way the world communicates. As it becomes possible to communicate quickly and directly with people in far-away places and unfamiliar circumstances, the world becomes at the same time larger and smaller. The lessons for both students and teachers can be dramatic. As Willy Snook said:

They learned some pretty tough things about the world. The educational piece of this and the slide show and presentation—very eye-opening and hard, hard stuff for kids—but also very motivating. So they learned that the world's not a perfect place and they see a lot of different things but they don't understand necessarily unless it's brought to them in a real way. They learned that the world *can* be helped. What's so neat about working with kids this age is that there's this eternal flame of hope that they carry. Call it naiveté or whatever but they do have hope and it's very inspiring. When you touch upon the kinds of things that we were dealing with in that project, you get really in touch with that and that there's power in that hope. I don't believe that they felt that they could heal the world but they do believe that they can affect it. They see the world as a lot smaller place after having been involved in this project.

For creative teachers who are not threatened by relinquishing control over what will be taught to students, who are themselves empowered, who care about their students' development as responsible participants in a democracy and as global citizens of the twenty-first century, the rewards for pioneering are worth the risks. Incorporating new technology is time consuming and difficult. Allowing students to become active, involved, decision-making learners is unpredictable and difficult, but for some teachers and administrators, neither is as difficult as watching early adolescents become apathetic, cynical, and powerless.

Against the obstacles of time, inflexibility of curriculum, and attachment to outdated methods, these attempts to use new methods are sometimes tentative and small, but they are a beginning. They are experiments using technology to explore the global village and the power of young people to make it a safer, cleaner, more just and peaceful place, and to see themselves as agents of positive change.

Note: For more information about I*EARN or to become a member, contact:

I*EARN - International Secretariat
345 Kear Street
Yorktown Heights, NY 10598
Telephone: 914-962-5864

▶ 8

New Horizons for Civic Education

A Multidisciplinary Social Issues Approach for Middle Schools

RONALD A. BANASZAK

H. MICHAEL HARTOONIAN

JAMES S. LEMING

TOWARD CIVIC RENEWAL

Amid a lesson on political primaries, one of Ms. Freguna's (a pseudonym) eighth-grade students at Collins-Riverside Junior High School, Northport, Alabama, asked a penetrating question.

"Why don't more people vote?"

A chorus of students responded:

"They don't need to. Voters don't really make any decisions that matter."

"Yes, they do. If they vote."

"One vote doesn't really matter."

"Lots of people don't care. Someone else will decide and it all seems to work out OK."

"Yeah, and voting doesn't seem to change anything."

These students' beliefs are partial evidence of a disturbing consensus emerging today regarding the health of the civic life in the United States. Evidence abounds regarding the sources of this negative view. Public participation in elections is low and getting lower each election. Frustration about politics and politicians is high and climbing. Americans appear increasingly apathetic about politics and a sense of civic duty is waning seriously. As Gans (1988) noted, "In the last two decades, fully 20 million people have dropped out of the political process." If current trends persist, nonvoters may soon constitute a majority of the electorate. In California, the most populous state, only 43.3 percent of the electorate registered to vote in 1986 did so. This represents a decline of almost 30 percent since 1960 (U.S. Has the World's Worst Voting Rate, 1987).

The young appear to be even more alienated from the political process than the electorate at large. In the past two presidential elections, 18- to 24-year-olds have voted at a rate 20 percent of the national average. A recent survey sponsored by the Girls Scouts of America found that only 39 percent of junior high students thought that voting in every election was the right thing to do (Coles, 1990). "My students show little interest in participating in civic events," commented Ms. Freguna. Coles (1990) has confirmed Freguna's impression by reporting that 60 percent of junior high youth said they would be unwilling to volunteer for the Peace Corp, Vista, or a similar activity.

The civic education of youth must share some of the blame for this apathy. Not only do youth leave schools without commitment to their civic duties but they also lack the necessary levels of knowledge about our political system. Periodic assessments conducted by the National Assessment of Educational Progress (NAEP) portray a generation of young citizens with little understanding of the institutions, events, personalities, and ideas that have shaped the nation's common civic past and future. For example, in the 1990 analysis of NAEP data, a national sample of eighth-grade students found that:

- Only 36 percent knew that the presidential candidate for each major political party is formally nominated by a national convention.
- Thirty-six percent could not correctly define a *boycott*.
- Only about one-third recognized examples of checks and balances and 42 percent could not select a correct definition of *separation of powers*.
- Fifty-six percent did not know that the right to religious freedom is found in the amendments to the Constitution.
- One-third did not know that freedom of speech has limits.

"Schools and teachers cannot be blamed entirely. Lots of changes in society are making it harder for youth," says Ms. Gaddy, a teacher at Central High School, in Tuscaloosa, Alabama. Indeed, she is correct. There are many trends in contemporary society that make the civic education of youth problematical and undoubtedly contribute to a growing sense of civic apathy. One such trend is an increasing cultural fragmentation resulting from a new emphasis on diversity; youth are understandably confused about what values we, as a nation, stand for. The changing family structure, with the decline of the two-parent family, makes it increasingly difficult for the family unit to teach civic values. The complexity of contemporary government and the issues that it must be concerned with undoubtedly create in many youth a sense that government is somehow beyond their grasp. Finally, television has replaced the print medium as the primary source of news for citizens.

Television, a medium that has unlimited potential to inform and educate, has for many youth become an agency that encourages passivity and the belief that there exist quick and easy solutions to all our national problems. "Television fills students with powerful negative images—problems, crime, wars, poverty—all sorts of things that are wrong," laments Ms. Gaddy.

The analysis that poor education and a changing civic environment have produced a generation characterized by civic apathy may be too simple an observation. A case in point is that a recent report by the Kettering Foundation, *Citizens and Politics,* based on focus group discussions with citizens held nationwide in 12 diverse communities, concludes with the following statement: "Apathy is not rampant among citizens. A sense of civic duty is not dead. Americans are not indifferent to public debate and the challenges our nation faces. Americans simply want to participate in this process we call representative government. They seek the possibility to bring about change" (Harwood, 1991, p. 63). Among the impressions taken from the focus groups was that people do, in fact, participate in politics, but only in arenas where it is possible to have a say and to bring about and witness change. People want to participate in the solution of public problems. The focus group respondents report that they have the desire and ability to participate effectively; they just want to know that their efforts will make a difference.

The Kettering Foundation portrait of the American citizen does not, then, detect a lack of interest in civic life nor a lack of interest in participating in civic life. Citizens care about politics; they are interested, but they need help in understanding specific complex public policy issues. When citizens were found to be apathetic, it was a rational apathy. That is, it was a choice based on an assessment of the relative benefits to accrue from the choice between participation and nonparticipation. The decision whether to participate was based on having confidence in knowing what policies to support and then knowing that one's participation would be meaningful. As one eighth-grade student commented, "They'd care if they thought it mattered." The obstacles to participation that citizens reported were the result of the perceived complexity of the issues faced and a lack of knowledge and skills of the means to effectively exercise influence.

If the Kettering Report is correct in its analysis, and we think that it is, then what is called for with regard to the civic education of youth is an approach that will develop skills and a sense of efficacy in dealing with complex public issues. If middle school students can begin to grapple with public policy issues *and* can learn effective strategies for developing and evaluating such positions, then they will have taken a necessary first step toward civic competence. The approach we propose uses social policy making that is designed to engage students in these important civic actions.

POLICY DECISION MAKING ON SOCIAL ISSUES

Frequently, middle school students voice awareness of the discrepancy between the ideals of U.S. society and reality. The students study the high ideals and compare them to the reality the students experience. For many students, notions of justice, equality, and freedom are almost laughable.

"You call that justice?"

"Is that fair?"

"He shouldn't do that!"

"What they did to my brother. That wasn't right."

"That's not right, but that's the way it is."

The Declaration of Independence boldly states that all people are created equal. Our students look around and ask, "Are you crazy? Can't you see the way it is?"

Some teachers have used the discrepancy between ideals and reality, between desired conditions and social reality, in an approach to social policy making that is appealing to middle school students. "Comparing the real and the ideal gives me a technique that captures student interest. It provides a bridge between 'book learning' and 'the way it is.' We use the gap between ideals and practices to identify where social policies can be enacted to bring practices closer to our ideals. I've been able to make this approach central to the way I teach my social studies classes," explained one eighth-grade teacher, Ms. Tunnell, at Collins-Riverside Junior High School, Northport, Alabama.

The basic steps in this approach are:

1. Define the issue.
2. Envision the preferred state of affairs.
3. Describe the current state of affairs.
4. Generate a policy position.
5. Apply evaluative criteria—comparing the policy position against other positions and potential consequences.
6. Decide what policy to implement.

Another eighth-grade teacher at Eastwood Middle School, Tuscaloosa, Alabama, who has used this approach, Ms. Smelley, commented, "I usually have to help my students define the issue. They may be able to identify an issue that interests them, but they are usually too vague in describing it. I ask them questions to clarify the issue and still often have to define it for them." One of Ms. Tunnell's classes recently discussed policies to reduce the number of fights in and around the school. She commented, "They should just find another way to fight. Maybe one-on-one basketball." Some others agreed, but Mike argued, "Yeah, but, when someone messes with you, ya gotta take 'em." Other students chimed in. "Yeah!" "You bet." "No, they don't have to. The one who starts it should think first." "It takes two to fight." Ms. Tunnell asked, "Why do students fight?" She then led the class to list causes of fights.

Students are much better at picturing the ideal. "Usually they are not shy about how they think the world should be," reports Ms. Freguna. "We use the Constitution, the Declaration of Independence, and other key documents to find the ideals of our society. Students are usually very sensitive about fairness and equality." Ms. Tunnell notes that "Freedom, that's what interests them. They are always asking about why they can't do this or that. Why a rule has to exist about . . . whatever. And they are not satisfied with the principal saying that 'It just has to be.' " Ms. Freguna challenges her students to "imagine a situation where, because people change the way they behave, the problem can be solved. Now, how can we get people to behave that way?"

"To help my students describe the current situation, I often duplicate readings. Sometimes the textbook is helpful, too. Usually, though, I have to go beyond the textbook. Articles from the newspaper and from magazines are most helpful. I do have to be careful, though, that the reading level is not too high," advises Ms. Gaddy.

Ms. Tunnell adds, "It is important that students clearly understand the details of the problem. I've even made getting information about it into a research project. Students are divided into teams and each team gathers information on different aspects of the problem. Then they all write up their information and share it with each other. Sometimes I find that I need to correct errors and focus students on the most important information."

Next, students generate a policy position. Students often need to be reminded that their policy should be feasible. More specifically, it should be one that would most likely result in a solution to the problem. Sometimes, they suggest policies that are not related to the problem. Other times, they may make a suggestion that is totally impractical. "Once a student wanted every person who drives while drunk arrested and placed in jail for one year. Other students pointed out that his plan would overcrowd jails," remembered Mr. Shamblin, a teacher at Northside High School, Northport, Alabama.

Consideration of consequences is part of the evaluative process. Each policy proposal needs to be evaluated by students to predict its consequences. "This may be the hardest part. Students keep wanting me to tell them what the consequences will be. I won't. I do ask them questions to force them to think for themselves," commented Ms. Smelley.

Students then make a policy choice from among those they have considered. "Sometimes, I have the students vote," Ms. Tunnell commented. "Other times, we arrive at a policy choice by discussing and agreeing—forming a consensus. I prefer that way." Ms. Banaszak, a teacher at Vance Elementary School, Vance, Alabama, reported, "Regarding litter around the school, students once decided to have a clean-up day. They didn't just want to talk. They wanted to take action! They invited students, parents and teachers to donate one hour on a Saturday to clean up the school yard and the neighboring empty field. They felt that if everyone joined in cleaning up the area, they would be less likely to litter in the future. They arranged for soda and cookies and played music on a portable stereo. And it worked! The area was clean and attracted less litter for a while."

The power of this approach can be seen in Ms. Kyle's sixth-grade classroom in North Central Wisconsin. Her room is buzzing again today. Two students have returned from the office with an additional 45 questionnaires from residents in northern Wisconsin. What's the cause of all the excitement? Three weeks ago, one of the students, Robert, mentioned a conversation he had with his father. His dad, an avid sportsman, had complained about the Timber Wolf Recovery Plan proposed by the Wisconsin Department of Natural Resources to reintroduce the Timber Wolf into northern Wisconsin. Ms. Kyle recognized immediately the high degree of student interest and decided to capitalize on it. Since she taught science and social studies back to back immediately after lunch, she decided to combine the times so students could take an in-depth look at the topic.

Ms. Kyle began by having the students write an essay on what they already knew about the timber wolf. Some typical responses were:

Whenever I think of wolves I think of bats, snakes, and spiders. They are mean!"

I think of bats, Frankenstein, mummies, and all the other wolves' monster buddies. I also think of a full moon, men changed into wolves, and Ozzie Osborne's tape, "Bark at the Moon."

I think of stories like "Little Red Riding Hood" and movies like *Teen Wolf*. The words I think of are *sharp teeth, scary, hairy, forest, claws, blood, full moon,* and *howl!* "

Ms. Kyle's conclusion was that students did not know much about the timber wolf so she assigned students readings and taught a few lessons on predator-and-prey relationships, forest ecosystems, the niche concept and population dynamics. But soon class discussion began to turn to the Timber Wolf Recovery Plan's impact on people. Robert kept raising the issue that his father had raised—namely that an increased timber wolf population would negatively hurt snowmobiling, trapping, and hunting. Ms. Kyle shared with the class a newspaper article on the potential adverse effects on tourism, and students had a heated discussion on the trade-offs between people and nature, and if a win-win situation could exist in this situation.

Ms. Kyle was able to get state Representative VanderKellen to visit her class and explain the political and legislative process involved in enacting this plan into law. Students were next assigned to engage in small group research projects on the different dimensions of the policy issue and to present their findings to the class. The students were slowly coming to recognize the ecological, legal, political, economic, and social dimensions to what had originally appeared to be a simple issue. To help students see the interrelationships, Ms. Kyle had the students construct a concept web (see Figure 8–1).

After much discussion and debate, students realized that ultimately the issue would be decided by how the people in the affected areas felt. They then decided to conduct a survey and constructed a 10-question instrument. Next, they randomly selected 350 residents from telephone directories. With each

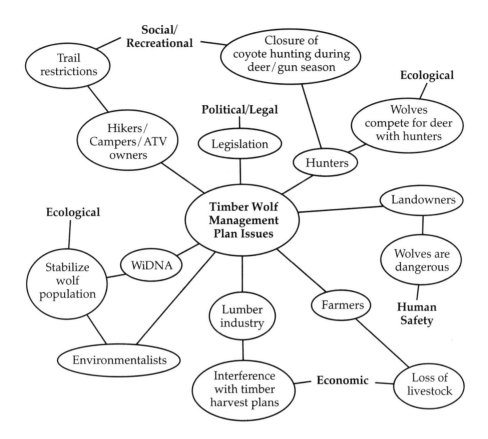

FIGURE 8–1   An Issue Web: Wolves in Wisconsin

survey students included a handwritten cover letter and self-addressed stamped envelope. The letter read as follows:

Hi,

My name is Kurt Warner. I'm a 6th-grade student from New School in Wisconsin. Our class has been studying wolves. As a special project, we decided to send out these surveys. We are hoping that you will help us with our project by taking a few minutes to complete the enclosed form. Send it back to us as soon as possible! Thank you very much for your time.

Sincerely,
Kurt Warner

Responses poured in. Many of the letters were accompanied by personal letters, newspaper clippings, drawings, magazine articles, and photographs. The letters contained many provocative perspectives for the students to consider:

It is ridiculous to introduce wolves into an area where they do not now reside and pay a ton of money to replace livestock and deer they kill. I personally will shoot any wolf, coyote, or domestic dog I see running a deer trail—legal or illegal, in or out of season.

I became acquainted with the timber wolf in 1929 when . . . [I assisted] in the establishment of the Nicolet National Forest. I have admired the timber wolf since he kills for food and not for sport. He is now an endangered species. I have not heard of one ever killing a human.

I do not support translocating wolves. The money spent on wolf resto-ration could be better spent. How about feeding the homeless in Wisconsin?

I, myself, think the Timber Wolf Recovery Plan is a good idea, but many people think it takes up too much land or is a waste of money. Most people do not have enough education about wolves.

By now, the students had done all the research they needed to understand the complex and multidisciplinary problem, and they wanted to make a deci-sion about the fate of the Timber Wolf Recovery Plan. Thus, Ms. Kyle assigned each student the task of writing a position paper that utilized all the information the students had acquired in the now month-long unit. They were required to define the issue, describe their desired state of affairs, describe the current situ-ation, articulate a policy, and explain its consequences. Each paper had to ad-dress a social policy and predict the expected consequences of the policy.

The class opinion was, overwhelmingly, to support the plan. Together, the class decided to raise money to donate to the Timber Wolf Alliance, a group working for the plan. Students raised more than $100 by selling buttons, pen-cils, and plaster-of-paris wolf prints. Robert and a couple of his friends did not participate in this fund raising, but did write letters to powerful legislators and interest groups in the state opposing the plan. "My students not only learned about wolves and social policy; they also learned that people of good will can honestly differ on a desired social condition," Ms. Kyle reported.

DEVELOPMENTAL IMPLICATIONS

This social policy approach fits well with the experiences, knowledge, and psychosocial development of young adolescents. Adolescence is a time of ambiguity when the individual is neither child nor adult and lacks a clear and satisfying definition of self. Adolescents, therefore, are at risk in terms of whether their decisions regarding future growth are adaptive or maladaptive.

Several current trends make adolescence more challenging today. "Few of my students come from a two-parent, undivorced (sic) family. I think that affects them a lot," observed Ms. Banaszak. Indeed, the divorce rate is growing rapidly. In the 1980s, about half of all marriages in the United States ended in divorce. Between 1970 and 1989, the number of families maintained by single women grew 389 percent! The period of adolescence has lengthened as puberty has begun to occur earlier, yet dependency has postponed the end of adolescence. Another challenge is greater access to health-threatening activities. Increasingly, youth are exposed to sexuality, alcohol, drugs, tobacco use, automobiles, weapons, and a variety of other temptations.

It should be no surprise that there is an increase in dysfunctional personal and social behavior among young adolescents. Death rates for motor vehicle accidents, homicide, and suicide have increased. The out-of-wedlock birthrate continues to climb, as does the proportion of teenage females reporting having sexual intercourse. Drug usage has stabilized, but at alarming levels. Delinquency rates are up and academic performance on most standardized tests has declined since the 1960s.

As mentioned earlier, student knowledge about the basic political, legal, economic, and social systems is fragmentary and incomplete. The *Civics Report Card* issued by the U.S. Department of Education found that 83.7 percent of eighth-graders could not show a knowledge of the structures, functions, and powers of American government as described in the Constitution. They lacked a detailed civic vocabulary and understanding of *separation of power, checks and balances,* and other basic principles. Tests of economic knowledge have also shown little understanding. One sample of 8,200 students showed only 25 percent could define *profit* and only 39 percent knew what *GNP* is. Though less information exists about student knowledge of our legal and social systems, every indication is that it is no more extensive.

Certain aspects of the psychosocial development of young adolescents can help us better understand how to meaningfully teach them citizenship. For example, adolescents are beginning to move from concrete to formal thought and are more able to consider a world of possibilities, test hypotheses, think realistically about the future, reflect on their own thoughts, and deal with abstract ideas like religion and justice. In any given classroom, students will possess these skills at various levels of sophistication. More uniform will be the expansion of students' relationships. More specifically, students will move from a world of parental bonds to one that includes peer bonds. This, in turn, reinforces their growing relationship with the world outside their home.

At the same time, adolescents become increasingly able to consciously examine the normative foundations of our civic life and examine the values they hold. They begin to realize that they are part of a social order. Paralleling the development of understanding of morality and society is the development of understanding of our legal and political systems. Young adolescents' understanding of political and economic phenomena is shifting from concrete and egocentric perspectives to more abstract and sociocentric perspectives.

Early adolescence is a singular opportunity for schools to positively influence the development of future citizens. Ms. Tunnell has observed that "children [at this age] are more interested in the world and are more able to learn about social problems and politics." It is a time of increased interest and capacity for learning about the social and political world. It is a time when an emergent morality and political ideology take shape. It is a time when appropriate civics instruction can serve as an impetus to a lifelong growth commitment to responsible citizenship.

MULTIDISCIPLINARY INTEGRATED CURRICULUM

Because social issues are not confined to a particular academic content area, they are naturally multidisciplinary. Students looking at school dress codes will need to use content from psychology, sociology, political science, jurisprudence, and history. Waste management issues require content usually thought of as economic, political, legal, social, geographic, and scientific. "I like using social policy making because it makes students use lots of different information. It gives students a reason to learn the information. They need it to understand the problem and to propose and evaluate different policies," commented Ms. Gaddy, a seventh-grade teacher. A social studies class that attempts to address authentic social/civic issues requires an integrated and coherent knowledge base. Thus, social policy making is consistent with the multidisciplinary curriculum goals of the middle school.

For social policy making, students need historical background and social studies knowledge, especially knowledge about the economic, political, social and legal systems. Understanding these four systems is critical. Figure 8–2 lists the basic concepts from these four systems. (For a more detailed content description, including generalizations that cross disciplinary boundaries, see Banaszak, Hartoonian, and Leming, 1991.)

But simply choosing concepts from these disciplines is not sufficient. These systems of knowledge need to be integrated in ways that illuminate the issue and provide alternative policies for consideration. The integration of knowledge provides a framework for observing, describing, analyzing, evaluating, and making policies about society that will lead to a healthier social climate for all citizens. As one of Ms. Smelley's students commented, "I'm confused. I think banning skateboards from the school yard is a legal issue. But its also social. We want to play with our boards and show off. And boards cost. So isn't it economic, too?" This student was beginning to realize how these systems overlap.

Political Concepts
Authoritarian Systems
Authority
Constitutional Systems
Government
Interest Group
Legitimacy
Political Culture
Political Party
Political Socialization
Political System Power
Social Control
State

Legal Concepts
Due Process (Procedural)
Ethics
Freedom
Justice
Law
Legal System
Privacy
Property
Responsibility
Social Contract

Economic Concepts
Competition
Economic System
Exchange
Factors of Production
Government Regulation
Incentives
Interdependence
Market Opportunity Cost
Price
Scarcity
Specialization
Supply and Demand
Trade-Off

Social System Concepts
Community
Culture
Group
Institution
Interdependence
Norm
Role
Sanction
Social Change
Social Processes
Socialization
Society
Status
Values

FIGURE 8–2   **Concepts**

"One reason I like using policy making is that it gives the students a reason to learn content. They have to know about the issue and be able to predict consequences. So often content is taught and the students have little reason to learn it, except to please me or for my test. When they are working to resolve an issue, they are motivated to learn. They have a reason to know," explained Ms. Freguna. The concepts and content do not have to be taught before students begin study of a problem. The content can be learned while engaged in social policy making, providing motivation for learning it.

Social policy making is always encased within a value system and attempts to move toward a valued end. In a general sense, values have to do with conduct, character, and community. Values also are another force for multidisciplinary content since they cross disciplinary boundaries and are naturally integrative of content.

Explicit teaching about values as ideals of society is an integral part of this approach. "It is important that my students reflect on what they are trying to achieve, their goals or values, when suggesting policies. I have to keep reminding them about the values we hold as a society," cautions Ms. Freguna.

As Ms. Kyle's students found, values held by society and by individual participants in it are not always consistent. Different individuals can desire to achieve different values through a social policy. Conflict among values is normal. In different situations, different values may be more valued and have a stronger influence on behavior. Additionally, individuals adhere to societal values with varying degrees of intensity. Such inconsistencies are normal and contribute to the rich dialogue about social policy. Notice the variety of values expressed in student comments during a debate in Ms. Tunnell's class about a proposed strict dress code.

"I wouldn't come to school."

"I'd change schools."

"I'd go to a private school."

"I went to a private school and we had to wear a uniform."

"I'd protest."

"We could kill the principal."

"Why not wear things we're not supposed to wear."

"That wouldn't work. They would suspend us."

"Not if everyone did."

"I'd carry signs, beat on things. Maybe throw rocks at windows."

"Or sign a petition. Give it the principal with an olive branch."

"If public school shouldn't make you pray, [and] prayer is only for private [school], not public school [then] dress code is for private. Then if there's no prayer in public school, there shouldn't be no dress code (sic)."

"If we have a dress code, we can't dress like you are—be an individual."

"My mama wouldn't want a dress code. She thinks we should have the right to express ourselves."

"My dad would probably like one. He doesn't like torn clothing, always wants everything to be perfect."

"My parents would fight the battle for me. You know, that's not right."

The values listed in Figure 8–3 have been identified as appropriate for instruction about social issues.

Policy making is also integrative in another way. It helps young adolescents see the relationship between the private (personal) side of their lives and the public (social) side. Young adolescents, and indeed most of us, are well aware of our private lives—that is, our friendships, and conflicts within families, work settings, recreation, and places of worship. On the other hand, most are only dimly aware of our public lives and how the private and public domains complement each other.

Yet they are related. Any decision we make within one dimension will have implications within the other. The personal choices we make in regard to jobs, lifestyle, and family have consequences not only within our personal lives but also within the public sphere. A personal decision to smoke cigarettes, for ex-

Basic Values	Social/Institutional Values	Personal Values
Human Dignity	Rule of Law	Integrity
Individual Freedom	Consent of the Governed	Reasoned Judgment
	Property	Responsibility
	Due Process	Participation
	Equality of Opportunity	Patriotism
	Freedom of Thought and	Tolerance
	Expression	Compromise
	Pluralism	Cooperation
	Authority	Courage
	Privacy	Truthfulness
	Justice	Fairness
	Promotion of the Common	Generosity/
	Welfare	Compassion

FIGURE 8–3 Democratic Values

ample, will carry consequences that are political, legal, economic, social, aesthetic, ethical, ecological, and medical. All of these consequences have larger public policy ramifications. Public policy decisions, from raising taxes to establishing Head Start education programs, will have personal consequences. Virtually any issue we act on will encompass both our private and public lives and we must become more aware of this relationship as we formulate policy.

Ms. Tunnell's eighth-graders realized this as they looked at the consequences of how students dressed. In a case study, students were told about fights and other problems resulting from the way students dressed at a middle school. They were asked what the consequences would be if shirts could have no writing. In their written responses, students commented:

"Kids would protest because of not being able to wear what the stores sell."

"People would have to buy a new wardrobe. The shirt sellers would lose money. Some other people wouldn't be offended."

"Parents would have to buy new shirts. If someone got a 'Vote for me' shirt for an upcoming political figure, they couldn't wear it."

"Well, for one, kids and parents would have to spend more time and money buying solid colored shirts, and the manufacturers would lose money because people weren't buying their shirts."

"Kids would try to change schools. The club tee shirts would no longer be used. Rallies against the new rules would be held."

Asked if the consequences related to the political, legal, economic or social system, all students indicated that consequences were part of at least three systems (many said all four). One particularly articulate student wrote, "Political—someone would have to enforce the rule. Legal—have to settle the fights about it. Economic—stop the buying of the shirts. Social—no messages." These students certainly saw how a personal decision about clothing can have considerable consequences for society.

MULTIDISCIPLINARY SOCIAL POLICY MAKING:
AN EXAMPLE

The multidisciplinary dimension of social policy making can be clearly seen in the students' study of waste management. (*Note:* This example combines the experiences of several teachers in the composite story of Ms. Jamison's class.) Her eighth-graders recently used social policy analysis to better understand an issue of growing importance across the country: garbage.

"I introduced the topic with several brief readings about the causes and nature of our current garbage and landfill problem. They were filled with lots of facts. Then I led a class discussion of them to be sure they understood the facts about the garbage problem," Ms. Jamison explained.

Ms. Jamison surprised her students by loudly thumping the classroom waste basket on her desk and asking, "How full is this basket by the end of the day?" After some discussion, the students decided that it was usually about half full. "How much trash do you think this classroom and this school produces?" she inquired. While one committee measured the basket to determine its volume, others estimated the number of baskets in the school. After some calculations, the class had an alarming estimate of how much trash one school produced.

With this fresh and personal understanding of the problem, Ms. Jamison asked, "Is a school or a city where people continually try to produce less garbage possible? One where citizens help protect everyone's environment? Where they recycle as much of their waste as possible? Can you imagine such a city?" Students were confused. "You mean no garbage?" "How could that be?" "Maybe everyone is careful about litter?" "I don't think so. How could that be?"

Ms. Jamison was not surprised. She asked, "What policies or laws could we pass that would encourage people to produce less garbage?" At first slowly, then with greater gusto, students fired suggestions at her.

"Charge a lot more for garbage collection for more than one small can."

"Pass a law limiting how much garbage a family can produce. Put the father in jail if the family makes too much garbage."

"Make every family carry their trash to the dump. That will make them want to produce less!"

"Pass a law that requires families to recycle."

"Fine any family that throws out items that could be recycled."

The students were constructing policies intended to help resolve the garbage issue. Some were practical, others were not. The key question remained: How can movement toward the imagined ideal be realized?

Ms. Jamison's students were constructing policies for both our personal and public lives that would help achieve the goal. "To cause my students to develop personal and public policies related to the issue of waste, I used the garbage problem of the mythical city of Plenty," explained Ms. Jamison. "Using this case study, I was able to simplify the situation and focus students on pertinent issues." In small groups, her students read the following:

Planning Waste Management

1. Imagine yourself as the mayor of Plenty. Your landfill must be closed because it does not comply with present standards for protecting the environment. What's Plenty going to do with all its garbage? As mayor, you are responsible for investigating new options for managing solid waste. You begin by forming a solid waste committee to study the options. Who do you think should sit on this committee (town treasurer, public works director, citizen representative, landfill developer, etc.)? Classmates can play these roles and decide on a name for the committee.

2. Call a meeting of the committee. Your assistant has prepared the table, "Managing Garbage from Homes," to help members see some options and impacts of managing garbage (see Table 8–1). Study the table and, as a group, consider the following questions:

   - At first glance, which waste disposal option seems best? Why? Do you all agree? Is there one best option? What are the economic costs? Political costs?

   - What criteria and values are you using to judge options? Are you pro-business, pro-taxpayer, pro-environment, pro-convenience? Discuss how your personal points of view might influence how you judge the importance of each potential impact.

   - For how many years into the future are you planning? Why is this an important consideration (population growth, long-term economic, and environmental impacts, etc.)?

   - How big is 52,000 cubic yards? How much space will you need if you choose to landfill garbage for that many years?

   - Compare the pros and cons of citizen convenience and environmental impacts for each option. Do you consider citizen convenience more important than environmental impacts, or vice versa? Why? How does your view affect which option you would choose? Should saving money be your only concern?

   - Does this table include the "costs" of each option's long-term environmental impacts or use of natural resources? What might these "costs" be? How much should your committee be concerned about these "costs" in making your decision? How easy is it to put a dollar value on environmental damage?

   - If creating jobs is a high priority, which option would you choose? What do you think about the often-made statement that recycling eliminates jobs? You have read somewhere about composting municipal solid waste. Where can you find out more about composting? Why might your community consider composting as a valid option for waste disposal? Which wastes could be composted?

   - What are the pros and cons of incineration? Do you think the benefits (landfill space saved, energy produced, convenient) outweigh the costs (landfill still necessary, toxic ash and air pollutants produced, expen-

TABLE 8–1   Managing Garbage from Homes: Options and Impacts*

Option	No. of Employees		Landfill Needs/Yr/ (cubic yards)	Net Cost ($/yr.) (includes sale of any energy produced)	
a) Landfill everything (landfill 15 mi. away)	Collection Landfill Total	40 2 42	52,000 yd^3	Collection Landfill Total	$1,300,000 520,000 $1,820,000
b) *Voluntary Recycling* Curbside pickup of glass, newsprint, plastic, aluminum, Landfill remainder.	Collection Recycling center Landfill Total	44 8 2 54	47,000 yd3	Collection Recycling (profit) Landfill Total	$1,400,000 10,000 470,000 $1,860,000
c) *Mandatory Recycling* (as in "b" above)	Collection Recycling center Landfill Total	48 15 2 65	42,000 yd^3	Collection Recycling (profit) Landfill Total	$1,500,000 60,000 420,000 $1,860,000
d) *Mandatory Composting* of yard waste. Landfill remainder. (#s assume 1/2 waste is composted at home)	Collection Composting Landfill Total	42 1 2 45	45,000 yd^3	Collection Composting Landfill Total	$1,350,000 50,000 420,000 $1,850,000
e) Incinerate for energy recovery. Landfill ash and nonburnables (incinerator in town).	Collection Incinerator Landfill Total	38 12 1 51	10,000 yd^3	Collection Incineration Landfill Total	$1,250,000 750,000 200,000 $2,200,000

*Example compares cost for a community producing 100 tons/day, 5 days/week.
  Numbers presented are realistic but not specific to any one community.
  Other options and combinations of options exist.

Amount of Energy (gallons of gas equivalent)		Environmental Issues	Critical Convenience
Collection	30,000 gal.	— Is unattractive	— Just put waste at curb
Landfill	13,000	— Uses land	
Total Used	43,000 gal.	— Can pollute water and air	
		— Can create hazardous gases (methane)	
		— Bury/lose natural resources	
Collection	33,000 gal.	— Reduces impacts at landfill	— Need to separate recyclables
Recycling		— Reduces pollution from manufacturing	— Builds good habits
(saves)	300,000	— Reuses natural resources	
Landfill	12,000		
Total Saved	255,000 gal.		
Collection	36,000 gal.	Same as voluntary recycling above.	— Need to separate recyclables
Recycling			— Requires enforcement for non-compliance
(saves)	600,000		— Builds good habits
Landfill	9,000		
Total Saved	555,000 gal.		
Collection	33,000 gal.	— Reduces need for landfill	— Need to separate yard waste
Composting	1,000	— Reduces methane gas pollution	— Builds good habits
Landfill	10,000	— Reduces strength of leachate	
Total Used	44,000 gal.	— Produces fertile humus	
		— Reuses natural resources	
Collection	28,000 gal	— Reduces need for landfill	— Just put waste at curb
Incinerator	840,000	— Produces fly ash heavy in heavy metals that requires special handling	
(produces)			
Landfill	2,000	— Produces air pollutants	
Total Produced	810,000 gal	— Consumes natural resources	

sive)? How do the experiences of other communities that already have installed incineration compare with those of recycling?

- Recycling newsprint sounds great. But some newspapers use ink that contains lead, a hazardous metal. What happens to this lead when the paper is landfilled? Recycled? Composted? Burned? What have newspaper manufacturers substituted for lead inks?

3. Investigate what is required by local, state, and federal laws for choosing the waste management option(s) for Plenty (e.g., public hearing, citizen referendum, environmental impact statement).
4. Do you feel you have enough information to make a wise decision? If not, where can you find more information?
5. Now that your committee has investigated and discussed the options for solid waste management plan, make a decision about which option(s) the city should enact.
6. List suggestions for what you can do to ensure the success of the new waste management plan (e.g., community education, providing containers for recycling).

Ms. Jamison explained, "This reading was used to guide the students through consideration of various policy options. I found that students need careful guidance or they get muddled in their thinking since they are just learning how to engage in policy making."

As her students suggested policies, Ms. Jamison repeatedly asked them to predict how these policies (usually stated as laws or ordinances) would affect citizens' patterns of behavior and the relative quality of the environment. We know, for example, that if we want most citizens to produce less waste, to recycle most of it, and to purchase goods in ways that will enhance these efforts, then their behavior patterns and assumptions about garbage will have to change. She asked, "How can city policy do this?" Next, she said, "I gave them a handout to help them think through their policies."

Consider the following questions as you plan your policy:

1. How would you change the behavior of citizens toward waste management? When considering changes in the behavior of citizens and the role of the four knowledge systems, list the economic, political, legal, and social concepts that should be used to understand and/or implement changes in behavior.
2. How would you change the cultural premises and assumptions of citizens and institutions relative to waste and waste management? When considering changes in cultural assumptions and the role of the four knowledge systems, think about what political, legal, economic, and social concepts should be used to understand and/or implement changes in cultural assumptions.
3. How would you show the demographic patterns of your community and its relationship to the waste management issue? When considering demographic patterns and the role of the four knowledge systems, think about what po-

litical, legal, economic, and social concepts should be used to understand these trends?

4. How would you enhance the conceptions of the ecosystem held by citizens? When considering the ecosystem and the role of the four knowledge systems, list the economic, political, legal, and social concepts needed to understand the environment.

Possible Answers

1. *Political:* Influence, power, decision making, etc. *Legal:* Court injunctions, due process, justice, etc. *Economics:* Prices, trade-offs, convenience, opportunity costs, savings, etc. *Social:* Peer pressure, social values, etc.
2. *Economic:* Long- and short-run costs and benefits, etc. *Political:* Grassroots support, majority rule, etc. *Legal:* Property rights, public responsibility, etc. *Social:* Public good, private conveniences, etc.
3. *Political:* Voting patterns, etc. *Legal:* Individual rights and responsibilities, etc. *Economic:* Capital, labor, employment, infrastructure, land use, etc. *Social:* Age patterns, social status, etc.
4. *Political:* Influence, power, environmental laws, etc. *Legal:* Property (water) rights, social responsibility, etc. *Economics:* Land use, trade-offs, investment, etc. *Social:* Public health and welfare, etc.

CONCLUSION

Policy making, in its broadest sense, is the fundamental activity of the citizen and it provides an operational definition of what it means to be civically literate within a democratic republic. The general policy-making strategy suggested here causes students to explore the dynamics between the ideal and real; between social and personal principles and the "facts" of life. Ms. Kyle's students faced choices about timber wolves. Ms. Jamison's class dealt with garbage. Others could address poverty, unemployment, inequality, and numerous other issues. Factual and conceptual knowledge of our basic systems is a necessary prerequisite, as are citizenship skills, democratic values, and the disposition to hold private and public notions together within a more inclusive sense of responsibility. The necessary conditions of classroom dialogue were described in this chapter, as was the importance of engaging the student/citizen in real issues that impact everyday life.

Finally, as we practice courtesy and concern, as well as take on a research and development mindset toward our civic obligations, the use of policy-oriented instructional strategies should prepare students to effectively carry out the responsibilities of citizenship. It is also worth noting that several teachers commented that their students enjoyed class more when using this process. "They were more motivated to learn and sensed they were dealing with real things, stuff that matters," commented Ms. Tunnell. "I think they learned some of what citizenship is all about."

REFERENCES

Adelson, J. (1971). "The Political Imagination of the Young Adolescent." *Daedalus, 100*(4): 1013–1051.

Adelson, J., and O'Neill, R. P. (1966). "Growth of Political Ideas in Adolescence: The Sense of Community." *Journal of Personality and Social Psychology, 4*(3): 295–306.

Anderson, L., Jenkins, L. B., Leming, J. S., MacDonald, W. B., Mullis, I. V. S., Turner, M. J., and Wooster, J. S. (1990). *The Civics Report Card.* Princeton, NJ: Educational Testing Service.

Banaszak, R. A., Hartoonian, H. M., and Leming, J. S. (1991) *New Horizons for Civic Education.* San Francisco: Foundation for Teaching Economics and Constitutional Rights Foundation.

Barber, B. R. (1989). "Public Talk and Civic Action." *Social Education, 53*(6), 355–356.

Boyer, E., and A. L. Levine. (1981). *A Question of Common Learning.* Princeton, NJ: Carnegie Foundation for the Advancement of Teaching.

Bragaw, D. H., and Hartoonian, H. M. (1988). "Social Studies: The Study of People in Society." In R. E. Brandt (Ed.), *Content of the Curriculum.* Alexandria, VA: Association of Supervision and Curriculum Development.

Callahan, W. T., and Banaszak, R. A. (1990). *Citizenship for the 21st Century.* Bloomington, IN: ERIC Clearinghouse for Social Studies/Social Science Education, Foundation for Teaching Economics, and Constitutional Rights Foundation.

Coles, R. (1990). *Girls Scouts' Survey on the Beliefs and Moral Values of America's Children.* New York: Girl Scouts of the United States of America.

Engle, S. H., and Ochoa, A.S. (1988). *Education for Democratic Citizenship: Decision Making in the Social Studies.* New York: Teachers College Press.

Gans, C. (1988). "Why Young People Don't Vote," *Update on Law-Related Education, 12*(3): 72–76.

Harwood, R. C. (1991). *Citizens and Politics: A View from Main Street America.* Dayton, OH: The Kettering Foundation.

Newmann, F. M. (1989). "Reflective Civic Participation." *Social Education, 53*(6): 357–360.

U.S. Has the World's Worst Voting Rate. (December 8, 1987). *San Francisco Chronicle,* p. A-11.

9

Future Problem Solving

**Preparing Middle School
Students to Solve
Community Problems**

RICHARD L. KURTZBERG   KRISTIN FAUGHNAN

Kristin (Coach): What do you think of the topic of teenage drinking?

Vance (Eighth-grader): It is an appropriate issue for us to work on, especially now. If you talk to older brothers and sisters, it seems to be getting worse in our community.

Nicole (Eighth-grader): It also seems like such a big problem. It's hard to tackle— it goes across many age groups.

Kristin: Is it possible to effect change in this area?

Nicole: I don't know. It's such a part of society—it's difficult to change society.

Lee (Eighth-grader): I know it's hard in our community. People say there's nothing else to do—they use it for an excuse.

Vance: It boils down to one important issue: Can we really change the way people act? You can't hypnotize an entire society.

On May 24, 1993, after a long day at John Jay Middle School, the 11 members of the Future Problem Solving (FPS) team met to continue work on the new topic of teenage drinking. These children, seventh- and eighth-graders, are a creative and intelligent group. They enjoy using the FPS process to solve problems. In this case, solving a problem will help their community. The structure is that of any normal club, except for the fact that the students are not always the normal club type nor is this the normal club activity. FPS participants are most often quite verbal and most are highly proficient at explaining and expounding on ideas. However, those who do not fit this mold are just as welcome; indeed, they can succeed to the same degree and often make unique contributions to our groups. We do not have any grade-point average or test score requirements for entry into our FPS program. All our middle-level students are invited to try the process, and those who wish to participate in the program select themselves. Since it is a thinking activity, it is not unusual for many bright and high-achieving students to choose to join FPS; however, this is not always the case. For example, of the 11 students involved in this project on teenage drinking, 3 or 4 might be termed "gifted," another 3 or 4 might be considered "bright average," several are average in academic ability, and 1 is a special education student. Another student is clearly gifted in social and organizational skills, but not in academics. As we hope you will see from their work on this project, the diversity of our students contributes significantly to the high quality of their efforts.

The discussion of May 24th was held at a picnic table at the middle school playground long after most everyone else had gone home. The students were working with their FPS coach [Kristin Faughnan], who is a high school senior with six years of FPS training. FPS coaches are usually teachers or veteran FPS students. Our middle school students were working on the very real problem of teenage drinking in our own community. Vance, an eighth-grader, is telling the others about a possible problem he has thought of related to alcohol abuse by teens:

Vance: When young adults are under the influence of alcohol, it is very likely they will commit acts of vandalism. These acts could include the defacing of public recreation sites, such as local parks, pools, sports areas, etc., and ruining it for the innocent users of the facility.—May 24, 1993.

On the night of Thursday, June 3, 1993, just 10 days after Vance's remark about drinking and vandalism, a large party was held at the house of a John Jay High School senior. The party involved 30 to 40 high school students, and a great deal of drinking occurred. At one point during the night, 4 seniors who had been drinking heavily got into a car, drove to the high school campus, cut down a number of trees that had been planted during the past 10 years, and spray-painted graffiti on the school buildings. This seemingly senseless incident devastated the school community and put a damper on end of the year activities, including the senior prom and graduation. The vandalism incident actually occurred *after* we had begun working on this situation.

Who is Vance and how could he know this might happen? Vance is an eighth-grader at the John Jay Middle School in Westchester County, New York, and he and his teammates were in the middle of a brainstorming session on teenage alcohol abuse as part of our Future Problem Solving (FPS) program. You will see many more ideas generated by Vance and his teammates in the following pages. These students see FPS as an opportunity to work in small "consultant" groups to address important issues. As will be explained in more detail later, FPS can be used as an extracurricular or pull-out program, such as the one

Vance and his teammates took part in, or it can be used by teachers right in the classroom to add realism to the curriculum and to train students to use higher-level thinking skills.

Although the project you will read about in this chapter was done by an FPS group as an extracurricular activity, teachers in our district use portions of the Future Problem Solving process in conjunction with the curriculum. One of our health education teachers splits his classes into problem-solving teams of six or seven students each, and presents them with school and community problems related to alcohol and substance abuse. This makes the problems much more real for the students and shows them how to at least begin to tackle complex issues. Many of our district teachers find other ways to use problem-solving activities in their classrooms in all areas of the curriculum. We are not intending this chapter to be a "How to Teach Problem Solving" manual, but we do hope to give you a good feel for the process and how it was used by one extraordinary group of middle-level youngsters to address a very real issue.

Before we show you some of the discussions our students had on this topic, we would like to introduce them to you: You have already heard from Vance, and yes, he really does speak as if he had swallowed a dictionary! When you read some of the writings of our middle level students on the topic, you may have difficulty believing that seventh- and eighth-graders can write that well. Vance is responsible for a good deal of that articulation. His teammates work hard to keep up with him. Vance describes himself as "vertically challenged." Most people think of him as short. He is certainly not short, however, when it comes to the capacity to work hard and do good research, to effectively problem solve, and to enthusiastically set high standards for himself and his teammates.

Lee, also an eighth-grader, brings a solid degree of common sense and practicality to her problem-solving group. She plays volleyball and lacrosse, is quiet by nature but commands instant attention and respect whenever she speaks.

Andrew is a seventh-grader who is new to our school and our FPS program. After one year, he seems like a veteran. Andrew is very creative and enormously gifted at generating ideas. Every problem-solving team needs at least some people who just seem to be able to turn on the creativity, and Andrew certainly fills this role for our group. He is a real thinker. He also has an excellent sense of humor, can be "wild and crazy," and keeps us smiling.

You will see a quote later in this chapter from Dana, a seventh-grader, about how every problem-solving group needs a "team-maker" (her phrase). Dana is our team-maker. Her sunny, vivacious manner keeps everybody on task, upbeat, and interacting in a positive, cooperative manner. When the going gets tough, Dana's ready smile and easy encouragement gets us all back on track.

Nicole is an eighth-grader who is unusually gifted in synthesis. Her capacity to integrate ideas is advanced far beyond her 13 years of age. Nicole can take the most divergent, flaky ideas and pull them together in a practical, useful manner. Just as effective problem-solving groups need wild and crazy types to generate ideas, they also need people like Nicole to make the ideas work.

J. B. is our resident skeptic. He questions everything. This is why we had him play a high school student with a "so what?" attitude about teenage drinking in the role-playing sessions you will read about later.

We had five other middle-level students help with this project. We cannot describe them all, but we hope the preceding has given you a feeling for the type of students who we are privileged to work with. Please also keep in mind that the "Coach" referred to in the discussions is Kristin, a high school student and one of the authors of this essay. A more detailed description of Kristin's work may be found at the conclusion of the chapter. Here is more of the discussion Kristin led when the students were brainstorming about teenage drinking (more of their work will be presented later):

Kristin: We've been talking about teenage drinking in our community. How do you think this affects them and those around them?

Lee: I think if teenagers drink, it would always affect the family—they might be more irritable or get depressed—the family might not like it.

Andrew: It might not be such a big deal if kids drink, as long as they don't show any other problems. Because teenage drinking is the norm, the family might not react.

Kristin: Should the family just expect it?

Lee: Every family should set their own standards—not approve or allow something just because most other kids are doing it. I don't think there are many kids on the fence. Because there's such a large majority of them drinking, most deciding kids would probably drink.

Andrew: It's mostly based on peer pressure.

Kristin: Is the drinking serious if you are not dependent on alcohol. Why does it matter?

Andrew: There are still the same effects. It influences your thinking.

Lee: It goes back to family standards, whether it matters if a child drinks once in a while.

This discussion is probably not very different from those that might take place at any middle school. What followed these discussions, however, is radically different, and can offer middle-level educators a new way to help their students address social issues. Please remember, although these students have been trained in small groups, classroom teachers can use the same principles to help their students to a systematic process of clear thinking and problem solving which, as we will show you, helps them approach serious social problems in an organized and carefully thought out manner.

The program we are describing, Future Problem Solving, when combined with an issues-oriented curriculum, can revolutionize the way teaching and learning is carried out. When you look at the work of our seventh- and eighth-graders, it is important to remember that the voices of our students, both in their discussions and in their writings, *were not edited in any way by the authors.* You may be surprised at the sophistication, and even professionalism of their work. Of course, some of this is due to their own abilities and talents. The training they have received in FPS, however, has given them a vehicle to structure their work and to allow them to see what it is like to function as practicing professionals.

We are not suggesting that every middle school teacher who uses the FPS process will see work like that produced by Vance, Dana, Lee, Andrew, Nicole, and others. They are unusually able and highly motivated students who have received intensive training in this model. They, and their coach, also had the rare gift of enough time to work on this project in detail. What you will see if you try this type of process, even in a setting of 25 students in a regular middle-level classroom, is better thinking, more creativity, and greatly improved ability to communicate thoughts to others.

In the following sections, we will: (1) describe the program for you with enough detail so that you can see how it changes the way middle level students think about problem solving and (2) show you how our students used this technique to address the issue of teenage alcohol abuse. For more details about how to implement the problem solving process, please see *The Future Problem Solving Program Training Manual and Coach's Handbook* (Jensen, 1993).

WHAT IS FUTURE PROBLEM SOLVING?

The Future Problem Solving process is a powerful program that allows students to understand and address important social issues that they might otherwise have trouble recognizing or dealing with. FPS helps train students of all ages to think clearly and flexibly, to work together in teams (usually consisting of 4 to 7 students) in a group "think tank" environment, and to address real-world issues, just as if they were consultants. Teachers who use FPS in their classrooms divide the students into small groups of 4 to 6 students for the actual FPS work. Thus, a class of 25 students might be divided into five teams. Teams should have a mix of thinkers, writers, and organizers, as our group did.

The FPS process can offer students many different skills that contribute to effective problem solving: flexible thinking in both convergent and divergent areas, analysis, synthesis, brainstorming, learning to listen to others and to work together, budgeting time, evaluating one's own work, and effective communication, to name just a few.

FPS was developed by E. Paul Torrance, who combined the Creative Problem Solving Process developed by Parnes and Osborn with the field of Future Studies (Torrance, 1979, Crabbe, 1991). The FPS process has developed in a variety of ways: It is used by the Future Problem Solving Program in state, regional, and national competition. It is used in classroom applications as a higher level thinking skills component of an issues-oriented curriculum (Pesce et al., 1995). It is used by advanced teams to address real world issues (Kurtzberg and Kurtzberg, 1993). The FPS process and the skills it helps to develop may be found in Table 9–1.

We asked some of our middle-level students to tell us what they had learned about the FPS process. It is important to realize that all the quotes from our students about both the FPS process and the alcohol abuse problems were spontaneous. Although they had all been in the program one or two years, we had never discussed the metacognitive aspects of FPS as a higher-level thinking skills program with them. Here is what they said about the process:

Dana: FPS is kind of like taking control of the future, even though we're not there yet. If you take FPS apart, it's trying to solve something that's going to happen, just like we said vandalism could be a result of drinking, and then it really happened.

Lee: It [FPS] helps you to think of things in different ways than you would otherwise.

Dana: If you did FPS by yourself, you wouldn't know how people would react to your ideas. If you worked yourself, your solutions would never satisfy as many people as when you work in a group.

Vance: You learn how to cooperate—to accomplish anything, you have to learn to work and cooperate with a group.

Dana: The team takes bits and pieces that you form into an FPS puzzle. You have the fuzzy situation [see description below]. It has all the pieces of the

TABLE 9–1   Thinking Skills Taught in the Future Problem Solving (FPS) Process

FPS Step	Thinking Skills Taught
1. Research and Discussion	Research, Comprehension, Speaking, Reading for Meaning, Selecting, Discovery, Clarification, Listening
2. Problem Identification	Brainstorming, Categorizing, Writing, Communicating, Flexible Thinking
3. Underlying Problem	Projecting and Combining Ideas, Selecting, Synthesizing, Analyzing, Discussing, Logic
4. Alternative Solutions	Brainstorming, Categorizing, Writing, Flexible Thinking, Projecting and Combining Ideas, Elaborating
5. Criteria and Evaluation	Selecting, Analyzing, Evaluating, Flexible Thinking
6. Final Recommendations (Oral and Written)	Discussing, Unifying and Combining Ideas, Presenting Ideas Orally, Selecting, Elaborating, Integrating, Writing

problem in it—they have all different colors, but no form. By doing the FPS process, you are putting form on it, one step at a time. You give it some form with the problems, more with the underlying problem, still more with solutions, and you complete the picture with the final recommendations.

THE FUZZY SITUATION

Ben: Most of the fuzzy situations are "What ifs"—you are trying to think of problems that could be happening in real life and solving them.

Problem solving begins when students are given a "fuzzy" situation, which may be set in the present or the future. The fuzzy situation is a short summary of an event, place, or condition. It is called "fuzzy" because problems in the real world are most often unstructured, ill defined, and sometimes downright messy. Some fuzzies are broad and encompass almost an entire topic, while others are more focused, but all give students the details from which they begin their problem solving. Our middle school English teachers pull fuzzy situations right out of stories the students have read. Social studies or science teachers can find fuzzy situations in almost every aspect of their curricula.

The fuzzy situation we have chosen for the problem of teenage drinking in our community was developed by the authors. We decided to use this situation because it is characteristic of a problem that has been of vital concern to our community. As you can tell, it became apparent that what our middle school children had been taught about alcohol abuse instilled a good deal of fear in many of them. Unfortunately, we found out from surveys of our older students that this fear does not carry them through their high school years, when drinking becomes the norm. When local high school students drink and discover that they do not become brain-dead, as they were told in the middle school, most of them tend to disregard much of what they had been taught. Here is the fuzzy situation exactly as we gave it to our seventh- and eighth-graders. Like the vandalism incident, this fuzzy situation really happened in our community:

FUZZY SITUATION: TEENAGE ALCOHOL ABUSE IN KATONAH-LEWISBORO

The John Jay High School Junior Prom was held on Saturday night, May 8th. A letter from the principal had been sent to parents of all the students attending. The letter discussed the problems of drinking on prom night. It asked the parents to check car trunks to make sure that students were not bringing any alcohol to the prom and it reminded them that students with Junior Drivers' Licenses were not allowed to drive to the prom. New York state gives Junior Driving Licenses to those between 16 and 18 years of age that prohibits them from driving after 9 P.M. The letter also reminded parents and students about the dangers of drinking and driving. Some of the students came to the prom in "party vans," which are small buses, holding 25 to 30 people. These vans were rented for the evening by the students, and driven by professionals. The students were charged $60 per couple for the vans.

A student from one of the party vans came to the prom showing the effects of drinking. He was questioned about how he got to the prom and who he came with. When it was discovered that he came in a party van, the van was searched and seven cases of beer were found. Word got around right away about this, and a great number of cars were seen quickly leaving the parking lot, presumably because they also had alcohol in their trunks. The students who had ridden to the prom in the party van with the beer were suspended from school for three days, even though not all of them had been drinking.

Research and Discussion

Research, as we use it in FPS, involves much more than looking up references in the library. Our middle-level students did a great deal of library research for this project, particularly on the physical dangers of excessive drinking (see Figure 9–1). They found much of this research to be consistent with what they had learned in seventh-grade health classes. As you can see from their comments, they also found some differences, especially in the manner in which the information was presented in health class and in the literature. Our students also interviewed high school students and teachers, and participated in seminars with some of our health teachers and substance-abuse counselors. By the time they finished this research, they had a very clear picture of the many deleterious physical effects of alcohol as well as the many other problems related to teenage drinking. Because they felt that it was unlikely that anything they might recommend would stop teenage drinking in our community, our middle-level students chose not to focus on the physical effects of teenage drinking. While they realized that physical problems are important, they decided, as you will glean from this piece, to turn their attention to dealing with a host of other negative effects of excessive drinking by adolescents. To do this, they focused their research efforts on our own high school.

Just as it is in many places around the United States, teenage drinking is a big problem in our community. When surveys of students have been conducted at our high school, they show that most John Jay High School students drink on a somewhat regular basis, even if only at parties. Drinking has become the norm for most of our young people. They feel that drinking is fine, and that it is what high school kids are supposed to be doing.

The school district puts in a good deal of time teaching students about the dangers of alcohol. These efforts are concentrated in health classes in grades 5, 7, 10 or 11. Teaching centers around the "evils" of alcohol, such as the destruction of brain cells, the addictive qualities of alcohol, the diseases it can lead to, and the pain it can cause individuals and families.

TEMPORARY EFFECTS:

Brain and Central Nervous System (CNS)

CNS Depressant	• Alcohol abuse lowers CNS functioning • Comprehension [understanding] is affected • Reactions are slowed down • Decision making and judgement are affected
Endorphins affected	• Reduces level of endorphins to brain
Short-term memory	• Ability to remember is impaired
Self-control	• Person can become more impulsive
Alcohol can kill	• If too much is taken too quickly

Rest of Body

Affects senses	• Slurred speech • Difficulty in hearing • Difficulty with vision
Inhibitions are affected	• People say and do what they normally wouldn't
Coordination is affected	• Loss of sense of balance
Increased tolerance	• The more you drink, the more you need

PERMANENT EFFECTS:

Brain and Central Nervous System (CNS)

Damage to brain cells

Long-term memory
  impairment

Damage to fetal brain cells	• Reduced level of endorphins in fetal brain
Fetal Alcohol Syndrome	• Increase likelihood of offspring becoming an alcoholic
Korsakoff's Syndrome	• Mental confusion and sometimes death

Rest of Body

Damage to liver	• Cirrhosis, hardening of liver
Addiction	• Dependency on alcohol
Delerium Tremens	• From withdrawal from alcohol
Affects immune system	• Interferes with immune functioning • Much more vulnerable to disease
Possible organ failure	• Can cause death

FIGURE 9–1   Results of Student Research on Detrimental Physical Effects of Alcohol Abuse

Our elementary and middle-level students take this education very seriously. In our rural-suburban community, they are often naive about these things, and the education in our middle school health classes does not seem to prepare them for what they are going to face when they get to high school.

Kristin: What did you learn about alcohol in health class?

Nicole: I heard contradictory things from my parents and from health class.

Kristin: What do you mean?

Nicole: They make you believe a few drinks will kill you—they really try to scare you.

Vance: Health classes are really, really boring. They don't tell us about the social effects, they just threaten you: "It will kill your liver." When kids see "Hey, it didn't kill us," all the teaching becomes void.

Andrew: I never really got much from the health classes. When we did our own research, I got a much better picture of the numbers of kids in our town who drink.

Most of the middle school students in our community come away from their health lessons thinking that all drinking is "bad." They cannot understand why anyone would want to drink, unless he or she is an alcoholic.

Dana: The statistics in health class aren't going to be a deciding factor.

Andrew: Because it [the fact that drinking was bad] was such a plain fact in seventh grade, it never affected me that much.

Lee: I was scared of drinking in seventh grade because health teachers exaggerated statistics so much. Now that I think about it, I know that losing a thousand brain cells a day is not too much.

Dana: Young kids believe everything. Later on, when they become teenagers, they may not believe the truth.

Andrew: Most teenagers may have already started to drink before they reach the mandatory health class in high school.

After the seventh-grade health classes, which include units on the dangers of alcohol abuse, our school district does not readdress this issue formally until students get to the high school health classes in tenth, eleventh, or in some cases, even twelfth grade. By this time, many of them view the lectures on the evils of alcohol as repetitive and tiring:

Dana: You're not drinking in seventh grade, and it doesn't apply to you. I would teach about alcohol in Freshman year. The facts that you get in health classes are boring.

Our high school health class surveys show that more than half of our students are already drinking on a regular basis. Only a few of those surveyed will acknowledge that their lives might be seriously affected by their drinking, which is usually done at weekend parties. They have now become part of the norm, and drinking has become part of their lives.

We set up role-playing situations, where some of our middle school students took the roles of high school students and argued that nothing was wrong with drinking, while others tried to "help them understand," using the model of teaching about alcohol they had been exposed to. In the following discussion, J. B., a seventh-grader, played the role of a high school student and argued that people ought not to fuss about teenage drinking:

J. B.: Why should it really matter if kids drink on the weekends?

Andrew: An overall problem of drinking is the thought of "why not drink?" If the majority drink, kids think it's OK to drink themselves. Then when the teenagers grow to adults, they realize the problem of drinking. They also realize that, unless they are alcoholics, they will be able to control their drinking.

Kristin: Certainly in high school and college, problems would not be noticed right away.

J. B.: Isn't it true that kids who drink still get done what they want to? It depends on motivation.

Lee: The kids might feel "this isn't doing anything," so they go ahead and drink. Teachers tell you the extreme, the end effects—they never say, for example, the first couple of times nothing might happen.

As you can see from this role-playing discussion, it was during this step in the process that we began to see a change in the thinking of our middle schoolers. After hearing the viewpoints of high school students as role-played by one of their peers, they began to question their own understanding of the issue. It suddenly seemed much more complicated, and simply saying that drinking was "bad" for you no longer seemed to be productive. As one of our seventh-graders commented:

Ben: The reality of the fuzzy situation becomes more and more clear as you move further along in the FPS process.

Brainstorming Subproblems

After the fuzzy situation has been researched and discussed, teams use the group brainstorming process to identify as many different types of problems as possible that come from the fuzzy situation. To show you how our students brainstorm, here are some excerpts from the process:

Dana: I think the kids who are going to drink will drink. If the education isn't really relevant to influencing a person's drinking, then it [the influence] comes from friends. Some kids might want to experiment, to try to be cool. Society influences this, such as beer commercials.

Andrew: Commercials, I think, have a lot to do with it. It's kind of subconscious. I would base my opinions on [the TV show] *Cheers.* You know, Norm. You watch these people who have failed in life, and they are destined to sit on a bar stool. For example, Frazier could probably be a successful psychologist, if he weren't in a bar the whole time.

Lee: I know what you mean. The impression that show gives is that you can drink all you want and you don't change. Norm drinks all the time and doesn't get drunk.

As you will see, the students' brainstorming of ideas leads to an increasing awareness of the complexities of this important social issue. As the brainstorming discussion continued, the students drew on their research and their training in using many different categories of ideas to explore teenage abuse of alcohol.

Andrew: People get a lot of their habits from commercials.

Dana: With beer commercials today, the ads refer to using alcohol as an option for teenagers, but the role models are adults. The music, advertisements, and endorsers, though, are focused toward teenagers. This may encourage teenagers to drink, even though the beer companies say they shouldn't drink.

Nicole: The person who sells the beer to the kids is most likely an adult and a negative role model for the kids—showing them it is all right to drink and buy liquor under age.

Vance: People will receive the wrong message from billboards advertising cigarettes and alcohol, and think that they will be more beautiful, have more fun, etc., if they use these things.

Andrew: When they are young kids who learn the facts about alcohol, they tend to believe everything they hear. But when they become teenagers who use alcohol, they may not experience all the effects and may not believe what they are taught.

Dana: Under the influence of drinking, people may be subjected (sic) to do things they wouldn't normally do. This may be a serious problem because you may be endangering yourself and other's lives.

Scott: Kids under "the influence" could get hold of firearms and put holes in people that don't belong there.

At this point, you may very well ask, "Where is the teacher in this conversation?" We have found that children who are experienced in brainstorming, as these students were, are easily able to carry on this type of creative discussion without interruption. This particular group of students has had lots of brainstorming experience. With students who are new to this type of expression, you may need to play a more active role than we did. Our brainstorming discussion continues with the results of some of the research our students did on how the legal system deals with DWIs (driving while intoxicated):

Rich: Many people, not just the ones drinking, could be put in jeopardy if there were drunk drivers.

Andrew: Don't you think it would be difficult for the legal system to act fairly when a teenager is arrested for drinking and driving?

Lee: Yeah. Especially because the court would be stuck between trying the adolescent as a juvenile or an adult.

Andrew: I bet some guilty people might get away to do it again, and some relevantly (sic) innocent people might be punished just because there's such a gap in the criminal court system in the adolescent DWI area.

Vance: It could be dangerous, if an official was addicted or was an alcoholic. Some people might begin to feel drinking was OK because a figure of authority they respect does it.

Nicole: It's the same with a parent. You see a parent drink and it's a role model for you.

Andrew: It's like a chain reaction.

Nicole: Kids who go off to college and come back—they can serve as a negative role model for high school kids.

Vance: But mostly it starts in high school.

Nicole: Kids are home by themselves a lot. Their parents don't monitor them. Liquor is always available in the house.

Dana: A high school person who is going out with someone who is drinking may start to drink or be morally torn about what to do if his or her parents don't want them to drink.

Lee: I think the teenager will become secretive about it, because of peer pressure. If she wants to stay with her boyfriend, she will probably start drinking and this can lead to more trouble.

Kristin: How?

Dana: When a teenager commits a crime under the influence, the guilt stays with them for the rest of their life. For instance, a death as a result of driving while drunk. Permanent psychological damage could affect the kid after such an incident.

Kristin: What other problems might teenage drinking cause?

Vance: Vandalism.

Andrew: A droppage in effort in school.

Nicole: It could start people lying to their parents and friends.

Dana: That would decrease family values. Also, it could cause a separation of social groups.

Kristin: Tell us how.

Dana: You could be friends with lots of people in sixth grade. By tenth grade, you sort of get split up by how much you drink or by whether you use drugs.

Vance: Wouldn't they be split socially anyway by then?

Nicole: Because of drinking it could happen at a younger age or to a greater extreme. You don't have anything in common with people who just talk about drinking or where to get marijuana.

Working in their small groups, the students refine their discussions into concise problems, in each case stating why they are problems in the context of the fuzzy situation.

In this step of the FPS process, students learn to state how each problem relates to the social issue, and to explain why each is a problem. They also learn to look for problems in a wide variety of categories, to encourage flexible thinking. Here are some of the categories that we use in identifying problems and in generating solutions: Education, Health, Social, Family, Physical Safety, Psychological, Legal, Economic, Environmental, Moral/Ethical. Our students find this step very valuable in helping them to think through all aspects of the issue:

Vance: From brainstorming you get lots of ideas—you get a wide view of the fuzzy. You start with a small idea, and then you look at all sides of it.

Scott: Everybody just tosses up ideas on what a problem or solution could be, and then it evolves into what it should be.

J. B.: Once somebody gets an idea and calls it out, it's like a chain—people get all these other ideas from it.

Dana: The problems are in many different categories so you can cover a lot of ground from the fuzzy—otherwise your problems and solutions might be too narrow and wouldn't apply to a lot of the problem.

Our students usually generate a minimum of 20 subproblems in a wide variety of categories. As you might imagine, this gives them views of the issue from a variety of perspectives. Once they have looked at the issue from many different angles, their next task is to combine all of these aspects into one focused problem, which, if solved, would also solve many of the other problems they had developed.

The Underlying Problem

Vance: The underlying problem is the thread that holds the whole quilt of the entire process together.

This step involves the convergent thinking skills of analysis, comparison, and synthesis. Students learn to focus on the most relevant issues and to write an underlying problem that lends itself to creative solutions. The underlying problem usually starts with a "How might we . . . ," contains *one key verb* (to focus the solutions), and a "so that . . ." phrase (to make sure the solutions are all relevant). Finding an underlying problem is the most difficult step in the FPS process but also the most significant and rewarding:

Marc: I've learned from FPS to focus on the one point that's making it a problem.

Lee: When you think of all the problems, they seem very different. When you bring them all together, you see the similarities in them.

Ben: It shouldn't be too broad, because you'd have no idea of what you're talking about. If it's too specific, it won't be able to solve all the problems.

Nicole: Without an underlying problem, the whole thing is kind of muddled and has no purpose.

Initially, our students tried to focus on eliminating teenage drinking in our community. They quickly realized, however, that this would be impossible:

Kristin: Can alcohol-related problems be prevented?

Vance: No, you can prevent some but not all. It's an impossibility to prohibit teenage drinking in our society.

Andrew: There's no way!

Dana: If we can't stop them drinking, we could try to make it better.

Kristin: What do you mean?

Vance: We could deal with the side effects.

The students came to the conclusion that their efforts would be better focused in dealing with the negative effects of drinking, rather than trying to ban it. They agreed on the following underlying problem:

> Knowing that the problem of teenage drinking cannot entirely be solved and eliminated, how might we deal with the negative effects of drinking so that people's physical and psychological health, social life, and property will not be damaged?

Brainstorming Solutions

After having decided that they needed to focus on the negative effects of teenage drinking, our students once again turned to brainstorming and flexible thinking. Using the same general principles as they did when they identified subproblems, the students developed a large number of alternative solutions to their underlying problem. We teach them to use the classic journalistic questions (Who? What? When? Where? Why? How?) in their writing, so that their solutions can be more practical.

Andrew: FPS shows you that there is more than one solution to every problem. You need wild, off-shooting ideas, but you also need good refining. Most people will say: "That idea's too wild! Why'd you even think of it?" A good refiner will take the idea and make it down to earth, using the same basic points, so it works.

Dana: When you work with your team in a think tank, you can't get the ideas fast enough. You feel like your solutions might actually help or save somebody some day. It's all very realistic.

The following discussion is typical of those our students had in generating solutions:

Kristin: Let's talk about how you think the education about teenage drinking could be more effective.

Andrew: Kids, once they feel nothing is wrong, will think they have been taught many lies. Tell kids the truth about the matter! Don't exaggerate!

Lee: I think they taught us about alcohol too early. In seventh grade, you think "it doesn't affect me," and the learning is not as significant. Eighth grade would be better, because they might be able to say, "This kind of thing is going to happen next year."

Dana: You're not drinking in seventh grade, so it doesn't apply to you. I would teach about alcohol in freshman year.

Lee: We had recovering alcoholics come in seventh grade, but by the time you get to high school you forget.

Nicole: The schools could make health programs more interesting so that children will listen. They might discuss the negative effects of drinking in a more realistic way. Just saying how bad drinking is might arouse a child's curiosity and lead to drinking.

Vance: I think that type of curriculum would be better than what is in place now, but high school students, even though attempts have been made to deter them, will still drink and do drugs, etc. I don't think there is that much you can do.

Andrew: I believe you could lower the percent, but you couldn't abolish it.

Vance: If the educational programs in the schools could be improved, the dangerous negative effects of drinking could be decreased. As the student moves to a higher grade, different information could be presented. As they get older, the information should address the effects rather than dealing with drinking as a broad topic.

In a similar manner, our students discussed other areas that might lead to productive solutions. Although they used many different categories in developing solutions, and tried to be as creative as possible, all their work was tied to the concept of reducing the dangerous side effects of drinking by teenagers, as presented in their underlying problem. Here are some examples of solutions that our middle schoolers generated:

Andrew: Lawyers and judges could volunteer time to talk to kids in small groups, to explain all the legal difficulties kids can get into because of drinking.

Vance: This might encourage them not to drink and drive.

Kristin: Should this be done in school?

Nicole: No, it would just be looked upon as a threat.

Vance: It could be done in libraries or homes.

Andrew: These kinds of workshops could also be held for parents to tell them of their legal responsibilities.

Kristin: How might we use technology to help solve these problems?

Nicole: We could use the information highway to help people teach other people about the negative effects of alcohol.

Kristin: How?

Vance: They could share experiences—you could have AA meetings over Internet, which would increase the communication . . .

Nicole: Once people start communicating, it gets the subject into the open and makes it less of a taboo to talk about.

Dana: TV alcohol commercials could have a public service message included, like a surgeon general's warning. It might decrease the amount of sales, and therefore cut down on the negative effects.

Kristin: What else?

Vance: They could develop a new scanner technology, which could measure alcohol in the blood stream. The scanner could be placed at any building entrance and if it beeps, you will not be permitted into the building. If it beeps in the entrance to school, you will not be permitted to attend classes. This would reduce the negative effects of drinking in school.

Andrew: You could also equip cars with a sensor on the dashboard to measure the amount of alcohol exhaled by the driver. If the reading measured a certain level, the car would cut off the fuel lines, enabling the car to move only a few feet. This would prevent drunk teenagers from driving, and therefore reduce the negative effects of drinking.

As you have seen, the Coach's comments, although brief, encourage the students to expand their thinking into many different categories and subject areas. In the preceding discussion, our students created solutions in the following categories: Education, Family, The Law, Public Relations and Technology.

Criteria and Grid

One of the unique aspects of the FPS process is that it allows students to analyze and evaluate their own work as they move toward pulling together a set of final recommendations. Teams develop five relevant criteria [e.g., cost, acceptability, feasibility] and use these to evaluate their solutions. They then determine which solutions are most promising by ranking them on each of the criteria.

Andrew: Finding solutions is easy—finding the best one is hard.

Rich: In life, FPS helps you with judgment skills, making the right decisions.

Nicole: Criteria is not judgmental—also, not just one person decides—it's a group decision. The five criteria all cover different areas, and it allows you to judge your solutions fairly. It helps because sometimes I think mine are better until we judge them.

In considering criteria for the teenage alcohol abuse problem, our students discussed many factors that could affect their solutions: Would students be willing to do it, and does it require too much from them? Will it cost too much? Is the technology available? Is it acceptable to parents, to the community as a whole, and to educators? Are there back-up plans for solutions that do not work? Are there too many negative side effects to the solution? Will the solution work in the long term? Is it applicable to many different ages? How quickly could it be put into effect?

After much discussion, the students synthesized these factors into the following five criteria:

1. Which solutions will gain the acceptance of the targeted teenagers in our community?
2. Which solution is likely to have the greatest long-term effect?
3. Which solution would be easiest to put into practice?
4. Which solution would have the least negative side effects?
5. Which solution would be most cost effective?

By ranking what they felt were their most promising solutions against each of the five criteria, our students determined which of these solutions were most likely to be successful. These highly ranked solutions formed the core of the final step in the process.

Final Recommendations

As previously mentioned, we train our FPS teams to act as consultants. They produce a set of final recommendations, explaining, elaborating, and integrating their best solutions, as well as discussing how they might be carried out. The set of final recommendations simulates a document produced by a think-tank group in the real world. We teach our students to present their final recommendations in both an oral and a written form.

In preparing their oral presentation, which is done before the written version, the students organize their solutions into themes that belong together. They also learn to "sell" their ideas by explaining the importance and relevance of their underlying problem, as well as how their recommendations can effectively solve this problem. The oral presentations are made to a panel of coaches, teachers, classmates, outside experts, and others. The team and panel carry out a dialogue, which allows the students to elaborate, expand, and justify their solutions. A recorder takes notes of the entire presentation, and these notes form the basis for the written set of final recommendations. Here are some excerpts from the oral presentation session in the students' own words:

Vance: As we pointed out in the problems, many students don't take health classes seriously. We would integrate the negative effects of drinking into other phases of the curriculum.

Panel: How might you do this?

Vance: You could, in English classes, read stories where the characters had their lives ruined by alcohol abuse—like *Long Day's Journey Into Night.*

Lee: Yes, and *Days of Wine and Roses.*

Dana: You take four to six kids, whose functioning is limited by use of alcohol.

Panel: How would you decide whose functioning is limited? Do they have to be totally impaired?

Andrew: No, it could be students where there is a suspicion that alcohol is a problem.

Vance: It could be like a big buddy program. Students could bond with a peer.

Panel: Someone their own age?

Dana: They could be assigned to an older peer who has gone through the problem. They could learn to have a good time without drinking.

Using their oral presentation notes as a basis, the students integrate and refine their ideas:

Andrew: You learn to take facts, whirl them around in your head, add things so they make sense, and then come out with them in a written form.

Vance: In the final recommendations, you elaborate on your best solutions. You sand the edges, add things, and get a real sense of what you have accomplished. If you have done it well, you can read only the fuzzy and the final recommendations and sense that you have done a lot.

What follows is the end result of our students' efforts in the area of teenage alcohol abuse in our community. Like the problems and solutions they brainstormed, our seventh- and eighth-graders wrote these final recommendations without any adult help. They decided to focus on their educational solutions, since they felt that these were the solutions that were most likely to be directly helpful in our community.

MEMO TO: KATONAH-LEWISBORO BOARD OF EDUCATION
FROM: 8th and 9th GRADE PROBLEM-SOLVING TEAM

There is a serious problem in our community with alcohol-related crimes, damage, social and academic difficulties. These create a scar on the community and present a danger to us all. Using John Jay High School as an example, surveys have shown that well over half of our students drink on a regular basis.

As we have learned from the past, alcohol abuse will never be completely eliminated. This is why we have chosen to try to reduce the negative effects of drinking as our underlying problem. We feel that the best way to do this would be to make changes in our education system, as it deals with young people drinking. In the new curriculum we are suggesting, varying amounts of information, with increasing amounts of depth, would be presented to the students based on their grade level. In the primary grades, a small percentage of time would be used to explain that alcohol is bad, and that they should shun it completely. Alcohol abuse education would take this tone until fifth grade. At this point, when the students would be getting ready for middle school, a new setup would be needed. More details about the negative physical effects of alcohol could be given.

In seventh grade, the students would be told that the effects of alcohol aren't quite as black and white as they might believe. This way, when many of them try alcohol in the near future, they will not disregard what they have learned. Hopefully, they will begin to understand that alcohol's effects are subtle and long term, and that they need to tread carefully.

In the next few years, they will be presented with more specific information about many of the negative effects of alcohol, such as mental, psychological, family, and social problems. This would allow students to get information about alcohol and its abuses on a need-to-know basis.

For the students who do fall victim to alcohol abuse, programs would be established to help. For example, a big buddy program could be started, where recovered alcoholics would take the students to fun, non-alcohol-related events.

A retreat could be set up for those who have become hard-core drinkers, in which four to six students would go away for a week, under the supervision of trained recovered alcoholics. At these retreats, the students could be taught to recognize and deal with depression, short tempers, and aggression in themselves and in others. This might help them to deal with both the causes and effects of alcohol abuse. After this week, they would continue to receive help to encourage them to stop abusing alcohol—they might even participate in these retreats again, this time as counselors.

Education about alcohol abuse could also be integrated into the entire school curriculum. For instance, in English classes, books that deal with the problems of alcohol abuse could be put on the required reading list. In the sciences, students could learn about the chemical properties of alcohol, as well as creating experiments that demonstrate the negative effects of alcohol.

We feel that with these necessary changes in our education system, and by using students at all grade levels to review the changes for relevance and impact, we can reduce the negative effects of alcohol abuse on our students. We also believe that the best way to communicate to these pupils is through our school system. By the development of these programs, we are confident that a positive change will occur in the near future.

After our middle-level students developed this set of final recommendations, a number of initiatives have begun in our school district. Our Assistant Superintendent of Schools has formed a districtwide group to assess the present health education with particular attention to drugs and alcohol. This Health Curriculum Study Committee includes administrators, health teachers, physicians, parents, and a few students from our middle and high schools—including Dana and Vance, two of the students who worked on this alcohol abuse project. As part of this committee's work, they will address the final recommendations presented by our FPS team. Our school has also begun an effort involving several different schools and their communities to discuss the problems associated with teenage alcohol use. In both of these efforts, our middle school students really will act as consultants to the groups trying to deal with this issue!

FPS IN THE MIDDLE SCHOOL CLASSROOM

The FPS process has been used by middle-level educators in a number of different ways. Teachers who become familiar with FPS techniques find that the techniques can be modified to fit their needs. This type of problem solving can be used in almost any curricular area. In addition, the FPS process lends itself to interdisciplinary curricular work. Our middle school students combined elements from the areas of English, social studies, science, and health in order to carry out their project on teenage alcohol abuse. This demonstrates the multidisciplinary nature of FPS.

Andrew: FPS enhances your school learning. Much of school learning does not require open-minded thinking. FPS requires open-minded thinking.

Scott: FPS is a challenge. It lets you apply yourself and be creative.

J. B.: You can use the steps for any problem and all subjects.

Although the FPS process can be used with any size group, it is best carried out in small groups of four to seven students, so that each student can be a major contributor. Teachers learn to balance stronger and weaker students on each team, as well as to create teams with a mix of skills:

Dana: You need some to be smart, but not all. They can all learn and get tips from each other. I'd look for some kids who are logical and some who are creative. You need real opposites. You need a thinker, you need a writer, a brainstormer, a team-maker. You need someone to come up with "stupid" ideas, which are usually the best ideas. You then get the writer and the brainstormer to turn the "stupid" idea into a stupendous idea.

Marc: It's more like a group of friends. You have a bond with them. It's not just like any other class—you work together more.

Teachers who are interested in implementing FPS in their classrooms should know that "it takes getting used to, but it's a great system" (Nicole, Grade 8). As Nicole says, the FPS process requires an investment of time and energy, both for the teacher and the students. Teachers can get initial assistance from the *FPS Coach's Guide* (Jensen, 1993). This manual will give you a good idea of the FPS process. For those who would like to get an idea of how you might carry out a project like this in your classroom, the following suggestions can help you get started in terms of organizing your class.

Tips for Trying the Future Problem Solving Process with an Entire Class

1. *Read the FPS Training Manual.* You do not need to be an expert in FPS, but you do need a fair understanding of the basics.
2. *Try some preliminary brainstorming activities with your students.* Teach the four rules of brainstorming.
   - No criticism is allowed while brainstorming.
   - The more ideas, the better.
   - The wilder the ideas, the better.
   - Students are encouraged to "hitchhike" or "piggy-back" on one another's ideas to make them better.
3. *Pick a project that will be of interest and importance to your students.* We often let students choose the project from a "menu," or brainstorm ideas for their own project. You can also use something right from your curriculum.
4. *Divide your students into groups.* A class of 25, for example, can be divided into five groups. Try for a mix of academic ability, motivational levels, and personality types. Successful groups usually have an organizer, a writer, and a mix of left-brain (analysts) and right-brain (creative types) students. The "organizer" can take overall responsibility for the work, while you run from group to group. At first, you will feel like you need four other teachers to be there with you, but as the students get the hang of it, your work becomes easier.

5. *Use the process in a flexible manner.* Some of our teachers only brainstorm subproblems and define the underlying problem. Others like to brainstorm and then apply criteria. You should feel free to use parts of this process or to modify it in any way you want.

In general, the teacher (or Coach) carries a good deal of the burden with students who are new to the process. This time investment decreases gradually, until, with really advanced groups, the Coach becomes responsible for logistics, pretzels and apples! Teachers who are experienced in FPS learn to take the process apart to meet their classroom needs. (Pesce et al., 1995) For example, if one step—such as criteria—is all you need in a given area, then just use criteria. Future Problem Solving is a hands-on program which can serve as an ideal vehicle for middle-school students to address social issues. As we have demonstrated, the FPS process can be used to allow students to experience real-world problems from the perspective of consultants. We feel FPS is particularly suited to middle level students because it is an active process, it is adaptable to all types of curriculum, and it encourages higher-level thinking in students. The flexible use of the FPS process can bridge the gap between the educational curriculum and the outside world.

Students who master the process can be given the opportunity to actually make an impact by suggesting solutions that may help to solve real problems faced by society, such as our middle schoolers did with the issue of teenage alcohol abuse. The value of these types of activities extend well beyond the academic; they allow middle-level students to feel a strong sense of having contributed to the world in which they live.

Vance: The FPS process prepares you for the outside world by teaching you how to solve real problems. You don't panic. It's a logical process that guides you through.

Ben: I'm proud to be in FPS because I know that I can use the steps to solve problems in real life. It's worked for me!

John Jay Middle School students who carried out the project on teenage drinking in our community were:

8th Graders	*7th Graders*
Brooke Benlifer	Dana Faughnan
Lee Carroll	J. B. Ferrarone
Rich Lynch	Andrew Goodwin
Scott Pfeiffer	Marc Mayer
Nicole Scholtz	Ben Pugsley

The authors would also like to acknowledge the assistance of Jeremy Younkin, a senior at John Jay High School, who helped in the research and discussion phases of this project, and Terri Kurtzberg, who helped with the final editing.

REFERENCES

Crabbe, A. B. (1991). "Preparing Today's Students to Solve Tomorrow's Problems." *Gifted Child Today. 14*(2): 2–5.

Jensen, B. (Ed.). (1993). *The Future Problem Solving Program Training Manual and Coach's Handbook.* Ann Arbor, MI: The Future Problem Solving Program.

Kurtzberg, R. L., and Kurtzberg, K. E. (1993). "Future Problem Solving: Connecting Middle School Students to the Real World." *Middle School Journal. 24*(4): 37–40.

Pesce, L., Faughnan, K., and Kurtzberg, R. (1995). "Addressing Society's Problems in the Global Studies Classroom." Submitted for publication.

Torrance, E. P. (1979). *The Search for Satori and Creativity.* Buffalo, NY: Creative Educational Foundation.

► 10

Alienation or Engagement?

Service Learning May Be an Answer

JOAN SCHINE   **ALICE HALSTED**

Who are these middle school creatures, variously described as early adolescents, transescents, or other less clinical and often more negative terms? They are curious and apathetic, energetic and lazy, tall and short, still children and almost adults, conscientious and scatterbrained, altruistic and self-absorbed . . . and so on.

Those who work or live with an early adolescent will have no trouble recognizing the description. Mood, behavior—even interests—alter often during this period, not only from day to day but also from moment to moment, making it a time of unpredictability—for parents, for teachers, and for the young people themselves.

This is understandable in that early adolescence is characterized primarily by change. Physical change is, of course, the most obvious, but cognitive and emotional changes, the loosening of ties to parents, and intensified importance attached to peer relationships are equally significant. The move, in Piagetian terms, from concrete to abstract thinking, periods of extreme self-doubt, and unpredictable and swift changes in mood—are all normal developmental shifts and all combine to make this period a time of extraordinary vulnerability, but a time, too, of equally extraordinary leaps in maturity and understanding. There is a dawning idealism and altruism, often seemingly at odds with a new absorption in self. A desire to reach out to adults other than parents and teachers and a drive to test values and to try on new roles are important developments of this period.

Involvement in service learning can meet many of the special needs of the early adolescent. Described by Dorman, Lipsitz,[1] Lounsbury, Toepfer,[2] and others, these include:

- Developing a sense of competence, testing and discovering new skills
- Discovering a place for themselves in the world, to create a vision of a personal future

- Participating in projects with tangible or visible oucomes
- Knowing a variety of adults, representative of different backgrounds and occupations, including potential role models
- Having the freedom to take part in the world of adults, but also to be free to retreat to a world of their peers
- Testing a developing value system in authentic situations
- Speaking and being heard, to know that they can make a difference;
- Achieving recognition for their accomplishments
- Having opportunities to make real decisions, within appropriate limits
- Receiving support and guidance from adults who appreciate their problems and their promise

As previously mentioned, these youngsters are changing quickly and dealing with many choices—not just the obvious ones or the day-to-day decisions that seem critical at the moment, but numbers of difficult choices that may determine the course of their lives far beyond the middle school years. Those of us who remember our own early adolescent years will recall facing a far simpler range of decisions in a world much less complex than the one today's young adolescents are trying to understand. We, too, were trying—often without being able to verbalize it—to figure out where we "fit in."

Young adolescents, then, are looking for entry points to the adult world, but at the same time they are fearful of joining that world. The institutions that serve these young people—and the school is surely the single institution of primary importance in the influence it can exert—face a formidable task and responsibility in helping their "clients" make sense of their world. We suggest that service learning is one strategy for addressing their needs.

Many young people must cope not only with the confusions and anxieties of adolescence but also with the very real stresses of lives lived in poverty and on the fringes of the "mainstream." For those, service learning can provide a kind of balance, a sense of the possible, and a feeling that they do have a stake and a place in a more hopeful world.

It is difficult to reconcile the needs of young people at this distinct developmental stage with the response that schools provide. At the precise moment when they require more freedom of movement, opportunities for independent choices, and role models outside of school and family to shape and test their emerging values, they are confronted with "a fundamental mismatch between the developmental needs of 13-year-olds and their classroom experiences in traditional junior highs."[3] Within a complex, rigid framework, the young person shuttles from one subject area to another, with a tightly prescribed agenda.

The isolation that can result from this solitary, individualized schedule may be compounded during the hours away from school.

> *Out of school hours constitute the biggest single block of time in the life of young adolescents. . . . About 40 percent of adolescents' waking hours are discretionary—not committed to other activities (such as eating,*

school, homework, chores, or working for pay). Many young adoles-
cents spend virtually all of this discretionary time without companion-
ship or supervision from responsible adults. They spend the time alone,
with peers, or in some cases, with adults who may exert negative influ-
ences on them or exploit them.[4]

Many young people are, in effect, raising themselves and/or each other
without the stabilizing influence of caring adults. How can we expect youth to
develop into productive adults and participating members of a free society if we
do not provide them with the education and preparation necessary to become
mature adults?

We often lament this widening gap between many young people and society by longing for the good old days. But, more constructively, we can face up
to the new reality, as exhorted by John Gardner:

Family and community have each suffered devastating blows, and to be
blunt about it, neither will ever be wholly reinstated in its old form. . . .
We wring our hands and wish that the reality would go away. But a
sounder course . . . is to say, "Given the reality, what can we do?" . . .
We see the loss of a sense of identity and belonging, of opportunities for
being needed and responding to need—and a rise in feelings of alien-
ation and powerlessness. People lose connection. More and more lost
and rootless people drift through life without allegiance to anything.
Too many of them lack any supportive network. But the sensible way of
dealing with the loss is to . . . stop lamenting the loss of old patterns
and ask what steps must be taken toward new patterns. . . . So where do
we start rebuilding community. My answer is "anywhere and every-
where we can."[5]

Although there is no one strategy that will magically reconnect young adolescents to America's institutions, service learning can be a powerful element in
an effort to "reinvent" community. In expecting young people to take on new
roles, develop skills and share their talent and energy in constructive ways,
service learning accomplishes multiple purposes, from exposing young people
to the world of work to making civic education come alive. But the most basic
accomplishment of a carefully constructed service learning program is the exposure of young people to the dual nature of caring, as they establish fundamental, human connections with caring adults, and at the same time practice the
behaviors of caring as they themselves serve in a wide variety of helping roles.

A DEFINITION

Descriptions of the glorious benefits of service learning can often be madden-
ingly vague, neglecting a basic fact that should be clear from the outset: Service

learning, by its very nature, is a complicated undertaking that requires constant attention and fine tuning. This is especially true of programs for the young adolescent. Establishing a rationale for the process and developing a detailed plan are essential to a program's ultimate success. In the following pages, we shall attempt to demystify the process. After 12 years of working with young adolescents in the Early Adolescent Helper Program, we know we can never be too concrete!

When we say *service learning* we mean the pairing of meaningful volunteer work with opportunities to reflect critically on the experience through regular group discussions. "There is strong evidence that a systematic reflective component is the factor that transforms an interesting and engaging experience into one which critically affects students' learning and development."[6] Our own experience suggests that, to be meaningful, the hands-on experience should cover a period of six weeks or more.

Reflection is the systematic preparation for the service experience and the ongoing provision for time to reflect on or process the service experience in a setting and climate conducive to learning and collaborative problem solving. Reflection is the factor that distinguishes service learning from community service. Collecting canned goods for the homeless or presenting a holiday concert at the local children's hospital are commendable activities, but they may or may not significantly add to the young people's understanding of others or of the world around them. In contrast, service learning offers a chance for substantial learning and the development of important human relationships so lacking in the lives of many young people today. In service learning, the collection of food may be connected to a geography unit in the social studies curriculum where water, soil resources, and the world food supply are studied. Or, in preparation for the hospital visit, a discussion of prenatal care and infant health needs may be part of a science class. A social studies unit on the local government that includes the rationale for statutes and ordinances that protect the welfare of children will open new ways of thinking about government and the role of laws in everyday life. The classroom as well as the hands-on experience will be enriched by making connections such as these, and the likelihood that lasting learning will ensue is increased.

Service learning can bring the curriculum to life for students *and* teachers. Jean Fazioli leads an intergenerational program at Bleeker Junior High School, a large, tidy yet undistinguished school building housing 1,024 students from seventh through ninth grades in Queens, New York. In sharp contrast to the mean streets of the usual urban landscape, modest detached houses with carefully manicured strips of lawn line the narrow streets of the middle-class community bordering the school. A stone's throw from LaGuardia Airport, the scene is surprising for its resemblance to many suburban settings. As in many other areas of Queens, the student population is drawn from immigrant groups from dozens of different countries.

Young people have been involved in service learning at Bleeker since 1991. Initially, the program was comprised of one class. Each year, it has grown; at present, it involves an entire seventh-grade house of 60 youngsters. Service has functioned as a vehicle to bring students together by emphasizing a common ability to help others. Work has ranged from Project TEACHER (Teaching Early Adolescents Child Care, Humanism, and Educational Responsibility), in which young adolescents work with children at the local elementary school and tutor their ESL (English as a Second Language) peers at Bleeker to Project WISE (Working In Senior Environments) in which students collaborate on a variety of projects such as creating an intergenerational quilt with senior citizens at a local community center.

When Jean Fazioli, a science teacher with 17 years' experience in New York City schools, talks about Bleeker's Helper Program, its impact on adults as well as students becomes clear. She speaks with enthusiasm about how the program has unexpectedly enriched her life. Jean was eager to become involved in service learning because of the benefits, both academic and social, that she thought the children would derive from the experience. But she was not prepared for the profound effect it had on her. She said,

> This has been an enormously enriching experience for me. First off, it has been a welcome change from the classroom. Just working in another setting, the senior center, has been stimulating. I enjoy thinking up projects with the children that they can do there. But the real surprise was the realization that I have made new friends and connections with the seniors. Teaching can be an isolating experience. This has become an important part of *my* week. I look forward to going and spending a little time with these wonderful people. They are the grandparents I never had. And my outlook has changed; I am more engaged in my work because it is an outlet for creativity.

When students and teachers collaborate in social action projects, they not only (perhaps for the first time) find common cause but they also discover each other as colleagues and co-workers. At Intermediate School 218, the Salome Urena Academies in Manhattan's Washington Heights, the Beautification Team exemplifies one such collaboration. At first glance, the neighborhood of the school looks like a perfect cityscape. A broad boulevard, with a lush park on one side, pre-war buildings with elaborate architectural flourishes, the occasional colorful awning of a greengrocer or bodega, lead to the schoolyard. But a closer look reveals the area's poverty and decay. Washington Heights has been characterized by *The Wall Street Journal* as the drug capital of the country. Tensions persist between the community of Dominicans and the local police. Despair is pervasive; young people face uncertain futures.

But I.S. 218 has brought hope to this troubled community. The school is a collaborative project of the New York City Board of Education and the Children's Aid Society. One of its four "schools-within-a-school" is the Community Service Academy. Its 300 students all participate in service through 25 different advisory groups. Raisa Vasquez facilitates the Beautification Team—a group of students who wanted to beautify their Washington Heights/Inwood neighborhood. Raisa Vasquez was able to guide the children to a more realistic, limited goal with which to start. After much discussion, they agreed that the gateway to the neighborhood was a subway tunnel connecting the Number 1 and Number 9 Broadway train platforms to the street level. This common entry to the neighborhood had become ugly and dangerous after years of neglect. The students wanted to change the first impression that people would have of their community.

The Beautification Team spent the school year trying to determine which city agency had jurisdiction over this tunnel. To their surprise, they discovered that no one claimed responsibility for its maintenance. Agencies played "hot potato" with their queries, each claiming that it fell to another to maintain the corridor. Students did research, made phone calls, wrote letters, petitioned the community board—all to no avail.

On a sparkling day in May when the Community Service Academy held its open house for parents and other interested community members, the Beautification Team invited Manhattan Borough President Ruth Messinger to attend a news conference in the subway tunnel. They were able to arrange for a news team from a local cable channel to tape an unforgettable scene as the Borough President presided over a conversation between representatives of the Transportation Department and the Metropolitan Transit Authority, who traded barbed remarks over who would step up to the cleaning and maintenance of the tunnel.

Ms. Messinger addressed the children saying, "You have done my job for me. It is my responsibility to see that good services are provided to the citizens of Manhattan and to do something about it when things go wrong. Neither my office or any other city agency was aware that the responsibility for the maintenance of this tunnel was unclear." The adults in the audience were astonished when the city officials finally promised to do a study and clean the tunnel. Cheers rang out. But the children were unmoved. They had been trying to get a straight answer for a year (to their minds, an eternity) and they would not be diverted. Lilly Trujillo, the spokesperson, a poised sixth-grader, took the microphone and queried, "What is your timeline for these repairs?" The children had learned their lessons well. As Raisa later explained, "I am learning along with the children. We are actually collaborating on this project. When we began, I did not know how to approach the issues. Together we developed a plan of action. Our questions are being answered together."

Incidentally, the city did clean and paint the tunnel in the summer of 1993. And although the graffiti has reappeared, there is surely reason to believe that the lessons of citizen participation will survive.

THE OVERARCHING IDEA

In order to derive the most benefit from service learning, it is critical to determine the rationale for its implementation. In other words, why are you doing service in the first place? This is not as obvious as it may sound. At the National Center for Service Learning in Early Adolescence, we often speak of an overarching idea for a service program. Over and above the belief that working in the community will be "good" for the young people, teachers need to examine their own reasons for introducing service. A program's overarching goal can be arrived at by tackling the following questions:

1. What are the pressing needs in the community? What are the students' most pressing concerns? How can the two be addressed in a mutually beneficial manner?
2. How will service make learning relevant? What connections can be made between the service experience and academic subject areas?
3. What impact will the service have on the children?
4. If the program is successful, how will the young people have changed as a result of their experience? What skills and sensitivities will they have gained in their community work?

Facing these questions in a disciplined, thoughtful, and honest manner will bring planning into focus. Young people should participate in the discussion wherever appropriate, so that their needs and abilities, rather than an adult perception of them, are central to the program.

Examples of overarching ideas are as varied as the schools and youth-serving agencies in which they operate:

- In an inner city middle school, a guidance counselor seeks a way to encourage youngsters with poor attendance records to find a reason to come to school. He makes a connection with the local Boys and Girls Club and places young people in every area of the Club's after-school program, from supervising outdoor play for pre-schoolers to providing homework help for school-aged youth.
- A science teacher wants to develop a hands-on environmental program. Research by her students uncovers a need in the local park for extra hands. Students plant bulbs and perform general maintenance for the park. Working side by side with a Parks Department worker who is developmentally disabled adds another dimension to their learning. As they work side by side, sharing a common purpose, the students' unease with some one who is "different," and his distrust of the young are replaced with mutual respect.
- A suburban middle school team is concerned about the apparent lack of caring and respect shown by students for each other and the faculty. The team develops an intensive intergenerational service program ensuring that the youth will collaborate with the same seniors each week on projects with tangible outcomes such as murals and cookbooks, giving each group an appreciation of the talents the others possess.

• The career counselor in a middle school situated near a large metropolitan hospital sees a need to counteract the impression that an M.D. is the only route to a career in the health field. To introduce young people to the array of health care careers and to encourage them to identify realistic goals, he arranges with the hospital's Director of Volunteers for a variety of service opportunities. Assisting in the kitchen, Mikhail becomes aware of the role of the dietitian; serving as a messenger between office and lab, Maria observes for herself the critical contribution the technician makes.

There are no guarantees, but a clear vision of the overarching theme and careful planning can forestall problems and ensure a successful start.

Identifying a rationale and focus for the service in advance facilitated the planning and implementation of a complex program at Wittenberg University in the 1992–93 school year. In order to receive a degree from Wittenberg, a small liberal arts college in Ohio, all students must engage in service to the community. Deborah Dillon, the Community Workshop Director, saw an opportunity for Wittenberg students to combat the growing isolation and "sense of estrangement" increasingly apparent among young adolescents. She envisioned linking college students, at-risk middle school students, and residents of a nursing and retirement home. She consulted with staff at the National Center for Service Learning in Early Adolescence, and applied to Ohio's Serve-America program, funded under the National and Community Service Act of 1990, for a grant. When funding was secured, Dillon set about involving staff members at Benjamin Franklin Middle School, the Community Workshop student coordinators, and the staff of the Ohio Masonic Home in the planning process. "Project Ben" was launched. She then invited representatives of the National Center to the campus for two intensive days of consultation.

The consultants met with the Community Workshop undergraduates and staff, middle school teachers, representatives of the Masonic Home as well as other community agencies, and finally with the eighth-graders. The two eighth-grade classes were wary, neither responsive nor openly negative. Jared sat with his cap pulled down over his forehead, head resting on the back of his chair. Kristin and Naomi hunched over a notebook, deep in whispered conversation. The college students were apprehensive, the consultants "cautiously optimistic." But as the college students became mentors to the middle school students, guiding them and helping them to prepare for their visits with the elderly, and as the residents of the retirement home welcomed the students, the weekly visits took on a party atmosphere. After a few weeks, positive comments began to be heard: "They're waiting for us when we come! . . . They really look forward to seeing us!" The Director of Volunteers at the Masonic Home reported that the student visits were "the highlight of the residents' week."

By term's end, students and residents had found "special friends." The middle school students brought youthful energy to the residents of the home, and in turn benefited from the connections made to two different generations. The linking of generations that had been part of the original theme did not end with the school year. During the summer, Shannon rode her bike, a distance of several miles, to continue her visits with Fanny at the Home. Also, serveral classmates corresponded with Sandy, student coordinator of the Community Workshop, as well as her fellow undergraduates in a continuation of the mentoring relationships that had been a part of Project Ben.

At St. Elizabeth School in New York City's Washington Heights, process and purpose appear to be quite different from the program we have just described. But the two have critical elements in common: Both started with a vision and a defined purpose (a purpose consistent with the broad goals of the institution in which the program would take root) and both have committed leadership. At St. Elizabeth, community service is a requirement, part of the preparation for confirmation. All seventh- and eighth-grade students are involved in service learning.

The Helper Program at St. Elizabeth is in its fourth year, and Sister Carmen Torres has developed a structure that works for the placement sites, the students, and (most of the time) even the school schedule. She says there are three key elements for a successful program: attention to interpersonal relationships, communication among all involved, and flexibility. She points out, "We're constantly having to change something," either because of a special assembly, a day of testing, a "snow day" or any of the multitude of unexpected departures from the usual schedule.

The seventh-grade service learning program is based on the Helper Program model developed by the National Center for Service Learning in Early Adolescence: The students have four "seminars" before they start. The first session is an overall orientation, It includes an examination of the meaning of *service,* the responsibilities of a Helper, and their own expectations. "Now," says Sister Carmen, "the eighth grade can give the first seminar, because they've had the experience." The next three sessions are devoted to introducing the work sites. A kindergarten or first-grade teacher arrives with a carton of books for little children. She models reading aloud, talks with the class about how Helpers serve in her classroom, and leaves the books behind for them to browse through and practice reading aloud as they will do if they elect to work with this classroom. The following week, a staff member from the preschool talks with them about early childhood and the differences between three-, four- and five-year-olds. And finally, someone from the senior center discusses what it is like to work with seniors from the community.

After the four introductory seminars, each seventh-grader submits an application that states, "I would like to work at ____ because. . . ." They also list a second choice. "It usually works out," says Sister Carmen, "that they get their first choice." Nevertheless, neither the opportunity to choose where they will serve nor the thorough introduction of the orientation seminars can entirely prepare the young people for the powerful experiences of working with younger children or with older adults. There are always surprises. After several weeks at the senior center, Maria wrote in her journal, "I have learned lots of responsibilities and ways in which I can care for other people. I have always cared for only myself, and service has helped me see that there are other people who need and can use my help." And Edwin made a different kind of discovery, one that may help him gain insights in a variety of circumstances: "Journal writing has helped me," he told a teachers' workshop audience, "because I didn't know how I felt about these kids until I started answering reflection questions."

In New York City's Community School District 5, Myrna Schiffman and Eileen Simon have developed service learning as an interdisciplinary initiative at the Mott Hall School. Ms. Schiffman teaches Home and Career Technology, a New York state requirement for grades 7 and 8; Ms. Simon teaches Communication Arts. The overarching theme unites their two areas and enriches both. Starting with the premise that to strengthen communication skills is a major goal of the middle school years, the two teachers have created a program that advances the goals of both subjects. They co-lead the weekly seminar in a classroom where, in large type, the bulletin board declares, "COMMUNITY SERVICE: A WAY OF LIFE." Beneath that heading, there is a list: "Workshops: Leadership, Dynamics of Working, 'Helping' Relationships, Communicating with Supervisors." Along with the permanent display are pages from *Community Reflections,* the student notebook the two teachers have created. It includes the guidelines for the multiple service roles open to the class, as well as pages for journal entries, a required assignment.

On a typical day, Ms. Simon opens the discussion: "Picking up from last week. . . . Some of you ran into trouble over handling the telephone. How do you call an agency, or answer when you're working at an agency? Can we have some volunteers to role-play what might happen?" Tata and Kesha conduct a brief conversation, complete with taking a message, spelling the caller's name, and repeating the number. The class critiques their technique. When Ian criticizes Tata for asking the message taker to repeat the number she had given, she points out that at the 34th Precinct, where she is a volunteer, they are required to repeat the caller's number. Ms. Simon occasionally interjects a comment, stressing the importance of communicating with clarity or suggesting that criticism should be substantiated by using an example. The pace is rapid; there is applause for a good performance and Ms. Schiffman quickly moves the discussion forward: "Today was much better than last week. We'll try it again next week."

"Now I'd like to spend some time on situations several of you mentioned in your journals that might occur in any site: You arrive at the center and the person in charge says your supervisor is not there, and there's nothing for you to do. How do you handle it?" Ms. Schiffman assumes the role of the Precinct House Desk Sergeant, and two students are the volunteers. Several solutions are proposed. The students offer to continue, on their own, the tasks begun the previous week, but the "Sergeant" says, "I can't let you be in that setting unsupervised."

The discussion continues. Students' suggestions include: "Go home," "Go around the Center and see if anyone needs help," "Call the school," and "Just sit around." Ms. Schiffman summarizes the discussion, points out that "going home is not an option. You're on school time, and to go home is to be truant," and goes on to praise the group's suggestion of offering to help elsewhere at the site, as a creative attempt to problem solve.

The 50-minute class period is drawing to a close, yet no one is gathering books, shuffling feet, or exhibiting any of the behaviors that those who know middle schoolers have learned to expect. In preparation for next week's discussion, Ms. Simon notes that several students have encountered some problems when serving as tutors. "How *does* a tutor connect with a child? What problems do you see? I see lots. What I want to get to is how a child gets to know you, because they'll learn better then. We'll talk about that next week."

In all these instances, the coordinators or program planners have a clear idea of why they are instituting service learning and how they want the young people to benefit. Clarity of purpose will facilitate orientation and training, planning for the reflection seminars, making the connection to curriculum, and evaluating the program.

Defining and narrowing the overarching idea is critical to the success of a program. It is tempting to set multiple goals, because service learning can indeed serve a range of purposes, from encouraging citizen activism to acquiring employability skills, and from teaching parenting to developing competence in math or reading. In thinking about the overarching theme, then, a healthy dose of realism is in order; no program, no matter how well conceived, can be all things to all people. In connecting school to community, service learning involves many different constituencies: young people, educators, community-based agencies, neighborhood residents, administrators, parents, and so on. The more the different groups are involved in the planning, the more smoothly the program will operate and the richer it will become. Planning takes time. It takes time to develop an overarching idea, to work with the administration in fleshing out that idea, to identify the funds for such needs as substitute teachers and transportation, to find a place in the school schedule, to connect with outside agencies and determine their needs, and to develop evaluation tools. But time and care devoted to planning at the start will pay lasting dividends in program quality and longevity.

To move beyond an initial positive response to the *idea* of service learning and to make it a *reality*, it will be useful to think about three separate phases in this transition. Phase I is critical; it builds the foundation for all that will follow. It is the time when support for the program should be identified and nurtured, when potential pitfalls or problems can be foreseen and forestalled. Phase II can be seen as the time for "getting down to brass tacks," for making the practical arrangements that may appear to be trivial but that often determine the success or failure of an innovation. It is the time for enlisting the adult leader(s), for completing arrangements with placement sites, and for recruiting or identifying the student participants. The start of Phase III should be used to clear away the "nuisance factors"—obtaining parent or guardian consent, completing forms the placement site may require, attending to transportation needs, and so on.

In the first flush of enthusiasm, it is tempting to overlook the step-by step mapping that is sometimes tedious and may seem to be ensnared in bureaucratic process. But because we have learned from our own experience how much grief can be avoided when each component receives careful attention before program implementation, we believe that it will be helpful to describe those steps in some detail, keeping in mind that no two schools or placement sites will have identical characteristics or requirements.

We have said that Phase I is critical to the success of the program; perhaps the single most critical element in Phase I is *identifying and inspiring support for service learning.* Parents, administrators, students and teachers who understand and value the power of service learning are its most effective advocates. The school-based program where the support of the administration (both the central office and the building principal) goes beyond the perfunctory, providing planning time and flexible scheduling is off to a good start. The Parent-Teacher Association, the local chapters of the American Federation of Teachers and the National Education Association, and community groups such as the United Way, Chamber of Commerce, and Rotary are all potential allies. They may be involved in proposing a theme or specific projects, in planning, and/or providing a wide variety of help, from guest speakers to transportation.

It is at this stage that the overarching idea should be developed. When students, parents, and staff collaborate to identify the theme or purpose, the next steps are likely to follow with a minimum of stress. Phase I concludes with a review of resources available in the service learning field. Materials and services already exist, and time and energy will be well spent in tailoring these resources to local needs rather than in "reinventing the wheel." The National Center for Service Learning in Early Adolescence has compiled a service learning bibliography, dealing specifically with programs for young adolescents. (To obtain the bibliography, write to: National Center for Service Learning in Early Adolescence, CUNY Graduate Center, 25 West 43rd Street, Suite 612, New York, NY 10036-8099.)

Phase II is the time for fitting the pieces in place. It sets the stage for program implementation, so that when the curtain goes up on Phase III the props and players are in position. The Program Leader, ideally a teacher or counselor who understands and embraces the role of *facilitator*, as opposed to that of dispenser of knowledge, is selected at this stage. The adult leader should be an individual who will *create a safe environment in which young people feel free to discuss their questions and concerns.* Young adolescents need the opportunity to test new roles and know that their successes and failures will be considered respectfully. The Leader creates a climate that ensures that learning will accompany service.

The process for recruiting students should be determined at this point. The Program Leader recruits the students. Some schools use a formal application process; some have students submit a resumé and references. We suggest that students be recruited from all academic levels. Almost without exception, those who have observed young adolescents in community service report that they seem more mature, focused, and competent in the service setting. One of the benefits of service learning is that it brings out the best in people. It allows youth to see themselves and be perceived by their peers and adults in new and more positive ways. This in turn improves their attitude toward school. Nowhere is this more forcefully demonstrated than in the heterogeneous group, where at-risk students often shine more brightly than the academic "stars."

In some schools, a language arts or social studies class becomes the setting for service learning, with all students participating. In others, a math or science teacher may find ways to enliven the curriculum by integrating a service component into his or her class. Where service learning is tied to a particular discipline, student involvement is automatic. (In the ideal middle school, where cross-disciplinary learning and teaching is the norm, the service component can enrich all aspects of the program.)

During Phase I, community agencies are informed of the program and representatives become involved in the planning. As Phase II draws to a close, those agencies and others can be approached as possible placement sites. The proposed program is explained, and the benefits to adolescents, to the populations they will serve and to the community are spelled out. *The young people, who frequently know the neighborhood more intimately than their teachers, can serve as resources in this effort.* With the proper preparation, young people can make the calls and line up placement sites, making this a part of the learning experience.

Finally, the painstaking planning and preparation is completed, and it is time for Phase III—the formal launching of the service learning initiative. At this point, it is important to learn from the experience of others: Many a well-conceived program has foundered because of unanticipated logistical problems that have little or no bearing on program content, but can nevertheless jeopardize a successful start-up. Again, because no two sites are alike, a final checklist will vary, but most Program Leaders will want to make certain that they have answered some basic questions:

Will transportation be required?

Will students need to be released from school?

Are parent consent forms needed?

Are arrangements with the placement site completed, and clear?

Is there agreement on the number of hours expected, the number of young people per day?

Are there supervisors at the service site who particularly want—or do not want—young aides?

Have guidelines for ongoing communication between school or agency and placement site been established?

Does the placement site require students to have a Social Security number, health certificate, or other forms?

With the all-important logistics taken care of, the Program Leader launches Phase III with a clear seminar plan. The seminar plan will reflect the overarching idea established at the start of planning. *Seminars will prepare young people for their service and introduce them to the background of the people they will meet.* The introductory seminars provide an excellent opportunity to invite outside speakers such as the volunteer coordinator of an agency where the young people will volunteer. The young people are venturing into unknown territory; the Program Leader and the placement site representative can help to allay any concerns they may have. In each reflection seminar, *a balance must be struck between the facilitator's agenda and the young people's need to solve problems about week-to-week experiences.*

As the service learning experience unfolds, theoretical concepts such as (1) the definition of *community* and the individual's responsibility to that community; (2) the meaning of service, altruism, or empathy; and (3) the need for problem solving and teamwork at the service sites will be considered in seminars. Because young adolescents are at the beginning of the transition from concrete to abstract reasoning, it is important, in order to ensure their understanding of the broader concept, to connect theory to reality. For example, to understand the role of empathy in working with the elderly, young people can role-play situations where they experience difficulty in grasping small objects. (Taping the thumb and first finger together can simulate a problem often associated with arthritis.) They can explore the idea of community by drawing diagrams of the different communities to which they belong —family, school, church or synagogue, clubs—and interpreting them for each other. The principles of problem solving and collaboration can be made concrete in the seminar setting by having students work in groups to build a three-dimensional structure and then examine the part each person played or did not play in the process. Exercises such as these make the *learning* in service learning conscious and heighten the students' awareness of their own growth.

Early in Phase III, the students will visit the placement sites. They may want to introduce themselves through letters and snapshots in advance. It is important, as the on-site work begins, to keep in mind the traits that uniquely characterize the early adolescent, as discussed at the start of this chapter. Because they are themselves going through a period of rapid change and of testing limits, they often demonstrate a particular affinity for preschoolers—especially the four-year-olds!—in day care. And because they are in many ways on the fringes of the larger society, too young for employment, too old for the play of childhood—they may find common ground with the elderly, who also find themselves on the sidelines.

When the school-based Program Leader and the agency liaison person can plan together for the students' first "official" visit, taking into account what we know about this age group, the odds for a program's successful start will be greatly improved. Remembering that these young people may be shy or, on the other hand, overconfident, that they will want above all to feel needed and accepted, will help the adults to structure activities for this crucial "get-acquainted" period.

Throughout the duration of the service learning initiative, the Program Leader visits placements sites to observe young people and to confer with site supervisors. During this time the seminars continue wherein the students share information, problems, successes, and observations from their site experience. They may also prepare special activities for the placement site. At the same time, the seminar provides a setting for discussion of some of the concerns typical of the middle school youngster—the struggle to make sense of their world and to think about where they fit in.

We strongly advise planners to include a special activity—such as a pizza party, a presentation about the program, or a book of essays or pictures—to mark the completion of the service learning project or program. Young adolescents respond to ceremony; rewards and recognition are important. Moreover, it is important for the larger community to acknowledge their accomplishments, which contradict the stereotype of the self-absorbed teenager that many adults accept.

As mentioned at the outset, these young adolescents are a bundle of contrasts, energy, and questions. They need to test, to have freedom within clearly defined limits. They need connections with adults in different roles. They need lots of opportunities to explore. They need a sense of their own competency, and they need to learn that they can succeed. But they need, too, to be allowed to fail, to learn from that failure, and to move ahead. Most of these learnings and experiences are difficult for many early adolescents to come by in the ordinary classroom. Service learning—interacting with others outside of their usual world and with the environment, creating change, learning and using new skills—provides a setting for these experiences. Combined with classroom preparation and ongoing reflection, it can be a powerful factor in helping youngsters negotiate the early adolescent years, and in making the transition to maturity and responsible citizenship.

ENDNOTES

1. Lipsitz, J. (1984). *Successful Schools for Young Adolescents.* New Brunswick, NJ: Transaction Books.

2. Toepfer, C. F. (1988, February). "What to Know about Young Adolescents." *Social Education, 52*(1):10–12.

3. Staff. (1992). "The Seventh Grade Slump and How to Avoid It." *Harvard Education Letter, 8*(1).

4. Carnegie Council on Adolescent Development. (1992). *A Matter of Time: Risk and Opportunity in the Non-School*

Hours. New York: Carnegie Corporation of New York, p. 28.

5. Gardner, J. W. (1992). *Reinventing Community.* Carnegie Corporation Occasional Papers. New York: Carnegie Corporation, pp. 4–5.

6. National Center for Service Learning in Early Adolescence. (1991). *Reflection: The Key to Service Learning.* New York: Author, p. 1.

11

Service Learning

A Catalyst for Social Action and School Change at the Middle Level

WOKIE WEAH   MADELEINE WEGNER

> *If you're coming over to help me, don't bother. But if you're coming over because you think your liberation is bound up with mine, let's work together.*
> *— AUSTRALIAN ABORIGINAL WOMAN*

Whether writing in the early or late twentieth century, working among American students or Brazilians who were illiterate, educational reformers from John Dewey to Paolo Freire have echoed the sentiment of this aboriginal saying. That said, teaching that focuses on creating independent thinkers capable of working cooperatively to fight oppression—in all its guises—is still relatively rare today. Instead, people merely retool the training of students to succeed within an educational system widely agreed to be both antiquated and ineffective as well as a socioeconomic system that suffers from a similar need for critical overhaul.

The latter concern has led us to wonder: What will happen if the most innovative, cooperative, interdisciplinary learning is not applied outside the classroom until students are finished with their education? and Why not allow real-world issues to drive students' need for academic, interpersonal and citizenship skills?

These questions need not remain rhetorical. In virtually every state in the country, a methodology that incorporates the best teaching/learning techniques and applies them to current social issues is taking hold: service learning.

- In New Mexico, for example, middle and high school students produced 1,000 adobe bricks to restore a crumbling 250-year-old church at Picuris Pueblo while applying their geometry, chemistry, and construction skills.

- In Michigan, elementary students practice writing and editing as they create books and deliver them to new mothers in local hospitals through the literacy promotion project Rock-n-Read.
- In northern Minnesota, students from 16 schools work cooperatively to collect, analyze and submit data on the St. Louis River to the Minnesota Pollution Control Agency. Throughout the project, while hip-deep in river water, rather than behind desks in a classroom, they learn about sediment analysis and water chemistry.

In each project, students see new relationships among academic subjects, demonstrate mastery of disciplines, and deepen their understanding of important social issues while investigating and implementing solutions to community needs. As education reformers Jim Kielsmeier, founder and director of the National Youth Leadership Council (NYLC),[1] and Joe Nathan, director of the Center for School Change,[2] noted in a *Phi Delta Kappan* article: "When teachers integrate service and social action into their academic programs, students learn to communicate, to solve problems, to think critically, and to exercise other higher-order skills. They learn these things because they are deeply immersed in a consequential activity—not a metaphor, not a simulation, not a vicarious experience mediated by print, sound or machine" (1991, p. 741).

Some of the most effective examples of service learning are practiced by a consortium (the NYLC-sponsored Generator School Project) of 38 K–8 schools around the country.[3] These schools serve as demonstration sites that build support for service learning by experimenting with, practicing, and sharing their curricular ideas on how to link academic learning to community service. Over the three years of the project's existence, educators in Arkansas, Michigan, Minnesota, New Mexico, Pennsylvania, South Carolina, and Washington have become a national community of service learning practitioners, all of whom are linked by regional centers in each of these states. These regional centers provide professional development, gather curriculum, and convene teachers and students to share ideas among themselves and with other interested school districts during regional and national conferences. Much of the material gathered from these sites will be disseminated beyond the Generator Schools through the database services of the National K–12 Service-Learning Clearinghouse/Cooperative, based at the University of Minnesota and managed by NYLC.[4]

The program descriptions that follow are representative of geographically diverse school settings, and the social issues studied reflect various communities' differences and needs. Although the schools' approaches differ, the goal remains the same: inspiring students to see new relevance in their education by applying their skills to pressing community needs.

In one case, developing a curriculum that blended current education reform recommendations with traditional Native-American values was the primary concern for a Bureau of Indian Affairs school in New Mexico. In another case, gender and race became the generative themes behind curriculum development for an urban Minneapolis school. And, in a final example, an empty school courtyard blossomed into a school/community "gathering place," in the process uniting a previously fractured school/community relationship. Each example demonstrates how service learning can be used to inspire action and how educators can foster learning that helps students become agents of change.

This chapter will explore the latter concern—profiling service learning ideas that have been developed at the aforementioned Generator Schools. The descriptions that follow are meant to be inspiring rather than prescriptive, for any service learning project is uniquely tied to its community and therefore defies lock-step instructions for implementation. All the projects, however, rely on the leadership of those who are rarely asked to serve others: young, often low-income students in urban, rural, and reservation schools.

CREATING A CURRICULUM THAT AFFIRMS CULTURAL PRIDE IN ACOMA, NEW MEXICO

For Native Americans, community service is an ancient concept, so integral to the culture that various tribal groups have their own words for it. In Cherokee, *gadugi* refers to the call to bring people together. In the Pueblos Keres language, *si-yu-dze* translates as "everybody's work," much like the Zuni expression *yanse'lihanna.*

McClellan Hall, Southwestern Regional Generator School Director, describes this Native tradition of community work as "a learning-by-doing process," usually under the mentorship of relatives and elders. He explained, "Customs, skills and languages were (at one time) transmitted according to locally determined priorities; the extended family clan system and larger community provided a safety net for all." Although the concept of communal work is deeply rooted in Native traditions, it has not been as deliberately fostered in the latter twentieth century as it once was. Yet, the need for this kind of service learning has been rekindled by contemporary issues of environmental degradation, drug and alcohol abuse, teen pregnancy, school drop-out rates and gang involvement.

Hall, who also is founder and director of the National Indian Youth Leadership Project (NIYLP)[5] and the teachers he works with have been breathing new life into the concept, instilling the community service ethic in a series of summer camps and maintaining it through school-based programs during the academic year. For the past 11 years, Hall's summer camps for middle schoolers based out of Gallup, New Mexico, have been providing Native-American youth with exposure to the traditional roots of community service. (Hall also has brought the camp model to states as wide ranging as Alaska, Michigan, Maine, Washington and Montana.) The focus of the camp is on *habilitation*—the process of becoming capable—not through self-centered individualism, but through interdependency. "We're about getting young people to use this up here," Hall says, pointing toward his brow, "getting kids to think before they act." Students often begin as middle school campers, return as high school students to be trained as counselors, and continue their involvement as adult sponsors of middle school groups.

Employing indirect teaching, camp staff use metaphor, story telling, and role modeling to teach team-building and leadership skills—skills that provide the foundation for effective community work. These techniques work well, Hall says, because in most traditional cultures, it is not common to discuss certain topics directly. Instead, he and his staff often tell stories that anthropomorphize animals (e.g., the coyote) to teach lessons of drug and alcohol abuse to the younger campers. "Education becomes a more open-ended process," says Hall. "We don't prescribe that everyone is to 'get' the same thing at the same time; we're not lecturing to kids about what they shouldn't do. . . . We're asking questions rather than giving answers." Hall contends that Indian and non-Indian students alike respond well to such an approach as it is more respectful than a teacher simply imparting answers.[6]

Throughout the camp, Hall and his staff are careful to model the kinds of behavior they are striving to instill. Deliberate role-playing is a part of the training, where emotionally and physically challenging situations are simulated, followed by a reflective session of questioning.

In an activity entitled *morals and ethics,* for example, participants experience the unequal distribution of resources and corresponding issue of personal responsibility. Although many options are possible with this activity, Hall often uses a situation in which students are divided into groups of "haves" and "have nots" and given varying degrees of equipment and food with which to get across a lake.

Processing this experience with the participants afterwards is critical. Hall is careful to begin the reflection on the experience with simple questions such as: What happened? and Who took the leadership roles? He then progresses to more interpretive questions on power inequities, asking: How did it feel to possess the better equipment when you knew your peers had less?

From simulation activities such as this, activities that emphasize team building and servant leadership, Hall aims to build in young people the value of doing something for others and for the greater community.

It is an ethic that Norbert Hill, Director of the American Indian Science and Engineering Society, recognizes as essential to traditional ways of living. "Service learning is . . . part of the fabric of our life, our well-being and survival. In my tradition, to be noble is to give to those who have less. . . . You are a servant of the people, and the people must come first."[7]

Building on these traditional notions of service, the culmination of each camp is a service project day. One year, camp participants and staff worked for the National Park Service, installing a composting toilet facility and information bulletin boards, helping build a year-round weather station, and clearing trails and weeding around Anasazi ruins. Another year, campers painted the administrative office complex of a pueblo, including the governor's office. While most of the staff and students painted, a smaller group taught songs and games to preschool children in the summer free-lunch program. An ongoing service project, begun six summers ago, involves planting trees on a nearby Navajo reservation.

After the camps, students are challenged to implement service-oriented projects in their home communities. For those students who return to NIYLP-affiliated Generator Schools, many of the camp's tenets are reinforced by their teachers who support the students in their efforts to address social needs and meet academic goals through service learning.

One such school is the Sky City Community School in Acoma, New Mexico. Located an hour west of Albuquerque, the original Acoma village (pueblo) is located on a mesa, 400 feet above the surrounding desert plain. A magical place of sandstone and yucca, it is the oldest continuously inhabited city in the United States and it has evidence of settlement dating to 1150 A.D. Most families in the nearby town still maintain family homes atop the mesa, and some still live there year round.

To tour the mesa is to believe the culture is alive and well; men still gather in their *kivas* (isolated rooms in the pueblo) for conversation; and Acoma pottery, distinguished by its fine geometric patterns painted with yucca leaves, is still produced by its residents.

But, according to tribal member and teacher Donna Boynton, the area is not immune to problems typically thought of as urban. She began a mentoring/ tutoring program three years ago, Buddy Works, in response to the rumors that gangs were beginning to recruit Native adolescents and to the increase of "irresponsible" behavior she saw developing among some of her students. She felt that if she could impress on adolescents the importance of positive approaches to child rearing, and the skills and responsibilities involved, she might have a way to influence their later parenting decisions and inspire an ethic of community childcare. Like Hall, she believes that "If I can get them to become responsible to someone other than themselves, if they can understand that there is someone who really needs them, . . . they will develop other skills that would go beyond their school years."

Through her elective program, middle school students choose at least one kindergarten or first grade "buddy" with whom they spend one class period each week. Prior to the weekly meeting, the older students develop lesson plans based on the developmental skills identified through the Prevention of Early Childhood Failure program: receptive and expressive language skills, auditory and visual skills, and gross and fine motor skills.

Primary goals of the program include:

- Transferring responsibility to seventh- and eighth-grade students to help develop their social and academic skills
- Teaching responsibility and child rearing skills to seventh- and eighth-grade students

- Creating an environment conducive to the development of readiness skills for kindergarten and first-grade students
- Providing a tutoring program for kindergarten students

Having taught the middle school students these skills and how to write a lesson plan, Boynton begins each week with a brainstorming session. Typically, she lists on a chalkboard the skill areas just mentioned. The students consider the skills they would like to introduce or reinforce with their younger buddies, then come up with ideas for activities that relate to a particular season, celebration, or reading. Activities often range from developing games or puzzles, to making accordion, pop-up, or shape books. The students choose an activity, discuss whether the activity selected will meet all the objectives of the developmental skills identified, and write out their lesson plans.

Lesson plans for Buddy Works look as sophisticated as any that a teacher might prepare. On the left-hand column, the buddy's name is listed, followed by the activity, its objectives, the methods to be used to teach the objective, and the materials needed.

In a recent session, students planned a Sandwich Day. One of the middle school students, Tahama, planned to first read the book *The Biggest Sandwich Ever* aloud to her younger buddies, Nicole and Dean. She decided that she would then help them complete a construction paper sandwich book to practice their fine motor skills. At the same time, the younger buddies would tell her about their favorite sandwich, so that she could write a story for them involving the sandwich—an exercise in receptive and expressive language skills. The biggest challenge, according to Tahama, was that "my buddy Dean did not pay attention very well, so that was something we had to work on throughout the year."

As Boynton attests, often the students discover that they are including most of the skill areas—even some they had not anticipated—and also are integrating multiple disciplines.

Another group of students read Pat Hutchins's book *Rosie's Walk* aloud to their students. The story involves a chicken that goes for a walk and is stalked by a fox. Following the story line, the middle school students developed an obstacle course for their kindergarten buddies, aiming to encourage motor and expressive language skills. The middle schoolers then took the process a step further, and labeled points in the obstacle course with "position" words and phrases (i.e., prepositions), such as *through the yard, under the fence,* and *around the beehive.*

Still another student's application of the preposition lesson involved creating a board game for his buddy. Eighth-grader Cletus created a trip across a deserted island, complete with shark-infested waters. In traveling across the island, his buddy not only learned how to avoid the sharks but also his reading, color identification, and counting skills were reinforced.

At the end of the activity, as with each Friday Buddy Works session, the students reflect on their experiences, assessing both successes and struggles, and scheming about their next project. As 13-year-old Nicole wrote, "I helped my buddy learn his numbers, colors, shapes, and how to write his ABCs; but the thing I like most about Buddy Works is having a good little buddy right beside me."

In essence, Buddy Works is designed to give those involved in the peer tutoring project "a sense of shared responsibility—to be caring, and nurturing, and to build a relationship which won't end at the end of the year, but will last a lifetime," explains Sky City School principal, Charlotte Garcia. An added benefit is that the middle school students reinforce their academic skills through tutoring their younger peers.

The program recently was deemed "exemplary" by the Bureau of Indian Affairs, and has been so successful that Boynton has had trouble keeping the students' generosity toward one another in check. When a student transferred schools last year, his buddy sent flowers to the new school. As she says, "It's a sharing that's positive. They're friends beyond grades 6, 7, and 8."

Boynton also has developed a Parent Works program. Kindergarten parents gather once a month to meet with the middle school students who model the kinds of reading and writing activities they share with their younger friends. This approach extends to the family the literacy promotion already underway. As Boynton says, "By having students work with parents, there's even a greater bond. Each group touches the next, the bond widens and gets out into the community." If the squeals in the Sky City library are proof, this approach is as effective today as it was a thousand years ago.

For the middle school student, being a buddy means he or she plays different roles—a friend in the hallways, a teacher in class, and a big brother/sister at a traditional feast. Along the way, the middle schooler also gets early exposure to possible career and parenting decisions. The exposure to teaching may have long-term benefits for Native schools, where non-Native teachers outnumber Native teachers by a large margin.

Of course, there have been benefits that outreach the original goals of the program. Many of the students remain friends not only outside of school but also beyond the year they are enrolled in the class. And the friendships that develop often bring out the best in otherwise troubled middle school students. "I've seen students be very ornery and negative with adults. But, for the moment they're with their buddies, they're patient and understanding. It's really touching to see them working so closely," says Boynton.

Like the students, the teachers at the surrounding Generator Schools in Gallup, Laguna, Taos, and Zuni share their struggles and victories. They gather during the summer for a residential teacher training camp, as well as throughout the year for curriculum development projects, regional and national workshop presentations, and school exchanges. In the spring of 1994, the National Service-Learning Conference was held in Albuquerque, so the New Mexico Generator Schools hosted visits from teachers and students representing other Generator Schools around the country. With these visitors from outside New Mexico, projects that first appear to be indigenous to New Mexico gained broader exposure and interpretation. In a program such as Buddy Works there are lessons not only for other schools serving Native populations but also for schools hoping to help nurture other cultural heritages and aiming to build understanding for other culturally based learning styles.

Lakota writer Vine Deloria Jr. (1990) has offered further testimony to the effectiveness of blending instructional methods that are at once traditional and new: "The old ways of educating affirmed the basic principle that human personality was derived from accepting the responsibility to be a contributing member of a society" (p. 16).

It is this principle that Hall believes has "much to offer the process of reforming Native education." In Buddy Works, when younger students understand and uphold the mentoring relationships that are traditional in their heritage, the hope of keeping these practices alive in the face of contemporary social challenges and numerous education reform initiatives—some of which do not enhance traditional ways of learning—is reinvigorated. By reestablishing traditional mentoring relationships, not only do students improve their academic skills through tutoring but they also experience the benefits of contributing to their school community—a step toward developing an ethic of positive social action that is lifelong and benefits the larger community.

BUILDING A THEMATIC YEAR-LONG CURRICULUM AROUND RACISM AND SEXISM IN MINNEAPOLIS, MINNESOTA

Four African- and European-American middle school girls chat, perched on urban schoolyard steps.

"Look at them black wannaabes," says one, glancing at two European-American boys dressed in oversized shorts. "And I know they can hear me," she says to her friends.

"I don't appreciate you talking about us like that," retorts one of the boys.

"I can talk to you anyway I want to," the provoker continues. "Boy, don't make me hurt you."

"I wish you would," the boy responds.

It is the sort of conversation neither educators nor parents want to believe is happening in schools. It contains the ammunition of an administrator's nightmare, and it could lead to headline-making violence.

Fortunately, however, the scene is staged. And the provokers as well as the recipients of these remarks are middle school student authors, actors, directors, and producers of a skit—part of a year-long study of gender and race at another Generator Project site, Webster Open School, in Minneapolis, Minnesota.

The action on the steps freezes and one of the girls interjects: "Has this ever happened to you? Let's look at what could have happened."

In the alternative ending to the skit, the girls ask the boys to go with them to a movie instead of instigating an argument by taunting them with assumptions. For these middle schoolers, social action begins with their peers and with their immediate world. The second ending to the skit may seem a simplistic answer to a charged situation, but it reflects defusing techniques the students have learned through simulation games, workshops, and artists' residencies held over the course of a school year.

This skit is just one of many student-produced artistic manifestations of a year-long study of race and gender entitled The Forum Project. To move the students from empathy to positive action, local artists worked with students in small groups, helping them draw from their own encounters to shape their performances and visual arts and teaching them professional techniques. The 80 students who participated in the Forum's training in turn trained 80 more fellow Webster students in a peer education model that resulted in significant gains in multicultural awareness for the direct Forum participants, and measurable gains for those students who were trained by the Forum participants.

One group produced a rap video entitled "Discrimination on School Grounds" in which a convincing rapper says, "Color, gender [bias], racism—just stop it!" as school scenes flash to the music. Another group created over-sized masks, representative of the cultures at the school. And a third developed a game show in which three of the four audience members/participants were systematically discriminated against.

Some groups have performed more than 15 times to audiences ranging from younger students at suburban schools, to a women's group from the YWCA, to students and teachers attending the National Service-Learning Conference in Albuquerque, New Mexico. Often, the student performers are an ethnically diverse, heterogeneous group performing for more homogenous audiences, as they did during a 1994 visit to the Hill City School—a rural Generator site in northern Minnesota. The postperformance discussions force the Webster students to further articulate their discoveries, to help audiences identify bias, and to develop strategies for confronting it. The middle school students' insights—developed over a period of nine months, and played out at home, in classrooms, and on stage—provide the backbone to the confidence the students exhibit as they lead these postperformance discussions.

In one such exchange, students recounted an incident of gender bias in the classroom. Commenting on a teacher's response to a map-making exercise, seventh-grader Natalie said, "One boy had his square perfect. So did a lot of girls in our class, but he only commented on the one boy's square."

Eighth-grader Tanya advised, "Then you ought to talk to him."

"Yeah, I know, but I don't really know what to say to him," Natalie responded.

Another girl, Jenny, chimed in. "If either sex is getting treated that way, I think that we have enough people that feel strongly about it to bring it up, to make something of it . . . to make sure that it doesn't get *not* noticed. . . . You can bring it to the teacher's attention. Or if you don't feel comfortable talking to that teacher, you can tell a teacher you do feel comfortable talking to."

Discussions such as this illustrate Kyra's, one of the student writer/actors, goals of the postperformance discussions with audiences: "I hope that we can teach people that they have the power to do what they want to do . . . that they shouldn't put up with stuff when people are treating them different because of their gender or race."

Teacher Phirun Fricke agrees that there have been both attitudinal and behavioral changes among staff and students alike: "If you (a teacher) say things like, 'Well, you know when you get married your wife can do your cooking,' you'll have 20 kids on you in a second. Whereas, before [The Forum], they might have let it pass by."

Audience member and sixth-grader Shane wrote in the school newspaper about his newfound understanding of prejudice based on training from the Forum students. "You may think there is no cure for the 'isms,' but you just have to fight them. Fighting them doesn't mean 'putting up your dukes.' It means learning about the 'isms.' "

The project grew out of drama teacher Cynthia Rogers's fascination with the idea of sustaining a thematic focus across disciplines. Like Harvard professors of education Howard Gardner and Vito Perrone, Rogers believes that students and teachers need to be able to immerse themselves in issues that transcend disciplinary divisions and that are relevant to their lives, particularly in this "information age." When she surveyed Webster teachers, looking for issues that were common across grades and throughout disciplines, she found that most felt that racism and sexism were recurrent issues for students. Rogers also believes that students need a community to turn to for regular discourse on those issues, so that they can arrive at new levels of understanding. With this newfound understanding, they become capable of teaching others—the point at which real learning, and service to others, occurs.

Teacher Char Johnson says she believes that the year-long study of racism and sexism will result in lifelong respect for diversity. "Students recognize that it's important. After all, they were able to teach someone how important it is." Of the students' culminating performances, she says, "To convey an idea, you have to have a certain amount of dedication to the project, so you put the effort into learning about it. At the beginning, I think students thought, 'Oh this will be too much work.' And then by the second time through, they sort of became infected with the idea. . . . That's the whole idea, to help them understand the benefits of responsibility, of following through." Teacher Bill Holden has already seen evidence that the students' ability to plan and execute a project for an audience seems to have "rolled over into other classes."

The Forum Project works particularly well at Webster Open School, with its tradition of community-based, interdisciplinary, thematic curriculum. In addition to the Forum Project, 25 to 50 service learning projects are underway on any given day, both inside and outside the school. Evidence of service-learning activities is everywhere. One classroom has become a community museum dedicated to the diversity of ethnicities that populate this urban neighborhood. Another houses seedlings soon to be replanted in downtown Minneapolis. In another, bat houses are under construction, which will be relocated to nearby islands in the Mississippi River so that their residents can provide a natural means of mosquito control.

The school looks like the "open" school that it is. A rampway, with a library at the mezzanine level, connects a series of brightly painted classrooms divided by movable partitions that rarely reach all the way to the ceiling. Classes (except for kindergarten) are composed of two- and three-grade level groupings.

The school also is a magnet for Ukrainian and Hmong students with limited English proficiency. It has a student population that reflects its urban setting: 26 percent Asian American, 18 percent African American, 5 percent Native American, 1 percent Hispanic American, and 50 percent northern European American. Children's voices, representing 28 home languages, dominate the hallways and classrooms.

But perhaps most critical to this project, according to Rogers, is the necessary mix of teacher attitudes: those willing to be problem solvers as well as letting themselves make mistakes. At the inception of Forum's planning, Rogers called these fellow teachers to a planning meeting and asked them to bring their syllabi and a teaching partner. She wanted to involve them in the kinds of "messy, elastic" discussions that she sees as essential to the process of curriculum development, in particular—and learning, in general. As Rogers says, "Teacher's lives [should be] a series of conversations that ask questions and move kids to really think. . . . When we ask hard questions of kids and guide them through various thinking strategies to reach logical conclusions, they develop deeper and more complex solutions. They are moved . . . to reasoning that allows them to see a variety of viewpoints. After all, life demands more than simple answers for fill-in-the-blank formats."

Out of that conversation, and the weekly teacher/student meetings that followed, grew the Project's focus on gender and race. The issues raised during those conversations became the Project's driving questions—its *generative themes:*

- Why are we so uncomfortable around people who are different from us?
- Can a multiracial and/or multigender community exist in harmony?
- What brings division or conflict to such a community?

From these questions, the teachers developed plans that incorporated the talents of artists and educators outside the school. Chief among the cooperating organizations were the National Conference for Christians and Jews, the Humphrey Forum based at the University of Minnesota, and CLIMB Theater.[8]

With these groups as collaborators, the teaching team devised a process in which students:

- Worked in student/adult groups to practice skills of clarification and negotiation
- Transformed their intellectual knowledge into visual performance with the help of artists, scholars, and teachers
- Were trained to discuss the "isms" with their peers and train them in the techniques they had learned
- Gave performances to local schools and organizations followed by question and answer sessions with audiences to further explore issues of prejudice and to teach conflict resolution skills

Thanks to various funding sources,[9] the teachers had release time to find relevant materials, team teach, and "keep the experience alive," as Rogers says. Two books proved especially useful in helping the teachers make connections to the Forum project within their other courses: *We: Lessons on Equal Worth and Dignity, the United Nations and Human Rights* and *Beyond the Suitcase: A Resource for Multicultural Teaching of History.*[10]

All of this activity happened over a six-month period, "so that it wouldn't be overwhelming," says Rogers, and involved scheduled times for further conversation and journal writing among the teachers and students. "We worked to create a philosophical base for exploration," she adds.

Early on, students were immersed in various activities intended to simulate prejudicial experiences. In one, former teacher and noted national speaker Jane Elliott divided students into two groups according to eye color. While the blue-eyed students were inexplicably sent to sit on the hall floor outside the room, the brown-eyed students were told that this was only a game, and to treat their blue-eyed compatriots poorly.

Once reunited, the blue-eyed students were ordered back into the room, to sit on the floor between two groups of seated brown-eyes. "Blue-eyes," Elliott told the group, "aren't as nice as brown-eyed people. They're not as smart, they're not as clean, and they are nasty, uncouth, and violent as well." Blue-eyes had to sign out to visit a blue-eyes only restroom. If a brown-eye saw a blue-eye chewing gum, the blue-eye was ordered to throw it away.

Suffering through such inequities, of course, has its lessons. Since 1985, Elliott has been leading similar sessions in schools and corporate settings. (For a more detailed discussion of Elliot's classroom experiment, see William Peters's *A Class Divided* [Ballantine Books, 1971] or see the ABC News documentary program *The Eye of the Storm.*) She cautions that teachers need to be careful how they use such lessons with children, but says that in her experience, adults have had the most violent reactions to the simulation.

One student, reflecting on the experience, said, "A lot of blue eyes felt that the discrimination was wrong; a lot of brown eyes did too. I realized there are a lot of stupid things that people do. The simulation sort of woke up some people to those things, and made them not feel so good about it."

At the end of each day's session, students discussed their impressions in small groups and wrote in journals—recording insights, memorable events and observations. As one student wrote, "When I first got there [to the simulation activity], I thought, 'Well, there are privileged people, but there's not too much anyone can do about it.' But after awhile, we figured out that we can [for example] call up TV people, and whenever there's a prejudiced TV commercial, we can ask them to change it. My friends and I did that."

Social action also took the form of skits (written, directed and performed by students and for students). One particularly sophisticated performance, "Battles of a Woman," was written and acted by four girls who appear too young to have experienced some of the heady issues they tackle. The play has an intricate format: Four friends unite in a restaurant after five years of separation. The course of their conversation leads to flashbacks on formative incidents in their lives, each of which involved confronting sexism: A woman, played by middle school student Regina, is forced to give her daughter the androgynous name "Toni" because her husband, played by middle school student Stephanie, was hoping for a son. Another struggles to prove her interest in woodworking over home economics, but is rebuffed by the shop teacher, again played by Stephanie, who says, "My boys, they're rough; they're tough. You couldn't handle it. Anyway, you're probably worried about getting your hair caught in a table saw, or chipping a nail."

Obviously, not all of the experiences reflected in this play are the students'. Many stem from conversations with parents, teachers, and other students—conversations about topics that might not have taken place had there not been the Forum as an avenue for discussion.

In a sense, the program has provided students with the language for discussing discrimination. As one middle school girl said, "My friends thought racism was something not to be discussed. Now they're more open about it. I think we're getting to know each other better than we already did. I mean, I know you're white and you know I'm black, but we also know who our inner person is. We don't intimidate each other about it. It's easier for us to stay together and be friends now."

The instruction on gender and racial bias so permeated Webster's culture that students developed a system for catching its teachers and peers in an act of discrimination. Holding up two fingers in an apparent peace sign (meant to signify the forked tongue of a snake), while hissing, indicates recognition of an insult, a stereotype, or other form of inappropriate behavior. As teacher Rosemarie Redmon says, "Everyone knows what it means. The recognition of the behavior gives us the opportunity to ask 'Why'? "

Indeed, a midyear school bus incident involving Webster students attests to the impact of this sustained study. As one student recounts, "There was an African-American kid, a year older than me, on the bus. All the white kids were goofing off. But he was the one to get in trouble. So all of us in the back seat got off the bus and walked home." Students then drafted a letter to the school board, explaining the incident. Ultimately, the bus driver was removed from the route. The busing incident is also indicative of the types of student gains endorsed by the Minnesota Department of Education: creating active learners, responsible citizens, creative problem solvers, and lifelong learners.

This kind of action was possible because students were given the time to "really change" over the course of the year, according to Rogers. "They got to practice taking on viewpoints, and began to see many ways to solve problems." Particularly through their interactions with audiences, the performers reached new levels of understanding of bias, making it imperative for them to act on their convictions—to get off the bus. As Rogers says, "If we want kids to become problem solvers, we have to teach them how to use their energy to make the world a better, safer place. We have to give them a chance to leave their mark on the world . . . to fail or to succeed, to collaborate with each other."

And, Rogers says, there were equivalent benefits for teachers. Referring to the creativity and initiative of the teachers involved, she adds, "Service learning gives teachers the broadest spectrum of possibilities to fire up their passions."

Overcoming School/Community Tensions through Public Art

Where once there was a bleak courtyard, containing only a sizable air conditioning unit for the surrounding 1950s-era school, students, faculty, and community members in northeast Minneapolis have created an inviting public space: a school/community "gathering place." Contemporary wooden structures, landscaped plantings, and student artwork fill this converted interior park. The cedar amphitheater, performance stage, benches, and picnic tables are connected by a winding brick pathway, and the air conditioner is nowhere to be seen—creatively concealed by a kiosk that advertises school and community happenings.

As eighth-grader James describes it, "It's sort of a small park, an indoor theater at the same time . . . sort of like a carnival thing, a festival thing."

It is anything but the drab space it once was, thanks to the efforts of this urban school's faculty and students, and the surrounding community. Since its dedication last spring, it has been used for science lessons on composting, for puppet plays and story telling put on for a nearby elementary school, for parent/ teacher organization meetings, and for summer sessions taught through the local community education program. Its potential uses are limited only by the constraints of the school's and community's imaginations, and Minnesota's sometimes challenging weather.

The genesis of the beautification plan began three years ago, when students painted a colorful 80-foot-long mural on their cafeteria wall, with the assistance of public artist Pat Benincasa. Transforming the wall into an exploration of cultures represented in the school—the largest, most ethnically diverse middle school in Minneapolis—proved to be a particularly successful way to get students talking about their differences, in turn finding their commonalties. This "diversity wall"—a profusion of ethnic symbols and color—also served to highlight the bleakness of the adjacent school courtyard.

Similarly bleak were the neighborhood/school relations, according to principal Larry Lucio. "When I came to this school six years ago, everything and anything bad that happened in the neighborhood was the Northeast kids' fault. The business strip two blocks over didn't want kids loitering, waiting for the bus in their businesses. There was a lot of stereotyping."

Much of this climate was attributable to escalating neighborhood/school tensions that developed when busing changed the composition of the student body in the early 1980s. Assistant principal Mary Spindler said, at that time, many neighborhood parents began sending their students to a parochial school just two blocks away. However, Spindler did not label the problem "racism"; instead, she said, "It's just an ignorance about diversity."

Of the 1,000 students that now attend Northeast, 80 percent are students of color. Approximately 60 percent have single parents, 84 percent are eligible for free or reduced lunches, and almost 25 percent of the student body moves each semester—all the more reason to foster a sense of community among this bused-in student body.

Not only do the students differ demographically from the school's aging Polish and Ukrainian neighborhood but the students themselves had little that bound them to each other, since 90 percent come from all over the greater Minneapolis school district. Furthermore, as Benincasa says, "If you ask most middle school kids, 'Do you have a place in this culture, in this society?' I hazard a guess that the answer would be 'Where?'"

Industrial arts teacher Lee Washington cites the attendant lack of an after-school sports program as part of the reason the school lacked a sense of common cause, "So any little bit of community we can have [through a project like the Gathering Place] is a good thing," he adds.

"When Northeast Middle School began its restructuring efforts six years ago, the goal was to make the school more of a community," says art teacher Rose Curran. The Gathering Place takes that idea one step further—toward fostering a sense of community that includes the surrounding neighborhood.

This courtyard transformation did not blossom overnight, however. "We started developing ways of projecting to the community that the kids here do care about more than drugs and rap—that they have a vested interest in the school they attend," says Lucio.

In the students' first efforts at community involvement, they raked leaves and shoveled snow for nearby residents. They went caroling over the holidays and spoke to the local business association about their projects. "We had to reach out, be assertive, to give them a complete perspective and not allow them to dwell on their assumptions," says Lucio.

Then, with some initial funding from the Generator School Project and from the Minnesota Department of Education's grants to schools from the federal Corporation for National Service, Benincasa and art teacher Rose Curran concocted a plan to manifest this need for community in a physical space. At the heart of the project was "everyday art—art for everyday places," says Benincasa.

The purpose of the Gathering Place is "for the community members and the school to get together," according to eighth-grader Amber. It is testimony to a successful public art, public education, and youth service learning collaboration. Benincasa quotes an Emily Dickinson line—"I dwell in possibility"—when describing the two-year metamorphosis of this space. "Any person involved in this project dwelled in possibility," she says.

The educational objectives of the project include having the school become a civic partner with the community, extending the classroom into the community, creating an interdisciplinary educational service learning experience, and fostering students' life skills, ownership of a project, and self-esteem. To secure students for these grand plans, Benincasa and Curran devised an application for involvement that asked students to find two teachers to recommend them, write an essay about what they could offer the project, and check a potluck list of interests that included soliciting money, educating others, building with wood, videotaping, pouring concrete, writing, speaking, helping with a green house, and creating time lines. They also asked parents about transportation needs for their children, assuming that as the project grew, after-school time would be necessary.

The project was especially well suited to a school that is divided up into six interdisciplinary teams composed of 140 students and five teachers, each with a different academic emphasis. In fact, the project could be considered "post-disciplinary," so intertwined and interdependent are its curricular pieces.

With Benincasa's architectural model for the space as guidance, a math class designed the courtyard's landscaping. They also provided the calculations for an industrial arts class, which built the stage, kiosk, amphitheater, compost bins, picnic tables, and benches from blueprints. Meanwhile, a science class was resurrecting a school greenhouse and learning about plant requirements as they raised seedlings for the spring planting that would fit the landscaping scheme of the math students. English students were busy writing for grants and documenting each stage of the Gathering Place's development—both on videotape and in scrapbooks—learning how to create a "visual narrative." And art students were practicing mosaic designs in concrete blocks for the eventual floor of the amphitheater and making cloth banners to be hung from the platform on the stage. While all of these activities were underway, other students were giving promotional talks at the local Kiwanis club, and researching prices of lumber, sod, and dirt.

Critical to the students' academic outcomes was their time spent discussing and writing about their experiences. As English teacher Katherine Kleingartner says, "In a service learning project, the skills are almost insidious—you don't necessarily realize you're learning them, so that's an important reason for reflection." Student evaluations of the project testify to the "painlessness" of this sort of applied learning. One wrote that "this is more fun than school."

Some of the more deliberate student reflections became part of a radio show, aired on Minnesota Public Radio. On the program, students described what it means to have a sense of place. To prepare for this writing, students considered different kinds of places in their community (a place with history, a happy place, an ugly place, a free place, a place where you have never been, a hectic place, a place where products are made, a place with animals, a place where people are helped, etc.). They then read a series of quotations on place, considering how strongly they agreed or disagreed with the statements. They also read through a list of characteristics of a place, and ranked where their community fell on a continuum.

Following this discussion of places, students wrote about what it meant to have a place they had revitalized themselves, and described the Gathering Place in poetry. The following was written by eighth-grader Shanita:

> The Gathering Place is like a common town.
>   It has very nice things to see, even things on the ground.
> The Gathering Place is a place for fun—
>   even with excitement, where you shall be stunned.
> The Gathering Place is a place of romance,
>   where everything in sight is in a beautiful glance.
> The Gathering Place is a place for all types of races.
>   It's a place to enjoy and meet new faces.
> The Gathering Place is a place of light,
>   The Gathering Place seems very bright.
> The Gathering Place isn't just for certain people.
>   It's a place where all people are treated equal.

Some wrote in teams, as did Danielle, Amy, and Jim:

> A place to build, a place to play,
> Everything should be this way.
> We'll make a place where everyone
> Helps one another in the hot morning sun.
> The thought came one winter day,
> A place to build, a place to play.

Industrial arts teacher Lee Washington also involved his students in small group work to accomplish the goals of the project. "Normally, my students work on individual projects, so I have a different set of instructions for each of them. In this case, 25 people worked on one set of projects, so I divided them into groups. For example, 5 students worked on a picnic table. They had to work together. Some weren't very good at math, so others would learn from those who knew a bit more. You would see them struggle from the start, but pretty soon you could see that they were learning."

As important as the skills instruction was to the project, Kleingartner says that some of the most important experiences for the students were social. "Because our school's divided into teams, kids work with the same 140 students for their whole three years here. By offering the Gathering Place as an eighth-hour (i.e., end of the day) class, it's intra-team, so kids are working with kids they've never met before. All of a sudden they have to depend on their social skills to have a successful interaction. They can't hang with a clique. That's really important for middle-school-aged kids, particularly in a school where they become very team-dependent."

As 13-year-old Amber attests, "It's kind of hard to be the shy type when you're working with the Gathering Place. . . . You don't just sit and read a book. You do a lot of action, you work with a lot of community." She goes on to say, "I've grown to be more attached to people. I used to be shy, and I'd never volunteer for anything. I've grown to see that I need to be with people. I've made a lot of friends."

In fact, Amber spoke to the local Kiwanis Club, describing the project and soliciting their interest. As she says, "I hadn't exactly volunteered to do it. I just kind of sat back and let somebody choose me to do it. . . . When I went I was shy. But by the time I left—it was only about an hour—it kind of broke the shyness and I was able to be open more."

Indeed, the Gathering Place is much more than its disciplinary parts. As Benincasa says, it takes the concept of service learning one step further: "It's about community building, not simply building something for the community." As Kleingartner describes the project, it "combines community volunteerism with public art. . . . Community volunteers are really mentors for the students."

This spirit was most evident during the four-day fall "Build-a-Thon." School and community members worked side by side in an effort to get all but the picnic benches built before winter. The school had plied the community with information about the event and requested help in the form of time, monetary donations, and/or food. When the building weekend hit, community members provided gardening, carpentry, and sewing expertise in such numbers that there were usually as many adults as students at work. Businesses donated tools, and students organized a tool "check-in" so that each borrowed implement was numbered, inventoried, and returned.

The event was poignantly timed. On a day when the Twin Cities' largest newspaper, the *Star-Tribune,* ran a cover story on its Metro section about a teen killing over a pair of sneakers, the inside story featured the Gathering Place's "Build-a-Thon." Thereafter, Benincasa attests, "The phones started ringing off the hook, and the publicity allowed the school to generate more funding." One woman even brought in a check on her way to surgery. Another woman dropped off a bag of apples. When asked whether she had any children in the school, she said that she didn't, but that she had stopped by "because there's so much meanness in the world."

The project also will have longer-term community-building benefits since, as Curran points out, "It brings the school/community together because they have to take care of it. It's not something the janitors are going to care for . . . it's a laboratory in some respects, because its use will evolve over the years."

Curran warns that the two-year project was not always easy to implement. As many struggles came from within the school as without. At one point, a "Bowl-a-Thon" fundraiser was threatened by teachers who felt this was pushing the idea of applied learning too far. In a letter that challenged those assumptions, Curran outlined the academic and life skills outcomes of the project, silencing her opponents and allowing the event to be held:

- Students will practice and develop math skills in a real-life experience.
- Students will develop organizational and leadership skills.
- Students will meet once a week to reflect on their learning and to set goals for the upcoming week.
- Students will record these reflection periods in journals to develop their writing skills.
- Students will learn about commercial art, advertising, public speaking and community outreach skills in a real-life situation.
- Students will gain a sense of self-esteem, ownership, and personal power as a result of their being productive members of the school community.

The significance of such hands-on learning is, as Kleingartner attests, especially important for middle school-aged students. "Information that is not immediately applied to real world situations does not become internalized."

Still, Curran admits, "As an art teacher, there are a lot of times when I just want to go back into the classroom and do little studio projects because they're easier. Previous to this, my art projects were pretty much studio or art historical projects. I didn't have to be as community involved and dealing with all the personalities of everyone. . . . But, once you get past all that . . . the benefits are so huge." Curran continues, "This took us out of the classroom, threw us into the school community, into politics, in the reality that art does not stand on its own—that it is interdisciplinary, and that it is not just a studio thing, not just something that happens and you put it in a museum. And so I think, in a lot of ways, I'm doing a lot to change people's attitudes about art education."

Arts extension service director Craig Dreezen, of the University of Massachusetts, shares this sentiment: "In a way, linking art to social action is a reintegration of the arts into life in a way that was once unquestioned. To connect art with education, for example, is to reconnect the arts with their historical role as basic tools of communication." These middle school students—whether creating a video documentary of the evolution of the project, compiling a scrapbook chronicling its development, writing poetry, presenting to the Kiwanis Club, or explaining to their peers how to dye concrete—have borne out the contemporary application of that theory.

At a time when middle schools have to be concerned about gang activity—

when a Northeast sign reads: "Please keep the following items in your locker: jackets, bandannas, hats, book bags, knapsacks, backpacks, purses"—the Gathering Place provides an oasis. It makes the more optimistic declarations, written on a sign near the school's central office, seem possible: "Be verbally appropriate; be physically considerate; be on time; be prepared for class; strive for best achievement; expect the best."

As Peter Hutchinson, the superintendent of the Minneapolis schools, said at the opening ceremony for the Gathering Place: "This is proof that dreams come true in Minneapolis schools, not somewhere else, but in Minneapolis schools."

Benincasa makes those dreams explicit: "Out of this collaborative effort, racial barriers blurred between students of color and the Northeast Community. This project evolved out of a need to bring the community and middle school students together so that the students would not be perceived as 'those kids.' Those kids are now recognized as community resources and participants."

One such student, who pounded nails, watered plants, and laid mosaic concrete blocks on the amphitheater floor, also wrote the following poem and read it at the Gathering Place's dedication celebration:

Wanting to serve community, the Gathering Place stands.
The place for peace and unity, the product of many hands.
The plans would never have come to be without work,
without we.
Rakes on air, they wouldn't be there
without we, without care.
We all were needed to lend a hand;
We all were needed together,
And all together, we present,
by nature's grace
The Gathering Place.

SERVICE LEARNING AND SOCIAL ACTION

Although these projects are only a sampling of the many service learning efforts underway in the Generator Schools, they illustrate the goals of the project: to integrate service and social action into academic programming by encouraging schools to develop curricula that connect life experiences with learning. The diversity of projects is representative of the many paths available in moving from service learning to social action.

The Generator School Project builds a national community of learners and practitioners who rely on each other for inspiration, resources, and problem solving through their annual national meetings, the summer National Youth Leadership Project camp, student exchanges among the schools, curriculum development workshops, and (soon) computer bulletin boards. (A projectwide effort to link all 38 schools electronically is currently underway; teachers and students can then share ideas more easily with other Generator Schools and with those linked to the National Service-Learning K–12 Clearinghouse/ Cooperative.)

These practitioners employ the strengths of such education reform initiatives as thematic instruction when they study race and gender in the Forum Project, "cooperative learning" when middle-schoolers team up with younger students as buddies, and interdisciplinary study when neighborhood/school relations become the impetus behind a school/community Gathering Place that includes instruction in six core curricular areas. As educator Audrey Cohen (1993) wrote in an issue of the *Phi Delta Kappan,* "As we abandon teaching by the disciplines, teachers inevitably face new roles with more challenging possibilities. Instead of teaching isolated subjects in isolated classrooms, they will find themselves working together to build curricula around significant social purposes. . . . They will see themselves less as storehouses of information and more as mentors, guiding their students through an empowering process that unites intellectual knowledge with effective action" (p. 795).

It is not only teachers who experience a metamorphosis through service learning. In recasting students from passive (often reluctant) information repositories to community problem solvers, they exercise their citizenship rights— by building parks, teaching their native tongue, and forging a sense of community by constructing a park. Through school-based service learning projects, students become experts, teachers, and resources as they assess community needs and develop plans for action—all within the course of their academic days. Along the way, they meet learner outcomes mandated by school districts, tackle social inequities, and perceive reasons to secure academic skills.

At the same time, the community gains a new point of entry into the school. Schools are no longer primarily the objects of community frustration. Instead, they provide a new forum for cooperation, uniting parents, students, and community members around common issues.

But perhaps most importantly, the power of service learning lies in its ability to help students in rural, urban, and reservation areas see how their liberation and struggles for social justice are—as the aboriginal saying goes—tied up with each other's.

REFERENCES

Bird, Traveller. (1972). *The Path to Snowbird Mountain: Cherokee Legends.* New York: Farrar, Straus & Giroux.

Cohen, Audrey (1993, June). "A New Educational Paradigm." *Phi Delta Kappan,* 74(10): 791–795.

DeLoria, Vine. (1990, Winter). "Traditional Education in the Modern World." *Winds of Change,* 5(1): 12–18.

Elliot, Roanne, and Sorenson, Mary Eileen. (1992). *We: Lessons on Equal Worth and Dignity, the United Nations and*

Human Rights. New York: The United Nations Association of the United States of America (UNA-USA).

Hutchins, Pat. (1967). *Rosie's Walk.* New York: Macmillan.

Kielsmeier, Jim, and Nathan, Joe. (1991, June). "The Sleeping Giant of School Reform." *Phi Delta Kappan, 71*(10): 739–742.

Stub, Helen. (Ed.). (1990). *Beyond the Suitcase: A Resource for Multicultural Teaching of History.* Minneapolis, MN: Minnesota Humanities Commission in cooperation with the Minneapolis Public Schools and the National Endowment for the Humanities.

ENDNOTES

1. The National Youth Leadership Council (NYLC) is an educational nonprofit program based in St. Paul, Minnesota. NYLC offers technical assistance, youth and adult training, and curricula and periodicals to teachers, community leaders and others who practice or advocate for service learning and youth leadership. For more information, call (612) 631-3672.

2. The Center for School Change is located at the Hubert Humphrey Institute, University of Minnesota, Minneapolis. It was established with support from the Blandin Foundation to help increase student achievement in selected Minnesota communities and to improve educational policy in the state. Call (612) 625-3506 for further information.

3. The Generator School Project is a collaborative effort that includes the NYLC in Minnesota, the Arkansas Department of Education, the National Dropout Prevention Center at Clemson University in South Carolina, the National Indian Youth Leadership Project (NIYLP) in New Mexico, the Michigan K–12 Service-Learning Center at Michigan State University, the Pennsylvania Institute for Environmental and Community Service Learning, and Project Service Leadership in Washington. Major funding for the Project is provided by the Dewitt-Wallace Reader's Digest Fund, the W. K. Kellogg Foundation, and the Corporation for National Service.

4. The National Service-Learning Cooperative: K-12 Serve-America Clearinghouse was established in 1994, with funding from the Corporation for National Service (formerly the Commission on National and Community Service). Sponsored by NYLC and the University of Minnesota, it offers a toll-free information number (1-800-808-SERV), a national database of service learning programs and resources, a materials library, an electronic bulletin board, and referrals for training and peer consultation.

5. The National Indian Youth Leadership Project (NIYLP) offers technical assistance, advice, and support to schools, programs and communities throughout the country interested in examining service learning in a traditional Native-American context. For further information, call (505) 722-9176.

6. For further ideas on the use of story telling, Hall recommends *The Path to Snowbird Mountain: Cherokee Legends* written by Traveller Bird (New York: Farrar, Straus & Giroux, 1972).

7. MacClellan Hall, *Something Shining Like Gold, but Better* (St. Paul: National Youth Leadership Council, 1991), p. 17.

8. The National Conference for Christians and Jews (NCCJ) works to promote peaceful conflict resolution. Contact Paul Sand at (612) 333-5365 for further in-

formation. The Humphrey Forum is a department of the Hubert H. Humphrey Institue of Public Affairs at the University of Minnesota. It runs a museum, offers courses that teach the concepts of government and politics, publishes a current affairs newspaper, and produces a television show on current affairs. Contact Steve Sandell at (612) 624-5799 for further information. CLIMB Theater is an instructive theater troup that works regionally with K–12 students. Contact Peg Endres at (612) 227-9600 for further information.

9. This project was funded through a grant by the Minnesota Department of Education, and received additional funding from the American Council of Learned Societies (ACLS) and the NCCJ.

10. *Beyond the Suitcase* is based on the work of the 1989–1990 Multicultural History Symposium organized by The Origins Program and supported by the Minneapolis Public Schools. Further funding came from the Minnesota Humanities Commission in cooperation with the National Endowment for the Humanities and the Minnesota State Legislature.

12

The Community as Classroom

Service Learning at the Louis Armstrong Middle School

IVY DITON   MARY ELLEN LEVIN

How did we justify our middle school students spending time visiting senior citizens, tutoring, gardening, or playing one-to-one with toddlers in a day care center as part of their school day at the Louis Armstrong Middle School? Middle school is a critical crossroads in the lives of our children. At this time, educators either engage them in learning, making school and career goals a vital part of their lives, or educators lose their interest, adding to the high drop-out rates in the nation's high schools. When lack of interest is coupled with other significant risk factors associated with growing up in a large city, many of these students are destined for lives of "rotten outcomes" (Schorr, 1989).

Charlie R., an African-American 13-year-old living in Jamaica, Queens (a section in New York City where a leading cause of death for young men is homicide) illustrates how an effective service learning program can inspire students to see possibilities of different outcomes. He volunteered weekly in a nursing home as part of his seventh-grade Home and Careers class. Charlie was a quiet, shy young man who has had limited contact with adult males. His household consists of a mother, grandmother, and two younger sisters. At the nursing home, he befriended a 72-year-old African-American man, Mr. M., who later became a significant role model for Charlie. Mr. M. had been a teacher who had lived through the desegregation of schools in the South.

During Charlie's weekly visits to the nursing home, he and Mr. M began sharing many intimate moments in the privacy of Mr. M.'s room. Many times, Charlie would be found sitting or lying on the edge of Mr. M.'s bed as they discussed personal experiences. Charlie expressed his fear and anger about living in New York City. He began to trust Mr. M. and look up to him for advice. As Charlie tried to paint a picture of the drugs, the poverty, and the violence that had become part of his landscape living in the city, Mr. M. began to describe his own life struggles against racism in the South during the 1930s and 40s. Charlie began sharing Mr. M.'s stories with others in the class. One story is noteworthy because Charlie told it to the class with absolute horror in his eyes. It seems that Mr. M. had narrowly escaped a lynching because he was in the wrong place at the wrong time. He had been jogging along a river levy in Alabama and was mistaken for a thief. Several white townspeople started running after him. He was not sure why they were running after him so he continued running. When they finally caught up with him, they were ready to kill him. Fortunately, one of the men recognized him as a mathematics teacher in the black school and this ultimately saved his life.

Charlie was fascinated with Mr. M.'s experiences. He could not believe that life had always been so difficult. He became more spirited as he began to see that even when things look hopeless there is always the possibility for change. Mr. M. pointed out that at one time blacks and whites went to separate schools and that blacks were overtly treated as second-class citizens in this country. Mr. M. taught Charlie how to find humor in the most difficult situations. Charlie was fascinated that, through all the difficulty, Mr. M. was able to maintain his sense of humor. Charlie, a shy young man at the onset of the program, became animated with hope for the future of African Americans. He became determined to keep Mr. M.'s struggles alive. In addition, Mr. M.'s life became spirited for the first time in years. The recreational director of the nursing home commented, "Charlie is like a fountain of youth for Mr. M. He's started dressing again and is asking for the newspaper daily. It's like he has a new lease on life." She just could not get over how close the two of them had become in just a couple of months and how positively they were influencing each other.

Subsequently, at a dinner honoring Ms. Joan Schine, the Director of the National Center for Service Learning, Charlie made a speech in front of hundreds of adults, sharing his experiences with Mr. M. at the nursing home, and talking about how these experiences had changed his life. In his public address, he stated, "You can learn a lot in school about history, but when you meet someone who 'lived' history it becomes real. Mr. M. showed me that times were never really good for any of us. I now know what I need to do with my life. This experience (service learning) changed the way I look at things. I know that even when life looks impossible, you need to keep working to make it better." The entire audience, including his teacher, were incredibly moved. After his teacher stopped crying, she said that she had always believed that service learning was an effective way to engage students in learning, but tonight she was certain. She later remarked at a faculty meeting that, "in college we learn how to teach students to read and do math and learn social studies and do scientific experimentation experimentation, but nobody ever teaches us how to help these students pull it all together and use this knowledge to improve society. Service learning may be that bridge. I have faith in the future when I envision all students engaged in some type of service learning."

Service learning is an instructional approach that encourages students to learn as they are given opportunities to perform valuable service within their communities. One teacher jokingly describes it "as a way to get two for the price of one," She says, "It teaches students valuable communication and technical skills, and at the same time teaches the students how to become participating citizens in society. What more can we ask?"

SCHOOL SETTING

The Louis Armstrong Middle School is a special place. Located in the heart of New York City, the student body, a population of approximately 1,400 students, represents the full ethnic, social, academic, and economic range. The school is a magnet school that recruits and admits students from the entire borough of Queens. Its program features an extended day and a college collaboration with Queens College of the City of New York.

At the entrance to the school is a wrap-around, colorful mural depicting jazz musicians, the New York City skyline, bridges, and other city scenes. The energy of the mural continues to be felt inside the school. Off the main lobby, a newly organized percussion band is playing in one of the classrooms. Some of the school's "serious problem boys" work earnestly to get the sound right. Next door a classroom fitted for adaptive physical education contains physically challenged students working with their teachers on swings, tables, and mats. A walk in the other direction leads one past the school museum, a busy place that displays the work of students, teachers and outsiders. Organized and maintained for the most part by Queens College teacher-interns, the museum hosts an average of seven different shows each year.

The school's classrooms are organized into "complexes" of four behind closed corridor doors. There, four classes and four teachers work for the greater part of the school day creating an interdisciplinary learning experience for those classes. These teachers are given time in their schedules to meet weekly. At these meetings, they discuss pupil personnel-related issues as well curricular issues. Since they share the same group of students for the entire day, they may also plan interdisciplinary units and activities for this common group of students.

The centerpiece of this busy school is the library. Staffed by two librarians who are devoted to meeting the needs of middle school students, the library does a tremendous business. Most periods of the day, one or two classes work there with their teachers on research or explore the shelves for reading materials. Other students work independently at computers, use the Chapter I mini-lab, or watch videotapes on individual video monitors. Teachers are likely to be working in the Teacher Resource Center; perhaps a workshop or meeting is in progress there.

Students are grouped heterogeneously in all subject classes. Service learning can contribute to the success of heterogeneous grouping, or "untracking," a recent focus of attention nationwide because of its potential for integration and providing access to knowledge. In that regard, it is worth noting that service learning also levels the playing field, as students contribute their own knowledge and skills to each situation. Maria R., a small and soft-spoken Hispanic sixth-grade student with learning disabilities, who in the past made slow progress in reading, became a volunteer reader to kindergarten students at a local elementary school. She was very nervous at first, but after studying and practicing, she was quite successful. She told her teacher, "Up until today, I always felt stupid. Now I know that I can read and help other kids, too."

The Carnegie Council on Adolescent Development's *Turning Points* (1989) recommends the Early Adolescent Helper Program (a model of an effective service learning program) as one way to establish connections between the school and the community.[1] Indeed, service learning fosters a sense of community in students who come to the Louis Armstrong Middle School from a variety of communities. Their parents were born in over 60 countries, and a large number of languages spoken across the globe are spoken by the students. Queens is a microcosm of a multiracial, multiethnic New York City. The students' economic statuses range from the upper middle class to the impoverished and homeless. Linguistic and cultural differences create barriers to meaningful interaction. Through weekly service learning activities, class meetings have become the ideal forum for these students to share their ideas and work together to try to change the ways in which these different groups interact. Indeed, the school's faculty takes the point of view that if multiculturalism can be made to thrive here, there is a distinct message in it for the rest of the city. In one group, Linda S., a bright and articulate first-generation Asian American, commented that when we (the class) volunteer at a community agency, we function as a cohesive group. She stated, "It is as if there are no more problems among us—we all work together to help others. It makes me feel part of a special caring group."

The Louis Armstrong Middle School is cited in *Turning Points* as a school where learning knows few boundaries because the school has "set aside traditional limits on when and where education can occur" (Carnegie Council, 1989, p. 53). Besides the Helper Program, the school maintains the tradition of sponsoring after-school and weekend mentorship programs in which individual students "report for work" in nonprofit service agencies at nearby LaGuardia Airport and local businesses. Through these programs, the community profits and the early adolescents engage in activities where they take on responsibility and assume work roles. Parents cannot get over how responsible their children have become. One mother tells a story about her son, Frank: "Early last Saturday morning my boss called and offered us four tickets to the Mets game at 1:00. Frank, an avid Mets fan, informed me that he couldn't go because he was expected at his job at noon. I said that I would make an excuse for him but he was determined to be get to work on time. I'm very proud of him."

Teachers also began to see noticeable changes in their students' behavior. Students involved in a service learning program were getting to class on time and were better behaved than their peers who were not involved in the program. Several teachers expressed an interest in changing the current curriculum to include a service learning component. After several meetings and lengthy discussion, it was decided to revise the Home and Careers Curriculum to include a service learning component. It was determined that the traditional curriculum lacked focus and connection to "real life." This is where our journey begins. This journey has shown us how powerful service learning can be for children, for community, for educators, and for society.

ADMINISTRATIVE CONCERNS

At the Louis Armstrong Middle School, our service learning program started small but grew fast. One reason it grew so successfully is that we avoided the pitfall of getting involved in after-school programs that involved credits, point systems, and extensive administrative tasks for teachers and principals. We included it instead as a component of the school day. In addition, we institutionalized the innovation in its third year by applying for and receiving a variance from the New York State Education Department. This waiver enabled us to transform a state-mandated seventh-grade course, Home and Career Skills, into an enhanced program, Careers and the Community.

The focus of Careers and the Community is personal and moral development through real-life learning experiences. Full classes volunteer in local daycare centers, senior centers, elementary schools, and nursing homes during the school day. These site visits are augmented by weekly group meetings (called seminars) in school that are designed to motivate and involve students through planning, active reflection, and discussion. These seminars are held during a regular school period of 45 minutes, once a week. Students learn as they strive to make sense of themselves and others by experiencing moral dilemmas and decisions involved in confronting real-life situations.

Getting the program started required significant groundwork. New curriculum needed to be written, schedules arranged, and placements found. Students were not initially involved in the process, but later they became vital members of the planning team. The Early Adolescent Helper Program at the National Center for Service Learning, located in New York City, was extremely supportive in providing the technical assistance necessary to create this exemplary program. They aided us with staff training, curriculum materials, and invaluable ongoing advice.

The first task was to arrange schedules. Two consecutive 45-minute periods were needed for the weekly field visits (preferably followed by a lunch period) and one 45-minute period was needed for the weekly seminar. In addition, as we will explain later in this chapter, planning time was arranged with the students' team of teachers, so that service experiences could be connected to the other curricular areas.

The next step was to find placements that would engage the students. The key to a successful program rests in matching the needs of the students with a desirable field placement. We were fortunate to find a nursing home with a recreational director whose concern for senior citizens dovetailed with the school's concern for early adolescents. Students were given opportunities to adopt "grandparents." To alleviate initial anxiety, we teamed two students to work with each "senior." Weekly activities such as baking, arts and crafts, oral histories, reading, movies, and parties were planned in advance for the students and the seniors. This was accomplished by establishing set meeting times between the program director of the school and the recreational director of the nursing home. At these meetings, the directors planned what would happen at each visit and developed a calendar for the students and the seniors so that they would be adequately prepared for each visit. The calendar covered two five-month periods: one from September through January and the other from February through June.

The director of a local day-care center was also more than eager to have our students volunteer their time, because cuts in day-care funding created large classes with fewer staff members. The preschool children ranged in age from 1 to 5 years old. Our students were teamed in groups of three, and worked as teacher assistants in the day-care classrooms. They were given the option of choosing a preferred age before they began, so that they would feel more comfortable.

STUDENT PREPARATION AND SUPPORT

Before students went into the field, we spent time in school preparing for the experience. The class that was to visit the nursing home focused on aging. Stereotypes about senior citizens were examined, and students role-played what it would be like to grow old. Jennifer said her mom's grandmother, who is very old, sits by the window all day watching people walk by. Ever since her husband died, she wants to die, too. Students role-play this scene:

Jen (Grandma): There isn't any work for me to do any more. I'm too old to go out. And I miss Grandpa. I'd like to die now."

Elisa (Grandma's daughter): Don't talk like that, Mom. We all love you.

Grandma: But what's the use? I'm useless. Just an old lady causing everybody a lot of trouble. There's no way I can help.

This role-play led to a discussion of whether there is a role for old people in our culture. Many of the children from immigrant families have grandmothers and grandfathers who do most of the child care. These students cannot imagine grandparents feeling useless. May, a first-generation Korean student with a very serious demeanor, states, "My grandmother doesn't have the time to feel useless. She takes care of my two younger sisters and my newborn cousin. She picks me up from school and cooks the family dinner. Sometimes she talks about my grandfather and life in Korea and gets a little thoughtful for her old friends back home. I guess she is a little lonely sometimes, but never useless." As other students continue to share stories about their own families, it appears as if the class is split between those who view seniors as an integral part of their lives and others who have little or no contact with senior citizens.

Values line-ups, which permit the students to expound their views, are also used. In values line-ups, statements are used to survey student attitudes (e.g., Growing old is horrible: 1—Strongly Agree, 2—Agree, 3—Unsure, 4—Disagree, 5—Strongly Disagree). Students choose the number that best matches their opinion on the statement. Numbers are placed around the room. The students move around the room to the number that corresponds to their choice. They then discuss their points of view. Issues of death and dying are discussed, and students share their own fears and anxieties.

Visualization is also used since it is an effective technique to encourage students to imagine themselves in 50 years. Students close their eyes as the teacher guides them through a visualization that encourages the students to see themselves in a mirror as they would look in 50 years. Student reactions are often pivotal and intense. During one session, Sara, a reserved and distant student, broke down in tears. She told the class that all she could see was an old, dying woman. She proceeded to tell the class that she did not want to grow old. Her reaction, more intense than most, signaled to the teacher that Sara was experiencing some deeper emotion. Sure enough, when the teacher called the parent to explain what happened in school, the mother indicated that Sara's grandfather was dying a terrible death from cancer. She was surprised that Sara had broken down because, she stated, "Sara has been a pillar of strength for all of us." The mother was very thankful that the school made her aware of the intensity of feeling that Sara was experiencing and assured the teacher that she would become more sensitive to Sara's needs and not expose her to the intense morbidity of the situation when it could be avoided.

The class that was to visit the day-care center focused on human development. Students examined their own personal development and discussed the changes that occur as they mature. They shared experiences in relation to their own changing bodies. In addition, they role-played anticipated situations so that they would be adequately prepared to deal with the young children. Here is the dialogue between a teacher and her students in preparation for a visit to the day-care center:

Teacher: How can we meet these little kids? What will we say to them and what will they say to us? Who knows anything about 3-year-old children?

Juan: I do! I have a 3-year-old brother. He likes to sing and play games where he claps his hands. He likes to build with blocks. He likes to play ball, even though he doesn't do it too good. He also likes to hear stories.

Teacher: Let's practice how we'll meet our friends. Who will volunteer to be the seventh-grader? The 3-year-old? (The pairs were quickly set up.)

Seventh-Grader: Hi, I'm Charlie. What's your nam*e?*

Three-Year-Old: My name is Cheryl.

Seventh-Grader: I brought a story about a duck, I wrote it for you myself. Would you like to hear it?

Three-Year-Old: No, I want to keep playing with the hamster.

Seventh-Grader: OK, I'll play with you. Maybe you'll want to hear the story later. It's a good story.

Teacher: What should we do if the little kids start fighting?

Allen: (jokingly) Knock both the kids down!

Teacher: We need to be serious because it may happen. May I have a few volunteer 3-year-olds? A volunteer seventh-grader? (The two 3-year-olds start fighting over a block.)

#1 Three-Year-Old: Give me the block back. I had it first.

#2 Three-Year-Old: No! I want it. You already had it.

Seventh-Grader: Hey! You don't have to fight over the block. Let's see if we can share it together.

#1 Three-Year-Old: I don't want to share."

#2 Three-Year-Old: I had it first.

Seventh-Grader: How about if we get another block?

Throughout the role-playing, positive reinforcement is encouraged and safety rules are discussed and demonstrated.

Admittedly, the students volunteering in the day-care center had an easier time becoming acclimated to the volunteer experience than those at the nursing home, a far more frightening place to visit. The first visit at the nursing home was an orientation, so students were given tours of the facility. We limited the students, for the most part, to floors where patients were ambulatory. They were not exposed to critically ill residents.

After the tour, students were encouraged to ask questions and share reactions and/or fears. The overwhelming response was a negative reaction to the antiseptic odor that permeated the home. They were also puzzled that many of the seniors did not get dressed during the day, even though they appeared to be healthy. One student noted and asked, "Some of the residents can walk. Why are they in wheelchairs?" Some of the students were visibly shaken up. On the way back to school, they voiced their concerns about growing old. Chris, an angry and sullen student, blurted out, "If growing old means living in one of those places, then I don't want to grow old." Another piped up, "You don't have to go to a nursing home; if you're nice to your kids, they'll take you in." During the bus ride back to school, a discussion ensued about what to do with old people in society. After about 15 minutes of bandying ideas around, the students decided that if a nursing home is the only choice for a senior citizen, then it should be made into a more desirable place to reside. A student summarized our discussion by stating, "What we should do at the nursing home is to make it a friendlier place for the seniors to live." The other students seemed pleased with this goal and were eager to return. One student, though, voiced concerns about meeting with the seniors alone. She wanted a teacher to be with her because, as she put it, "The old people scare me." Because of that, she was made the teacher's assistant for the first couple of visits. On the third visit, she informed the teacher that she felt comfortable visiting the seniors on her own.

The day-care center orientation was quite different. The students started "playing" with children the first day. They were brought into the day-care classrooms in groups of three and were introduced to the young children. Within minutes, they were joining the children at the blocks, in the dollhouse, at their tables, helping them play, cut, paste, and read. The middle school students felt important and needed. Several students commented, "This is the way school should be; big kids helping little kids; we'd all learn so much more." It was difficult getting the students back on the bus at the end of our visit, and the preschoolers cried when we left. Our students were elated and could not wait to return. The discussion on the bus was quite lively. Students were sharing stories about what they did with the preschoolers. One student started describing a little girl who would not play with the other children in her class. She was concerned that this behavior was anti-social and asked several of her classmates for advice. The students started giving her suggestions. Some suggested that she talk to the teacher while others gave her concrete recommendations. One student boldly stated that maybe the little girl wasn't "ready" to play with other children yet. More specifically, she said, "Give her some time. Little kids are funny that way. When she is ready to play with the other kids, she will. Don't worry so much." Other students described the behaviors of the children they worked with. One student asked, "Did we look and act like the little kids when we were that age? They're so cute and lovable. I can't remember being that small." Another student described the experience as "an opportunity to see how much we have grown." The students were beaming. We were off to a wonderful beginning!

We recommend that teachers eat lunch with students following the service activity in order to get spontaneous reactions to the students' experiences. Writing these reactions down is a good idea, so that they can be recalled during the classroom meetings. For example, the issue of what to do with seniors in society came up on the bus. This topic was written down and brought back to the students the following day at our weekly class meeting. The discussion continued with more thought, depth, and reflection.

Teacher: We've seen and talked about the problems old people face. How can we describe them?

Alexander: They're poor. They can't earn any money. If they didn't save up, they need their children to help them.

Paul: Some of them don't have children. Some of them are on welfare.

Maria: Some of them are sick. They aren't strong enough to take care of themselves. Their husband or wife has died, and they're all alone.

Amar: They're lonely; they don't see anything to live for.

Teacher: What are some of the things we can do for seniors? (Class brainstorms ideas: visit them, write them letters and cards, send them books or gifts, invite them over, take them for walks or rides)

Teacher: What are some of the things seniors could do, so that they'd feel more wanted and needed?

Kevin: They can read to one another or to little kids. They can be like grandparents to kids who don't have any.

Recalling experiences can be a useful tool when something disturbing occurs, such as the time when a nurse in the nursing home refused to dress one of the seniors. In fact, the nurse yelled and humiliated the senior in front of seventh-grader Jennifer, who later came to one of us in tears to discuss this problem. She was too embarrassed to bring it up in class and asked if we could discuss it with the nursing home director but not mention her name. This situation was used as a role-playing activity with other classes to better prepare them for similar situations.

Socializing with the students after the service activity is always delightful, because they are bubbling over with enthusiasm and excitement. They tell stories and share experiences with each other and discuss everything from ways of disciplining to ways of motivating young children. One student boldly commented that she discovered "giving the children food helps them focus on their work better." This is a wonderful insight into children's behavior, and we recommend rewarding middle school students with ice cream or soda to reinforce their positive behavior as well. We usually go out to a Carvel or Burger King after a service visit. Adults comment that they have never seen a group of adolescents (usually about 30) so well behaved in a fast-food restaurant. The new maturity carries over to other situations. Dr. Roland Yoshida, Dean of the School of Education at Queens College of the City University of New York, came with us on a field visit to a day-care center. The students assumed the role of tour guides. They shared their own insights and instructed him how to behave with the little kids. One student told him, "If one of the day-care children starts to cry or bothers you, just let me know. I'll help you out."

Weekly group meetings are informal classroom discussions. Chairs are arranged in a circle so students are better able to share their experiences and learn from one another. Starting with a "go-around" is recommended. This helps to break the ice and to get the students thinking. Topics vary, based on the site visit, and have included, "When the nurse yelled at the senior citizen, I felt . . ." or "When the 3-year-old cursed, I . . ." or "Caring means. . . ." The discussion usually begins with events that occurred at the site, and then shifts to broad topics such as family, children, career, and the future. One day, the students started debating the issue of child rearing. One student began to talk about how she was beaten as a child by her father and how horrible it made her feel. Another student asserted that all children need to be hit to learn how to behave. She told the group that her mother told her that parents who do not hit their children do not really love them. This point was instantly debated by a majority of the students who strongly disagreed with that standpoint. These stories were a wonderful catharsis for the group.

The teacher then moved the students to another level of thinking by asking how they would raise their own children. Juan, an articulate and outgoing seventh-grade student, stated, "I'm not sure I want children because it is really hard to be a kid today. Maybe we should all think about whether or not we want kids before we have them so we don't end up beating them up." Other students were a bit more hopeful. Michael, a quiet and bright student, projected his lessons into the future when he said, "At the day-care center, I learned what challenges will become (sic) of me when I am an adult. . . . I will already know something about parenthood. . . . I hope I will remember what I have learned to become a caring parent. I want to give my children lots of opportunities."

At times, intrinsic values that arise during the discussions—such as honesty, respect, love, unselfishness, kindness, discipline, and friendship—become the focus of the session. These seem to be the recurrent values that have grown out of our experiences. Very special friendships have developed as a result of this program. Students develop unusual bonds with each other as they assume helpful roles outside the school. Students have commented that they feel part of a group of kids who care about other people. Many have continued their involvement over holiday weeks and summer vacation as volunteers in senior centers and nursing homes, and as counselors in summer camps. Love is a recurrent urgent theme and topic of discussion. One student commented, "Receiving love feels nice, but learning how to give love to others feels even better."

Teachers who are new to the program often express unusually close feelings toward the students in the program. One teacher, a veteran Home and Careers teacher who was very resistant to changing the curriculum, stood up at a faculty conference and proclaimed,

> When I first found out about changing the program, I was very angry. I had been doing the curriculum for 20 years and was very happy with it. I grudgingly began with one class at a local elementary school. We made crafts in school and then went to share them with kindergarten students. The attitude of my students changed immensely. Knowing that someone would be receiving their work made them more conscientious and caring. This made the class more enjoyable and made my work more rewarding. I now know that you can have honest and respectful relationships with these kids. Once they are given the opportunity to do something meaningful, they rise to the occasion.

Group meetings are supplemented with material from local papers, books or magazines that deal with contemporary issues in society such as euthanasia, teenage pregnancy, and drug abuse. Students learn the skills necessary to teach young students or to read and talk to senior citizens; for example, they practiced reading story books clearly, showing the pictures as they read, and asking the young children questions to motivate or check comprehension. One teacher showed her students the same videotape that was shown to teachers during an in-service course on whole language. Those going to the nursing home worked on "speaking up" and speaking clearly, and developing questions to ask and anecdotes to tell so as to be good conversationalists. In addition, students are required to reflect in a journal at least once a week. Daysha, a defiant seventh-grader, wrote the following about her experience at the day-care center: "They make me laugh, smile, and feel good about myself. I am learning how to get along with them [the preschoolers] better. It takes a lot of energy to be nice to them all the time. I know I have to keep working at it."

Amelia reflects on her experience at the nursing home when she states, "I'm learning that growing old isn't so bad. I like getting to know Mrs. C. She's cool and the best person at the home. She really knows how to listen to me. She's not like other adults I know." Teachers read the journals as often as possible and make comments when appropriate. Students are permitted to staple or fold back the pages that they do not want to share. One student told a teacher that she would rather not share the journal at all. Flexibility is another important aspect of the program. The teacher and the student agreed to have private bi-weekly meetings to discuss progress and/or any concerns.

SOCIAL AND CURRICULAR CONCERNS

These service learning activities provide opportunities for educators to develop curricula that are based on both the developmental and academic needs of the student. Middle school students are intense about relationships with peers. Service projects allow them to work together on constructive activities. They read, write stories, make up directions for games, and create new activities. They learn to interview and to tape the interviews. They also read and clip articles about issues related to their service projects. Together, these activities truly result in an interdisciplinary learning situation.

Early adolescents undergo intense physical changes. This causes much anxiety in middle-level students. It is not uncommon for female students to be ashamed of their developing breasts or their "underdeveloping" breasts. Our teachers have witnessed male students comparing hair density on their legs and arms. Intergenerational programs encourage the discussion of physical change without the embarrassment of focusing solely on the challenges of puberty. During seminar, Erin, an articulate and sensitive student, shared a story about her adopted grandmother, Mrs. M., at the nursing home. She described how

Mrs. M. told her how young and beautiful she once was in her youth and that now she sometimes doesn't recognize herself in the mirror. Erin told the group that she had the same experience when she looks at pictures of herself because in her mind she is still a child but in pictures she is beginning to look like her older sister. Other students chimed in how fast they are changing. Katrina, who is proud of her own aging process, proudly claimed, "I don't know why some people don't like to get old. I know that I get prettier as I get older."

Students volunteering at the day-care center focus on the changes that occur during early childhood. As part of the seminar, students prepare a case study for one day care child of their choice. Students observe and record changes in speech patterns, increasing vocabulary, use of volume, tone, and pitch; increased dexterity; physical growth and strength; and any other notable behavior. They are also asked to discuss this child with their mentor teacher in order to gain insight beyond their own observations. Here is Sydney's first observation sheet of Tawana at the day-care center:

> *Name*: Tawana
> *Age:* 3 years, 2 months
> *Physical Description:* About the same size as the other girls in the class; short hair in pretty bow; very active, can run and jump very fast
> *Speech:* Can say her name very clear, talks a lot but a lot of words are not clear; talks loud
> *Notable Behavior:* Likes to get her way; very bossy with other kids; seems very smart and likes me a lot

During seminar, the student's findings are shared with the class. Students are amazed to observe the changes in the children's behavior. During seminar, Ramon, who frequently uses vulgar words as part of his vocabulary, was appalled that his case study student at the day-care center was also using profanity. He asked the students in the group what he could do about this problem. Together, they did some creative problem solving and speculated about the reasons why this child was cursing. (For the teacher, this process is delightful. What better way to address the problems of early adolescence than by having early adolescents focus on the same problems in younger children?) The discussion went on for about 30 minutes. One student suggested that the young child heard Ramon use a bad word himself. Another student suggested that the young child has no other words to use. The teacher helped guide the students but did not interfere with the discussion. By engaging in such discussion, the students are developing problem-solving skills as they work collaboratively on real-life community problems. Thus, social learning takes place both at the service site as well as in the classroom.

Students volunteering at the nursing home have an opportunity to observe the final stages of the life cycle. At first, this can be frightening. Debbie, a seventh-grader, describes the initial experience as "scary and heartbreaking." The students are sensitized to the experience by role-playing the physical limitations of aging. In addition, the seniors often describe their own feelings about aging and how difficult it is to have a frail and tired body. In seminar, the students are able to make comparisons between the seniors and themselves. Jasmine, another seventh-grader, commented that "as humans, we constantly change." She said this as though it were the first time she had ever thought about her own changing body. Once the subject was raised, other students felt more comfortable discussing their own physical development, which may have been causing them anxiety. This kind of discussion is often difficult between middle school students and their teachers, because large classes that meet for 45 minutes are not settings that lend themselves to intimacy. We know that our students desperately need positive role models and constructive relationships with adults. This service learning program supports that relationship.

These experiences lend themselves to wonderful units for other subject areas that engage students in their own learning, another middle school goal. As part of their Home and Careers curriculum (a New York state-mandated middle school subject), students learned about child development through a series of elementary school visits. A seventh-grader named Roberto commented, "One child came up to me and told me he wanted me to come with him, so I did. He brought me over to the hamster cage and told me the animal's name was Creampuff. I was surprised that he had the guts to come up to me." Another student, Neela, was analytical about the teachers in the day-care program: "They should do songs sitting in a circle and read them stories. They should bring them to our school to know what they will be doing a few years from now." (This was successfully arranged.) Marissa commented, "I learned one important thing about being a parent. You don't buy kids sharp toys."

The three-part spiraling activity—discussing and predicting ("I think they'll be shy"), then living the activity, then reflecting on it in a journal ("I was surprised that he had the guts to come up to me")—constitutes a wonderful whole-language experience. It involves the child in listening, speaking, reading and writing. It is organic—a seamless experience that unfolds all year long.

Interdisciplinary teams of teachers can use the service learning experience to enrich their own curricula. For a unit on human development that began with the day-care center and nursing home projects, the science teacher focused on changes in cell structure during the process of aging and the English teacher focused on literary accounts of the life cycle through novels and poetry. Students interviewed older Americans, particularly immigrants, about changes they have seen or experienced. One particularly touching interview is transcribed here:

Jon: Could you tell me about when you were a boy?

Mr. K. (an 80-year-old Russian immigrant): I was a Jew in Russia—not an easy thing to be in those days. I remember the pogroms.

Jon: What is a pogrom?

Mr. K.: It was a time when the Russian soldiers would try to round up and hurt the Jewish citizens.

Jon: That sounds terrible.

Mr. K.: I remember a Pogrom that almost killed me. We were running across the ice. The ice broke and I fell in. Someone grabbed me by my knapsack, still on my back, and pulled me up. I was freezing but alive. (The interview continues about Mr. K's Russian history.)

Jon: Would you say something in Russian for me?

Mr. K.: (Says a sentence in Russian) That means you're a wonderful boy. I enjoyed this interview.

Another excellent interdisciplinary approach that can be related to service work with seniors is stereotyping. An English and social studies teacher developed a wonderful unit. Students examined the stereotypes associated with various populations, particularly the elderly. Students are accustomed to discussions of stereotyping, but think of it more in connection with race, or religion, or gender. The idea that there are "ageists" who hold stereotypes about seniors was a new idea to them. But they quickly generated some stereotypes that they realized existed. Some stereotypes included, "they're mean," "they're grouchy," "they're ugly," "they're slow," "they're sick," "they smell," and "they dress funny." These stereotypes were written on oak tag and left hanging in the room. As the students began visiting the seniors at the nursing home, these stereotypes were "revisited." In addition, students read literature in English class written by seniors that describes the process of aging (Erma Bombeck is a wonderful source). In social studies, they focused on contemporary issues related to aging: homelessness, institutionalization of the elderly, other cultural responses to aging, and economic factors pertaining to aging (e.g., Social Security benefits). Study of culture or community with interviews and oral histories is also successful. Students from a predominately Hispanic community conducted interviews, transcribed them to monologue form, and then worked with the school's museum staff to coordinate an exhibit entitled "La Bodega," a spectacular exhibition of student work. The music and art teachers further enhanced the unit. For example, as another culminating activity, student volunteers at the nursing home sang Christmas carols with their adopted grandparents.

Young teens seek power and adult status, but at times can assume it through "macho" behavior and inappropriate talk and action. Service learning naturally encourages students to become independent and to develop a sense of responsibility for themselves and others. To illustrate this point, students have actually called in sick on days that they were unable to attend a service activity. This shows an unusual commitment for middle-level students. This sense of responsibility comes from feeling needed, valued, and respected by the people at the placement site.

Seniors are as disappointed as the little children at the day-care center when our early adolescent volunteers are about to leave. Some seniors try to cajole our students to stay by offering them candy or other inducements. The most heartbreaking time for one teacher and class was the day a senior cried and begged our student volunteers not to leave after the party that marked the conclusion of the program.

Urban youth are isolated from the life of their cities. They often experience an equivocal sense of what community is all about. Service learning encourages a sense of civic awareness that lets students know how valuable they can be. One of our experiences made this clear. Funds allocated for day-care centers in New York City are diminishing. To address that issue, last spring we planned a street fair with the day-care center. Student volunteers served as hosts and hostesses. They painted the faces of the little ones, sold cookies and balloons, and helped supervise the children. The center raised over $1,000. The students felt very proud of themselves. At the next group meeting, students shared the pride they felt as active participants in the street fair. Jackie captured the spirit of the day in her journal:

> Today is one the best days I've ever had at school. . . . The center needs repairs for holes in the wall and a new paint job. The little kids need toys and stuff. We got there early in the morning. . . . It started to rain and I felt sick that no one would show up. But after a little while, it started to get real crowded. We were the people in charge; the ones who welcomed people and showed them around. It was great. . . . The center made a lot of money. I can't wait to see the center fixed up and everything. I'll know that it looks better because of me.

Another important benefit of the service learning program is caring. Students are not simply told to "care" for others; they learn through their experiences. Anthony is a quiet, sad student. His mother died several years ago, and he lives with his grandmother in a housing project in Queens. Violence and drugs are no stranger to this boy's experience. His initial attitude about service was negative, and he made it clear that he had little interest in visiting the "old" people at the nursing home. During the first seminar in class, he jokingly remarked that senior citizens "smell funny." We were a bit concerned about his reluctance, and discussed his case with the director of the nursing home. She said she had the perfect "grandparent" for this child. She matched him with a resident who had been a jazz musician in his youth. He was a warm and friendly man who had no family. He was delighted to have Anthony visit with him. Mr. B. was very talkative and helped break the ice. Anthony did not have much to say when we returned to school. The following week, Anthony asked one of us if it would be okay to bring his radio to the nursing home, although students are not normally permitted to carry radios or "walkmans" in school or on field trips. When asked why he needed to bring it, he told me that he wanted to share "rap" music with Mr. B., his adopted grandparent. This was a real breakthrough for Anthony. The two of them really hit it off. Anthony became friendlier in class. He began to participate during class discussions. His behavior began to improve in other classes as well. At the end of the year, students were asked to reflect on the service experience. He wrote, "I learned to care and to be kind. I feel proud of myself."

Another outcome of a service learning program is noticeable changes in student behavior. Jerry, a large and overage seventh-grader who is classified as emotionally disabled, enjoys working with a 3-year-old buddy so much that his school behavior has improved tremendously; he doesn't want to lose the privilege of going to the day-care center. Another teacher describes a seventh-grade class chosen to volunteer at the day-care center as having been extremely rowdy before the program began. Getting this class to pay attention usually required a stern look and a loud voice. Following the first field visit, the teacher walked into the seminar to find the students sitting quietly waiting for her to arrive. Since this group was usually yelling and running around the room, she asked them if everything was all right. One student spoke up and said, "After volunteering at the day-care center and seeing how hard it is to control the little kids, the class couldn't be bad in our own class. It just wouldn't be right."

EVALUATION

Evaluation is an important aspect of a successful service learning program. In our program, reflection is ongoing, as students share and critique one another's work and write journal summaries of their experiences. Written reflections can be structured so that both concrete learnings and increased self-esteem are documented. Katara, a witty student with a cherubic face, states that she "has learned to be much better with kids" than when she started the program, because of her newly discovered patience. In addition, she writes in her journal, "I think that this experience has helped me with my attitude problems that I sometimes get when I get mad." Through real-life experiences and role-playing, the students have an opportunity to practice socially acceptable behavior. Jennifer writes, "I think the children in my group enjoy me. . . . We play and read to them and do other fun things. We also help them tie their shoes and put on their coats. As the weeks passed, we have to help them less and hug them more. It is like they are becoming family." Students volunteering at the nursing home develop new perspectives on living. Linda reflects that she "learned to take advantage of life . . . and realize how good it really is. Instead of feeling down, I try to look at the bright side of things. One person can bring a lot of happiness into other people's lives. I'm glad I had this opportunity."

Last fall, three of our students were invited by the National Center for Service Learning to present their service learning experiences at the National Society for Experiential Education Conference in Providence, Rhode Island. These students had been chosen because of their extraordinary work in the field. Sydney and Nick volunteered at the day-care center and Vanessa volunteered at the nursing home. Together, with two adults from the National Center, we took the train from New York to Rhode Island. On the train, the students were busily practicing their presentations. Sydney, an extremely articulate and precocious 13-year-old, was busy asking me questions about the conference. Vanessa, a very attractive and soft-spoken student, was busy studying everyone around her as she contemplated her notes on index cards. Nick, quiet and reserved, was fidgeting with his notes and asking to go to the eating car every 15 minutes.

When we got to the convention center, the students became a little nervous. First, Sydney worried that no one would come to hear the presentation, and then Nick worried that they would not be well received by the audience. After their initial anxieties were assuaged, they assumed their roles as presenters with ease and distinction. They charmed their audience of approximately 20 adults with their knowledge, insight, and introspection. Sydney shared her expertise in conflict resolution as she became a "pro" in breaking up fights within her 3-year-old group at the day-care center. She stated, "Part of my job at the Day Care Center was to make sure the little kids were safe. Not only did we have to make sure they weren't playing with anything dangerous but we had to watch them every minute . . . they were always fighting with each other. I became a fair referee in their fights and they would come to me. Now I know how my parents feel when I fight with my brothers." Vanessa shared her insights about senior citizens. She stated, "Getting old doesn't mean that you become a new person. It just means you change a little, that's all. At first I was real nervous, but my adopted grandmother made me feel so comfortable. We even like some of the same things. She loved astrology and so do I! I'm not so afraid of growing old anymore." Nick was a little shy but answered audience questions astutely. At one point, a college professor asked him what he liked least about the experience. He quickly responded, "The end of the semester." They maintained these distinct adult attributes until we got into a cab to take us back to the train. Then, all of a sudden we were seated with three very giddy early adolescents. They literally giggled all they way to the train station. Once again, it became clear to us that given the right context and motivation, these middle-level students are capable of accomplishing so much!

The students are also trained as "evaluators" by the National Center for Service Learning, and conduct their own program evaluations. They interview various constituents—including school staff and students, parents, community members, nursing home staff and clients, and day-care staff and children—and then compile their own data (see Figure 12–1). Of the nine seniors interviewed in the Spring of 1992, seven (78 percent) liked having the students come to the nursing home, one had mixed feelings and one didn't like them coming. Five (55 percent) felt the Helpers were doing a good job, three (33 percent) had mixed feelings, and one felt the Helpers were not doing a good job because "they are always bothering me." Other seniors were more positive and their comments included, "The students are pleasant," "We talk about my past," and "They try hard and are always helpful and courteous, not like other children I know." Seniors also report that they would like to talk more with the students and learn about the world outside of the nursing home.

Interview questions for *Helpers* working at the Franklin Nursing Home:

1. What do you like about the program? What don't you like?
2. What do you do with the seniors?
3. Do you feel that you make the seniors happy? Yes _____ No _____
4. Do you get along with seniors better now than before you participated in this program? How?
5. Would you rather work at a day-care center? Yes_____ No _____ Why?
6. What can we do to make the program better?

Interview questions for the *Principal* about Helpers working at the Franklin Nursing Home:

1. Do you think that having students work at the Franklin Nursing Home is a good idea? Yes ____ No ____ Why?
2. Do you notice changes in the students who are participating in the program? Yes ____ No ____ What are they?
3. Do you think the students are doing important work? Yes ____ No ____ How would you describe that work?
4. Do you think the program should continue next year? Yes ____ No ____ Why?
5. Is there anything that you would change abou the program? Yes ____ No ____ What would it be?

Interview questions for *administrators and nurses* at the Franklin Nursing Home:

1. Do you think that the Helpers' Program is a good idea? Why?
2. Do you notice changes in the seniors after our visits? Yes ____ No ____ What are the changes?
3. Do you think the students are helpful? Yes ____ No ____ How?

FIGURE 12–1   Student Evaluators: Louis Armstrong Middle School

Students volunteering at the day-care center had a difficult time interviewing the young children because they (the children) did not understand the questions. Middle school students also interviewed their peers about the day-care center experience and discovered that the only times that bothered them were when the little children would not listen to them and were too active (90 percent). Most students (95 percent) felt that the only thing needed to improve the program was to visit more frequently. Day-care personnel were also very positive. Everyone questioned felt that the middle school students were very helpful (100 percent). They felt that the students needed no special supervision and that they responded very well to the needs of the young children. These findings, it should be noted, were presented at the annual conference for the National Center for Service Learning in Early Adolescence. Any school interested in rewarding the student volunteers could arrange an in-school conference with proud parents as the audience.

We gleaned from the responses to the student questionnaires what service learning programs contribute to the middle school program. We learned that students would like to spend more time in the field. We learned that students enjoyed the day care center more than the senior center, but felt that the senior center was an important part of the their service activity. They recommended that students spend half a semester at a day-care center and half a semester at a senior center, in order to get a diversified experience. We learned that community perceptions of the school improved as students went out into the community to do service. We learned that parents are supportive and glad that their children have an opportunity to participate in the program. We learned that most senior citizens are happier because of this experience, and that the day-care students looked forward to the weekly visits. We learned that day-care staff relied on the students as valuable assistants in their classes. We learned that student volunteers are willing to continue these activities during their own time. We learned that senior citizens, teachers, students, and little children can have a fine time together. Indeed, we are learning a great deal about the human spirit.

CONCLUSION

Schools can become a place of hope for many children. They can be empowered with opportunities to develop into caring adults, capable of taking control of their own lives and improving society at large. To do this, bold changes need to be incorporated into the educational program by restructuring the role of the school in the community. Schools cannot and should not exist within a vacuum. They can use the community to encourage learning, motivate students, enhance their self-esteem, connect them with community life realities, and nurture and stimulate their hopes for the future. Indeed, the community can use the school to develop its citizens.

It is time for service learning to become an accepted part of the middle school curriculum. Our future as a society depends on it.

ENDNOTE

1. Service learning is a form of experiential learning that connects meaningful work in the community (community service) with content curriculum in the school. Students are then encouraged to examine these experiences through active reflection led by experienced teachers. The reflection is structured so that the student has time to think, talk, and write about what he or she did and saw during the actual service activity.

REFERENCES

Carnegie Council on Adolescent Development. (1989). *Turning Points. Preparing American Youth for the 21st Century.* New York: Carnegie Corporation of New York.

Schorr, Lisabeth B. (1989). *Within Our Reach: Breaking the Cycle of Disadvantage.* New York: Anchor Press/Doubleday.

Wheelock, Anne. (1992). *Crossing the Tracks.* New York: The New Press.

13

Incorporating Service Learning into the School Day

JULIE AYERS

KATHLEEN KENNEDY TOWNSEND

Mary Ann Hartshorn is passionate about service learning. Hartshorn, a social studies teacher at Southhampton Middle School in Harford County, Maryland, says, "At the middle school level it is so important to do service learning. Kids have so much energy. It's important to let them know that someone is willing to let them use it in a way that they think is important. They are looking for a place to shine and service learning gives them a place to do that." Hartshorn represents a growing number of Maryland educators who believe that engaging students in service learning activities during the school day ensures their intellectual, personal, and social growth.

WHAT IS SERVICE LEARNING?

Service learning is one of the latest manifestations of experiential education. It has captured the imagination of kids, teachers, communities, and politicians because it has multiple benefits. It helps students learn and it helps solve problems in communities. President Clinton, at a Summer of Service rally in College Park, Maryland, in August of 1993, said, "I think every state should include community service as part of the curriculum."

In Maryland, *service learning* is defined as a structured learning experience. Time is set aside for preparation and for reflection. Students learn about problems in their community, provide needed services to the community, connect their actions to their duties as citizens, and reflect on what they have done. Service learning differs from community service and volunteerism, where individuals undertake activities expecting no compensation, financially or *educationally.*

Service learning is increasingly popular because it "fits." Service learning fits the developmental needs of middle school students for active learning as well as the need to apply learning to the "real" world. Service also fits communities by meeting their needs.

In 1992, Maryland became the first state in the nation to make participation in a service learning program a requirement for public high school graduation. The requirement stands on the foundation for service learning established in the state by the Maryland Student Service Alliance (MSSA). MSSA has trained more than 2,200 Maryland teachers and 500 community agencies to engage students in service learning projects as part of the school day.

MAKING SERVICE PART OF THE SCHOOL DAY

Service learning fits into virtually any school, academic instructional unit, or course. It may be directly linked to course curriculum or it may complement a variety of course curricula. In whatever way service learning is incorporated into the school day, it reinforces or builds on many core educational objectives by helping students improve their problem-solving and communication skills. Service projects may be carried out within the school building or at sites in the community. The main goal is to meet real community needs through service learning projects.

This chapter describes how four Maryland middle schools are using service learning. It represents a progression of programs from those more loosely tied to course content to those directly linked to classroom curriculum. The models featured range from programs carried out within the school day that complement educational objectives to programs that directly infuse service learning into course curricula. An urban school that alters its school schedule twice a year to offer service learning mini-courses for students is highlighted first. This model features a program that incorporates service projects into the school day without infusing them into specific courses. Instead, by performing these service projects, students gain general educational skills such as problem solving and team work. Next is a suburban school which uses advisory periods for service learning work. Service projects are also linked to social studies classes. Third is a suburban school that has special education and regular education students working together on an infused service learning project in a science class. And finally, a rural school is featured that offers a model of interdisciplinary infusion projects.

MODEL 1: MINI-COURSES

Canton Middle School is tucked into one of Baltimore City's oldest residential neighborhoods. The three-story brown brick school building is surrounded by the narrow streets of East Baltimore's famous old, red brick row homes. They are each about 11 feet wide and house families who are predominately working class, descendants of Polish immigrants. The tourist attractions of this neighborhood are the polished marble steps and the hand-painted pastoral scenes on the screen doors of most of these homes.

Canton Middle School is showing its age with worn steps and cracked sidewalks. But the people who fill the building each day give it vibrancy with their energy and diversity: 65 percent Caucasian, 30 percent African American, and 5 percent Native American and Asian American.

Canton has a reputation for innovation. The principal, Dr. Craig Spilman, is always seeking and implementing new programs that have the potential to help his 775 students. The majority of Canton's students come from blue-collar families, many of whom are suffering from the prolonged recession. Many students have serious educational as well as economic needs; 105 are special education students and 550 students qualify for the free or reduced-price lunch programs. Canton's students often have a poor attendance rate and many drop out of high school.

How the Program Started

For many years, Canton had been offering mini-courses for students. These mini-courses, held twice a year, brought small groups of students together during the school day with a teacher to work on arts and crafts projects—painting, jewelry making, guitar lessons, and so on. These mini-courses were unpopular with students. Students would often cut school when courses were offered or act up and not participate in the groups.

After teacher involvement in MSSA-sponsored workshops, school administrators decided to change the focus of the mini-courses.

"We began our community service learning program five years ago because we felt our students should be more aware of their community's needs and should play active roles in meeting those needs," said Bailey Trueman, program coordinator, who makes one think of an Irish Santa Claus as he speaks. "We also felt by involving students in service learning, they would begin to view themselves in a more positive light. They would discover they can make positive changes in their neighbors', and their own, lives. We changed our traditional mini-course program from arts and crafts to service learning. Each year, our service program has gotten stronger. We still do mini-courses in the fall and the spring, but it's a thousand times more educational now!" said Trueman. "Canton's service learning mini-courses are designed to help students meet general educational objectives such as problem solving, communication skills, and development of a positive self image," adds Trueman. This program meets Maryland's definition of service learning as it engages students in preparation, action, and reflection activities for each service project they carry out. That said, it should be noted that the depth and breadth of the preparation and reflection activities at Canton are not as extensive as the other three models highlighted in this chapter that incorporate service learning projects into course curricula.

Prior to implementation of the mini-courses, a coordinator conducted staff development and training to introduce the rest of the teachers to service learning. Once they understood the "preparation, action, reflection" model, they began to develop their own programs to fit the mini-course structure.

That first year, a group of students at Canton began serving meals weekly at Our Daily Bread soup kitchen. According to Trueman,

> It was everything an educator could hope for. The students involved benefited tremendously. They would go to the soup kitchen and see these people who were in need, and the students would fill at least one of those immediate needs by giving them a warm meal. This was a powerful experience. The students realized they could make a difference in someone else's life. They have the power to solve problems. This was a revelation to many of the kids. They are so used to being told that they're too young to do anything important. Kids are also told frequently by adults that they themselves are problems—certainly not problem solvers. We realized helping students discover their power to make positive changes in their communities was a valuable experience for *all* of our students, so we began making plans to expand the program.

Student response to the program has been overwhelmingly favorable. Students look forward to mini-courses and take their work very seriously. Katrina Geeorgiadis, an eighth-grader during the 1992–1993 school year, sums up the typical student reaction to the program when she wrote in her journal: "I think community service learning is something that is fun to do, and it also gives you the opportunity to help other people. For the past three years I have been doing service at a local nursing home because I like to help elderly people. It also makes me feel good about myself. It helps to not take so many things for granted, like I have always done."

Scheduling

By participating in mini-courses, all students at Canton get a chance to do just what Katrina described—help others and feel good about themselves—at least twice a year. On mini-course days, normal classes end by 1:15 P.M. Mini-course activities last from 1:15 to 2:35 for at least three consecutive days.

Six weeks before mini-courses are scheduled, teachers select issues they care about and develop a mini-course around that theme. They develop appropriate preparation, action, and reflection activities for students that complement educational objectives rather than meet specific core subject course objectives.

During the service learning mini-courses, students take on every imaginable service project. They monitor streams, paint city storm drains with "Don't Dump: Chesapeake Bay Drainage," paint the school gym, serve meals at soup kitchens, write pen-pal letters to children in the hospital, create and perform a pregnancy prevention skit for peers, sort clothes at Goodwill, clean the neighborhood, plant trees and flowers, visit senior citizens at a nearby nursing home, collect supplies for the food pantry and clothes closet students created in the school, read books on tape for blind students, collect and repair suitcases and photo albums for children in foster care, sew quilts for babies born with AIDS, and much more. One of the most popular service projects is playing chess with senior citizens. Once the students have learned about aging and its physical and emotional effects, and how to play chess as part of their preparation, they visit nursing homes to challenge the elderly residents. In reflection, the students discuss and write about their visits. Through these reflection activities, students discover they have improved their own cognitive and problem-solving skills, while stimulating their opponents' minds.

"One of our main objectives is to have 10 or fewer students involved in any activity. This allows the teacher to work with the children on an individual basis," says Trueman. In order for these numbers to remain low, all faculty members and nonteaching faculty, except administrators, take part in sponsoring a service activity.

Student Choice

Students have a voice in all aspects of the mini-course program. This fall, 12 students coordinated a "college-style" registration in the gym where all students signed up for mini-courses. "It's important that students be allowed to select the type of project they want to work on," says Rachel Rhodes, the young, enthusiastic coordinator of the school's mentoring program who helped Trueman organize mini-courses this year. "When students are allowed to choose what they will do, they are much more invested in the project. Both the teacher and students need to be working on their project because it is important to them."

Transportation and Liability

Many projects are conducted at the school or at service agencies within walking distance of the school, so transportation is not a problem. If transportation is needed, Trueman arranges in-kind donations from the agency that will receive the service. For example, Greenery Extended Care Center sends its agency van to pick up students for the projects. Trueman and other teachers occasionally drive students in their own cars as well.

All activities are covered by the school's insurance policy since they are part of the school day. In addition, agencies that students visit carry volunteer insurance.

The entire mini-course model operates with minimal funding. School resources are used to cover small expenses for supplies. Local businesses occasionally lend the school equipment to carry out projects that require special materials.

Preparation

Day 1: This year, guidance counselor Carol Ford sponsored a mini-course called Sunshine Kids Feeding the Homeless. On the first day of the mini-course, students began to prepare for their project by watching a video about hunger and homelessness in America. Then they discussed what they could do to help. They decided they should make bag lunches for people who were homeless. They talked about where they had seen homeless people in the city and selected an area where they would go to hand out the lunches. Their teacher contacted Beans and Bread, a soup kitchen in the neighborhood the students had selected, to set up the visit.

"The students discussed nutrition and what kinds of foods to give to people who are homeless," said Rhodes. "Should we give them potato chips or apples? Someone said protein foods help keep you warm, so they decided it would be important to make sure the lunches included a protein and a fruit. They also talked about where homeless people could store food, and soon realized the food in their bag lunches should be nonperishable." They developed a menu of peanut butter and jelly sandwiches and apples. Everyone selected an item they would bring in the next day so they could begin to make the lunches.

Action

Day 2: A lunch table in the cafeteria was transformed into an assembly line. Bread here, jelly next, then peanut butter. Another student stuffed the sandwich into a plastic bag. Then an apple and the sandwich were placed carefully into a brown paper sack. Fifteen students made short work of creating the 200 lunches. "They were taking it seriously because the preparation helped the students see why this was important. They weren't goofing off. They understood that this mattered. They made sure to make the layer of peanut butter on each sandwich nice and thick so the recipient would get plenty of protein."

Day 3: It was a sunny day, a great day for a nice long walk. The bubbly group of sixth- to eighth-grade students and Ms. Ford filled their arms with brown paper sacks and walked the half mile down to the harbor area in Fells Point to the soup kitchen. There was a line of clients standing on the sidewalk to get into the small soup kitchen. Students timidly walked up and asked the people if they'd like a bag lunch that they'd made themselves. Most people in line smiled and said thank you. A few were less gracious, and looked away as students approached.

Reflection

After they had delivered their lunches, the students and Ms. Ford came together to discuss and write about their experience. They talked about why some clients were not very friendly. Students speculated that some clients might feel bad since they were homeless and needed help. They talked about how they would feel in that situation, about how good they felt being able to help someone, and about what they had learned through the experience.

"One man growled at me! I was so scared. But I just went up to someone else who was nicer. I guess he was just embarrassed or angry that he had to be at the shelter in the first place, " wrote eighth-grader Angela Naumann.

Through reflection, students began to understand the importance of their contributions and what it had taught them: "I joined a group of students who delivered toys and food to needy children in the area of our school. While out that day, we stopped to help Miss Bea Gaddy distribute food at her center. I hope that when I become an adult, I can make the kind of difference in my neighborhood that Miss Bea makes in her community. Through service, I have come to realize how thankful I am because I have a loving family and friends. Through my community, I can show my appreciation," said eighth-grader Katrina Geeorgiadis in a letter she wrote reflecting on the projects.

"I enjoyed the mini-courses because it gave me a chance to help out in school. I helped get clothes for the poor and helped down at the Canton Public Library. The best part about it was it was fun because I helped someone in need," said seventh-grader Royce Lamp.

MODEL 2: ADVISORY PERIODS

Magothy River Middle School in Arnold, Maryland, is circled by a wide, green lawn that is surrounded by trees and a stream. The school is located in a middle-class residential neighborhood sprinkled with detached and semi-detached homes. There is a medical center, community college, and child-care center within walking distance. Unlike Canton Middle School, at Magothy there is little diversity in the neighborhood and the school building. Of the 1,063 students attending Magothy River, 90 percent are Caucasian. Most students are from middle-class families. Only 7 percent of the students receive reduced-price or free lunches. Students with disabilities are included in this school.

At Magothy, every two weeks an advisory period is scheduled by shortening class times for one school day. The advisory period is held during the first period of that day and lasts 30 minutes. Students and teachers use the time for service learning projects. The service learning activities complement core educational objectives, and direct curricular links are also instituted whenever possible.

How the Program Started

Craig Offhaus, Dorothy Weddington, Janice Lake, Jackie Sachs, Mickey Lloyd, Jeannie Hillman, and Tim Hopkins are the teachers that head the OWLS team at Magothy River. The OWLS team is comprised of 150 seventh-grade students. The acronym OWLS is formed from the first letter of several of the team leaders' last names. These teachers are proud of their team. Dorothy often wears a gold owl necklace and is quick to explain why. She is proud not only of her students but also her professional peers. "Our team is great. We really support each other and work well together," says Weddington.

After four members of the OWLS team attended a MSSA training institute, the teachers decided they had found a solution to their advisory period problem. Their school had recently begun scheduling advisory periods designed to bring small groups of students from the team together to assist them in developing social, coping, and other group dynamic skills. The teachers were unclear on how to focus the advisories and make them useful and meaningful for students.

During advisories, the team is allowed to bring all of their 150 students together for large group activities or to break them into small groups. They like doing some of both. After attending MSSA's training, they decided to use the advisory time as a catalyst to get students organized to work on service-learning projects.

Preparation

During the MSSA training, the teachers met Betty Russell, a spokesperson for Action for the Homeless. Russell is a recently retired English teacher with more than 20 years of classroom experience and has the gray streaked hair to prove it. She has turned her passionate concern about homelessness into a second career—visiting schools all across the state educating students about it. The OWLS teachers invited Russell to speak to their students during a large group advisory.

As Russell stood on the stage in the cafeteria, she asked the young faces in front of her, "Who are the homeless?" Students shouted out answers: "Old people," "Drug users," "People who don't want to work." Russell patiently recorded their responses on a flip chart. Then she showed them a film called "Shelter Boy" about a young boy from the Midwest who ends up living in a shelter with his mother, father, and sister after a tornado destroyed their home. Russell then asked the students the same question again: "Who are the homeless?" Now, as hands flew up in response, the descriptions that followed painted a very different picture of a homeless person: "They could be children," "They could be looking for work," " It's not always their fault." The students quickly grasped that homelessness affected many diverse groups of people in various situations.

Dorothy Weddington says the key to preparation is research. She had students clip articles on homelessness from newspapers and magazines to bring to social studies classes to be discussed.

During the students' next advisory, they met in small groups to brainstorm ways they could help the homeless. The newspaper articles about homelessness in their own school district were distributed to each group. Each group completed a sheet entitled "Portrait of the Homeless," filling in information from the article. The students read in order to ascertain who was homeless, why they were homeless, and what a possible solution might be to this specific example.

Back in the large group, they shared their ideas and picked projects they would all like to work on. They unanimously decided to help homeless children, whom they dubbed "the innocent victims." To help these children, the students developed plans for an advocacy project and an indirect service project. As their advocacy project, they decided to educate other students about the realities of homelessness and try to dispel common myths. As the indirect service project, they chose to provide supplies for children who live in local homeless shelters.

"While doing this, the students found out one of the families from our school was homeless," said Weddington, a social studies teacher with a commanding presence and a voice used to reaching across large rooms filled with noisy 11-year-olds. "It was a harsh reality for them to find out that it hit so close to home. They had thought that homeless people were poor, lower class, mostly black, on drugs, and wasted money. The realization came to them, after studying the issue in more depth, that there is more than one way you can become homeless. It could happen to anyone." She also said students "didn't feel enough was being done to help the homeless using resources that already exist."

Action

Now it was time to get to work on the projects. During advisory periods, students divided themselves into committees to work on different parts of the two projects.

"We allowed the students to choose the groups they wanted to be in and we, the teachers, picked what group we wanted to work with. In doing so, we regrouped our advisory period," explains Weddington.

Students enjoyed the regrouping process: "You also worked with other teachers that you would think are mean but weren't once you worked with them," explained an animated seventh-grader named Leah Smearman.

"When we changed advisory based on interest, it cut across friend groups, incomes—it exposed them to other students," said Weddington. "Now in advisory we worked on our projects."

Students divided themselves into seven working groups. Two groups, named Kid & Play and A Play for You, created skits about children who were homeless. Students working on skits decided that advisory periods did not give them enough time to polish their "masterpieces," so they would often come in before school to write and practice. They wanted the plays to be perfect, to really express what it was like to be a child who is homeless, before they presented them to the rest of the student body. One skit was about a brother and sister who were homeless and afraid to let their classmates find out. When the sister does reveal to her best friend that she is living in a shelter, the other girl shuns her and tells everyone else in school. Another skit explored the reasons why families might live in shelters. Students depicted a family in crisis: The father loses his job, the mother does not make enough money to cover the rent and other expenses, the son needs new shoes.

"I was able to see new leadership," said Weddington. "One student directed, wrote and acted in the play group. She was a real leader. In the classroom I had never seen that side of her. They were able to discover new talents and skills. We more or less let the groups direct themselves. All of them really came through."

At the same time, two other groups, Speak for Yourself and Signed, Sealed, Delivered, focused on locating shelters in their community. Betty Russell gave them names of shelters; students surveyed adults and community directories to find others. Then they wrote to the shelters to find out what kinds of supplies they needed for children living there. One of the request letters said in part:

> The students of the OWLS team would like to help make homeless shelters better. We are planning fund-raisers to raise money for the shelters. We would like to be informed of the supplies you need, so that we can contribute the scarce items. The OWLS team feels strongly about the nationwide issue of homelessness. We are hoping our efforts in such activities will help to solve this problem. Homeless people need many things that others take for granted. These people, less fortunate than us, need school supplies, clothing, food, and medical attention. These people need support from peers when they are in trouble or have a bad day.

Another group of students, Post It, sponsored a poster contest for the 150 students on their seventh-grade team. Students created colorful posters that showed that many children are homeless. These posters depicted many situations in which children, just like themselves, could find themselves without a home. Hung in the school cafeteria, these posters reached the entire school population and became an impetus for discussion.

The last two groups, Fun Raiser and Loose Change, raised money to buy the supplies that the homeless shelters said they needed for their child residents. Fun Raiser held bake sales and raised $50. Loose Change filled a giant jar with jelly beans and students made donations each time they submitted a guess on the number of beans in the jar. The person with the closest guess would win the jar and all the candy. Loose Change generated $86.08 worth of guesses.

Once everything was ready, all the groups came back together to share their efforts. The play groups performed their productions for the other students. The posters that had been on display in the cafeteria were judged and winners received prizes. The results of the letter-writing projects were shared. The shelters had asked for school supplies and for play equipment for older students. The group based their purchases on the needs of the shelters using the $136.08 they raised.

To purchase the items the shelter needed, students contacted local businesses for donations or price reductions. The Magothy students also purchased notebooks, pens, pencils, volleyball and badminton equipment, basketballs, and croquet equipment for the shelters.

Reflection

To reflect on their service, students took photos of their progress throughout the project. At the end, they made a poster out of the photos to display in the school. The pictures showed the various stages of preparation and action. Students were shown baking the goods for their bake sale, writing letters to the shelters, purchasing needed items, and creating the cafeteria posters. With captions, the photo poster described the entire project. Students also held a closing ceremony for their project to which they invited community members, the press, and shelter representatives. At the closing, each group reported what it had done. Students also performed their skits, presented the prizes to the winners of the poster and jelly bean contests, and gave donations to the shelters.

"You felt like you were doing something," said Leah Smearman, age 13. "Taking charge! Helping someone. You felt really good inside. All bubbly. You feel responsible. Adult-like. The best thing about it was the feeling of accomplishment and pride."

"Seeing the kids give their energies to something that's important because they thought it was important was great," said Weddington. "They saw it through from beginning to end. Since advisories only met twice a month, it was a long process. They wanted to do it badly enough that they gave of their time and stuck with it."

MODEL 3: INCLUSION AND SINGLE-SUBJECT INFUSION

Driving through Columbia, Maryland, one is immediately struck by how clean, green and the orderly everything is. The streets and buildings have all been carefully and tastefully laid out. Harper's Choice Middle School is located in this planned, suburban community between Baltimore and Washington, D.C. The school is located on a quiet street in a village cluster and is within walking distance of a special education school, businesses, restaurants, residential communities, and day-care and senior centers. The one-story brick school building was designed to be an open school, classrooms flowing into one another. Through the years, walls and partial walls have sprung up in the building to close off areas. As one walks down the carpeted hallways, one sees these walls covered with student artwork, samples of classwork, and displays created by students who come from predominantly middle-class or upper middle-class families. The centerpiece of the school is the media center. Each morning, the school's 600 students (83 percent Caucasian, 5 percent African American, 5 percent Asian American, 5 percent Hispanic, and 2 percent Indian [students from India]) gather to watch their own TV station, HCTV. All programming is produced by students and often features service learning projects underway in the school.

How the Program Started

Harper's Choice Middle School uses an inclusion and single-subject infusion approach to integrate service into existing courses and established curricula. It is the Howard County Public School philosophy to provide inclusive educational programming students with and without disabilities in the same instructional environment. Single-subject infusion is incorporating service-learning activities into a particular course to meet that course's educational objectives. At Harper's Choice, service learning has been successfully infused into the seventh-grade Life Science Curriculum.

David Patterson is an energetic yet soft-spoken special education teacher with 10 years of experience at this school. Patterson, who gives the impression of moving in many directions at once, attended a MSSA training in the summer of 1991. He decided that involving students in environmental service learning projects would be a great way to bring special education and regular education students together to work toward a common goal. About 80 students at Harper's Choice are part of the special education program representing levels from mild to profound. Some have physical disabilities.

His project encouraged his school to develop inclusion programs in which special education students participate in general education courses such as math, science, language arts, and social studies. This program provided a first opportunity for the Science and Special Education teams to pioneer inclusion, the first to prove that children of all abilities, backgrounds, and experiences can learn together.

Scheduling

Because Patterson's special education students are included in general subject courses, he teamed up with science teacher Karen Doerrler, the seventh-grade team, and other staff to work on service projects. Patterson decided to work with Doerrler because the listed service topics were so readily infused into the existing science curriculum.

Doerrler teaches 200 students a day in five environmental education classes. Several of these classes include five special education students with mild to moderate disabilities. Patterson and Doerrler analyzed the science curriculum to identify places where service learning would enhance lessons. They selected four projects that would reinforce lessons about erosion, habitat, eco-systems, and pollution, and that could be carried out at intervals during the school year. Doerrler concentrated on teaching the content while Patterson did the legwork to set up the projects.

Preparation

Doerrler used her usual lessons on the water cycle, natural habitats, eco-systems, and pollution as preparation for the service-learning projects. "We had a guest speaker from the Environmental Protection Agency (EPA) address the students about environmental issues as a preparation activity," said Patterson. The speaker discussed pertinent recycling procedures and policies, and used interactive methods such as videos and student discussions to describe what happens in the students' own neighborhoods.

A slide presentation from Save Our Streams of Maryland was used to explain the scientific and practical components as to why " Don't Dump: Chesapeake Bay Drainage" should be painted on local storm drains.

In meeting curricular objectives, students learned theory about how things grow, adopted a tree for a year, and discovered the environmental benefits to planting marsh grass. Erica Pencak, age 13, said she liked doing the preparation for the projects in class. "We had a unit from science on plants," explained Pencak. "The service trip allowed us to plant flowers and marsh grass. We also did a unit on the Bay to prepare for our service project."

Projects

As students were learning more about the environment with each curricular unit of instruction, a variety of service projects were infused into each curricular application. They painted storm drains with the dumping warning and planted marsh grass and trees. Students tested the water quality of streams near their school and reported the data they collected to the Columbia Association and Save Our Streams of Maryland. They also collected litter and recycled what they could. These projects were done twice during the year—once in the fall and once in the spring. Patterson arranged for 100 students to do the projects on a half day in the fall, and the rest of the students did their projects in the spring. To leave school to do the projects, the seventh-grade school schedule was changed for two half days. This decision to change the schedule on those two days was made by all seven teachers on the seventh-grade team.

In shifts, students painted the storm drains. Every 40 minutes, a new class would arrive to continue the project. "We were lucky because of the location of the school in a village center. We had lots of storm drains to paint!" said Patterson. "It was a real high-energy day. Karen and I were exhausted by the end of the day but it was a blast!" The students were so charged by the information shared, they said they would never throw a cup out of a window again. Another student showed his frustration about how people could dump motor oil into a storm drain. Other students were eager to assist their peers who are disabled with tasks that were new and different.

Christine Descends, age 12, liked it because "it made it [the lesson] more fun. We actually got to see the product. It was a good idea."

Based on Patterson and Doerrler's success, all of the other team members rallied behind them and decided to go on an overnight service learning camping trip with their 200 seventh-grade students on a Thursday and Friday in May.

"Our team loves working together. Our theme was service. Each school team has a theme. Ours has been service for the last two years. We wanted to pick a theme that was meaningful," explains Patterson.

Funding and Transportation

Patterson found out about potential funding sources for service projects at MSSA's training. He wrote grant proposals to the state's Chesapeake Bay Trust and solicited donations from local businesses to cover the cost of the project. "I loved doing that," said Patterson. "It was fun to be able to raise several thousand dollars." Patterson said:

> Every teacher on our team did a monumental amount of work. Students and members of the PTA were also enthusiastic participants. Through months of preparation, students joined their parents at evening meetings to plan integral parts of the overnight trip. They actively wanted to be part of the decision-making process about what activities would be implemented at the camp and work sites. Another exciting factor was the "true inclusion" that occurred throughout the trip. Our cabin assignments were inclusive for the first time and quite successful with genuine student interactions throughout the day and night.
>
> We did two solid days of environmental service in May. We built a wildlife refuge by planting marsh grass, cleaned up three dump truck loads of recyclables off the beach, and we also planted wetland plants, built duck boxes, and toured a sewage treatment facility. It was really a good learning experience. We did a service project for the campsite as well. We built a jetty, cleaned up the beach, and planted a vegetable garden. We brought plants with us. They were donations from nurseries. We also built flower gardens around buildings at the camp and did trail maintenance. It was incredible. We had a large group of parents with us. We had 200 kids, probably 10 to 15 teachers, and 20 parents. We had 8 students with severe to profound disabilities and all our school's students with mild to moderate disabilities as well.

The trip was a great success. "Now our team loves doing service," said Patterson. "They loved seeing what the students learned and the comments they heard from students during and after the trips. They heard things such as 'I'll never throw trash away again' and 'I've never planted a tree before.'"

"I learned to plant marsh grass, which stops soil erosion" said 12-year-old Christine Descends. "I feel I am a better citizen." Erica Pencak, age 13, "learned how strong marsh grass is and how it holds the soil on the beach."

Reflection

Patterson, who was once introduced to a school visitor as David "Service" Patterson, is sold on inclusion and infusing service into his school's curriculum. "The service projects gave students a practical experience—an experiential component to skills they already learned in the classroom," said Patterson. "It broadened the classroom." When students returned to school, they had a great deal of "real" material to discuss in class. "Students had a new understanding of the impact of pollution on the environment. In class, we discussed the amount of trash they'd collected, and related that to our own behavior. Every time we throw something on the street, out the car window, or in the garbage can, it has to go somewhere," said Patterson.

The students built a Howard County landfill in the hall showcase. The display contained all recyclable materials such as glass, aluminum, tires, and paper. The adjacent showcase contained recycling trivia and photographs from the year's service activities. Patterson's students really enjoyed the project. "I think it's a nice way to learn, as opposed to textbook lessons, and it promotes service to the community—a good part of education," said Erica Pencak. "I thought the trip was great because we got to do fun stuff and service. It was well planned and we looked forward to it for a long time."

The community also seems sold on service. The school received recognition from their County Council and local media coverage for the environmental service projects.

MODEL 4: INTERDISCIPLINARY INFUSION PROJECTS

Southhampton Middle School is located on a large campus, more than 50 acres, in a rural county in Maryland. Ten acres of this land is devoted to an environmental center started by students in 1990 as part of a science class project. Since 1990, students have transformed that flat, grassy space of land near the woods and a stream into a colorful nature center filled with plants, tall grasses, and wildflowers. Students have constructed picnic tables, benches, and bird houses that are sprinkled throughout those 10 acres. There are pathways for students to explore on nature walks. In the spring and fall, many teachers hold classes outside in this area. The 1,485 students at the school are mostly Caucasian; only 1 percent of students are not. Very few students receive reduced-price or free meals. Approximately 40 students at each grade level are classified as special education. All special education students are fully mainstreamed at this school and have peer helpers.

Recently, Southampton got a new principal who restructured the school into teams. There are four main subject teachers on each team. Each team is assigned 120 to 125 students. In the daily schedule, those 120 students are locked into only three things: a 50-minute unified arts period (music, art, home economics), a lunch period, and a physical education period. The rest of the day, those 120 students belong to the team. "We can divide them up any way we want to," says Mary Ann Hartshorn, a petite woman who is bursting with so much energy it seems as though her small frame may burst into dozens of whirring pieces at any moment. "So we can spend all day on social studies if we want to. We have an integrated team time, this advisory period, which our team has made into a 40-minute period. Thus, we use those 40 minutes for service learning each day."

Preparation

To prepare their students to do service, the teachers took their entire team of students to the lecture hall at the beginning of the school year. "We like to give the kids a choice," says Hartshorn. "We start off our preparation by giving them choices of projects we think they might be interested in. We do this by giving them examples of successful projects students have done in the past by showing them slides. We also have them fill out an interest inventory and show them a film about 500 ways kids can help the environment. Then we ask them if they are interested in anything special."

This year, students came up with several project ideas. Some, after learning about water sampling, sediment control, larvae census taking, measuring flow rates, and creating scale drawings, wanted to clean and monitor the stream behind the school. Others wanted to make the school more beautiful and inviting by planning landscaping blueprints and preparing soil for the planting of 2,000 tulip bulbs. Still others wanted to educate the public about the need to protect the environment by researching and creating public service announcements with the cooperation of a local radio station. The last group, which researched nutrition and good eating habits, wanted to teach students about the importance of good nutrition through posters, brochures, announcements, and development of a healthy snack break during the school day. Each teacher on the team headed up one project. Students selected which project they would work on. Since most projects had the same environmental theme, it made it much easier for all teachers on the team to infuse the projects across the curriculum into classroom lessons.

"I think it's pretty hard not to find a way to connect any project to the curricula if you want to," says Hartshorn, who teaches social studies and language arts. She adds:

> If you really look for it, a connection is always there. We have never done a project yet that has not involved research, writing, and reading, which are all objectives of the language arts curriculum. And anything that has to do with good citizenship ties into social studies. The objective of any good social studies class is to end up with a good citizen. And I think a good citizen is a person who learns how to work with others toward a common goal. The more we do service learning, the more we find ways to link it to our classes.
>
> Actually, I think performing service learning projects is almost like a trick at getting the curriculum covered, because the kids don't realize that they're doing what they're suppose to be doing at the time. They're having so much fun they think it can't be 'good for them.'
>
> When they are writing a letter to a person for a purpose—like when they adopted a stream, or created a script for radio announcements, or wrote thank-you notes to people who helped us with our tulip-planting project—the task itself is so important to them that they want to do a perfect job—and they do.

Action

Hartshorn, who worked with her students on a school beautification project, said:

> This year, the group of kids I worked with wanted to do something to feel more a part of the school. They felt the school is kind of an ugly place, sterile and not as inviting as it could be. They talked about what rooms in the school they liked—rooms that looked homey. They came up with ideas on how to make the school more inviting. Someone came up with the idea of making the front of the school look prettier so we might want to be here more. They wanted to feel like it was their building—that they had something to do with making it more beautiful. The kids got together and wanted to plant tulips in the school colors all around a huge circle in front of the school to make it dazzle. They used their math skills to measure the space and found out we needed 2,000 bulbs.

Ashley Plumly, a quiet, attractive, seventh-grade student who helped plant the 2,000 purple and white tulips, said, "I learned from the experience that when you work together, you get a lot accomplished. That's why we're called a team. I also learned that hard work hurts!"

Myesha Douglass, one of the few African-American students on this seventh-grade team said: "This was a great opportunity. It taught us how to live, work, and rely on one another to get a job done." Myesha was in charge of planting one of the flower beds. "She accepted the challenge of being a leader well, even though she is usually quiet," said Hartshorn. "She really enjoyed working on the project and I think it raised her self-esteem because we were so successful. We planted 2,000 tulips!"

Next year, the students want to plant more seasonal flowers in front of the school and wildflowers in the environmental center.

Steve Cigal, a bright, energetic student in the advanced algebra class, said participating in service learning projects "really builds character and skills and knowledge that a person can use in life. By the way, this is a lot more fun than a teacher reading from a text."

Hartshorn learned a great deal from the projects as well:

> I'll tell you one of the most valuable things I have learned from doing this. We mix kids up into heterogeneous groups to work on these projects and there are no fights. They work in groups that they would never choose—learning disabled kids mixed with kids with behavioral reputations mixed with kids known for their physical prowess. The usual social acceptance or gender issues don't seem to matter. They respect each other and learn to appreciate each other for what they are because we all are working together for the same end. And nobody seems to not want to do it.

Kids with behavioral problems in my team became leaders on the projects and they exhibited no behavioral problems. They got rid of all their energy in this positive way. One teacher said to us, as we walked out of the building carrying hoes, "You dare to arm those kids with hoes?" He was serious! But they were great. They were my leaders. They know they're doing something important.

Reflection

Throughout the projects, teachers and students set aside time to reflect on their progress. Teachers asked students to respond to questions such as What did you get out of this? and Would you recommend this experience to others? Initially, the students discussed these questions in large groups, and then they wrote down their individual responses and broke into small groups for further discussions. Sometimes students would reflect on their experiences by visiting another team in the school to describe what they were doing and advocate for their projects.

"It felt very good knowing what we did as a group helped a lot of people. We enjoyed what we were doing and had fun while we were helping other people," said dark-haired, olive-complected Dimitri Mathicudakis.

Twelve-year-old Richard Park, a member of the adopt-a-stream team who is of Korean descent, said, "It feels good to be able to do something you know is going to help other people and the environment. The things we are doing are important and that makes me feel good, too."

Students also wrote letters to thank our guest speakers, and the letters reflect some of their new-found knowledge. For example, Amanda Biscontini wrote the following letter of thanks to the Department of Planning and Zoning:

November 15, 1993
Department of Planning and Zoning
220 South Main Street
Bel Air, Maryland 21014

Dear Mr. Meyer:

My name is Amanda Biscontini. I am a seventh-grade student at Southampton Middle School. I am participating in Mrs. Ketelsen's adopt-a-stream class and would like to thank you for sending Ms. Bernhardt to talk to us. She taught us a lot of things. I learned that wetlands need to have hydric soils, hydrophitic vegetation, and hydrology. I also learned about watershed and ground water recharge.

The maps we received were really neat. I especially liked analizing (sic) the topographical maps.

I'd like to thank you once again for sending Ms. Bernhardt. Her presentation was very informative and we welcome her to come back again.

> Sincerely,
> Amanda Biscontini

Students also wrote reflected pieces on their experiences. For example, Danielle LeCompte, a 12-year-old seventh-grader, wrote the following "Discovery" paper:

> Team 7-3 has done many projects this year and my opinion is that tulip planting was the most creative idea. It shows togetherness and a team spirit (team 7-3 spirit) and our team takes pride in our team work and we hope the bulbs turn up in the spring.
> I think that the community around Southampton Middle School is proud of the excellent work we all have done. As the buses ride into the school's driveway we all will know that team 7-3 took "pride" in their school.
> All of us have learned that our school is like a 2nd home. I learned that if we all work together it pays off.

"I hope what I'm doing will make a difference in my students lives, as well as in the world which I think needs some help," says Hartshorn. "I really believe that this is the answer to the problem. Having students learn how to work together toward a positive end is the answer to our problems."

CONCLUSION

Service learning has the potential to transform students and schools. As students feed an elderly woman, plant a garden, or advocate for a cause, they awaken to a new world. "It helped us understand about people we didn't know about," said Jamie Voss, a seventh-grade student at Magothy River Middle School. It teaches students how to be active, engaged citizens and it builds their sense of competency. As Jamie Mankiewicz, a seventh-grader at Magothy River Middle School, said, "You feel really good inside because you're helping someone." Service learning also promotes student leadership: "You were making decisions. Someone wasn't making decisions for you," Lauren Zang, a seventh-grader at Magothy River Middle School, explained.

In recognition of the power of service learning, many organizations have recommended its use. Among these are the National Association of Secondary School Principals (NASSP); the National Council for the Social Studies (NCSS); the Carnegie Foundation for the Advancement of Teaching (in both its middle school and high school reports); and the Educational Commission of the States. The Association for Supervision and Curriculum Development (ASCD) has also endorsed mandatory service learning. The National Governor's Association has set for one of its "America 2000" goals that every student engage in service. Also, Goal 3 of the National Schools' goals for year 2000 recommends service-learning as a means to citizenship education.

There are as many models for incorporating service learning into a middle school as there are middle schools. No matter which model is used, it is a great way to harness the energy and enthusiasm of students and to show them that they can, *and do*, make a tremendous difference in their communities.

14

Science-Technology-Society

An Approach to Attaining Student Involvement in Community Action Projects

CURT JEFFRYES   **ROBERT E. YAGER**

JANICE CONOVER

As the programs in the Creston School System (Creston is a rural community of about 10,000 people located in the south-central part of Iowa) began to be examined for strengths and weaknesses, science education was singled out as one of those areas in need of a major overhaul. Indeed, during the latter 1980s and early 1990s, many of the stakeholders (teachers, parents, and students) voiced dissatisfaction with the science program and recognized that changes had to occur. The greatest difficulty facing them, though, was that no clear solution seemed to be looming on the horizon. Some teachers were so frustrated that they were actually thinking of leaving the profession.

Ray Courtney, the eighth-grade earth science teacher at Jones Middle School, says, "I was boring the kids to death! They were hating science and I didn't know any way to make it better. I was becoming so frustrated with what I was doing that I began to seriously look for other employment." Ray had been a teacher and a coach in the district for about 10 years and felt tied to a book and a curriculum that neither he or his students liked. Ray goes on to say, "I wanted to change how I was teaching, but I didn't know how or even if I could do it."

Joy Spargur, the seventh-grade life science teacher at Jones Middle School, echoed similar sentiments, "The students just didn't care anymore. They seemed to have become bored with science and had no incentive to learn. They hated the book we were using and quite frankly so did I." Joy had been teaching in the Creston system for about 20 years and felt trapped in a situation about which she could do nothing. Her attitude toward teaching had reached a low point and the stress of the situation showed in her reaction to students and colleagues.

Curt Jeffryes, a 12-year veteran in teaching sixth-grade science at Jones Middle School, felt many of the same the things. "I was beginning to look forward to when I would not be teaching anymore. I never liked teaching from a book and always felt like somewhat of a maverick for not wanting to do so. I was not a traditional student growing up and I was becoming increasingly frustrated working in a system that I had rejected. I saw that same frustration in the eyes of the students I taught and I didn't see any real solution to the problem. I wanted science to be enjoyable and meaningful but it was anything but that."

The students were equally adamant in their criticism of science education at Jones Middle School. Common sentiments were: "I hate science! All we do is memorize vocabulary words, do worksheets, and take tests. What possible use is this? How will I ever use any of this stuff in real life?" "Science ought to be fun. I think it would be neat if we did real experiments and messed around with things, but instead all we do is read the book and take tests." The students of the district wanted science to be something different. They saw science as something you did instead of something you read about or heard about via a teacher delivered lecture.

Did the old system of teaching ever work? Parents of students seemed to echo the same distaste for science in their past. Verle Manson, a mother of one of the sixth-grade students, stated, "I hated science as a student. I wasn't smart enough to do well. I remember all those tests that I could never pass, besides the fact I didn't see any use for it." Verle was a life-time resident of Creston who grew up on "the wrong side of the tracks" and had little success in school. Another parent, Denise Brown, had a different recollection of science: "About all I remember of science classes were the endless lists of vocabulary words that you would memorize for a test each week and then forget by the next day. Science must not have been much fun since I don't remember much about it."

The picture of science education in Creston was a bleak one. Parents, administrators, teachers, and students perceived both the curriculum and teaching strategies as miserable failures. Each of the science teachers at Jones Middle School had reached mileposts in their careers where education seemed to be heading down a one-way street to no where and all had lost the drive and enthusiasm for teaching.

Jones Middle School is not unlike many middle schools in the United States. The building was constructed during latter 1950s and added onto during the middle 1960s. At the time of construction, it was a junior high school and became a middle school (in name only) in the mid 1980s. The rooms are small and more clearly suited to a traditional lecture format than to active hands-on instruction. What exacerbates this situation is that the majority of the teachers and administrators are veterans of at least ten years and were educated in the more traditional style of the 1960s and 1970s.

This situation began to change when Curt Jeffryes was invited to participate in the Iowa Chautauqua program in which a new methodology for teaching science was presented to a group of teachers from across the state. This new methodology was called Science-Technology-Society (STS) and focused on the teaching of science in a social context. Here are Curt's own words about the reaction of parents and students to STS:

> My entry into STS was slow at first. I thought it sounded like a good logical way to teach science but I was skeptical about whether or not I could actually do it. Even though I knew the practices I had learned as a traditional teacher were not making it, they are hard to give up. It was difficult to accept the idea that students should have a voice in their education. I was afraid that I would lose control and that I would not be able to meet my school district's curriculum that I was mandated to teach. My fear subsided though when I began to see the results and the comments from parents, students, other teachers, and administrators. I feel more confident now, but there is a lot I still don't know.

But how do students and parents react to this style of teaching that focuses on the student and the community in which they live? What do they see as positives and what are their concerns? Linda Smith, a parent and the wife of a school board member, made the following comments about her son's experiences in Curt's STS science classes at parent teacher conferences:

> I had heard about STS through conversations with my husband. I didn't know what to think about it but I was noticing that my son Travis was coming home and talking about all he was doing in science class a lot. I also found that he was spending evenings in my husband's workshop building and testing all sorts of contraptions that related to his experiences in class. Personally I never got that much out of science, but I was curious to see what Travis was so excited about. I decided to accompany them on a field trip they were taking and I found myself learning and having a ball doing it. I am kind of envious of my son—I wished my science classes would have been like that as a child.

Levi Burton is a sixth-grade male student with average ability. Levi's dad said that Levi had a great interest in science but had never had much success before arriving in Curt's classroom. Levi comes from a single-parent family and lived in a rural area outside of Creston. Here are Levi's own words about his experiences in an STS constructivist classroom:

> In fifth-grade science was boring. All we did were worksheets, watch movies, look at pictures, and take lots of tests. We never spent much time on anything. It always seemed like we were in a hurry to go on to something else. I don't like listening to teachers talk all the time and that is usually what they did—talk. I like to do things and in fifth grade we didn't get to do that very much.

In sixth grade, we got to do things. We worked in groups lots of the time and we didn't do a lot of worksheets or have as many tests. I liked having assignments that I could do lots of research on. That makes them fun. I liked the variety of things that I could make choices about what I wanted to do. I also liked having more time to complete things. I liked science relating to my home. In other years we heard about all the things that are happening in far off places like Brazil and California and I don't care about those places much. I am more interested in what takes place here.

I liked the way we were graded in sixth grade. We were graded on what we did and on what we learned instead of just on tests and worksheets. In sixth grade, science was fun—you didn't sit and listen to the teacher. You got to get out and do things and find answers to questions you had.

In STS, issues relevant to the students' lives, application of science concepts, creativity in problem solving using the processes of science, and community action are the cornerstones of instruction. In an STS classroom, students do "real science" through direct experiences in which they apply the concepts of science in an attempt to understand or solve problems centered in the context of the real world they lived in, and, finally, action is taken on those principles they believe in.

STS has been an exciting movement in the United States, with the National Science Teachers Association (NSTA) proclaiming the efforts to integrate science, technology, and society as the major new direction for the 1980s and 1990s. The STS philosophy of teaching science is in harmony with the position statement from NSTA that STS is:

> *the teaching and learning of science/technology in the context of human experience. It represents an appropriate science education context for all learners. The emerging research is clear in illustrating that learning science in an STS context results in students with more sophisticated concept mastery and ability to use process skills. All students improve in terms of creativity skills, attitude toward science, use of science concepts, and processes in their daily living and in responsible personal decision-making. (NSTA, 1990–1991, p. 47)*

The move in Creston to an STS style of teaching was gradual, for the changes at hand were monumental for the teachers. Not only did the Chautauqua program offer a new methodology for teaching but it also offered an alternative to the traditional beliefs about how students learn. In order to teach an issue-oriented student-centered, action-based science, a different theory on how students learned had to be adopted. That learning theory was *constructivism*. Martin A. Simon and Deborah Schifter (1991) offered a clear and concise definition of the

Constructivist Learning Theory: "The core idea is that learners actively construct their own understanding rather than passively absorb or copy the understandings of others. The construction of new understandings is stimulated by a problem situation; that is, a situation which disturbs the individual's current organization of knowledge" (p. 310).

Nolan and Francis (1992) offered a comparison of the traditional view of learning and its implications for teaching and the constructivist view of learning and its implications for teaching. The traditional view of the learning-teaching process, which has dominated instruction in most schools, can be captured in five fundamental beliefs about learning (Nolan and Francis, 1992). These five fundamental beliefs are:

- Learning is the process of accumulating bits of information and isolated skills.
- The teacher's primary responsibility is to transfer his or her knowledge directly to students.
- Changing student behavior is the teacher's primary goal.
- The process of learning and teaching focuses primarily on the interactions between the teacher and individual students.
- Thinking and learning skills are viewed as transferable across all content areas.

During the 1980s, the shape of educational practice slowly began to change, creating a new mindscape about human learning. This new view of learning and teaching can also be encapsulated in several interrelated beliefs about the nature of learning and teaching (Nolan and Francis, 1992). The five new beliefs are:

- All learning, except for simple rote memorization, requires the learner to actively construct meaning.
- A student's prior understandings of and thoughts about a topic or concept before instruction exert a tremendous influence on what he or she learns during instruction.
- The teacher's primary goal is to generate a change in the learner's cognitive structure or way of viewing and organizing the world.
- Because learning is a process of active construction by the learner, the teacher cannot do the work of learning.
- Learning in cooperation with others is an important source of motivation, support, modeling, and coaching.

A third component in the transformation of the middle school staff was assessment of student learning. In traditional classrooms, assessment is isolated from instruction. The student might possibly take a multiple-choice pretest focusing on facts and terms related to a predetermined unit of study. At the end of a unit of study, the teacher normally gives a summative evaluation which, again, is often in a multiple-choice format eliciting student recall of the terms/facts that were presented in the unit. The goal of instruction is *mastery of content,* and *not the construction of new knowledge* leading to more complete understanding (Brooks and Brooks, 1993).

In an STS constructivist classroom, the goal of assessment is different. The instructor uses assessment as a tool that enables the student to achieve understanding. In the traditional classroom, assessment often drives the curriculum, but in the STS constructivist classroom, assessment and instruction are inseparable. Brooks and Brooks (1993) term this as "teaching through assessment" where it is difficult and unnecessary to differentiate between instruction and assessment.

Assessment embedded in instruction is authentic by nature and emerges from the interactions between students and the teacher. The teacher uses assessment as a means to achieve understanding through nonjudgmental questioning, problem solving, and the performance of tasks generated in the context of the instruction. Instead of focusing on the number of questions answered correctly, the teacher uses assessment as a means of gaining access to student thinking.

What does this view of STS, constructivism, and assessment tell us if we seek to use the STS approach in engaging students in community action projects? Karen Vertanen, a parent of a sixth-grade student, had this to say about her son's experience in Curt Jeffryes's STS and constructivist science classroom: "Constructivism (and STS) may be one way to encourage that creativity latent in so many children. This method seems to meet the needs of all students, not only the fast learners. This method allows children the freedom to learn and to think for themselves, rather than teaching them how to manipulate the system with a minimum of work."

Let us now elaborate on these generalities with some specific examples of STS at work in Creston. Part of the story involves how Creston has become a center of STS activity and how every teacher has been involved—even those who do not teach science.

When students are engaged in problem identification, planning for solutions, conducting investigations, and using information to resolve problems, education and schooling are viewed differently. It is almost as if the purpose of education changes from the transmission of what is promised to be useful information to one of student empowerment to work on real problems—which frequently results in students taking actions in the community as a result of the school learning and activities.

Curt Jeffryes's own words illustrate what this means and what it entails:

> In the fall of the year, the entire Jones Middle School sixth-grade class goes on a field trip to Talmage Hill County Park. The field trip was supposed to be an multidisciplinary experience in which teachers from all subject matters work cooperatively together in an outdoor class-

room environment. (We would discover that we really hadn't known the meaning of multidisciplinary teaching). On previous trips, I generally had the students do some sort of classification activity in which collections were made of such things as animal signs, micro-organisms, leaves, wild flowers, or edible plants. From my point of view, the field trip was always a success as the students were doing "hands on" science and it was being done in outdoor setting. I was certain that I was meeting the students' needs by providing them a real experience based in the context of a setting that was familiar to them. In retrospect, the students probably were more excited about getting out of school for a day than with the actual experiences I planned for them.

This year, however, turned out to be different. About three weeks before the planned trip, I decided to lay out what I had planned for the students to do. I had presented my initial ideas to the class and asked if there were any questions. The classroom was as quiet as a tomb and none of the students looked excited or even interested in what I had been saying. I looked around the room for some indication of life but there was still no response. At this point, I was rather frustrated and became agitated for I had already started to plan what each class was going to do on the trip. These were activities that I thought would be exciting and interesting to the students and they seemed like they couldn't have cared less. Finally, I asked if there was some sort of problem with what I had suggested.

Slowly, and without a great deal of confidence, a hand began to rise. The hand belonged to D.J., a very large and mature boy, who was noted for being one of the terrors of the sixth grade. His normal interaction in class often took the form of some sort of misbehavior, but his hand was the only hand up and I felt obligated to call on him. "Mr. Jeffryes," he began slowly and sheepishly, "These activities you have planned really don't sound like too much fun. From what you said earlier, I thought we were going to help plan the activities."

I was taken back by what he said. I replied by telling him that I thought I had let them be a part of the activities because I had let them choose from a list I had compiled. I stopped short, for as I heard my own words I realized that he was right and I was wrong. Just getting to pick from a list is not student ownership at all—rather, it was teacher ownership. I said, "D.J., you're right. I promised that you would be able to help plan our field trip. I mistakenly thought that my ideas would be the same as yours and that was wrong. Let's start over again and this time you tell me your ideas."

I think the rest of the class was in shock at this point. I couldn't ever remember admitting I was wrong to the class, and besides, here was the orneriest boy in the sixth grade getting me to admit it. That seemed to break the ice. The ideas from the students began to flow and

I recorded the responses on the board. The list on the board was long and I asked the students if it was possible to do all the things they had listed. Tyler, who was a buddy of D.J., said, "Why don't we split up into groups and find two or three things we want to do the most." I was about as leery of Tyler as I was D.J. Being D.J.'s friend was not a vote of confidence in matters related to academics; however, normal rules didn't seem to be in effect.

I replied that I thought he had a good idea and so I numbered the class off into groups of three or four students and each group narrowed their list of ideas to two activities. I sat back rather amazed at how well they were working together and I noticed that each student was involved in the process. At the end of class, each group presented its ideas. We were running out of class time, and still we had 10 different ideas on the board. Annie, who normally is a class leader and rather outspoken, suggested that we vote on the topics tomorrow and then develop a plan.

With the ringing of the bell the students departed. My next period was free and I began to reflect on what had happened. I began to understand what student ownership really meant. To own something, you must have a personal stake in it. My activities were good—well thought out and well planned. I began to see, however, that my ideas were just *my ideas*. The students had no stake in them, so they found little or no relevance in them. After D.J.'s statement, everything changed. The class became not only interested in the field trip but they also became genuinely excited. They now had a personal stake in the success or failure of what we were about to do, and that made all the difference in the world.

I also felt comfortable with the role I was beginning to take. I found that I enjoyed watching the students work. Their ideas were good and probably better than mine. I began to feel like I was getting to do something I had dreamed about as a teacher, and that was to assist students in their learning rather than dictating it. As the day proceeded, I followed the same format with each ensuing class and I took the role of being a mediator and troubleshooter as the students worked together.

The next day in class, the students were to vote on what they wanted to work on at the park. Prior to the actual voting, I thought it would be wise to discuss the options listed on the chalkboard. I tried to ask questions that brought out their point of view and I tried to resist stating my own. I was careful with the questions I asked, for I wanted to know what they thought and I didn't want anyone to feel put down for what he or she said.

In the midst this brainstorming session, D.J. once again came to my rescue. All the negative things I had heard about his behavior had given way to a new-found respect in his ideas and worth as a student. It was easy to see that his image of himself was changing as well. A product of a broken home, D.J. lived with his grandparents and had few positives in his life. He was like a new person in his commitment to what he had started. D.J. raised his hand and said, "Mr. Jeffryes, I think all of the ideas are very good, but I was thinking about something you said the other day about the park belonging to all of us, and I think we should just adopt the park and do things to make it better."

To my surprise, the other kids in the class echoed his sentiment. Talmage Hill was a park located in a remote part of our county. Because of its location and the fact that it is a county park, the use of the facility was limited. Tara, a normally reserved girl who rarely ever contributed to class discussions, said, "We should rethink our ideas about the nature of the field trip. Everyone should be working for the same goal of making our park better."

I told the class that I thought they had finally came up with an idea that everyone could live with. I then asked them what it meant to "own the park" and what responsibilities they had. The classes came to the following conclusions:

- Adopting the park means we need to take care of the park and keep it looking nice.
- Adopting the park means that it is ours and we need to do things that will make it better.
- Adopting the park means that we need to protect it from being harmed.

Our next discussion now turned to what we were actually going to do to meet our responsibilities as park owners. Another brainstorming session started, and Mike, who was a Boy Scout, said, "In scouts, we have camped at Talmage Hill several times. I have been all over the park and I think it is terrible that there are so few trails for people to walk on. The ground is very hilly and full of deep gullies. I think it would be really neat to build a trail over there so more people could use the park."

Ryan, another Boy Scout, emphasized the point: "Mike is right. Building a trail would be a good idea. We have built trails at summer Boy Scout camp and on some of the steep hills we have even put in steps to make it easier for people to walk."

Jesse said, "Yeah, we have ridden horses over there and I think they are right." Jesse is a young lady who doesn't fit into the traditional female stereotypes. She considers herself equal in every respect with the boys in the class. She continued, "When I was with my dad, he told me somebody ought to do something to stop all the erosion in the gullies. He farms and he told me that they put in terraces and ponds to stop that kind of erosion. Do you think it would be possible to do something like that?"

My job as a teacher was now to try to get a handle on what the students were saying and to assist them in bringing this dream to reality. In the ensuing days, I began to question them about their ideas and again to get them to narrow their focus to something that was achievable and realistic. Each class embraced the ideas presented and each class added to the plan. Their list of things to improve the park had now been brought down to more a workable list:

- Build a segment of trail on a problem area.
- Build trail steps on some existing steep trails.
- Build erosion control devices in the gullies.
- Have a litter clean-up activity.

I realized that the job outlined by the students was too big for me to handle. I decided to ask for help from the other teachers in the sixth grade who also go on the field trips. This would be quite a step, as each had already planned an activity of his or her own. In a middle school team planning session, I outlined what the students had done and asked the other teachers if they would agree to help with carrying out the whole affair. To my surprise, the students had been talking to the other teachers long before I even thought of it. The other teachers had already quietly become "converts" and each saw it as an opportunity to do something interesting and unique as related to their particular subject matter. Frankly, it never occurred to me that even my fellow staff members would become excited and interested in the project if they, too, became stakeholders.

The sixth-grade staff was beginning to understand the real meaning of multidisciplinary teaching. The team was working to meet a need and was formed in the context of student relevance. The sixth-grade teachers had thought that simply working together was multidisciplinary teaching, and we discovered that was wrong.

Each teacher picked an area to work with and set about developing a curriculum that would match the goals of their class. Each developed ownership in the project and each added his or her own individual flair. Mr. Weaver, the social studies teacher, had talked to students about mapping the park, so his project centered around doing this and developing compass skills with the students. Mrs. Stine, the English teacher, agreed to help with building erosion control devices, which we named check dams. Her English activity was soon to emerge from the investigations we were undertaking. Mrs. Snyder, the reading teacher, took on the task of litter clean up. She thought her students could possibly write poems/slogans about littering and possibly develop posters. Mr. Veitz, the math teacher, agreed to take on the trail- and step-building enterprise and would work with Mrs. Hilger, the special education teacher. He saw this as a good math activity, as questions about slope and other types of measurement were sure to emerge as they built the trail.

What had started with a single comment had somehow grown into an all-school project. With so much going on, it now became a regular practice for me to reflect seriously about each day's events. I was concerned with being able to "see" the science in what we were doing. I began to think in terms of broad-based multidisciplinary science themes and concepts that would be a part of the investigation and came up with this list (Rutherford and Ahlgren, 1989) that I thought would emerge as a result of the students' experiences:

Themes: Systems, Models, Patterns of Change, Scale, Evolution

Concepts

Soil conservation	Topography	Water percolation
Soil permeability	Soil compaction	Water shed
Soil formation	Erosion	Water conservation
Soil texture	Erosion control	

Another goal that I had was that I wanted each student to be involved in a scientific inquiry where he or she would develop questions that could be answered as a result of his or her investigations.

Through further discussion and negotiation, the students and I developed a plan of study and research. Each class was divided into research groups. The groups picked areas of study from our list of investigations. The next step was for the students to develop questions that were to be resolved as an end result of their investigations. These are some of their questions:

- Is a check dam like a terrace?
- How do you build a check dam?
- Will the dams really work to stop erosion?
- Do the check dams hold water like a pond?
- Where do you put check dams?
- Do farmers build check dams on their farms?
- How do you build a trail?
- Does it matter what the trail looks like and where it goes?
- What is slope?
- How do you know where to put the steps?
- How do you build trail steps?
- Do the steps stop erosion? (They kind of look like little check dams.)
- Are there different types of soil?
- Why is it so hilly at Talmage Hill?
- What happens to litter after people drop it?
- Is it against the law to litter?

The questions the students asked and my questions of them served as a preassessment and a formative assessment through which I could see their level of understanding. Some of their questions and responses to questions revealed misconceptions about the science concepts. Their questions then became the vehicle by which their own inquiries proceeded. This ongoing process gave light to what would be their final or summative assessment. The students and I developed what we call a "contract" or what is commonly known as a rubric. Through this contract, we were able to develop a criterion for what would constitute a successful completion to their investigations. Involving the students in their own assessment was essential in their role as stakeholders.

Each class decided that it would have one group investigate each of the four park projects. It was decided that there were four parts to the basic contract: (1) preliminary planning and research, followed by (2) completion of the park project, resulting in (3) the development of an experiment to test hypotheses, concluding with (4) a presentation of the groups findings. This simple rubric became our assessment instrument.

It would be nice to say that all of our investigations went flawlessly and without problems, but that was not the case. The students discovered that to do projects at the park required the permission of the county conservation board. Mrs. Stine helped the students in her English class develop letters stating their case to the conservation board and Park Supervisor John Tapken. Mrs. Stine said, "I think that this project is great. This gives students a real need to know how to write letters and to express themselves clearly. Often, what we do in English has no apparent relevance to the students. The attitude of the students was noticeably better when they were doing something [that served] a real need."

John Tapken, the park ranger, and Barb Busenbarrick, the park naturalist, seemed excited about the interest the students were taking in Talmage Hill. They did, however, state that there were several problems to be overcome. Since this park was designated for use as a natural area in which hunting and fishing were allowed, the development of the park was limited. Any improvements had to be consistent with the natural setting and anything constructed had to be of natural materials. Trails and trail steps could be constructed only in areas with severe erosion problems and could not be obtrusive. As Amanda stated in frustration, "It seems as if everyone seems to be making this as difficult as possible. All we want to do is help out and it seems that no one wants to let us!" For Amanda, these were strong words. She was one of those students who sits in class for a whole year without you knowing she is there. Normally shy and retiring, her commitment was plain to see.

After some pretty convincing lobbying, the students persuaded John to allow them to build some trail and trail steps on one small hillside to help prevent further erosion that was being caused by heavy foot traffic. He also agreed to letting the students build a few check dams to help curb erosion. He did, however, add one stipulation: "If you are allowed to do these projects, the conservation board would like evidence that what you are doing is truly going to benefit the park over the long term."

The students could have easily given up at this stage, but they were more committed than ever. Amber was an A student and the daughter of one of our middle school teachers. The rules seemed to keep changing and she was becoming frustrated and confused. She summed up the class's feelings when she said, "We really want to do these projects in the park. Even though we are just kids, we still think we can do a good job." She was really frustrated with all the red tape we kept running into. Amber was our consummate perfectionist and researched to the point of obsession. She was sure she was right and just couldn't understand the delays.

The problem with building the trail was considerable. No one had any degree of experience in building trails, including the students' teacher, the park ranger, and the park naturalist. Luckily, Nathanial came to our rescue.

In class, we were discussing how to go about building the trail and not having much success when suddenly Nathanial's hand shot up. Another person was speaking as he waved excitedly and impatiently. I wondered if he was sick or in dire need of going to the bathroom for he seemed as if he were about to burst. Nathanial never raised his hand in class. In fact, I often wondered if he knew what was going on at all. Nathanial was an adopted Korean refugee who lagged behind in school because of language difficulties. I finally interrupted the other student and asked, "Nathanial, what is wrong with you?"

Nathanial didn't bother to answer my question but excitedly replied, "I think my Dad can help us. Every summer he goes to national parks and helps them build trails and things like that. In fact, last summer I even went with him. I could ask him, if you think that would be OK?" Nathanial was so excited and the words came out so quickly that I barely understood him. I had to ask him if he could slow down and tell us the whole story again. He related to us that his dad, Rick, had been a volunteer trail builder with the Sierra Club for several years. It was decided that Nathanial should try to get his father to help us.

Later that same night, I got a call from Rick, who offered to help work with the students in building and designing the trail. He told me that he was uncomfortable working with students but it was the first time he had seen Nathanial become excited about school. He said, "At first, I didn't want to do this, but Nathanial was excited and felt so important when the other students had asked him to do this—I just couldn't turn him down."

With Rick's guidance and expertise, the students once again looked at nature for the clue as to where they should build the trail as well as how it should look. Several of the students' dads were deer hunters and they suggested that deer trails would be a good model to copy.

The trail building was a massive job. Mr. Veitz and his crews constructed approximately 200 yards of switch-back trail through some of the most formidable terrain found in the park. Rick Rice helped the students lay out the course and showed the teams the basics of trail building. The students were divided into groups of 20 and worked in two-hour shifts for two days. After many a blister and sore back, the trail was finally completed.

When discussing how to construct check dams, the students decided that they would be built from natural occurring materials. The students got a hold of Mr. Zumbach, the agriculture teacher at the high school, and he gave them suggestions and books to use in researching their ideas.

Most of the research conducted by the students was completed at home or during study halls. Actual class time evolved into a forum for discussion, a time for reporting results, and a place where the group attempted to solve problems collaboratively.

After considerable discussion and research, they finally came up with an idea from reading about beaver dams. The modified beaver dam approach appeared to blend into the natural setting more effectively than earlier solutions. John Tapken seemed most satisfied with this decision, as it would not destroy the natural beauty of the park. The students then decided not to make specific check dam designs. They felt that the natural features and availability of construction materials would dictate the design of the individual dams and that each one would be unique.

The check dam project went extremely well. In fact, it went better than anyone had anticipated. The students, again, divided into teams and planned on building one check dam per crew. The teachers' contributions to the project was in heavy lifting power, which was indeed needed. All other facets of the job were done by students in a cooperative manner. The check dam research teams anticipated that each crew would be able to build one check dam. They thought that if we built a total of 5 dams, the project would be a success. It ended up that their calculations were off, as each team built 10 dams, resulting in a total of 50 instead of the predicted 5.

The trail step teams ended up building close to 10 steps per team. They found the work to be extremely hard, for terrain was steep and the ground very hard. Rick Rice again provided the expertise, as he showed teams how and where to build them for maximum erosion control effect.

The litter project ended up being a great deal of fun for the students. They worked with Mrs. Snyder and turned the project into a scavenger hunt in which they looked for different types of litter items. This team had contacted the Iowa Corn Board prior to going out to Talmage Hill and secured some biodegradable trash bags to use for cleaning up the litter. The students decided that they would bury the trash in these plastic bags and see if they really did degrade over time. They also buried some of the trash in paper bags to compare against the plastic ones. Each bag was carefully cataloged and maps were drawn to ensure future location.

When we got back to the classroom, the kids were still excited and interested in what they had accomplished so far. I then asked them what I considered to be a key question: Did the things we did at Talmage Hill ultimately help or hurt the park? Their immediate answer was that they thought that only good things would come of there work. I then asked: Well, you all think what you did was good, but could you tell me some things that might happen that are not good? What followed in each class was another brainstorming session that resulted in the following comparisons:

Trails

Positive	*Negative*
Park more accessible	Increased use and wear
Stop bank erosion	Possibly created new erosion patterns
Safer travel	Disturb animal environment

Dams

Positive	*Negative*
Control gully erosion	Create new erosion
Create new shelter area	Loss of habitat
Clean up forest floor	Disturb natural processes
Improve water quality	Alter how park looks

Litter Pick-Up

Positive	*Negative*
More attractive setting	Less food for scavengers
Safer for animals and people	Loss of soil-building materials through decomposition
More public pride in parks	Burying garbage could contaminate soil and ground water

After weighing the pros and cons, each class then decided that our ideas and projects needed to be tested, data collected, and conclusions drawn. The students were proud of their work and determined to prove that what they had done would have a long-term positive effect on the park. Each group then set to work to develop tested models in which they could conduct experiments to predict the long-term effect of their projects.

Subsequently, each group constructed models that would closely resemble their full-size Talmage Hill counterparts. Experiments were constructed, data were collected, and demonstrations were given to the class. John Tapken was also invited to witness these presentations so that he could report back to the county conservation board.

Not all the results were what we expected. We found problems with our check dams and were able to correctly predict that some would not survive. The trail builders also found a flaw in one part of their design and construction and successfully predicted a new erosion problem resulting from it. After all the hard work on the steps, the students were able to predict that the trails would fill in in a short amount of time. The trash experiments were the most disheartening. The experiments showed us that in landfills little if anything decomposes. The bio-degradable trash bags were a dismal failure.

After all the work and planning, the project finally came to a close. What started as a two-week project had turned into over one month's work. Even after I thought we were finished, Talmage Hill kept coming back to us in one form or another for the remainder of the school year.

I decided to reflect on the experience as a whole. What had happened surprised and astonished me. The student ownership in the project was a key to success. What had been a good outdoor classroom activity was now a great multidisciplinary educational success. Each student and each teacher in the sixth grade had become a stakeholder in the project with a desire to see it through to a successful conclusion.

Mr. Weaver, the social studies teacher, was already talking about next year. The students developed maps of the park and learned orienteering skills during their park forays. Mrs. Stine had taken the task of building erosion control devices and wove it into her writing curriculum. The students wrote business letters, friendly letters, different types of descriptive paragraphs, journals, and research papers in the course of doing a science project. Mrs. Snyder, the reading instructor, involved the students in the writing of poetry and developed listening skills activities on the field trip. Mr. Veitz used the trip to teach estimation, perimeter, surface area, and calculations of slope.

As for myself, the students met all of the curriculum goals I had anticipated and more. Listening to students and valuing what they say took on a whole new importance. Each student I taught successfully satisfied his or her "contract." For probably the first time since I had become a teacher, I felt satisfied that I had met the needs of each of my students. I had wanted the students to do "real science" in which they would act like scientists in finding the answers to questions through a process of inquiry. I felt satisfied that they had.

A commitment was made to monitor the projects over an extended period of time. Ensuing sixth-grade classes have built on the work of these students, and over time we have found that the long-term effects of the students' projects have been positive. The Talmage Hill field study project has become a tradition in the Creston sixth grade. D.J.'s message still rings loud and clear as the students still retain ownership. The program changes with each ensuing year as new ideas and new projects arise out of a simple commitment of ownership and pride.

The excitement over our science projects at Talmage Hill didn't go without notice. The local newspaper and radio covered the events and administrators heard lots of positive comments from students and the teachers who participated in the Talmage Hill experience. Reggie Sands, who was Jesse's dad, accompanied the students on the field trip and said, "It would be hard to tell who learned more—the parents or the kids. I think we all learned more in one day out here than you could get in a month of classroom work."

Even with the accolades, the administration and school board of the Creston School District looked at the project with interest but also with a reserved skepticism. This was a form of teaching and learning that was clearly different from the norm. They wanted to see evidence that curriculum goals were being met, that attitudes were truly changing for the positive, and that standardized test scores were improving. Curt Jeffryes's own words tell this part of the story:

Just like the administrators and the school board I, too, wanted to know if STS and constructivism really worked. Were the students really learning more, as I suspected they were? Was their attitude improving? To find the answer to these questions I looked in two different places. To see if the students were learning more, I decided to look at the Iowa Basic Skills test scores and see how my students compared against other students in Iowa. We didn't have a long-term pattern to compare against since our school was in the first year of taking the science tests. To look at changing attitudes, I decided to use the attitude survey found in the *Iowa Assessment Handbook.*

The basic skills scores worried me a great deal. I knew the ITBS primarily focused on knowledge of facts and principles with a small degree of application questions. The test format was all multiple-choice questions, which was different from my performance-based assessments.

I was concerned about how well the students would do on questions that primarily focused on terminology, as it is deemphasized in constructivist and STS practice. To my surprise, the students' average scores on areas related to our study (Nature of Science, Earth's Surface, Forces of Nature, Environment/Interaction, and Earth's Resources) were considerably higher than the national or Iowa average.

The attitude assessment was even more revealing to me as a teacher. I was confident that the students were enjoying science class but I didn't realize how much. Ninety percent of the sixth-grade students rated science as their favorite class, even when physical education was included in the survey. This trend in student attitude toward science has continued with little deviation over time. The message was loud and clear that STS science based on constructivist principles of learning was a clear success in the sixth grade.

Creston's administrators began to echo the same point of view. Keith Langholtz, my first building principal, said, "This style of teaching science through problem solving and hands-on experiences is the only way it should be taught. I think teachers are too concerned with following the exact course of a textbook. Science is everywhere in the community in which we live and we should take advantage of it." Gene Lust, who became my new principal when Creston moved to a middle school concept, said, "STS is totally compatible with the philosophy of middle school. Having students engage in hands on experiences with science phenomena and looking at issues related to science is a natural common sense way to teach science. I am also excited at the multidisciplinary opportunities STS science presents."

These two administrators and Curt Jeffryes began work on engaging other teachers in STS constructivist teaching. Through their efforts and the Iowa Chautauqua program, nearly all of Creston's 100 plus teachers now adhere to the principles of STS and constructivism. One teacher summed up STS and constructivism in this manner: "I have trouble with the acronym, but STS could be labeled more clearly as just good teaching. The principles of STS apply to all subject matters and not just science. Getting students actively involved with issues and topics relevant to their lives just makes good sense."

The move to STS constructivist teaching has had the effect of renewing the Jones Middle School staff. Rather than looking for ways to get out of teaching, the middle school staff has been revitalized and looks with anticipation toward science teaching and education in general. Ray Courtney, the eighth-grade science teacher now says, "There is a level of excitement mixed with fear in my teaching now. I am fearful for not having sufficient knowledge in certain areas and excited because each year and each unit is new and different. I look forward to working with the students and with my other colleagues in the area." Ray continues, "There is a lot I don't know about what I am doing, but it is exciting for me and the students. It is exciting to learn right along with the students and comforting to not have to know all the answers."

Joy Spargur has also noticed the changes as well. Three years ago, she was extremely skeptical about STS: "I remember when I first became involved with STS. I think you can still see the furrows I left in the ground from being drug (sic) into it. That seems like a long time ago, for now I could not imagine teaching any other way. In fact, I would refuse to do so."

What is different about STS teaching that catches the fancy of veteran teachers to the point of their changing their teaching methods? Ray, Joy, and Curt came up with the following comparison of where they were before STS and where they see themselves now:

> When teaching an STS unit or module, there are key points for a teacher to keep in mind. Teaching science in a social context dealing with issues related to science is different than traditional textbook-oriented curricula. The first major difference is that textbooks tend to be linear in the concepts covered. The concepts are presented in a specific sequence and grouped in narrowly constructed categories according to specific science disciplines. The teacher, local curriculum, or textbook normally control the time and direction of study. Relevance to the students is often incidental or contrived by the teacher, resulting in science being more abstract than concrete.
>
> In STS, concepts tend to cover a broad range and cross traditional discipline lines The curriculum is less reliant on textbooks and therefore covered in a nonlinear-, nondiscipline-specific manner. Issues and real problems rarely tend to be classified specifically as biology, earth science, physics, or chemistry. Often, elements of all the science disciplines are found in each STS unit. In an STS class, the focus and direction of study is based on issues or situations that are a part of the students' real lives. Relevance to the students is clear for the class centers in the real concrete world in which they live.
>
> In traditional classes, the teacher imparts most of the knowledge to the students. The teacher tends to be the only authority on content and direction of study. In an STS unit, the teacher moves to a role that more closely resembles a facilitator. The student becomes more actively involved in the decisions relating to the direction of study. The teacher will also facilitate use of experts outside of the classroom to present specific science content or to instruct in specific science processes (e.g., doctors, engineers, applied scientists, and researchers). This does not constitute an abolition of classroom control but rather a sharing of ownership in the work.
>
> In traditional science classes, laboratories are often done for the sake of doing some type of hands-on work with science and to verify knowledge disseminated by the teacher. The labs may or may not be

relevant to the context of instruction and often do not reflect the true nature of scientific inquiry. In STS classes, laboratories are more often inquiry based and assist the student and teacher in finding answers to questions. The labs emerge as a part of instruction in which the students seek to collect data in pursuit of resolving an issue related to science.

In traditional classes, assessment of student learning often revolves around a test that focuses on the rote memorization of concepts or vocabulary. If preassessment is attempted, it normally consists of a concept/vocabulary test. Mastery of material is accomplished by additional worksheets or tests given at the completion of a unit of study. In traditional classes, the students have little or no voice in the assessment of their learning, and the types of assessment are limited in scope and variation.

In an STS class, assessment is an integral part of instruction and is ongoing. Through the careful use of questioning skills, the teacher assesses the student in terms of prior knowledge and misconceptions at the beginning of a unit, during instruction, and at the unit's completion. In an STS constructivist-based classroom, remediation is immediate, as the teacher derives instruction from assessing student growth and understanding. Evaluation in an STS classroom tends to be multidimensional and centers around not only concepts of science but also attitude, process skills, application skills, and creativity. In an STS class, the students are actively involved in the assessment of their learning. Students are often evaluated on task completion (performance-based assessment) and the compilation and progress of work completed (portfolios). An STS teacher searches for ways to demonstrate when learning has occurred, so the form of assessment is variable and tends to adapt to a variety of learning styles.

Science-Technology-Society focuses on the teaching of science in a social context. During the 1980s the goal of science education was to develop scientifically literate individuals who could understand how science, technology, and society influence one another and for those individuals to be able to apply their knowledge in everyday decision making. The goal was to create a life-long appreciation for science and its resultant technology in society and understand its limitations (NSTA, 1982, 1990–1991).

Harm's (1977) NSF-supported research project called Project Synthesis also established STS as a major new direction in both science and social studies. Project Synthesis established four goal clusters for school science. These goals stated that science education should prepare individuals to use science in improving their own lives; to prepare citizens to deal responsibly with science-related social issues; that science education should give students an awareness of the nature, scope, and variety of science and technology-related careers; and that science education should allow students to acquire adequate knowledge to pursue science careers.

Project Synthesis provided clear evidence that the only goal for which teachers and schools were concerned was the acquisition of adequate knowledge to pursue science careers. Most justified their program and their teaching on the textbook, the curriculum guide for the school, and the expectation of students, parents, administrators that they cover what they cover because it will be needed at the next academic level.

The STS movement has been an attempt to balance the goals as well as the curriculum, teaching strategies, and assessment to provide direct attention to the first three goals. We know that few really learn by going over textbook information, performing verification-type laboratories, listening to teachers talk, and being evaluated on the ability to repeat information and skills practiced.

Cognitive science has revealed that even the most successful students (e.g., university physics majors and engineering students) have not internalized the ideas and the skills that they find so interesting and with which they are viewed as being most successful. When confronted with real-world problems and issues, they cannot use the information and abilities seemingly learned in school. When these successful university students have been studied more intensely, cognitive scientists have found that real learning (though it is often discongruent with what scientists know) arises from personal explanations and constructions. These personally constructed ideas are stronger than any of the teachings from schools—even for the best students who seemingly know perfectly what the teacher and the curriculum outline as essential.

The use of social issues, service learning, and community service has become the cornerstone of Curt Jeffryes's sixth-grade science class in Creston, Iowa. The tenets of STS and constructivism have provided the philosophical basis for this transformation. Again, Curt's own words describe the change:

> The experiences of Talmage Hill have changed how I view my role as a teacher. I have come to realize that my science classes must be centered in the real world of the student and must be personally relevant. Issues and community service projects not only allow me to satisfy those two goals but they also provide a means for students to exercise their rights and responsibilities as citizens. My focus has shifted from trying to cover and master a large amount of material to helping students gain understanding of a limited number of key concepts.
>
> The Burton R. Jones Middle School correlates state, "Every student has the ability to learn and to the right to succeed." The sixth-grade science students believe this. Recently, a teacher visited my class, and while questioning my students, I heard Annie, a somewhat outspoken girl who "tells it like it is," respond to a question about failure by stating, "The only way you can fail is by not trying. In science, its all right if you make a mistake—I ought to know cause I makes lots of them—but I don't fail."
>
> Tanner, a very talented student, stated in response to the same question, "In science class there is no failure. You can take a risk in doing a

project or experiment and if it doesn't come out the way you think it should, then everyone helps you to see what you could have done differently. We're not graded on how well we can take a test; we are graded on what we can do and on what we know. Science is my favorite class!"

REFERENCES

Brooks, J. G., and Brooks, M. (1993). *The Case for Constructivist Classrooms.* Alexandria, VA: Association for Supervision and Curriculum Development.

Harms, N. C. (1977). *Project Synthesis: An Interpretative Consolidation of Research Identifying Needs in Natural Science Education.* A proposal prepared for the National Science Foundation. Boulder, CO: University of Colorado.

National Science Teachers Association (NSTA). (1982). *Science-Technology-Society: Science Education for the 1980's.* Position Paper. Washington, DC: Author.

National Science Teachers Association (NSTA). (1990–1991). Science/Technology/Society: A New Effort for Providing Appropriate Science for All (Position Statement). In *NSTA Handbook* (pp. 47–48). Washington, DC: Author.

Nolan, J., and Francis, P. (1992). Changing Perspectives in Curriculum and Instruction. In C. D. Glickman (Ed.), *Supervision in Transition* (pp. 44–58). Alexandria, VA: Association for Supervision and Curriculum Development.

Rutherford, F. J., and Ahlgren, A. (1990). *Science for All Americans.* New York: Oxford.

15

Calling Students to Action

How Wayland Middle School Puts Theory into Practice

STEPHEN FEINBERG   **RICHARD SCHAYE**

DAVID SUMMERGRAD

One-hundred-eighty bicycles head north along Route 126 from Wayland, Massachusetts, to Walden Pond. Legs churn, helmets gleam in the crisp October air. Is this an international bicycling event? A giant camp excursion? A bike-touring extravaganza? No, it's the Henry David Thoreau House of Wayland Middle School—the entire sixth-grade—embarking on one leg of their journey toward responsible citizenship. The students, broken into groups of 10, accompanied by their middle aged teachers, huff and puff as they complete the final miles. One girl remarks, "There was one part of the ride where we went through a grove of trees, and the light was just streaming through the leaves."

During their day at the pond, the students will retrace the footsteps of Thoreau as they begin to consider the majestic nature around them and the power of Thoreau's words: "I came to the woods to live deliberately." Students will also encounter "Mrs. Ralph Waldo Emerson," portrayed by the middle school band director, who will regale the students with tales of mid-nineteenth-century life in Concord. Away from the routine of bells and 41-minute periods, the students collect leaves, visit the site of Thoreau's cabin, and, along with their teachers, take a deep metaphysical breath.

After a quiet day at the pond, students and teacher once again climb aboard their bicycles and begin the 10-mile journey back to Wayland Middle School. Approaching the school, one can hear a feeling of individual accomplishment. "I never thought I would make it!" shouts one excited 11-year-old. "I've never biked more than 5 miles, and today I did 20! " another exclaims. Yet, at the same time, there is a noticeable pride in the collective accomplishment. "We did it!" exclaims a group of 10 students arriving with their winded teacher. Although tired from the long day, the beginning of a bond among students and teachers has begun to develop. The start of a three-year adventure in personal growth and individual social responsibility has begun.

It has often been stated that one of the primary goals of public education is to develop a responsible citizenry for our democratic society. Although there is general agreement over the positive nature of this goal, there is less agreement on how it is to be realized. Some have argued that responsible citizenship can be cultivated primarily by examining selective lessons of the past, usually in a chronological manner. This approach contends that citizenship skills are best learned by scrutinizing past models of good citizenship. Others concerned with citizenship education have argued that a close inspection of the political branches of our democracy will enhance citizenship skills; familiarity with the structures of our democracy will deepen our commitment to a democratic system.

At Wayland Middle School, we believe that educators, especially middle school educators, risk failure in their attempt to develop a responsible citizenry if they make the assumption that they can rely solely on an analysis of the past or a study of governmental structures to educate future citizens. Standing on the brink of adulthood, adolescents unconsciously seek empowerment. Although we realize that the middle school experience is but a small part of our students' education in citizenship, middle school represents the first solid opportunity to connect the lessons of the past with specific well-planned activities that use this emerging knowledge of how to live democratically. Further, we believe that when students stay with an issue, study that issue, analyze it, and approach it from a variety of perspectives, they are not only learning about that particular issue, but more importantly, they are internalizing a model for learning about other issues.

A visitor to Wayland Middle School watches warily as 25 youngsters, wearing black T-shirts and buttons that say TCC, get their final instructions from an energetic teacher. "Remember, enter each room quietly, remove the boxes carefully, and move quickly. Go get 'em!" The students disperse and the visitor approaches.

"Excuse me," he asks, "what was that?"

"That was The Crap Crew (TCC)," the teacher replies. The students, members of the seventh-grade Rachel Carson House, are taking the classroom lessons on the environment that they have learned and are applying these lessons in a practical manner. Two times a week the students run a school-wide recycling program that has become a model for other middle schools.

Reading excerpts from *Silent Spring,* students and teachers were inspired to put Rachel Carson's belief into action. This led to the birth of The Crap Crew, our recycling commando team. Boxes are left in each classroom. Teachers and students are encouraged to separate trash into recyclable paper and nonrecyclable items. In cooperation with the management of the environmentally conscious Wayland Town Landfill, the contents of the boxes are brought to the dump twice a week.

An unintended consequence of this program has been positive student/teacher interaction. In a traditional school, the sight of students wheeling enormous bins down a school hall, entering classrooms at will, and stomping around in a bin to compress the paper would raise the hackles of most teachers and administrators. At Wayland Middle School, through the collective teaching efforts of science teachers and students, the spectacle of TCC illustrates the allure of empowerment—individual action can make a difference.

Some 20 years ago, Wayland Middle School, then known as Wayland Junior High School, was a typical school for early adolescents. In many ways, it was a miniature high school. Departmental structures dominated the school, and tracking based on "ability" levels was widespread. Students in the upper-level courses were deemed successful, students in the middle-level courses were often given less attention unless they were behavior problems, and students in the lower-level courses, while often receiving additional services, were seen as "not achieving" in the academic world of school.

Beginning in 1978, in an attempt to more successfully meet the needs of all of the students, the structure of our school began to evolve. Under the leadership of the former principal, who was highly skilled in methods of organizational management, the school underwent major restructuring. While departmental structures were retained for academic purposes, teams or "houses" were developed within each grade to help us meet the social and emotional needs of early adolescent students. As Wayland is closely connected to the powerful historical heritage of the Boston area, each of these houses was given a name associated with that history: Emerson, Lowell, and Longfellow.

Within a short time, it became clear that the house structure was beginning to better meet the needs of our students. The house system was effective in facilitating our understanding of students, but we began to discover the limitations of the names we had chosen. Students attached no meaning to the names associated with each house. We realized that while seemingly unimportant, the names we selected for our houses could have a profound impact on our students and on our courses of study, our curriculum. If the staff selected names that reflected important symbolic themes, we would be able to organize units around those themes and integrate them into our existing courses of study. Students would see that they were involved in issues that had current and active meaning, rather than passive involvement in successive exercises in memorization.

Beginning in 1984, the eighth grade became the Martin Luther King House. The study of social equity issues and racism began to be interwoven within existing courses. The seventh grade became the Rachel Carson House. Environmental issues became the focus of this house. The sixth grade became the Henry David Thoreau House. Using the unique individualistic approach of this famous writer, issues of personal conscience and respect for the serenity and beauty of our local environment were folded into the existing curriculum.

These three Americans are all heroes. Their lives are proof that individuals can become meaningful contributing citizens through their actions. In effect, concentrating on these individuals over a three-year middle school period, first in our neighborhood and then in our larger physical and social environment, serves as a wake-up call for civic responsibility. We have developed courses of study and specific activities around these themes, with many opportunities for individual and group actions related to these themes. Parental support for this integrated approach to education has been remarkably positive. Many have identified our middle school as the place that begins to make sense of the world for their children. As one parent put it, "Our dinner time is no longer the inevitable discussion of what do you have for homework tonight. That question now shares time with what we as a family can do about the environment or why full equality is so difficult to achieve. It has helped us to see our children as future adults." We firmly believe that middle school students need a curricula of empowerment in order to develop skills for responsible citizenry in a pluralistic, participatory democracy. We believe that our model provides multiple opportunities for such empowerment.

> One sunny June morning, four yellow school buses roll up the driveway of Wayland Middle School. As 100 kindergartners pour out, they are greeted by Elizabeth J. Fontana, a poised and engaging seventh-grader who has organized a special event. As she finishes her year in Rachel Carson House, Elizabeth wants to leave a legacy that reflects what she has learned.
>
> She, along with three friends and a small group of teachers, has organized a tree-planting ceremony. They held bake sales, arranged for a pine sapling to be donated by a local nursery, and invited the entire kindergarten class of the town to celebrate the symbolic planting of a tree. As Elizabeth leads the youngsters in singing "Plant a Tree," she demonstrates that she has internalized the action-oriented ethic of Wayland Middle School.

The three-grade progression at Wayland Middle School is quite deliberate. A conscious attempt has been made to mirror the progress of the emerging adolescent. Starting locally, students in the sixth-grade Thoreau House begin to maintain personal and academic journals. At the Walden Pond visit, students sit in small groups in the autumnal splendor of a New England fall as they sketch and write their observations. Students are encouraged to explore the world of Walden Pond using all five senses. "If you listen carefully to the sound the leaves are making when the wind blows through them, you can hear a soft hum.

I can see the leaves dancing their way to the water where they float like little rafts for fairies," writes one student.

The lessons of the pond are brought to the school building through a heightened awareness of the connection between individual thought and the environment. This is highlighted in the English and science curriculum in grade 6. In-class journal writing, reflective in nature, is a required part of the English course of study. This has a proven effect on improving the fluency of student writing. In addition, these journals provide a wonderful outlet for students to record their reactions to many of their academic experiences. Respect for nature is rekindled through the study of natural forces in the sixth-grade science course. Units on fire, electricity, wind, and other aspects of physical science form the core of the sixth-grade science program.

The social context of Thoreau House is accentuated by the involvement of all sixth-grade students in Teacher Advisor Groups (TAG). The TAG groups, which meet weekly, foster self-worth by encouraging students to express their opinions and points of view on a variety of school, personal, and social issues in a respectful, safe, and nurturing setting: "Why do we have so much homework?" "It's not fair that we can't watch TV on school nights." "Sixth-graders ought to be able to go to dances." "Why is our school cafeteria still using Styrofoam trays?" "How can we stop teasing at lunchtime?"

Students leave the sixth-grade with a strengthened sense of belonging in the school and in the world around them. "Students, like all of us, feel a need to be heard," observes one sixth-grade teacher. "The TAG groups afford a great opportunity for students to express their feelings and for teachers to listen." They have also learned that Thoreau did not always "go along with the crowd"— an invaluable lesson for middle school students who exist in a subculture of extreme peer pressure. Most importantly, by June of their sixth-grade year, we hope they have rediscovered what Rachel Carson termed "a sense of wonder."

The principal and assistant principal call out the names and start to pass out the sponges and brooms. The daily ritual of cleaning the lunchroom has begun. But wait! This is no ordinary custodial crew. The sixth- and seventh-graders, during the first of Wayland's two lunch periods, are taking their turns in the cleaning rotation. Initially a response to the cuts in educational financing across the land in the 1980s, student involvement in maintaining the cleanliness of the building has become an integral part of school life. Before the end of the school year, each and every student at Wayland Middle School will have helped clean the school lunchroom.

Upon entering Wayland Middle School, students quickly learn that they are as responsible for the maintenance of the building as are the teachers and the custodial staff. Parental response to this involvement has been overwhelmingly positive. "It's great. Just tell me how I can get them to help more at home," quipped one parent. The principal adds, "The kids have a tough time complaining to me about their turn for clean-up when they see that I'm using a broom too. One thing they all agree on is that I drop less food on the floor than they do." He goes on, "Both parents and students have heard me say many times, 'Learning how to clean up your own mess is one of the most important life skills we teach in our school.' "

As students move through the seventh grade, their courses of study gradually begin to broaden their social horizons. Through the study of world geography, students are made aware of environmental issues. Their life science course introduces them to the splendid variety of life forms. In English, each student does a year-long "Rachel Carson Project" that highlights one of these environmental issues. Among these issues are endangered species, toxic waste sites, air and noise pollution, acid rain, beach erosion, deforestation, and the impact of population on environments. Beginning in September, students make weekly visits to the library where they do research to help them become experts on their topics. Each student uses this research to prepare a written report and an oral presentation that is shared with the class. Letters are written to environmental groups such as Greenpeace, Sierra Club, and Save The Whales, asking for information that will later be used in their presentations. Letters are also sent to "offending" corporations and businesses, as well as to legislators and policy makers in charge of environmental concerns. In these notes, students elicit information as well as share their own personal points of view.

Jennifer Hughes's letter represents a first step toward integration of the "call to action in learning." Her research forms the basis of her new found convictions:

Dear Gillette Company,

I recently got hold of a list with companies that test on (sic) animals. You were on the list.

Whether it is true or not, you should know that testing your products on animals is cruel. It shows that the Gillette Company only cares about making money when they really are taking the lives of millions of animals.

I want you to stop testing on animals because I am letting people know that you use animals in laboratories and nobody wants to buy products that have been in the eyes and skin of innocent animals.

I did some research on the subject and there are many alternatives. One, you can use artificial skin cells of humans. I know of three companies who do that and have extremely high sales.

Two, use human volunteers, autopsy reports, studies, and use ingredients which have already been proven safe without animals. By the way, testing on animals has been proven far more inaccurate than without animals.

Another way you can prevent the selfish murder of animals is by SIMPLY PUTTING A LABEL WITH A WARNING ON YOUR PRODUCT that says it has not been tested. After putting the warning label on, you can proudly stick on a
"NOT TESTED ON ANIMALS"
sticker like the (sic) many other companies.

Enclosed is a petition which many of my friends have signed. Thank you for listening to my complaint and I hope that next time I'm shopping for products, a sticker will be on your products reading (sic) that you have listened to me. If I see that, I'll give out the word you have given up murder.

Against Animal Testing
Jennifer Hughes

It is striking that Jennifer tries to offer a solution to the problem in her letter. The students are trying to push beyond protest toward constructive change. The Rachel Carson House theme encourages these early steps in activism. A second letter illustrates this point well:

April 25, 1994

International Fund For Animal Welfare (IFAW)
Box 193
Yarmouthport, MA 02675

Dear Madam or Sir:

My name is Jennifer McKay and I am doing a report on the pollution and clean-up of Boston Harbor. I have to take action in some way that will help Boston Harbor.

Several years after the Massachusetts Water Resource Authority (MWRA) started cleaning up Boston Harbor, there is a conflict. The Boston Harbor outfall pipe is a tunnel twenty-five feet in diameter and ten miles long. The pipe will carry lightly treated sewage out of Boston and forty-two surrounding communities. The sewage quality will improve by the year 2000.

This pipe will bring lightly treated sewage practically right into the North American Right Whales feeding grounds. The population of this endangered species is down to no more than three hundred. Right Whales use Massachusetts and Cape Cod Bays as a nursery ground, where mothers and calves feed for at least three months in the summer and fall.

I am interested in starting an Adopt A North American Right Whale program at my school to make sure these endangered species don't become extinct. Please send me any information that could help me with starting this project. Thank you.

Sincerely,
Jennifer McKay
Grade 7, Age 13

The students' year-long environmental focus culminates in a three-day trip to Cape Cod and the Cape Cod National Seashore. Students and teachers stand ankle deep in the tidal flats as together they explore the rich marine life in the intertidal zone. Biking on Martha's Vineyard, students realize the tremendous impact humans have had on the environment. While on a whale watch off the coast of Provincetown, students stand poised at the boat's railing trying to catch the first glimpse of a humpback or right whale. As the vessel cruises slowly along Stellwagon Bank, traditional feeding ground for whales, seventh-graders marvel at the amount of paper and plastic garbage visible in the choppy water. "Can you believe all the junk way out here in the ocean?" one girl remarks. "No wonder we're studying about this stuff."

"I see one!" screams an excited student. Everyone on board rushes to the railing for a better look. They are rewarded with the rare sight of a humpback whale "breaching," leaping completely above the water's surface. It is truly spectacular. "Once the humpbacks were a common sight here and all along the coast. They are only recently making a return," the guide for the whale watch explains.

Later that same day, students visit Woods Hole, where Rachel Carson did much of her research and writing. Afterward, they walk the beach nearby. "Look at all the erosion at the Cape," one student says.

"People should do something to save these dunes," another responds.

"What do you mean 'people'? We're people, too. *We've* got to do something."

Ingrid's letter to President Clinton shows that the students are including themselves in the debate about the environment. As the the following letter indicates, the students are nearly ready to assume a role in the struggle as they seek to influence national policy:

President Clinton,

I am in 7th grade writing from Wayland, Mass. I am immensely concerned about global warming and the greenhouse effect. All year I have been researching and collecting information. What are we going to do to reduce the amount of carbon dioxide that we release in the atmosphere? What will happen when glaciers melt, raising the sea levels conceivably up to 24 feet? Or when precipitation patterns alter, causing the Mid-west and regions of Russia to dry up and no crops will grow? Why is it that North America is the continent emitting the most carbon dioxide?

I know you have many other problems and concerns, but this effects (sic) the way we live. I have already written to many other organizations without receiving a reply. If you could send me some answers or information on global warming, I would be deeply gratified.

Sincerely,
Ingrid Keller

Slowly but surely, students begin to have an awareness that they are both part of the problem and, potentially, part of the solution. For12-year-olds, this is a profound revelation.

Strange lights play across a sea of "enchanted" students dressed in an array of improvised costumes; some are fish, some are gulls, some are fishermen and fisherwomen, and still others—coated with haphazard bits of refuse—are "polluters." The entire seventh grade has been transformed into actors and actresses as part of a day-long theater experience. A traveling drama troupe, the Grumbling Gryphons, has created an entire seascape using all of the members of Carson House. With the help of the cast, students perform for each other a series of skits replete with environmental images. Dozens of students slip into their costumes showing undersea life. Some are dressed as fish skeletons that float to the surface; they are the victims of those who are wearing assorted pieces of trash representing pollution in the ocean. The skits form a story whose ending is yet to be written. Students begin to understand that the ending is literally left up to them and their generation.

Some 200 12-year-olds, who normally cringe at the thought of donning a "childish" costume or performing in front of each other, are able to transcend, for a few hours, their inhibitions as they actively explore the all-too-real drama of the battle to save our planet. Voices are raised in an excited cacophony as "environmentalists" battle "polluters" to determine the future of the sea. The day is filled with a level of engaged learning which makes it the highlight of a year filled with classroom and field experiences that have deepened student understanding on complex environmental issues.

The realization of the threats facing the environment produces not only a sense of wonder but also a sense of concern. "What can I do," a student wonders, "to reverse the damage?" This individual worry soon broadens into a realization of the need for collective action, and students begin to ask, "What can we do?" As part of their English and science courses of study, students begin to put their book learning into action by organizing Earth Day clean-ups, building compost piles, engaging in neighborhood beautification projects, and promoting the schoolwide recycling program. The transition from classroom to community, so difficult to achieve in a traditional school setting, becomes a natural and inevitable progression. An outgrowth of this transition is that students begin to question environmental injustice as they begin to see the need for social actions. This questioning facilitates the transition to the social concerns highlighted by teachers in the eighth grade.

> Thirty sets of eyes are riveted on the red-haired woman standing in the front of the room. All are hushed as she speaks of Nelson Mandela, the Sharpsville Massacre, and the struggle to end Apartheid. Tracy Blues, a visiting teacher from St. Barnabas School in South Africa, patiently answers each question about the situation in her homeland. "Many of the students in my school are boarders because their neighborhoods have too much violence for them to commute to school safely." Students and teachers alike are awed by her tales of courage. "I would never be able to work in a government school, having been blacklisted due to my political activities as a student. I faced many threats during that time in my life."
>
> But most importantly, students are impressed by the power of their own letters, which have brought her to our school. As part of her visit to the United States, Ms. Blues has journeyed to Wayland to meet the students in Martin Luther King House. The thoughtful pen-pal letters from Wayland to her students have begun to build a bridge of friendship half way around the world.
>
> Students ask questions that transcend national and racial boundaries as they try to understand the lives of their pen-pals in the townships of South Africa. "Is there violence where you live?" asks one student. "Do the police bother you, even though you are white?" asks another. A third demands, "What can we do to help end this injustice?" Even after the bell sounds, the students continue to bombard Ms. Blues with questions. Teachers, standing around the room, listening to any of her five presentations, are impressed by the passion for justice they hear in their students' questions, as well as by her answers. As one student commented, "The way they set up those racial categories under Apartheid seemed really stupid. How can you call Japanese people 'white' and at the same time call Chinese people 'coloured'? Maybe someday all people will have the same rights."

As their third year at Wayland Middle School begins, not only have students grown physically but they have also begun to see a change of emphasis in their courses. The relationship between individual actions and social issues is now accentuated. Dr. Martin Luther King, Jr. told us: "Injustice anywhere is a threat to justice everywhere." Using Dr. King's life and work as a foundation, students explore issues of justice and injustice in the world today in greater depth in both their social studies and English courses.

The entire eighth-grade social studies curriculum is organized around the concept of justice. The first unit examines the Foundations of Justice. The purposes and origins of democratic governments are explored through detailed examination of the U.S. Constitution and the Bill of Rights.

A car slows down as it approaches two teen-age girls on the chilly Boston street corner early on an October morning. A man rolls down the window and, as he passes the girls, yells, "You two should be in school!" The girls exchange a surprised glance.

Moments later, a second car slows long enough for a woman to stare at the two girls and then give them "the finger" as she drives away. Are these people reacting to delinquents or runaways? Are they simply intolerant of teenagers? The two girls, although puzzled by the reactions of passers-by, continue to stand on the corner for the next two hours holding a sign for Clinton/Gore. They, along with 160 of their eighth-grade classmates, are participating in the biannual Social Studies Election Field Trip.

Across the city, students are spending a few hours immersed in the excitement of a presidential election campaign. Twenty youngsters are stuffing envelopes in the Bush/Quayle headquarters, and another 25 are distributing Perot election flyers to the early-morning commuters. One bus-load of students is interviewing both a columnist and a political cartoonist at the *Boston Globe,* while another group is meeting with the news editor and anchor of the local NBC affiliate. In both cases, the students hear the same message: "Stay on top of current events and get involved." The columnist further encourages them to work on their writing: "The written word is a powerful tool."

These eighth-graders *are* in school, although the passing motorists did not realize it. They are applying first-hand the lessons of democracy by participating directly in the campaign process of free and open elections. It is certain that come election night, these youngsters will be tuned in to the election results with a keener interest due to their hands-on experiences.

The first social studies unit is followed by a unit entitled Justice Delayed. This is an examination of the African-American experience that culminates in a detailed study of the modern civil rights movement. Through extensive use of videotapes and interactive media programs, students are introduced to and interact with this piece of American history. Each year, Martin Luther King House rents a local movie theatre for a private screening of "The Long Walk Home," a fictionalized version of the Montgomery bus boycott starring Whoopi Goldberg and Sissy Spacek. The film takes our collective breath away as many students realize for the first time that they are looking at a piece of their own history.

"I knew that blacks had to ride the back of the bus, but I never understood how they had to pay in the front, then get off, and then get on again in the back. It must have been so humiliating," one student observes. This movie experience begins our investigation into the history of African Americans.

Students examine West Africa prior to the advent of the European-dominated slave trade. They learn where in Africa most of the slaves came from, what nations were involved in the slave trade, and when the slave trade occurred. "I always thought that the English were the only slave traders. I never knew that the Portuguese, Spanish, and Dutch were also involved. And I *never* thought that the Swedes and Danes were also slave traders." The economic basis of slavery is explained through a study of the Triangular Trade and the growth of regional economies in the British colonies. The disputes over the expansion of slavery that eventually led to the Civil War are studied. As one student put it, "I thought the Civil War was originally fought to end slavery. It turns out that the expansion of slavery, not its abolition, was one of the causes of the war."

Also included in this study is the reaction of African Americans to discrimination in the period after Reconstruction. Not only are the students told of Booker T. Washington's response to white bigotry but they are also told of W. E. B. DuBois's reaction. Students are encouraged to trace the historical threads connecting African-American leaders of the nineteenth and early twentieth centuries to those of today. Included in this study are Sojourner Truth, Harriet Tubman, Marcus Garvey, Thurgood Marshall, Martin Luther King, Jr., and Malcolm X. Some students begin to see the connection between the beliefs of an earlier leader, such as Garvey, to a more modern leader, such as Malcolm X. "Malcolm X was more like Garvey than King was," one student says, as she realizes that both men were black nationalists. "But King wasn't like Booker T. Washington," another quips. Both white and black students find it enlightening that there is more than one black voice speaking to the issue of race in America. Through our study, students have seen the connections between the diverse black voices of the past and the voices of today.

This experience is summed up in the "Flesruoy" essay assignment. Modeled on the famous pseudo-anthropological study, "Body Ritual of the Nacirema" by Horace Miner, students are asked to take the perspective of an alien who is describing how justice is meted out in our culture. Drawing on the wealth of information presented, students produce essays that attempt to synthesize the history of African Americans. Like Robin Williams's alien TV character, Mork, eighth-graders are puzzled by the inability of humans to achieve a perfectly just society. At the same time, they are aware of the continuing attempts to achieve that just society. This tension between what **is** and what *should be* is at the heart of any serious study of the American past. Our students make the connection between past and present as they consider America's future.

A woman's mournful voice rises out of the darkness. As the lights come slowly up, the audience is mesmerized by shadow puppets portraying the treatment of slaves in early nineteenth-century America. The eighth grade of Wayland Middle School, the King House, has traveled a short seven miles to Arlington, Massachusetts, but a long 150 years across time, to Bucktown near Cambridge on the Eastern Shore in Maryland, the birthplace of Harriet Tubman. Conductors and participants accompany the students as the journey north from bondage is recreated. All strain their eyes looking for the North Star as they try to "Follow the Drinking Gourd."

For 90 minutes, the students and staff are regaled with the sights and songs of the life of Harriet Tubman as performed by the Underground Railway Theater. Their understanding of the present-day issues in civil rights is deepened as they learn about the roots of this struggle. As the students reboard the buses, they blink, due to the unaccustomed light, and in disbelief at the moving piece of history they have just seen brought to life.

The third unit, Justice Denied, is a study of the Holocaust. Building on both their understanding of the foundations of our democracy and their knowledge of African-American history, students are made aware of the potential for enormous human suffering when individual rights are ignored. The study of this history is often controversial due to the horrific nature of the Holocaust. Yet, it is essential to clearly focus on this history, for it shows that it is essential for a citizen in a democracy to act to protect that democracy. As Edmund Burke so clearly stated, "All that is necessary for the forces of evil to win is for good men to do nothing." Any teacher who has ever witnessed students being teased while their classmates did nothing to stop the teasing understands the relevance of this curriculum.

Waiting for the speaker to arrive, 170 students are quietly sitting on the floor. They have been carefully prepared for this visit, but no amount of preparation is sufficient. Rena Finder, a Holocaust survivor, enters the room and quietly, with much dignity, and begins to tell her story. "I was 11 years old when my nightmare began. I lived in a beautiful town in Poland, Krakow. When the Nazis entered my town at the start of World War II, my life changed forever." The students sit absolutely still, riveted by her tale.

"We were forced to leave our home, a pleasant place, and move into the small constricted place known as the ghetto. I couldn't bring much into the ghetto. Most of my things remained in my old house." Disbelief begins to appear on the faces of the students.

"Daily, I saw the destruction all around me. People were starving, people were dying." Tears form in students' eyes. Their teachers' faces reflect their own sense of injustice. Rena goes on to explain how she and her mother were taken from the ghetto and sent to a work camp. Eventually they arrived in the Auschwitz death camp. "We were two of the 'lucky' ones. We were *Schindlerjuden,* Jews who worked for Oskar Schindler, a German who miraculously helped save over 1,000 Jews."

After 40 minutes, she asks if there are any questions. A sea of hands waves in the quiet air. Question after question is asked. It is as if there will be no end to the questioning. "How can this have happened?" The starkness of the absolute denial of justice has permeated the consciousness of the students. One African-American girl is stunned by what she has heard. She interprets this in the context of the previous unit, Justice Delayed, when she says, "I never knew that white people did such terrible things to *other* white people."

As Rena indicates it is time for her to go, she is surrounded by students who continue to ask questions. "Do you think something like this can ever happen again?" wonders one student.

"The future is in your hands," answers Rena simply.

Complementing this course of study is the English curriculum. The writing program at Wayland Middle School, using the process approach, emphasizes the importance of purpose and audience in each writing task. The best writing happens when a writer can clearly posit the internal audience for the assignment as well as the reason for the writing. Each of our units develops a rhetorical situation to maximize these two factors.

In the eighth-grade unit Understanding Differences, we foster the belief that one individual can make a difference. Students are encouraged to write letters to well-known individuals about a continuing American issue: racism. Students have written for information and advice to such diverse citizens as actress Whoopi Goldberg, Senator Bill Bradley, Presidents Bush and Clinton, director Spike Lee, Commissioner Pete Rozelle, baseball player Mo Vaughan, journalist Diane Sawyer, Archbishop Desmond Tutu, and dozens of others. Each time students receive a response, it not only increases their knowledge but it also reinforces their belief that their voices are heard—that individual action matters!

If students are to become active participants in the democratic process, this belief is essential. If you do not believe that your voice will be heard, then why participate?

Through reading, letter writing, and journal writing, the issues of racism and justice are explored. Selective nonfiction readings, such as *Streets of Memphis* by Richard Wright, *Not Poor, Just Broke* by Dick Gregory, and Maya Angelou's *I Know Why the Caged Bird Sings,* along with a variety of novels such as *Roll of Thunder, Hear My Cry, Sounder,* and *Native Son* deepen students' understanding of these concerns.

In the past, students have sent letters to New Hampshire legislators in support of a bill to make Dr. King's birthday a state holiday, and they have sent letters to a Cub Scout leader in South Carolina whose troop was denied access to a water park because one of the boys was black. They have written to burn victim Christopher Wilson, an African American who was nearly killed in Florida in a hate crime, and they have written to the family of Yusef Hawkins, a black teenager who was killed by a gang of white youths in Brooklyn, New York. Some students write letters to the editor of the local newspaper describing what they have learned. One student explains how the curriculum has called her to action:

I live in Wayland. I have lived here all my life. I am13 years old, and I am in the eighth grade. This fact might not mean much to some people, but older graduates of the Middle School should realize the significance. It is a year of learning, of growing. It is a year when we are introduced to racism, prejudice, and the glorious teachings of Dr. Martin Luther King, Jr. Harsh facts are brought to life before our eyes; the stereotyping, discrimination, and exploitation of minority groups such as African Americans. I was appalled and shocked when I read the stories of degradation that made me question the goodness of life. Do I want to bring my children into a world of hate and shame? Does anyone? I certainly hope not. Are people in Wayland making an effort to help the world? Well, even if no one else is, I am. I doubt that there are many people who think about things like racism and discrimination these days. I know that there is not a big focus on racial issues within our community.

Black children being denied the right to enter a water park in South Carolina, Yankee outfielder Mel Hall being stopped by drug enforcement agents on his way to a game because he "looked like someone," the diminishing quality of African-American health care, the stereotypical outlook on careers of black people—these are the things that eighth-graders are learning about at the Middle School. Now, of course, the question "Why?" arises. Why are we learning about these things? Because we have to try to improve this world as the future of tomorrow. I hope to God that this world will be a heck of a lot better place than it is now by the time I die, and if you are going to improve something, first you have to know about what it is that you are improving. Do the people of Wayland know about these things? Well, if they do not, they should.

A major focus of the eighth-grade curriculum is leadership. Each grade represents a person who has made important contributions to the world and deserves to be remembered. The eighth grade represents Dr. Martin Luther King, Jr., a great leader of the civil rights movement. We must realize that we will have to take over to be the leaders of the future because there does not seem to be anyone who will do it for us. If we can take charge of this pitiful situation that the world is in, then perhaps we can create a world of peace, harmony, and justice as the generations before us lose power and we raise our children to be good people with values.

On the first day of school, we read one of Dr. King's speeches, "The American Dream," where he speaks of how America is always pictured as a land of freedom and justice for all. But this land does not really exist, he says; it is merely a dream of what we wish the world would be like. Where have all the great people like Dr. King gone? I hope that eventually some more people with outstanding qualities who will make a difference will emerge from this endless throng of normal, boring people, because it is sad to think that all the great heroes who make marks in history are gone.

If we do not try to improve the world, it will not get any better. Abolishing racism and prejudice would be one way of helping. Everyone should just accept everyone else for who they are. We have to realize that you cannot judge people by their skin color, gender, eye color, or hair color. You cannot just think that all people with dark skin are the same or that all people with light skin are the same, because it is as far from the truth as you can be. It is the same as saying that all people with blue eyes are the same, but unless you were born on the same day, at the same time, and in the same exact place as someone else, you are not the same as anyone. I think that the purpose of life is to be happy. Will being cruel to people for no reason really make you happy? In my English class, we studied a quote that said, "No one is free while others are oppressed." If so, how can anyone be happy while others are sad? Come on people, help the world. It is the only one we've got, and we only have one chance.

Thank you for listening.

In each case the students' awareness of racial injustice has been heightened, and their desire for change has been strengthened. They use each of these exchanges to broaden the definition of the boundaries of their own community. Students begin to realize that they exist in a larger community than the town of Wayland.

Congressman Martin Meehan of Massachusetts expects to spend 5 minutes—enough time for a "photo-op" and a few hellos—when he comes out to greet 170 visiting eighth-grade students from Wayland Middle School on the steps of the U.S. House of Representatives. Instead, he is treated to the equivalent of an aggressive press conference as the students ask questions about the economy, gays in the military, the environment, women's rights, and his views on abortion. A poised 14-year-old boy so impresses the Congressman with his questions on health care that Meehan invites him to return to Washington in two weeks to attend a committee hearing on this issue. Some 45 minutes after the meeting began, Representative Meehan is finally allowed to leave the House steps, but only because he is late for a committee meeting.

Across the street at the Supreme Court, in a small ornate meeting room directly behind the Justices' Chamber, Associate Justice Sandra Day O'Connor faces questions from some of these same Wayland students. Again, the intensity and thoughtfulness of the students' questions impress the Justice. Although she allows no pictures to be taken, she willingly fields all of their questions during a half-hour private visit.

Meanwhile, at the other end of Pennsylvania Avenue, another group of eighth-grade students sits in the first floor corner office of Eli Segal, director of President Clinton's Office of National Service. For close to an hour, drawing on their increased understanding of the many problems facing contemporary America, the students ask Mr. Segal, a former Wayland resident, a broad range of questions about his vision of National Service. One perceptive student later says, "Well, we've managed to cover all three branches of government, haven't we?"

When students meet face to face with the policy makers whose decisions affect all of us, they come away with an excitement that simply cannot be achieved in a classroom back at school. "Before we went to Washington, we read about it and saw pictures of the monuments and buildings, but it didn't seem real. When we got there everything seemed to come alive!" wrote one student. As they stand on the steps of the Lincoln Memorial, not far from the very spot where Dr. King delivered his "I Have A Dream" speech, students can be heard to utter the word *Awesome!* in a way that sounds truly appropriate. With Abraham Lincoln seated behind them and the Washington Monument in front of them, the students think about what they have learned. "This country was built on so much hope," says one student. The themes they have pursued have served to awaken their dreams for the future.

This awakening occurs within the context of a week-long journey to our nation's capital in May. Plans for this journey begin in November when all eighth-grade students are involved in a major fundraising effort. Building on their experiences in seventh grade, the fund raising involves the sale, not of chocolate or candy, but of citrus fruit shipped north from Florida. After the annual "citrus sale," students choose from a list of themes connected with either Washington or contemporary social or political issues. The project groups include themes such as Bearing Arms: A Right or a Wrong, Homelessness and Hunger in America, Space—The Final Frontier, Women and the Law, To Hill with It: A Study of Capitol Hill, and The Holocaust. These project groups, led by all the eighth-grade staff members—including the mathematics, foreign language, arts, and specialty teachers—serve to build an enthusiasm for learning that cannot be matched by staying at the school. "It was extremely gratifying to see our daughter so excited. The trip was an incredible trip for her both academically and socially. She came back from Washington with a zeal for her project which we have never seen before. She had us up until 2:30 in the morning sharing her experiences—from the Holocaust Museum to the hotel room. This is probably the most information she's shared with us in the past two years!"

Beyond enthusiam, students make connections to the units they have studied back at school. A dramatic example of the power of these connections occurs during the students' visit to the United States Holocaust Memorial Museum. Every eighth-grader visits this moving and unique memorial during our stay in Washington. One student shares the profound effect this visit had on him in a letter to the museum's director:

> Recently I visited your museum with twenty other eighth grade students.
>
> Before we visited the museum, we, in school, studied the Holocaust and all the events surrounding it. I thought I knew basically what went on inside Europe during this time. I found out I was wrong. When I studied the Holocaust, I realized that this happened and to how many, but in my head it didn't click that these were people. It seemed that the people involved weren't people, but objects that couldn't be hurt, but could die. When the elevator doors opened and I saw the charred remains of people in a pile, all previous thinking left. I saw that they were once living like me and could feel pain.
>
> The thing that moved me the most was the video images of pictures taken when medical experiments were performed. I will never let the images of what I saw there that day ever leave my mind or soul unitl the day that I die.
>
> I thank you for making me realize that feelings died and not just people.

From January through May, students prepare their projects so as to be able to maximize their learning during their week in Washington. That week marks the culmination of the adventure that began three years earlier with their bike ride to Walden Pond.

The principal sits at his desk one afternoon in early June sorting his mail. Just as he is about to toss aside what looks like yet another piece of junk mail, the name in the corner of the envelope attracts his eye: Bun Baldwin. Intrigued, the principal opens the envelope and discovers a neatly typed personal letter.

> Principal
> Wayland Middle School
> Wayland, Mass. 01778
>
> Good Morning:
>
> On May 2nd, a gang of boys from your school and I moved onto the 4th floor of the Washington Hilton Hotel, in D.C.
>
> Being a grandfather, I was concerned about the noise and carrying on that was going to disturb my stay.
>
> NOT SO! You and the parents of these young men are to be complimented on their behavior and friendliness. I was never dis-

turbed and it was "hi or hello or good morning" everyday— a happy surprise and a welcome happening!!
    You can be proud of these boys.

Sincerely yours,
Bun Baldwin, Jr.

While the letter is a surprise, the content reaffirms what the principal and the staff already know: The three-year tapestry of experiences in Wayland Middle School have a positive effect on behavior as well as on academics.

At the end of their three years at Wayland Middle School, our students are by no means fully formed. We have no illusions that our house organizational structure is a panacea. Students still call each other names, leave gum under the tables, and stand awkwardly at dances. Nor would it be accurate to imply that these three heroes—Thoreau, Carson, and King—and their ideas infuse all that we do in our school. Much of the daily routine at Wayland Middle School is similar to what one would find in most middle schools across America. The core academic program continues to be the bread and butter of the student experience. What is distinctive is that we use these three themes to continually and consciously make connections between in-school study and out-of-school problem solving.
    We are confident that our graduating eighth-graders feel empowered by the themes and heroes they have studied. As one parent wrote:

If you ever need evidence to support the 8th grade Washington trip, feel free to use our daughter as an example of the value of this experience. Clearly, Washington was educational and stimulating. What was so special for her, however, was her sense of independence, empowerment, and responsibility in dealing with the outside world; her realization that being on her own was exciting and fun. This was the culmination of her three years at the Wayland Middle School, her true graduation.

We have biked together in the spirit of Henry David Thoreau; we have collected trash from the woods with the passion of Rachel Carson; and we have confronted racial injustice bolstered by the courage of Dr. King. The models of Thoreau, Carson, and King have set our students on the course to responsible citizenship. They have learned that as true citizens in a participatory democracy, they need not be afraid to take individual actions nor to hold on to their own personal beliefs. They are also aware that, collectively, they can change the world.
    In the words of one juror in Reginald Rose's classic courtroom drama *Twelve Angry Men*, a play read by all our seventh-graders: "It takes a great deal of courage to stand alone." It is our hope that on our best days, the ethos of Wayland Middle School makes each of our students a little more courageous.

Hundreds of "artists" atop a dizzying structure of scaffolding and extension ladders are scurrying to put the finishing touches on their enormous painting. Their efforts cap off a three-month collaboration among 400 students, parents, teachers, and professional muralist David Fichter. As the final dabs of paint are applied, a hush spreads through the workers as if guided by some unseen signal. Even artist Fichter, who designed the mural along with 35 student artists (with input from hundreds of others), is awed as the project nears completion. The entire southeast wall of the school gym, which for 20 years has greeted every visitor to the school with a blank white expanse, is now covered with colorful scenes of daily school life. All three grades are represented through images of their respective activities and trips. There are depictions of students at play, as well as students with books, binoculars, and globes engaged in learning and living. Finally, there are glorious portraits of Carson, Thoreau, and King, who greet all students, staff, and visitors with determination, inspiration, and hope.

SPEECH TO GRADUATING CLASS OF WAYLAND MIDDLE SCHOOL

On a hot day in June, the eighth-graders of Wayland Middle School are gathered together for a farewell breakfast. They have completed three years of rigorous academics, engaged in a variety of exciting field trips, and begun to internalize some of the "call to action" we value in our school. On this, their final day at Wayland Middle School, the principal addresses them one last time:

> My fantasy as your principal is that on the final day of school, each of you finally listens to me. Suddenly, everyone in the cafeteria is instantly quiet as you carefully weigh my words and decide that what I have to say is just what you needed to hear.
>
> I know it's only a fantasy. Many of you would rather talk and listen to each other; after all, you probably have heard everything I have to tell you many times over these past three years.
>
> Like Sisyphus in Greek mythology, who keeps pushing the rock up the hill only to have it roll back down again (or his modern counterpart, the Energizer bunny), I'm going to keep trying and trying and trying until I get you to listen carefully.
>
> If I would give you one final exam before you leave, what questions would be on my exam? For starters, I would ask you about three important people in our lives: Mr. Thoreau, Ms. Carson, and Dr. King. My exam would begin by asking you:
>
> 1. Are you an individual like Thoreau, prepared to stand up for your own beliefs? Or are you a person who only knows how to do what

your "friends" tell you to do, even if it means giving up on one of your own beliefs?

2. Do you take care of our physical environment only when someone is watching? Is it just a game to recycle your trash? Or, as Rachel Carson taught, do you understand that your life and the lives of all of us who share this planet—Earth (not planet Reebok, planet Earth)— depends on each of your actions?

3. Do you pretend that you care about people of all races and religions? Do the words and actions of Dr. King teach you how to respect all people, or are his words heard one day and forgotten the next?

My questions don't have easy answers. They cannot, like a vocabulary quiz, be learned in a week or a night of cramming. My questions take a lifetime to learn and on some days we *all* answer them poorly. Indeed, all of your teachers have tried to ask you hard questions. If you can analyze a science problem, recite Shakespeare, solve a math equation, keep a Holocaust journal in school, but learn nothing from the needless fighting of Montague and Capulets, have you learned anything at all? If you get an A on a social studies test and fail to give your friend courageous—not easy, courageous— advice, does your A really matter? If you answer a health quiz perfectly and destroy your body with cigarettes or alcohol, does the quiz still count?

For, you see, the real purpose of middle school education is to give you the tools that will help you be serious learners. But the tools are irrelevant if you ignore the meaning of our school's mentors—Mr. Thoreau, Ms. Carson, and Dr. King.

In the next few years, your teachers and I will hear many stories about your achievements in the classroom, on the stage, and on the athletic fields. You have probably noticed this week that we welcome and love the visits we get from our former students. But the stories we hear are not just about achievements. Too often they are about a seatbelt not fastened, a taunt of someone because he or she is gay, a put-down of a classmate just because he or she is not in your group of friends.

I would ask, therefore, that each of you take from this school, from these superb teachers and from me, just one lesson that summarizes all the other lessons that we teach. It is simply that you treat others as you would wish to be treated by them—not some others, but all others. If you succeed in this lesson, it will outlast every A on a test, three-point basket that you make, and every fine musical performance that you give.

I have discovered a secret over these past 12 years of being a principal. As the years go by, I remember students by their kindness more than their achievements. As the years go by, I remember students by the courageous decisions to help a friend in a timely fashion or, for that matter, to help an enemy as well.

Your extra large class has impressed all of us many times over with its energy, vitality, hard work, and capacity to help each other. Of course, you have disappointed us as well. That's what middle school is all about. Leave us knowing that we care about you deeply and look forward to your own future discovery of the Thoreau, Carson, and King inside each of you.

Thank you.

Dr. Richard Schaye
June 22, 1994

▶ 16

Our Forest, Their Forest

A Program That Stimulates Long-Term Learning and Community Action

PATRICIA McFARLANE SOTO

JOHN H. PARKER

GEORGE E. O'BRIEN

THE HISTORY OF THE OUR FOREST, THEIR FOREST PROGRAM IN SOUTH FLORIDA

John Parker often tries to reduce his carbon dioxide emissions by commuting to Florida International University using an environmentally sound mode: bicycling. One morning in the fall of 1988, while he was biking through an area called Horse Country, he was pondering about the need to make people more aware of the rapid rate of destruction of tropical rain forests. Perhaps Aldo Leopold's phrase *Act Locally, Think Globally* triggered the phrase *Our Forest, Their Forest*. It was clear to him that this was an exciting and appropriate phrase to use for an environmental education campaign dealing with tropical deforestation.

The basic premise of the Our Forest, Their Forest concept was that children might better understand the characteristics and ecology of a tropical forest eco-system if they could compare it to a local forest eco-system that they could study and learn about firsthand. From that original idea, Our Forest, Their Forest (OFTF) evolved into a comprehensive and successful program involving more than 80 schools in Dade County, Florida. More specifically, the program was particularly well received at several junior high schools[1] in which it significantly enhanced the learning of science, societal, and environmental concepts by the students. It also resulted in the preservation of about 1,600 acres of pristine rain forest in Costa Rica.

In its initial stage, the primary goal of the OFTF idea was to stimulate students to learn more about the science and environmental issues dealing with forest ecology. In the late 1980s, it had become evident that tropical deforestation was taking place at an extremely rapid rate. In fact, it was estimated that tropical rain forests would disappear from the earth during our lifetimes unless something was done to reverse the trend. However, teaching about an environmental problem that is thousands of miles away is a difficult task. Thus, the OFTF concept tried to enhance the students' understanding of the local forest ecology while addressing one of the crucial environmental issues of our time: tropical deforestation. The locally developed curriculum included instructions on how to develop a small forest eco-system of native plants on the school grounds. As the forest began to grow, students would describe the botanical and ecological characteristics of "their" forest and, through research and reading, find out how those characteristics differed from a "typical" tropical rain forest.

Shortly after John Parker began developing the educational curricula in 1988, an article appeared in a magazine telling the story of how, following a slide presentation by an American plant ecologist named Sharon Kinsman, some young students in a rural town in Sweden started a rain forest preservation effort in Costa Rica. The article indicated that the students' concern and anger about the level of destruction of rain forests was in part related to their love of their own local forest. This appeared to be a clear verification of the premise of the OFTF concept.

The next step in the evolution of the south Florida program occurred a month later when John Parker told the story of the Swedish children's preservation project, *Barnes Regnskog* (*Children's Rain Forest* in Swedish), to an ecology club at a Miami high school and at an environmental seminar at Florida International University. Students at both meetings responded enthusiastically to the idea of developing a network of students and teachers "to save the rain forest."

At a follow-up organizational meeting, several middle-level teachers attended and participated in the formation of an organization called Students for the Children's Rain Forest. The organization decided to educate teachers and students about tropical deforestation and to raise money to preserve a pristine tropical rain forest in Monteverde, Costa Rica, an area now called El Bosque Eterno de los Ninos (the International Children's Rain Forest). It was immediately clear to one middle-level teacher that her students would jump at the chance to participate in such a project, and another middle-level teacher voiced her excitement about the possibility of planting a native eco-system on her school grounds.

To educate students about deforestation and to stimulate interest in participating in the OFTF program, a tropical rain forest slide show was developed by faculty and students in the Environmental Studies Program at Florida International University. Two different versions of the slide show were developed: a shorter, simpler version for primary students, and a longer, more comprehensive one for middle level, junior high and senior high school students. The script and slides depicted various plants and animals of the Monteverde Cloud Forest. The next part illustrated the causes and results of the destruction of tropical rain forests. After this somewhat depressing message, the final segment was about the Children's Rain Forest showing how children in south Florida and around the world were writing letters to stop this destruction and raising money to preserve that pristine rain forest in Costa Rica. Then the students were encouraged to learn more about tropical rain forests and to participate in local efforts to save the Children's Rain forest through fund raising.

In order to raise money to save the rain forest, the OFTF program focused on the development of a new concept called "environmentally sound" fund raising. This concept involved a blending of the original OFTF idea and Leopold's "Act Locally, Think Globally" philosophy. Environmentally sound fund raising focused on projects that have positive environmental impacts in the local area while the funds obtained were used to save a tropical eco-system that was far away in Central America. A primary example was an effort by middle school and senior high school students to remove invading exotic vegetation from a natural coastal eco-system on Key Biscayne. The "clean-a-thon" idea was developed in which students collected pledges for the hours they worked removing the exotics, with the proceeds going to the Children's Rain Forest. Excited about the project, the middle-level students readily found sponsors to support their clean-up efforts.

The middle-level students also raised funds through recycling programs and sales of environmentally produced rain forest products and recycled paper products. In the middle-level schools, students excitedly purchased Children's Rain Forest T-shirts to demonstrate their support for the project. According to some students, the Children's Rain Forest "label" became more fashionable than Gap or Banana Republic labels.

One of the most successful environmentally sound fund-raising techniques was a direct extension of the original OFTF concept. Students and teachers worked with a local nursery to design and implement an Our Forest, Their Forest program at several middle schools. It involved the planting of butterfly gardens and/or native hardwood eco-systems on the school grounds. These planting projects were made into fund-raisers by getting parents or teachers to "adopt" (i.e., donate money for) trees at a retail price (e.g., $60 for an 8-foot tree). However, arrangements were made with the nursery to obtain the trees at a wholesale price (e.g., $30 for an 8-foot tree) and the net proceeds were used by the students to preserve acres in the Children's Rain Forest (see Figure 16–1). The usual result was that about half the money went for the purchase of the plants and half went to the Children's Rain Forest. Thus, local "forests" were planted on school yards while a forest in Costa Rica was being preserved: Our Forest, Their Forest!

An additional local/global aspect of this school yard planting program was the connection to global warming. The trees were planted as a part of the Global Releaf campaign, a national effort by the American Forestry Association to plant 100 million trees in the United States within four years to absorb carbon dioxide—the primary cause of global warming. It is worth noting that recent scientific studies show that tropical deforestation may produce about one-quarter of

OUR FOREST, THEIR FOREST

Plant Adoption Order Form

Our school is participating in a program that will provide (1) plants for our school-yard and (2) the purchase of tropical rain forest land for preservation on behalf of our school.

Our plan is to: (Teachers should describe their plan on the form.)

1. Plant a miniforest/hardwood hammock area on school grounds. (An outdoor classroom area may be included.)
2. Plant firebushes and a variety of pentas that attract butterflies.
3. Plant trees and shrubs to shade school buildings with the intent to reduce air conditioning requirements.

You are being offered the opportunity to adopt a plant for our school ground plan. You have the choice to select from three types of plant adoptions: (1) a large tree (6- to 8-foot tree) at the donation of $80.00, (2) a small tree/shrub (2- to 4-foot sapling) at the donation of $20.00, (3) ground cover plants and shrubs at the donation of $10.00.

Order Form for Plant Adoption

Name of Purchaser _____

Phone _____

Type of Plant to be Adopted _____

Cost _____

Dedication Plate (Maximum of 10 Characters) _____

Other _____

Make checks payable to The Florida Rain Forest Alliance.

For more details about our school's participation in the Our Forest, Their Forest Project, please contact _____ , phone _____ , during the time of _____.

FIGURE 16–1   Our Forest, Their Forest Program Plant Adoption Order Form

global greenhouse gas emissions. Thus, the combination of tree planting and rain forest preservation involved in the project is an important example of effective local action to reduce global pollution.

Patricia Soto, seventh-grade teacher and science chairperson at the G. W. Carver Junior High School, was in attendance at the first meeting of "Students for the Children's Rain Forest" during the winter of 1988. As she witnessed university and high school students organizing and enthusiastically sharing their visions of the OFTF concept, she could not resist the optimism, vitality, and positive actions that these young people were suggesting. She wanted to include her 200 seventh-grade students (five sections) in this movement of rain forest preservation by making that local connection through tree planting. Additionally, she wanted the project to be integrated into the curriculum of the other five science sections. Concurrently, she had a vision that included multidisciplinary dimensions for a project that could increase collaboration among faculty colleagues, more involvement of families with her students' projects, and even positive community impact. Another component of her vision was the development of an outdoor classroom area. Subsequently, she began to implement one of the most successful OFTF projects at the G. W. Carver Junior High School.

G. W. CARVER MIDDLE SCHOOL: THE TRANSITIONAL YEARS

G. W. Carver Junior High School was built on the boundaries of two cities: Coral Gables and Miami, Florida. For 30 years preceding the 1970s, G. W. Carver predominantly had African-American students enrolled in grades K–12. In the early 1970s, as part of a racial desegregation plan, Carver was designated a "seventh grade center" through which all students in the six elementary schools within the feeder pattern were channeled. From 1973 through 1988, G. W. Carver Junior High School housed those seventh-graders who did not enroll in private schools to avoid attending there. A strong Parent, Teacher, Student Association (PTSA) increased the morale and quality of the school; however, much effort was spent selling the idea of integrating the seventh-grade center to the more affluent community members. By 1988, Carver, with an attendance of only 400 seventh-graders, was targeted by the Attendance Boundary Commission of Dade County for its underenrollment. At the time, 47 percent of the students were Hispanic, 27 percent White non-Hispanic, 25 percent African American, and 1 percent Asian. Change was coming. Speculation about establishing a magnet program was high. Concurrently, as part of a countywide policy on the establishment of middle schools, the county changed its name to G. W. Carver Middle School. Carver became a middle school in September 1990. Full teaming began in 1991. Today, G. W. Carver Middle School houses 300 students in grade 6, 280 students in grade 7, and 150 students in grade 8.

CURRICULAR ACTIVITIES AND INSTRUCTION

Laying the Groundwork for the Outdoor Classroom Project

Initially, the G. W. Carver OFTF project began with a strategy meeting between the science department chairperson and the principal in December 1988. Decisions were made about the proposed site for an outdoor classroom area, and instructional goals and expected outcomes were established (see Figure 16–2).

Underground structures, facilities access routes, water pipe locations and other ground's issues dictated detailed involvement by the principal. School-wide curriculum connections were also explored in order to incorporate some multidisciplinary activities. Patricia Soto suggested to Principal Samuel L. Gay that the Curriculum Council could assist in making the project schoolwide. After all, as Soto stated, the resulting outdoor classroom would benefit any class wishing to use the area. The faculty collaboration and teamwork in designing certain activities and components was essential to the successful completion of the project.

The processes of faculty, students, and family interactions and the carrying out of the project were blueprints for later development of team approaches and networking after the 1990 change to a middle school format. Since this project required educating the instructors in order to develop student motivation, a rudimentary "teaming network" was developed. Furthermore, brainstorming techniques used at the school for the first time helped faculty and students gain access to new ideas and ways of conducting multidisciplinary investigations and activities. For example, the PTSA forum brought Ms. Soto's ideas before parents and students, asking for direction and input for a plan of action. In this way, many parents were able to contribute to the success of the project. Students suggested the poster as a vehicle to reach staff and students about tree adoption and using the Intraclassroom Television Network to teach the student body about rain forest destruction. Faculty invited speakers to enrich geography lessons with rain forest habitat information. A science teacher and her students developed an instructional video about how to plant a butterfly garden. These ideas were implemented with successful outcomes. Additionally, teach-

---

From participating in the OFTF project, students demonstrated successful outcomes of the following goals. The students were able to

1. *Identify* local flora and fauna.
2. *Identify* rain forest characteristics, citing typical flora and fauna.
3. *Draw* conclusions about dominant populations, food chains, human influence, and energy flow within a site.
4. *Describe* the role of the rain forest in the global ecological balance of the system.
5. *Explore* problems and solutions to deforestation.
6. *Discuss* the positive steps students can take in their communities to make a difference in environmental quality.
7. *Involve* and *interact* with family members and other community members in the outdoor classroom project.

FIGURE 16–2   Instructional Goals/Outcomes of the G. W. Carver Junior High School OFTF Project (December 1988–June 1989)

ers exchanged ideas at nontraditional planning times such as during 30-minute lunch periods and during preschool coffee hour.

Logistics for the OFTF project included formulating a time table for ordering, planning, and dedicating the area. Teachers from several disciplines voiced an interest in helping with OFTF. Some of them attached their own curricula's outcomes to the project. For example, one science teacher at the seventh-grade level, Phyllis Learner, had been awarded a grant to plant a butterfly garden. She suggested, "Let us use my butterfly garden as a focus for all of the students to study the interactions between plants and animals. Everyone in the school passes by my butterfly laboratory and we can point to this garden as a micro-habitat which can help the students visualize rain forest needs."

The art teacher also eagerly accepted the challenge to incorporate the rain forest theme in her classes. "The brilliant colorings and lines of the animals and unique plants within the rain forest are 'naturals' for us in art." Her students depicted brilliantly colored Macaws, Toucans, an array of colorful insects, and lush tropical plant species. Also, she utilized the rain forest habitat informational posters that her children created as a vehicle for teaching elements of design.

Geography teachers capitalized on the rain forest theme to awaken students to the unique environments in Central America and South America and Malaysia. It personalized and energized their map skills and biome diversity lessons.

Mathematics teachers included problem-solving activities such as helping students perform calculations to project from hourly destruction rates (i.e., 6,000 acres per hour) to daily, weekly, and yearly rates.

Patricia Soto recalled that her efforts also stimulated other instructors' interests in the project. "This effort to make connections throughout our school was the precursor to the coordinated efforts that are standard in current middle school strategies."

OFTF was a frequent lunch-time topic in the faculty lounge. Over lunch, a geography teacher said, "I'll display maps of rain forest locations in the Western Hemisphere." When two math teachers heard how many acres of rain forest were being destroyed each minute, they said they would have their students make calculations of the problem in class.

The high-energy PTSA members were quick to pick up on the plans for schoolwide awareness. "Just tell us when, where, and what, and we'll be there for any activity" said PTSA President Lucy Petrey.

It was agreed that the trees would have name plaques to motivate the sales of the butterfly gardens and trees that students could plant. Student representatives in the student council developed information sheets for the homerooms so students would know how to go about adopting a tree while contributing to rain forest preservation. Parents who heard about the plans suggested long-range ambitions in the future, such as the PTSA raising money to put benches and tables under the future tree canopy. Thus, the first stage of a scope and sequence for implementing an outdoor classroom while promoting rain forest preservation was accomplished (see Table 16–1).

TABLE 16–1   A Scope and Sequence for Implementing an Outdoor hile Promoting Rain Forest Preservation

Step	Activity	Purpose
1	Project meeting with administration	Define goals and purpose
2	Collect classroom research materials on local plants and animals	Provide access in classroom to updated, varied sources
3	Begin schoolground naturalist study	Acquire observational skills
4	Introduce rain forest habitat and issues	Provide background information
5	Organize fund-raising strategies with sponsoring organizations	Plan timetable, options, and delegate responsibilities
6	Assign informational posters about rain forest issues	Generate information to disseminate to all students, faculty, staff, and community
7	Begin public relations plan to develop interest in purchase of plants (and plaques) as rain forest land is purchased	Prepare support for project
8	Organize a dedication ceremony to showcase area and summarize the project's achievements in presentation	Involve a wide spectrum of student body, parents, and the community

Getting Started

The perpetual challenge to "cutting edge" current-events education is the rapid location of accurate informational sources to use in the classroom. At the time of this project, there was not a plethora of rain forest knowledge readily available for use in the middle-level classroom. Thus, the quest began. The media specialist at G. W. Carver Junior High School was overheard to have said, "In other words, Mrs. Soto, you want everything in the media center for your classroom research project. Perhaps we could build a tunnel for direct access."

When *Time* magazine's "Planet of the Year" (January 2, 1989) issue appeared on the newsstand, Patricia Soto began gathering copies of that issue with the idea of using them as a learning resource. Students were asked immediately to collect neighboring newsstand copies for class use. Parents also helped locate some issues. Patricia soon discovered that magazine distributors gather all unsold copies and destroy them at their warehouses. After a trip to the Southeastern Periodicals distribution center, she managed to get 50 copies of the coveted magazine just as they were bound for destruction. (How availability changes! Much later, the collection of environmental articles in that issue of *Time* were reprinted separately because of the demand by educators.) These magazines were boxed up and carted to school, where Patricia numbered the magazines and set about analyzing the potential lesson plans to be drawn from the charts, graphs, maps, photos, and narratives assembled in the issue. Other valuable sources included Beriault (1988) on planning and planting a native plant yard; Cerulean, Botha, and Legare (1986) on school yard habitats for Florida's birds and beasts; Fitzpatrick, Snyder, and Showalter (1984) on development of an outdoor classroom; Gann (1979) on planting a hammock; Meerow, Donselman, and Broschat (1989) on identifying and classifying native trees of south Florida; and Braus (1989) on the study of the tropical rain forests. Articles in the *Miami Herald* by Georgia Tasker (1986, 1989) concerning local student projects (which included ideas on beach clean-a-thons and park plantings) offered great stimuli for discussion as well. Patricia also called the Dade County Public Schools Science Education office to find speakers available for presenting rain forest issues. The first guest speaker at the school addressed all social studies classes, which were in the process of studying South America at the time. Two students could not get over how live hermit crabs crawled all over speaker Mabel Miller's straw hat as she spoke. "Creatures have a margin of adaptability as well as a limit. Notice the hermit crabs crawling about my hat here. Obviously, this is not their preferred environment. Yet, what does the hat have that allows them to at least temporarily scoot about on it? The rain forest inhabitants do not have a wide scope of alternatives. If the canopy is disrupted, the levels of life habits are also interrupted."

Brilliantly colored slides were shown of the variety of animals found in the rain forest. "I'm going to use that poison arrow dart frog for my art project" blurted out a voice in the group. "I'm painting a sloth" added another.

Dade County's Public Volunteer Office was contacted. Speakers were invited. Students particularly enjoyed several presentations made by college students working on their own projects at Florida International University.

A great coordinated effort by several teachers and students to secure information was happening at Carver. At least a dozen students brought in *National Geographic, Ranger Rick, World,* and other periodicals in which rain forest information was found. One student was intrigued by the announcement that the science textbook was not going to be directly used for a month. A grin came across his face as he remarked, "So, it's up to us students to find what we are going to study? Is it legal?" The search and upwelling of support for current rain forest topics reinforced the energy and vitality with which students explored the issues. Primary resource guide and materials used in the OFTF program are listed in Table 16–2.

Activities

One of the primary challenges was to have students make connections between local and global environmental issues. OFTF logically guided students to learn about their own habitats and ecology as they carried out field studies of their home environments.

TABLE 16–2   Primary Resource Guides and Materials for the Our Forest, Their Forest Program

Resource	Purpose
* 1. Executive Summary	Overview of program
* 2. Guide for Community Group Involvement	Description of program and ways community organizations can support a school's project
* 3. Teacher's Guide	Detailed description of what a teacher should do for successful implementation
4. Plant Adoption Order Form (see Figure 16–1)	Explains program to parents/teachers and facilitates donations for plants/rain forest preservation
5. Butterfly Gardening Guide	"How to" manual on butterfly gardening
**6. Rain Forests Educational Resources	Annotated bibliography of curricula/references on tropical rain forests
7. Rain forests—Help Save Their Layers of Life (1993)	Educators Guide for National Wildlife Week

* Available from the authors of this chapter.
**Available from The Children's Rain Forest, P.O. Box 936, Lewiston, ME 04243.
(207) 784-1069 and/or The International Children's Rain Forest, Monteverde Conservation League, Apartado 10581-1000, San Jose, Costa Rica.

Several pamphlets, such as How to Plant a Butterfly Garden and Global Releaf in Your Community, were used by the students in class. Ms. Lerner described her butterfly garden project to the 100 members of the science club one afternoon. "If you want Monarchs, you must have milkweed. Now, I know of an expressway cloverleaf covered with milkweed over by the airport; who wants to come?"

Patterns of similarity and difference between the local habitats and those existing in rain forests were explored in the science classes. For example, groups of students had to prepare habitat drawings showing the plants and animals of one of the 10 south Florida's natural environments. With this, they drew birds commonly found within the habitat. Mrs. Soto had compiled an index of all the animals featured in the previous 10 years' worth of the magazine *Florida Wildlife* and this index proved invaluable to assist students in gathering well-illustrated, life-like information within the classroom. As the group drawings evolved, a common comment from the students was, "That bird sure gets around. It's in our habitat of study too!"

Another curriculum connection was made with the butterfly. The butterfly garden on campus became a focal point of study. Phyllis Lerner and her 120 students (three sections) had designed the garden's layout based on the pamphlet given out by students from Florida International University. Inspired, others wanted to plant the correct plants that would increase butterfly activity in the yards of students' homes.

Ms. Lerner held her classes in the surrounding butterfly garden and would point out the mimicry of some leaf structure such as the passion vine. One enthusiastic student of Mrs. Soto's joined in the plant observation one day and really connected with this eyes-on experience in plant observation. "I never really looked at the plants this way before." Freckled-faced Chris pointed at the sky, remarking, "I never noticed the path the sun takes across this area. Look Mrs. Lerner, this plant is never getting direct light; don't you think you ought to move its location?"

Erica, a quiet, blonde-haired, shy student, commented "Our group has come up with 20 different shades of green for leaves." As the students assisted in the search for information and sought geometric shapes in the local flora, this process opened their eyes to the uniqueness of the local habitat dynamics. The science, the math, the art, the patterns—all revealed their interconnectedness.

Students told their parents about the butterflies being grown in some of the classes, and that brought parents in to see them. "I understand that soon my child will be mapping our backyard. We have so many unidentified trees there that I will purchase a few native tree-identification books that you may use in your classes," said Mrs. Kernish, a parent of a seventh-grade student. Mrs. Kernish then asked, "Where can we get more information about plants that attract butterflies? We wish to attract more to our backyard." In some cases, such questions stimulated further activities. In this particular case, Phyllis Lerner and her students were stimulated to produce an informational/instructional videotape for other teachers and students so that they could learn about the different stages of butterfly development as well as plants necessary for the development of a successful butterfly garden in south Florida. The videotape shows students and teacher providing instruction on different stages of butterfly development.

From the videotape, students are heard saying,

First is the food for the caterpillars' larval stage. Native passion vine provides larval food for zebra butterflies. Dutchman's pipevine will feed the Damask swallowtail. Milkweed is the food for monarch butterflies. Second, they need flowering plants that provide nectar. Wild citrus fruits such as lime will provide nectar for a variety of butterflies. Adult butterflies use a long curled-up tongue called a proboscus to get nectar. Flowers are needed of different color, shapes, and sizes to provide different-sized food types. Here are pink, red, daisy-type flowers, and milkweed flowers—all good nectar foods. Here is Cortia, it has tiny white flowers used by butterflies with short feeding tubes. This has been a little introduction to planning variety in a butterfly garden.

Meanwhile, a variety of more specific activities were planned and carried out.

Activities in the Science Classroom

Cooperative groups in the science classes studied the plants and animals found on school grounds. These groups were asked to identify local native plants, make rubbings of their leaves, and search for other locations where these native plants could be found. During the science class, Mrs. Soto escorted her groups of junior naturalists outside to the fields and buildings on the school grounds. Additionally, the groups took naturalist walks on the residential street adjacent to the school. As Monica, a seventh-grade student, heard about how many ornamental trees are poisonous, she remarked, "I have almost all poisonous trees at my house. I wonder whether my mom knows this!" Back on campus, Alejandra was in charge of carrying the crayons and paper for the leaf rubbings. Miguel and his team were marking the places where the common anole lizards were sighted. Jesus was marking off the distance between two trees that his group was trying to put accurately on their map of the study area. Meanwhile, Paul, slightly distracted, found it fun hopping over the string, much to the dismay of Jesus.

To transfer some of the value lessons of the uniqueness of life in a specific area, the seventh-graders did ecological studies of their backyards. They had to draw a bird's eye view of their home property and mark in all trees, bushes, garbage cans, fixed items, ground coverings, and other parts of the yard's features. Then, over the next month, they wrote observational journals and listed the day and night animals seen. Journal entries included such comments as:

> Here I was, ready to hit the flashlight on whatever was near the trash can when dad popped on the back porch light and away the unknown noisemaker scampered.

> I cannot believe how the rats use the high wires between houses like a highway.

> I followed an ant for 15 minutes on the pavement and it turned into the grass and disappeared.

> I saw two anoles, both with their mouths tugging on a large black beetle. The struggle ended with the little anole taking the prize and swallowing it whole.

> I am certain the reason I found no living creatures in my back yard was because of Scamp, my pit-bull.

> What I cannot figure out is why I keep finding mangoes gnawed on in my yard when there is no mango tree for two houses down. (Instructor and student inferred the squirrels transported them to eat.)

> My swimming pool is a bug graveyard.

Often, some students would run into class, describing a mystery creature sighted the night before, which anxious group members would help them identify using reference materials set up in the classroom. From that knowledge, students had to construct logical food chains and food webs, and discuss the types of interactions they either saw or inferred. Class reports using large colored diagrams provided a synopsis to all students of each other's surveys.

Families of students were actively involved with most home assignments. For example, as Michael's mom was moving a series of flower pots, she noticed that several nests of ants with eggs had been disturbed. She stopped working, went inside the house, and roused a late-sleeping Michael, saying, "I found several ant nests you'll want to put in your naturalist study. Come see what I found." One parent remarked, "Now, when my child hears television news stories discussing the rain forest, he comes rushing in to the room to hear the details." Another parent volunteered, "Your oral homework assignment for my child to explain the importance of the rain forest to the global health of our planet has been enjoyable. I learned a lot from my daughter."

Resulting conclusions from the study included Cammie's observation that "now I know why the cat sits in the corner of the porch; that is where the lizards sit sunning themselves." Carroll, a boy fascinated with the discovery of unidentifiable creature footprints by a garbage can, made plaster casts of them and deduced they belonged to a raccoon. The biome study allowed students to discern why we could not plant an actual rain forest with the trees and plants we were assembling for our outdoor classroom area. The importance and uniqueness to our own climate's character helped the students know why we were planting a tropical hardwood hammock, something suitable to Coral Gables and Miami, Florida. For example, the rain forest vegetation receives much more rain, and the internal humidity is trapped under the dense, tropical canopy. A tropical rain forest could not successfully be achieved in Miami because the rainfall is less and the opportunity for sizable, impenetrable forest areas is unattainable.

Multidisciplinary Activities

Numerous multidisciplinary activities were a focus of the OFTF project. For example, the seventh-grade students accomplished the following:

- *Art* (100 students): Paintings of rain forest and local indigenous plants and animals were done.
- *Music* (100 students): The works to be played by the band at the dedication ceremony were selected.
- *Geography* (200 students): Habitats, climate, regions, and biomes were studied.
- *Civics* (200 students): Preservation laws and environmental regulations were examined. Focus topics included: (1) local tree ordinances were being changed that restricted homeowners' and land developers' rights to remove trees natural to the south Florida environment and (2) national, state, and local car pollution regulations.

- *Mathematics* (400 students): Rates of destruction were calculated and acreage for sustainable populations was computed.
- *Language Arts* (400 students): Poetry writing and other creative writing activities occurred. One creative writing activity had the students writing a first-person essay such as "I Am a Tree Frog" or "I Am a Mahogany Tree" from the point of view of describing its surroundings and the needs of that organism. Poems composed by students included:

> Nature Nature,
> I wish I could have seen it,
> It was once a big and magnificent tree
> It saw the seasons
> Spring, summer, winter, fall
> Who stopped it?
> A dangerous, thoughtless, greedy animal
> None other than man
> Who will stop him?
> That tree still before,
> Yet a different form
> Still stacked high
> I can't get a splinter
> Just a paper cut.
>   —Shante Haymore

> Escape
> I want to escape
> I want to be swallowed up in my own tranquillity
> I want to retreat into my own thoughts
> I want to relax in my own being
> I want to sprawl in grass yet to be trodden by mankind.
> Undisturbed and independent
> Surrounded by peace.
> But there is concrete under my feet
> And pollution overhead
> Buildings around me
> Squeezing me tighter and tighter
> Born here, raised here, living here,
> Will I die here?
> I want to leave it all
> Yet it holds me under its spell
> I am its captive
> It is my captor
> I want to escape
> But I can't
>   —Tabitha Mallory

Dreamland
A land much unheard of
Where sorrows and worries are never mentioned
Where rejoice and hope is called upon
Where beautiful distinguished palm trees protect
the land and the sea
Where none of nature's creations are ever disturbed
Where the sky is never gray and the sun is never hidden
Where the blue of the ocean lets fish do as they please
Where the blue lagoon sits in serene silence
This land so placid and tranquil sits far away
Only seen in our dreams.
  —Luz Lacouture

Schoolwide Activities

Guest speakers on rain forest destruction addressed the entire student body. Additional resource people spoke on local plants and animals. The issues behind the school's involvement with planting a local area and purchasing rain forest land for preservation were presented through the morning and afternoon announcements. The science club organized these informational moments and spearheaded the promotional sale of the trees and butterfly garden flowers that the community was asked to purchase. The Science Club President exclaimed "We've got to get them [the students] so excited about what we're planning that they won't want to be left out!" Fliers were prepared to take orders for the trees and other plants that were to be located in the outdoor classroom as well as for home plantings. The art instructor suggested and helped organize a poster contest on rain forest issues that helped to heighten everyone's knowledge. The art instructor later commented, "'Can I prepare more than one poster?' has been the most frequently asked question by the students about this contest."

A particularly attractive and important aspect to the fund-raising success was the promise to place an attractive weather-proofed memorial plaque in front of the plants that the students, families, and others purchased. Homerooms and groups of friends were caught up in the decision as to what should go on the plaques they purchased. Successful outcomes of all of the plans soon became apparent. One student said, "My family is Chinese. It is a tradition to plant a tree for an ancestor. For this reason, we intend to purchase a tree and plaque to honor my grandmother." One parent commented, "Each person in our family wanted to have a tree named after him or her, so we wound up purchasing four." Ultimately, close to 100 plaques were placed in the outdoor area!

Activities in the Community

Several associations participated in the donation of plants and/or served as consultants and tree planters. These included the Native Plant Society, Florida International University, and a private nursery. Not to be left out, the PTSA members brought in hoses, shovels, and orders for plants from other places in the city. About this time, Phil Donahue had the rock star and environmental activist Sting as a guest speaker on a morning show. Patricia Soto remembers, "We educators knew that the rain forest lessons had reached the home front via our students because over 10 parents independently started calling our classes to let us know that the rain forest issues were being discussed on television. Many taped the program [for us], not knowing others were doing the same."

Culminating Activity

As the time for the outdoor planting approached in May 1989, the school had various activities in progress. Many of the multidisciplinary aspects were happening in class. The band director and his students were putting together a group of songs about nature. The PTSA had several moms baking cookies shaped like trees. The art department faculty supervised students who created a backdrop for the dedication ceremony comprised of bright, colored images of the flora and fauna of the rain forest. Posters created by students (based on the graphics from *Time* magazine's environmental issue) were hung around the school. Meanwhile the cheerleaders were busy making up a rap lyric called "The trees . . . save 'em."

The following rap song was performed by students on Arbor Day at the outdoor classroom dedication ceremony:

> The Trees . . . Save 'em"
>
> I'd like to thank you all for buyin' a tree,
> All you had to do, was save some money
> I'd like to thank the girls for telling the boys,
> and I'd like to thank the boys for telling the world,
> Now we all have our reward,
> and anyway you see the goal we've worked toward
> Ohhhhhhhhhh, the trees, save 'em!
> Ohhhhhhhhhh, the trees, save 'em!
> Oh we thank the teachers for saving the trees,
> and you did that with your lessons very easily.
> We're glad now that you did make a big fuss
> you taught and also motivated us.
> Ohhhhhhhhhh, the trees, Whew!, save 'em
> Ohhhhhhhhhh, the trees . . . save 'em!
> We thank you all parents for also for helping us,
> Your purchases provided trees—a whole great bunch.
> Without you this spot would never have been
> A place of shady joy to share with a friend.
> Anyway you see it, without you this wouldn't have been
> anyway you see it, we automatically win.
> Ohhhhhhhhhh, the trees, Whew!, save 'em
> Ohhhhhhhhhh, the trees . . . save 'em!

Now we got what we really want,
We've got small trees, and large trees and even more.
Because of everyone's help, from this great community,
Our future is better and our optimism will restore.
Ohhhhhhhhhh, the trees, Whew!, save 'em
Ohhhhhhhhhh, the trees, save 'em!
Mrs. Soto, this part is just for you
Thank you for all that you do.
Thank you Mrs. Soto for spending your time,
It's because of you, for you, we're making this rap,
Love you Mrs. Soto so very much.
Because you tell us about the trees.
Ohhhhhhhhhh! Mrs. Soto! Whew! the teacher.
Ohhhhhhhhhh! Mrs. Soto! Whew! the teacher.
Thatde datdat ed dat de dat datteacher, Mrs. Soto.
        —Composed and performed by The Female Edition

The day of the planting was, as can be expected, both chaotic and exhilarating. The middle-level students, teachers, and parents worked diligently with the volunteers from Florida International University and the Florida Rain Forest Alliance. The native hammock was now installed and ready for its dedication (see Figure 16–3).

At the dedication ceremony, dignitaries and all Carver students and teachers were entertained and informed about the project's important accomplishments. Some of the interesting commentary heard at the event included:

The plants this student body has purchased in honor of my deceased son are a living testimony to his memory. Thank you for making his memory central to your outdoor classroom planting project.—Father of a student who lost his life to leukemia during the school year.

We made all the cookies for this reception in the shape of trees. Those are the only trees we want this generation to destroy!—PTSA Mom

You've brought into focus an important global issue and taken action to do something about it. Costa Rica thanks you.—An official from the country of Costa Rica attending and addressing the student body at the dedication

This outdoor classroom area is going to be part of Carver's outdoor education program for a long time.—Ms. Heise, Assistant Principal

It is great to see the students rally their neighbors, their parents and the community.—Lucy Petrey, PTSA President

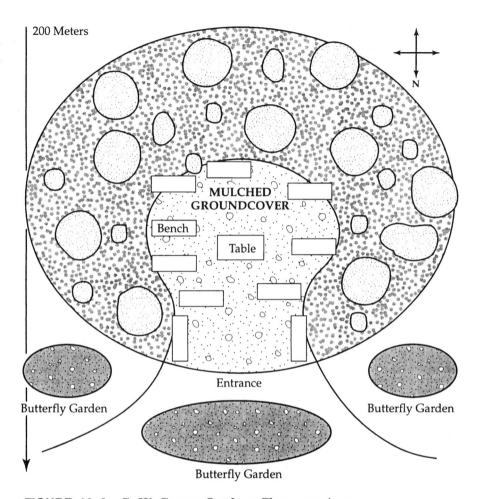

FIGURE 16–3   G. W. Carver Outdoor Classroom Area

I proudly dedicate these trees in memory of Raphael Sequiera.—Nicolas (in memory of his best friend Raphael Sequiera who passed away during the school year from leukemia.)

We are touched to see that you have planted two tall trees in your outdoor classroom area because Ralph who was less than 5 feet tall stood tall in courage and character.—Father of Raphael Sequiera.

Our forest had been created while their forest had been preserved!

LEGACY OF THE OFTF PROJECT AT G. W. CARVER MIDDLE SCHOOL: FOUR YEARS LATER

Now that the dedication of the outdoor classroom is four years behind us, the trees and plants are beginning to shade our outdoor classroom area. The planted semi-circle of trees and the islands of butterfly gardens have changed from a spindly planted site of promises to a lush, canopied, inviting refuge. Four years after the first photo, the backdrop of fence and walls is no longer visible as the area has matured. Secretaries eat lunch under the shade. Drama groups practice their lines there. French classes sit on the benches, and teachers have begun to check with one another so that they too can bring a class outside.

The legacy of the classroom also extends to those who ordered the name plaques peppered about the bases of the trees and shrubs—the Petrey Family, the Kanor Family, and so on. People come to the area to see their plaques. "See that tree?" says a school staff member to her little 5-year-old boy, "It has grandma's name on it. It's her tree."

Birds have begun to make their homes in the branches. On some days, there are so many orange gulf fritillaries and zebra butterflies that we cannot count them all.

The backyard study that seventh-graders now do at G. W. Carver Middle School has a new entry point of field study. These students of the natural surroundings practice their identification, mapping, and observational skills together in cooperative groups in an area they have in common. This study in the outdoor classroom area helps students sharpen their observational skills before they tackle their naturalist study of their own homes.

Additionally, people from the community who shared this project's evolution are now traveling to Monteverde, Costa Rica, to see the International Children's Rain Forest. They come back and tell those of us who haven't been there how lovely and special the area is. It is nice knowing your group helped secure the perpetuity of a little piece of heavenly rain forest habitat.

Students and Their Families: Four Years After the Project Had Begun

Four years after the initial planting and related activities, interviews were held with high school juniors who participated in the OFTF Project at G. W. Carver Junior High School in 1988–1989. The first student, interviewed by telephone, remarked to the interviewer, "I can't believe you're calling this afternoon. I just arrived home from planting over 100 trees with my service club this morning."

Another student, living outside the state now, recalled how competitive the students were during classtime, in the outdoors preparing for the tree planting. "I still remember the blisters [from digging in coral rock]. During class, everybody wanted to be out in the butterfly area, watering trees, and putting up new information posters."

A third student offered a different perspective: "I had my first experience developing a computer data bank while working on that project. After learning how to keep track of the school community members who purchased the plants and ordered nameplates, I used that computing skill innumerable times in high school. I don't remember any lessons as well as that computer work I did for OFTF."

One parent visiting the Outdoor Classroom Area for the first time in four years asked, "Where is our family's name plate? I want to show my young children our tree." A few students related that one of the reasons for their current volunteer "habitat restoration work," including post-Hurricane Andrew activities in South Dade, was their experiences as seventh-graders in the OFTF project.

At least a dozen former students remembered the accompanying plaque that they ordered when adopting a tree. "You've put them in the ground now? I'm coming over to see the one I ordered."

A rededication ceremony of the Outdoor Classroom Area held in June 1993 brought back numerous family members of the former and current seventh-grade classes. The spirit of the OFTF project has endured the four years and is captured by one parent's recent summation: "My family learned so much about our environment [during the project] and we are still learning today. We care about what happens and we want to make a difference in improving our world."

Today, new sixth-, seventh-, and eighth-grade students are taken to the Outdoor Classroom Area and told about the legacy in which they are sitting. The engraved nameplates serve as a memorial to those who purchased nameplates—The Breakfast Club, Genesis 1:1, Homeroom 7-3. These nameplates number close to 100. They are there as a reminder of an effort to make a difference and to serve as inspiration for students to continue their involvement.

ENDNOTE

1. Most schools with grades 6–8 in the Dade County Public Schools (DCPS) were referred to as junior high schools prior to November 1988, when the DCPS School Board voted for the process of changeover from junior high schools to middle schools. Since the inception of the OFTF program in 1988, most middle-level schools have changed both in name and philosophy in Dade County.

REFERENCES

Beriault, J. G. (1988). *Planning and Planting a Native Plant Yard*. Orlando, FL: The Florida Native Plant Society.

Braus, J.(Ed.). (1989). "Rain Forests: Tropical Treasures." *Ranger Rick's Nature Scope, 4*(4).

Cerulean, S., Botha, C., and Legare, D. (1986). *Planting a Refuge for Wildlife: How to Create a Backyard Habitat for Florida's Birds and Beasts.* Tallahassee, FL: Florida Game and Fresh Water Fish Commission.

Educator's Guide for National Wildlife Week. (1993). "Rain Forests, Help Save Their Layers of Life." Washington, DC: National Wildlife Federation.

Fitzpatrick, G. E., Snyder, W. B., and Showalter, L. E. (1984). "Development and Implementation of an Outdoor Classroom Using Native Vegetation." *Proceedings of the Florida State Horticultural Society, 97,* 227–230.

Gann, J. (1979). "Everything You Always Wanted to Know about Planting a Hammock." *Fairchild Tropical Garden Bulletin 34*(2), 15–26.

Meerow, A. W., Donselman, H. M., and Broschat, T. K. (1989). *Native Trees for South Florida.* Gainesville, FL: The University of Florida Publications Distribution Center.

Tasker, G. (1986, September 21). "The Vanishing Rain Forest." *Miami Herald*, pp. 1–4.

Tasker, G. (1989, March 5). "Kids' Pennies Help Save Rain Forests." *Miami Herald,* pp.1H, 12H.

Rain Forests Educational Resources. (1992). "The Children's Rain Forests." Lewiston, ME: Author.

Time. (1989, January 2). "Planet of the Year." *133*(1).

Every Step Counts

Service and Social Responsibility

LARRY DIERINGER   ESTHER WEISMAN KATTEF

Dear readers,

Our fifth-grade class has been working on a serious project. We have been talking about helping the homeless and trying to learn more about homeless people. One of the students in our class found out that Ms. Kattef and other Brookline teachers and principals worked at the Long Island Shelter in Boston. Last year, students from 5K helped out there also.

We wanted to help out, too, but we really had to think about why we wanted to do this. Many of us wanted to know more about homeless people so we wouldn't be so scared. Others wanted very much to help and talk to homeless people directly. We realized we had to make a serious commitment for the entire year. It couldn't be just a passing impulse or just to make us feel good.

We came to consensus as a class to commit ourselves to baking about 400 brownies a month. Every month we would bring $1.00 of our own money to buy brownie mixes. Some of us are responsible for buying the mixes at the best price, which so far is 99 cents. We then bake the brownies at home a day or two before we go.

Four of us at a time will go with Ms. Kattef to the shelter to help serve dinner and dessert. We also plan to have a tour of the shelter and get some of our questions answered. We can't wait to hear what the first group has to say about their experience. We hope other people will give in some way to homeless people.

Sincerely
The Students in Class 5K

About eight years ago, a small group of administrators and some teachers from Brookline Schools volunteered their time one night a month at a shelter in Boston Harbor. They called the project LIFE (Long Island Shelter Food Effort). These adults baked meatloaf, bought and cooked vegetables, and served at the shelter, while responsibility for baking 400 brownies rotated in one school among eighth-grade classes.

Jerry Kaplan, principal of the Edward Devotion School, had enough interest among teachers and parents in his school to form another group to serve at the shelter one additional night a month. One of the teachers, who had been involved with the LIFE project, Esther Weisman Kattef, had been concerned about the nature of student involvement:

> My fifth grade class became involved when our principal formed a group at the school to serve an additional night at the shelter. Prior to this, the brownies had been made by students who knew little about the project or homeless people, and who never came to the shelter themselves. I saw an opportunity to create a more powerful learning experience for students. So I initiated a different process for the involvement of my class in which students not only made brownies, worked at the shelter, and learned about homelessness, but would also get deeply involved in organizing the project.

The Devotion School project has continued since the day of Jerry Kaplan's initiative. For the past eight years, Esther's fifth-grade class has been responsible for preparing dessert and helping to serve the evening meal.

Service and Social Responsibility

"There is more than intellectual growth at stake in the teaching enterprise. Teachers, like parents, want to produce good and happy persons, persons who will support worthy institutions, live compassionately, work productively but not obsessively, care for older and younger generations, be admired, trusted, and respected" (Noddings, 1987, p. 6). Esther Weisman Kattef has a number of things she hopes will result from the children's involvement in this form of community service: a greater sense of care about other people; thinking skills for understanding the complexity of issues; a commitment to helping where one can; a belief that one can make a difference in the world; an action orientation to social problems; and a deeper understanding of homelessness. These goals are addressed not just by the act of working at the shelter. Equally important are the various ways in which students participate, how the project unfolds, and the connection of the project with larger goals and with the culture of the classroom.

The shelter project is an important vehicle for learning social responsibility. Students explore their own convictions and have the opportunity to act on them, supported by the adults in their lives.

Classroom Meeting

We assume schools are communities, when, in fact, they are merely institutions that can become communities only when we work at it. We can create an experience for students that demonstrates what it means to be a compassionate, involved citizen. For it is only within a community, not an institution, that we learn how to hold fast to such principles as working for the common good, empathy, equity, and self respect. (Wood, 1990, p. 33)

Last year, the homeless project was introduced to students and developed in much the same way as in each of the previous seven years. Early in the school year during a class meeting, Esther Weisman Kattef raised the topic of working at the shelter. The class meeting is a fundamental part of Esther's class. The service project is integrally linked to the meeting. The purpose of the meeting is to create an opportunity for the class to come together as a group to share ideas, events, and feelings, and to solve problems in and out of the classroom. The way a meeting is run is meant to reinforce shared participation and responsibility. Esther talks about its importance:

> I would say that the grand purpose of meeting is to foster a strong sense of community. The specific content is secondary to the process of the meeting. Meeting is a microcosm of life in the classroom. It is a time when we come together to talk and share, while at the same time practicing taking responsibility for creating a safe and successful learning community.

A classroom meeting is held daily for the first four months of school, and three to four times a week after that. It is one-half hour long during which three topics are brought up. The topics are signed up for in advance on an agenda, which a student is responsible for having ready every day. Any student or teacher may suggest a topic. The person presents the topic during the meeting; anyone else may then comment or share his or her own ideas or feelings once the topic has been brought up. Each topic lasts for 10 minutes. Students do not raise hands; rather, they determine when and how to speak. The teacher's role is the same as the students.

Immediate problems arise, which the students need to take responsibility for: Who decides who will speak next? What if more than one person tries to talk at a time? What if no one talks? How is time kept track of? How are disruptions taken care of? Who keeps us on the topic?

These problems are a regular part of meetings and of classroom life. However, usually it is the teacher who is expected to handle them. The structure of the meeting, particularly not raising hands, is meant to shift the responsibility for the smooth running of the meeting to the students, and further underscore the need for shared responsibility among the students. Esther elaborates on her role, saying, "I try not to answer most of the questions, solve concerns, or comment on students' opinions. Rather, the dialogue is among students, and I join in periodically with a comment or question." These same skills are necessary for learning and living in the classroom, where shared participation, community, and responsibility are valued.

GETTING STARTED

A few weeks into the school year, Esther brought up the shelter project by telling the class that this was a project that some people at the school had been involved in and that her fifth-grade class had done for a number of years. An open discussion ensued. Students talked about homeless people and reasons for working at the shelter. Students' questions tended to focus on their concerns about homeless people and the nature of their own responsibilities.

For example, Doreen, a 10-year-old Asian girl, asks, "Can you get sick from living with homeless people. My mother says homeless people can give you diseases." Sammy, a 10-year-old Indian girl, asks, "How do you bake brownies? I've never baked them before." Others ask, "How often do we go?" "Who gets to go?" "Are homeless people mean?" "Are they crazy?" As these concerns and questions were raised, other children responded based on stories they had heard or actual firsthand experiences with homeless people. It was through this initial discussion that stereotypes about homelessness began to be acknowledged and questioned. Esther describes a typical conversation:

> A student might tell a story about people she knew who had lost their home in a fire and had to go to the shelter. Another would ask: "What if your parents lose their jobs?" Because they lived in the city, students would talk about homeless people they saw daily. Nick, an 11-year-old "city" kid, asks, "Who's seen the man who talks to himself and wears a lot of coats outside the school on Harvard Street?" "Oh yeah," many kids respond. Some laugh. Michelle adds, "He's OK, you know, he doesn't bother anyone. I used to be afraid of him, but he doesn't bother anyone. He's just lonely. It's so sad." James adds, "Yeah, he once said 'Study hard' to me. I thought to myself, 'This guy is weird.' But I wasn't scared."
>
> Such questions and discussions continued during the course of a series of classroom meetings. The challenging of loosely held beliefs seemed to heighten the students' interest and desire to work with homeless people. It was as if they were drawn to test some of these new ideas that have been raised by their own classmates.

As concerns and questions began to be dealt with, the focus shifted to students' responsibilities and logistical issues. Esther explains, "I informed the students that if they were going to do this, they must make a commitment as a whole class, for 'once you begin, you'll be counted on.' In subsequent class meetings, students discussed this commitment and eventually came to consensus about working at the shelter for the year." (Coming to consensus will be discussed later in the chapter.)

Students had experience coming to consensus with other issues. Early in fifth-grade, Esther talked about the difference between consensus and majority vote decision making. She then asked questions that got the students to think about when each process was useful or particularly important. "For example, I asked, 'Can anyone think of a situation where voting is how decisions are made?' 'Why is voting used in these situations?' 'What kinds of decisions are best made by voting?'"

One student responded, "When you have to decide something quickly or when the choice is between a couple of things like 'Do you want to go on the playground or the tennis courts?'" "Or," Ian added, "when there's a lot of people deciding, like the presidential election." The same kinds of questions were asked about consensus.

Esther relates an instance when the difference between consensus and majority vote was illustrated for the class around a real issue:

> We were talking about whether or not to wear costumes to our Halloween party, and students had different opinions. I asked, "What happens if 12 people want to wear costumes, 8 do not, and 4 have no opinion? Does the whole class wear costumes?" "Well, you can if you want to," one student said. "But you might end up being the only one and you'll feel stupid," said another. "So, do we wear costumes or don't we?" asked a third. I asked, "Will everyone have fun if we make the decision by majority vote?" "No," interjects a student, "we should try to come to consensus on this. Who doesn't want to wear costumes? They should speak." Students went back and forth like this for several minutes, discussing people's concerns and the pros and cons of wearing costumes. Time ran out. The topic was picked up at the next meeting where the decision was made to wear "easily prepared" costumes such as putting on a mask or a hat. Through discussions like this one, students identified some of the times that consensus is especially important: when the whole group wants to have fun together, when there is long-term responsibility and commitment, and when most people really care and want their voices heard.

Organizing the Project

In the next phase, students formed committees to canvas local supermarkets for the best price on brownies, wrote letters home about the project, and created a time line for buying and baking.

Dear Purity Supreme,

We are from the 5th grade at Devotion. We bake brownies every month for the Long Island Shelter. We will be buying 20 boxes of brownies each month. And we would like to buy them from you at the lowest price possible.

Please let us know as soon as possible, since we must bake for the first time on October 16th.

Sincerely,
The Students in Class 5K and
Esther Kattef—Teacher

Dear Parents,

5K would like to share with you some information about a subject we are getting involved in.

For the past two weeks, we have been having a very serious discussion about a very important matter, homelessness. For six to seven meetings, we have brought up the subject. We have decided by consensus that we will bake brownies and serve dinner once a month at the Long Island Shelter in Boston. This is a shelter Ms. Kattef has been volunteering at for a couple of years.

This is not a passing impulse to help the shelter. We have talked very seriously about why we want to help homeless people directly, and have written about our feelings and concerns. We have decided that doing this just to feel good ourselves isn't enough. We have to really commit ourselves to this project, and we also want to learn more about homeless people directly. More specific information will follow. For now, we need to bring $1.00 in to buy brownie mix for November. We think we should raise or earn this money ourselves.

Sincerely,
The Students in Class 5K

Discussion of working at the shelter continued to take place during meetings where Esther regularly asked the class, "What do we need to talk about next?" Open-ended questions like this one continued to place responsibility for thinking and planning with the students. The class moved to the issue of buying and baking brownies. They wanted to know how much brownie mixes cost and who bought them. Esther let them know that prices varied and that "we'd like to get the best price." Many students offered to go to a supermarket near their home or one they were very familiar with. They discussed the best way to present the project and to ask for a "deal." They decided to speak to a manager and to clearly describe the project. Committees were formed to go to different stores according to who lived nearest to each. Each visit often resulted in a different deal and better prices. The committees then reported back to the class, and discussed and chose the best arrangements. Esther describes one dimension of this phase of the project:

> Students seem very excited about being a representative for the class and school, and going to speak with a store manager to ask for a good price. In one instance, Talia came back very excited from her visit to Purity Supreme where she talked to the manager and got a great deal. On the board she had posted: "What a deal!!! 20 boxes for $19.00 from Purity Supreme. That's less than one dollar a box!!! Details at meeting tomorrow."
>
> On two occasions, the managers would quote a price only if the principal wrote a letter or called. The discussion and responses that followed turned a potentially disempowering experience into a positive one. Students talked about how difficult it was for kids to do things that adults think only other adults can or should do. Discussion then moved to all the things that kids already did. "I call a taxi to get to my piano lesson, because my parents work." "Me, too, but I get a taxi from school to where my mom works." "Sometimes I write notes for school and checks for trips and my mom signs them, because she forgets otherwise." Esther wrote a note to the store manager, explaining the children's role and asking that he deal with them. The principal did not write or call. This part of the process was empowering for the students— even the spin-off discussions about children's credibility.

Through organizing the project and dealing with obstacles that arise, students learn lessons that will be valuable throughout their lives.

Next, a discussion took place about who pays for the brownies. "Do we ask our parents?" "Do we fund-raise?" "Do we pay for it?" "Do we collect money from the school?" In the discussions of helping the homeless, different ways of giving and being involved were talked about. Students discussed how some people didn't do anything to help others, some wrote checks or gave money, others gave their time, and still others organized people to give time or money. In light of the previous discussions about why students should be involved in such a project and how one can help others, the students came up with the idea of paying a dollar, themselves, once each month. This usually covered the cost of a box of brownie mix.

A committee wrote a letter home, informing parents of the project and summarizing the process the class went through to decide on helping homeless people. Esther and the class then baked one batch of brownies, going over directions, size of pans, and so on. After the brownies were baked, they were cut and wrapped. This became an interesting math lesson on how to get the best size and at least 20 brownies. After reviewing the steps, the class quickly unwrapped and ate the brownies!

Efforts often continued, depending on different students' interest, to get better and better deals. Some children reported on sales they saw advertised on store windows or in the newspaper. One student wrote a letter to Pillsbury asking for a donation:

Dear Pillsbury:

We are in the fifth grade at the Edward Devotion School, a public school in Brookline, Massachusetts. Our class makes and serves dinner at a homeless shelter in Boston Harbor once a month. Since September we have been purchasing our brownies at a local store to make for dessert. We bake over 400 brownies each month. We buy the boxes of brownies with our money.

Would you be willing to donate 24 boxes of brownies each month until June? We would appreciate any help you can give us.

Sincerely,
Chris Bennett

Pillsbury wrote back:

Dear Ms. Bennett:

I am sorry to inform you that we are unable to respond favorably to your request for Brownie Mix. Our contributions guidelines target funding almost exclusively to direct service programs serving economically disadvantaged youth in areas where we have a plant or another large business presence.

All product donations are made through the Second Harvest Food Bank Network. I suggest you call their affiliate, the Boston Food Bank (617) 427-9738, to see if they can assist you.

I wish you the best in your endeavors.

Sincerely,
Kristin K. Larson

When Chris got over being mistaken for a female, he reported Pillsbury's response to the class. Students understood Pillsbury's policy of helping where they do business, but thought Pillsbury was big enough to help out.

Other children suggested recycling cans and donating these to help pay for the rest of the meal, or using the money to buy brownies if some children could not afford the dollar every month. Parents often got involved and bought sale-priced brownies, and either sold or donated them to the class. "We all became very brownie-price sensitive," claims Esther.

Working at the Shelter

A group of parent and/or faculty volunteers baked meatloaf and served the evening meal at the shelter on the second Thursday of each month. Esther's class was responsible for the dessert and for identifying four students to help serve the meal. A week before, the class drew four names to decide who would help serve the meal that month. Esther reports, "During class meeting, we had two students sign up for 'drawing names for the shelter.' Two boys and two girls were chosen. There's always a lot of excitement in anticipation of the drawing, and many students often offer to be substitutes if someone gets sick."

Students brought in their dollar for buying brownies during the week before they went. A student was in charge of collecting this money, and a committee took responsibility for buying the brownie mixes after school, bringing them to school, and handing them out on Monday of the shelter visit week.

The students baked the brownies at home on Tuesday or Wednesday, and everyone brought them in wrapped and packaged by Thursday. A student took responsibility for checking off students as they brought in their brownies.

The prospect of going to the shelter raised a mixture of feelings for students. Some admitted to feeling nervous or unsure. Others talked about it as "an adventure," "exciting," and a "cool thing to do," because it was "different" and "a new experience." Esther described how the day of going to the shelter was special for the four students:

> The students were full of energy. Typically, the group made plans to do some homework together after school for an hour before they went. They also arranged to get a snack together or to bring food to share. I found this time to be relaxing and fun as we laughed, ate, and worked together before driving to Boston. What was apparent to me was that a strong sense of community was forming in these small groups. The students talked more intimately to each other than they did in the larger classroom setting. They asked about how a sick pet was doing or for a person to "tell more of those jokes you were telling after school." They asked me about my car and talked about their own family cars, and got into family stories that were often emotional. We discussed our class and what we liked, and things that we might do and/or change. I looked forward to this time because of our sense of common purpose and togetherness in an informal setting.
>
> At the shelter we were enthusiastically greeted by Jerry, the principal, and his wife Nancy, who were always there before us with Bob Kondel, another committed teacher. They brought in and cut all the meatloaf, and we began to prepare bins of mashed potatoes and lay out all the brownies. The staff at the shelter was friendly and excited to see us each month. They took all the new people on a tour of the facility. Some of the students asked questions about how the shelter was run and how it worked for people.

When the buses arrived, the children, along with adult volunteers, had all chosen the part of the meal they first wanted to serve, and changed jobs throughout the hour. These included pumping milk, serving mashed potatoes, gravy, vegetables, bread, and brownies. "I want to do the milk. It's fun and you have to be fast because the people can take as much milk as they want!" "Can I do the mashed potatoes? I like using the ice cream scoop." "Will you switch with me now? I've never served the gravy." A second shift came to relieve the group and to handle clean-up. After grabbing bread or brownies to eat, Esther dropped each child off at his or her home by 7:00 P.M. For these children, the shelter had become their "school" for the evening.

As George Wood (1990) coordinator of the Institute for Democracy for Education and author of *Schools That Work,* states, "Schools with a civic mission open their doors to the world around them. This is how they keep the school community from closing in on itself and how they show their young people the needs and possibilities that will confront them when they leave school" (p. 36). The class continued to work at the shelter over an eight- to nine-month period.

Classroom Discussions and Other Follow-Up Activities

Back in school, children often shared their experiences in the class meeting the next day. "We brought up 'shelter' because we wanted to see if you had questions and to share stuff." "Yeah, the people are so nice. They tell jokes and thank us." "Yeah, one guy said, 'Bless you sonny,' to me." "Oh, a lot of people asked me where I went to school." "Some had real nice clothes on." "I didn't see any kids, did you?" There's an explosion of discussion around observations and comparisons of experiences.

As the year went on and experiences became more common and familiar, this discussion became repetitive. They brought up the topic of "shelter" less often in the class meeting. However, they did continue to be "homeless sensitive." Students made connections with books they read. For example, Matt found a newly released book called *Maniac Magee* about a homeless boy. "I wanted to read this because it looked exciting and it's about a real homeless kid," he later told the class. He also shared parts of the book with the class in a topic called "book sharing" he brought up in meeting. Several other students were familiar with the book and brought their copies, which encouraged others to find more books related to the topic of homelessness. Soon there was a homeless book section in the reading area totally created and managed by the students. On another note, Esther and her students began to link the topic of homelessness to various subject areas. Speaking of this effort, she says:

> Other connections are made with our social studies curriculum when we discuss immigrants coming to this country and the resultant competition for food, housing, and jobs in the cities. Our study of slavery, reconstruction and the civil rights movement always cause us to reflect

on and make connections to the class system in our society and to the less fortunate. "Where does poverty start?" "What structures serve to create or help solve the problem?" "If you don't get a job, or are not skilled, you may not be able to live anywhere."

Increasingly, the students approached the curriculum with a sense of awareness and caring for others less fortunate. They began to see homelessness and poverty as more complicated issues. They realized the homeless were not just drunk, sick people who deserve what they get. They began to see that there are many poor people, as well as many people who are small steps away from being homeless. Specific journal assignments about the shelter experience were also given: "What has been most important to you in working at the shelter?" "Has your thinking changed? How?" Excerpts from the journals are included here and illustrate how students make meaning of the experience.

Learning and Growth

The learning and growth that take place for students through working at the shelter occur on many different levels. Former fifth-grade students, now in sixth, seventh, and eighth grades, were interviewed for this chapter. We also read the journals of current fifth-graders and listened as they spoke about their experiences in class meetings shortly after each visit to the shelter. Students usually spoke first about the things they were surprised by and described how the experience debunked myths and stereotypes: "They looked normal," "They were real people—not dirty, drunk, or in rags," "They were well dressed," "You wouldn't recognize them as homeless people if you saw them on the street," "They were not talking to themselves," "They have the same feelings as anyone else," "They were nice to you," "There were so many people," "Many kids were there," and "One person had shoes that I've wanted for a long time."

For some students, deeper understanding resulted from personal connections they made with people at the shelter. Heath (eighth grade) talked for 15 minutes to "a big wrestling fan, just like me." Talia (seventh grade) got to know "a retired seaman who had been there for many years, waiting for a place where he could live. He said, 'People think of this as home,' which is upsetting for him."

The experience also provoked extended thinking about the complexity of homelessness and the surrounding issues for some students. Heath told how "another student asked me why they dress so nice. I guess some of them have [received] donated clothing and others have jobs." Danny (sixth grade) talked about how he realized "they're just people with problems like anyone else, only different problems. It's not like they're a different species. They're portrayed differently, made fun of, and made to seem like they're not as important as other people." Andy (sixth grade) described how he "got rid of his stereotypes. . . . As you get older, it's harder to get rid of (them). Some never have jobs. Others made a bad choice or had bad luck. It shouldn't mean they can't try again. It's not fair." Jamie (eighth grade) told a story he heard "about a guy in Cincinnati who let people live in his barn for free. He helped them and then they built the Fleishman's Company, which makes yeast. It's a good example of why not to prejudge." Heath shared his analysis of homelessness: "Some people are really sick and can't get a job. I sympathize with them. Some people just do it to get money from the government. I have no sympathy." Jessica (fifth grade) felt she "learned a lot from working at the shelter. I realize how much I take for granted. It makes me realize that people less fortunate than I am are people too, but they have more obstacles to go through. They deserve the same treatment."

When students responded to what was most important or how the experience affected them, they talked about "helping people who don't have what I have," "giving my time and not just money," "serving food because they really need and appreciate it," "seeing that homeless people are being taken care of," "giving people who don't have a home hope," and "knowing that one person can make a difference."

Students talked about feeling "good," "special," and "satisfied." Heath described how "helping and seeing people smile gives you emotions you have wanted to show . . . it (reaches) something deep within you . . . do it if you don't care about recognition." Danny asked, "Why help them? Because they're just like us . . . you help your friends." Andy "learned that it is so easy to serve and help." Talia told the story of giving someone an origami crane. "He still has it . . . since last Christmas. That's what it's all about—making people feel better." James (fifth grade) said, "I feel I made a difference in people's lives, and also that they approved of me being there helping them." Josh (fifth grade) wrote, "The most important thing for me is serving the food to homeless people because for them it's like a Thanksgiving dinner. Also I like serving food because you feel like you're the head of a restaurant!"

In his essay, "Educating for Social Responsibility," Berman (1990), the former Executive Director of Educators for Social Responsibility (ESR), describes the link between such feelings and student empowerment: "Schools must help students fight their feelings of powerlessness by developing their sense of community and their confidence that they can make a difference in the world" (p. 75).

The experience encouraged self-reflection and greater appreciation of one's own circumstances among some students. Jamie said that he now "sets lower standards for things like clothes and shoes. They're not important." Cicely (eighth grade) claimed the experience made her "more compassionate, to think about my own life and to set goals." Andy talked about the Golden Rule, "Do unto others. . . . If I ever became homeless, I would want people to [take care of me]." Dara (fifth grade) shared, "I think this project has really helped boost my self-esteem. Just being a kid helping all these homeless people makes me feel I can do anything I want to if I put my mind to it." Michelle (fifth grade) admitted, "When I was little, I thought that everyone gets what they want when they grow up. As I got older, I realized it wasn't true. Now that I've worked at the shelter, I understand, sort of, how people, who don't get what they want, feel." Jon (fifth grade) said, "Showing homeless people that there *are* people who care about them, making them feel cared about, is what is most important to me. I feel that I greatly affected another person's life for the better, and I feel like a better person now." Joshua (fifth grade) wrote, "Being in this project has made me think about how homeless people live, feel and act. I thought it would be fun, but when I got there, I saw it was pretty serious. It was sad to see so many people in need of help. They are normal people who need help. It's great for them to know people care and I liked working with them. I learned a lot from that." Nilah (fifth grade) shares, "What they really need are jobs. If they get a job they might still be homeless for a little while but soon they will have enough money to buy a home and they will not be homeless anymore. Feeding them for one night is better than letting them starve, but it doesn't solve the problem. It's still better than nothing."

One of the most powerful testaments to the impact of the project on students is the extent to which, years later, some students integrate the shelter experience into new learning. For example, Heath created an interview about the meaning of working at the shelter for a writing project in his eighth-grade computer class. He used this interview with students and adults throughout the school and with people at the shelter. The end result was an article he wrote for the school newspaper. This example illustrates the extent to which the project provides the relevant substance for traditional subject areas.

However, conversations with several of Esther's former students also revealed some disturbing cross-currents in their thinking and beliefs. One might expect that many of these students would get involved in more efforts to help other people or address social problems. In fact, some are doing so. Several continue to go to the shelter on their own initiative. Others talked about volunteering during a marathon, raising money at camp for children with disabilities to go to camp, or collecting cans for a food drive. However, Annie's (seventh grade) comment that "I know I could do things, but I'm not" was typical of some students. Even more troubling were the number of statements about young people not having any power. Jamie (eighth-grade) said, "It's hard. We're young. No one listens. We'll be more likely to do something as adults." Chris (sixth grade) stated, "If a kid says don't do drugs, no one listens. If a kid does a bake sale, people say it's cute. I'll have more power when I'm older. People will take you seriously." He then tempered his statement, "I can make a difference. It's not big now, but (will be) when I get older."

In his book, *Transforming Power: Domination, Empowerment, and Education,* Kreisberg (1992) described how young people learn to be submissive in our culture and how schools reinforce this understanding:

Schools are places in which relationships of domination are played out extensively every day between teachers and students. . . . Students are

confined to places where they are told, and too often accept, that some-
one else knows what is good for them, where someone else controls
their lives and daily choices, and where their voices are patronized or
ignored. (p. 6)

It seems that these young people have learned and are struggling with the belief
that only adults can have real power.

Parental Response

Parents have generally been supportive and excited about the shelter project. In
fact, many volunteer their own time, services, and money. Not everything, however, is straightforward, says Esther:

> This year, one parent did not approve of our work at the shelter because
> he felt that it did not get at the root causes of homelessness, and that our
> work only masked the real issues. Furthermore, he felt that it led the
> children to believe that their work was enough, when, in fact, much
> more has to be done to solve the causes of homelessness. This perspec-
> tive made for interesting discussions with me and with the class, but we
> felt that our work was necessary and appreciated, and we would con-
> tinue, knowing that the problem is bigger and deeper than serving a
> meal once a month.

Other concerns revolved around the actual baking and ingredients of the
brownies. Some children in kosher homes could not bake certain brands of
brownies. Others were completely unfamiliar with brownies as a food, or the
pans necessary to bake them in. In every case, students offered each other solutions, such as baking together at one student's house, buying the necessary number of kosher brands, or, occasionally, some students baking for ones who could
not. The process the students went through to solve these issues was far more
rewarding than actually having all the brownies baked.

SERVICE AND THE CULTURE OF THE CLASSROOM

Esther strives to create a classroom culture that reinforces, on a day-to-day
basis, the values and practices of community service. "I feel strongly that service opportunities should not be isolated events in young people's lives," says
Esther. "Students can experience caring, helping, thinking about real-world issues, and making a difference in the classroom, too." Noddings (1987), a Professor of Education at Stanford University, has described just this link between
service and classroom culture: "Service can be rendered in either caring or noncaring ways. In a classroom dedicated to caring, students are encouraged to

support each other; opportunities for peer interaction are provided, and the quality of interaction is as important as the academic outcomes" (p. 7).

Such a classroom model is one that emphasizes student participation. Students take responsibility for the management of the classroom, creating a safe and successful place for all students to learn. The development of a caring community is at the core of this participatory model, where students take responsibility for their own learning, as well as for the success of the group as a whole. Only after a strong sense of community is formed can the students truly commit to each other. There are several components needed to fostering this sense of community. One is having class meetings regularly. Another key component is that the content of the curriculum should be used to highlight issues around interdependence, cooperation, active participation, trust, and responsibility. Still another major component is the structure and management of the classroom, which is directly related to the latter concerns.

At the core of this approach to teaching and learning is a major assumption. When the values and practices just mentioned become familiar habits of heart and mind, young people will more likely carry the skills and attitudes into their adult lives. It also seems more likely that they will become active, responsible citizens who can both develop healthy and productive relationships with other people and help address larger social problems. As Berman (1990) has noted, "Social responsibility—that is, a personal investment in the well-being of others and of the planet—doesn't just happen. It takes intention, attention and time" (p. 75).

CLASSROOM STRUCTURE

"Social observers often decry 'me-first' individualism and lack of concern for the common good among young people. If we wish to strengthen ethical cooperation within society, we should strive to make it a character trait of children, as they live and work in the small society that is the classroom" (Lickona, 1988, p. 422). In addition to the central role that the class meeting plays, the class is structured so that most of the activities are facilitated by students individually, in pairs or in small groups. Students take attendance, lunch count, make announcements, correct homework on the board as a group, facilitate transitions in a timely and orderly fashion, monitor their own use of time in reading and math, and facilitate small group and individual work in curriculum areas. In order to facilitate these activities, Esther uses lessons and role playing activities that teach her students how to "help" someone without just giving the answers. These are also used to illustrate both acceptable and unacceptable ways of supporting each other. At the beginning of the year, Esther's class also creates rules and consequences for work and behavior, as well as for how to help someone and what to do if the individual cannot or does not have the time.

Academically, students work at their own pace in math and in reading/writing, and in small groups in social studies, writing, and science. In small groups, students are often assigned roles, such as facilitator, recorder, checker, or encourager. Again, the notion of shared responsibility for learning and creating a safe learning environment is emphasized and practiced throughout the day and across the curriculum.

CURRICULUM CONTENT

The content of the curriculum in any subject area emphasizes problem solving, critical thinking, multiple perspective taking and role-play, dilemma discussion techniques, and an action orientation. It is in this context that working with homeless people is discussed. Journal writing is an integral part of each curriculum area. (Specific examples in social studies and literature were given earlier in the chapter.)

As students both learn and live in this participatory community, they begin to take on more and more responsibility for their own and each other's learning. They also develop a sense of caring, interest, and responsibility for social problems.

SERVICE AND THE CULTURE OF THE SCHOOL

Just as the classroom culture reinforces the values and practices of community service, the school culture also reflects these same values and practices. Esther's principal, Jerry Kaplan, models these values by his own work at the shelter and by the opportunities and structures he sets up in the school for teachers and students to actively participate in this project or other service projects. Esther explains the added benefit of having a supportive, active principal:

> My own work in providing a supportive classroom environment in which students become caring, active participants almost mirrors, and is reinforced by, the supportive school environment Jerry creates for the teachers, students, and parents in the school community. In the same way I bring up my work at the shelter with my class, Jerry offers the staff and parent community opportunities to work with him at the shelter. He provides a clear, well-organized structure in which staff and families can choose to participate either monthly or one time. Carol and Linda, the secretaries, help out by keeping this structure intact, making sure the different roles and tasks are filled each month.

Jerry believes that teachers, in general, "have a feel for giving" and that, given the opportunity and the right time, teachers will get involved in helping others. Because of his own democratic style and the voluntary nature of the project, people do not feel obligated to participate. Some teachers, in fact, prefer to pursue their own service opportunities. For example, two kindergarten classes make and sell calendars and give the proceeds to Oxfam (a national relief organization). The health teacher works with seventh- and eighth-graders baking food for Ronald McDonald House, a home for terminally ill children. Others collect "Pennies for Peace."

Esther explains the importance of Jerry's role:

> The fact that these various projects go on in the school is testimony to the importance of modeling active participation as well as for providing a context to do service work. My class and I would not still be involved in the shelter project without Jerry's involvement. However, the fact that he values such work himself and transmits that throughout the school community via newsletters as well as by his own actions, creates a stronger, richer experience for us all. We are fortunate to have such congruency between the culture of the school, the classroom, and individual behavior. Just as students need adult support and opportunities for involvement in community service, teachers need administrative and other adult support and opportunities for community service. Jerry is always looking for more opportunities for involvement in helping others. As he says, he feels that "action is important. It's the way we get rid of the me-first attitudes that are so pervasive today."

ISSUES FOR TEACHERS

During most of the past eight years, Esther has made a conscious decision to raise the topic of serving the homeless by bringing up her work at the Long Island shelter in class meeting. On three occasions, siblings of past students in Esther's class have also brought up the issue or it was brought up in the context of current events in an election year.

There are several dilemmas built into the decision to take the initiative. Esther is committed to student-centered learning, yet, in most cases, the initial impetus comes from her and not the students. Esther is also sensitive to the issue of encouraging choice and divergent opinions, and not advocating causes.

Teacher Initiative

There are many reasons why teacher initiative in raising service opportunities more than counterbalances the problems mentioned here. First, children at this age are eager and enthusiastic about helping in the world. They are hopeful and optimistic that they can make a difference. However, they have little sense of what can be done and how to go about helping. In response to the question, "If the teacher hadn't shared her experience at the shelter, do you think you would have done other projects where you could help people who need it, or work on a social problem?", Jesse (fifth grade) said, "When the teacher asked if the class was interested in working at the shelter, I felt the answer was a definite 'yes'! I wanted to work at the shelter. When I got the chance to, I took it." Dena (fifth grade) admitted, "If my teacher hadn't raised the idea of going to the shelter, then I probably wouldn't have done anything because I didn't know how to get involved. I'm glad Ms. Kattef told us about the shelter. I really like this project." Doreen (fifth grade) shared, "I always wanted to help homeless people even though my parents thought I would catch cold. I made them take me to a shelter when I heard about it. I also donate money to the Salvation Army, to Ronald McDonald House, and to a leukemia shelter." Other children said: "No, I wouldn't have known how to get involved." "No, I never thought about poor people much, but now I think I'll do a lot more and even come up with ideas for what to do myself." "Since people don't think kids can do this kind of thing, we're never given a chance. It's never a possibility." "I couldn't do this without help from an adult." As these comments indicate, many children are aware of social problems and want to do something about them. By presenting the possibility of working at the shelter in conjunction with an existing program, Esther offers a channel for the energy and optimism of the children.

Second, students need adult models and support. They need to know that adults care about problems in the world and are doing something about them. Dara (fifth grade) said, "I think our teacher helped a lot by introducing this project to us, but we can work for ourselves and accomplish things with a little moral support." They are particularly enthusiastic and hopeful about change when they see adults actively taking responsibility and working on these issues.

A third advantage to this approach is that there already is a program in place in which the school community and faculty are involved. Students work hand in hand with parents, teachers, and administrators. Also, the whole class is involved in the same experience. This common experience further leads to a strong sense of community among the students. Such a sense of community might never eventuate if each student worked by himself or herself on an individual project.

It is worth noting that Esther has developed the model and structure for working at the shelter over an eight-year period. She claims that she is more confident of shaping a successful learning experience with this kind of planning and forethought. It is also more efficient for her than an approach of developing new service projects every year.

Finally, although Esther realizes bringing up working at the shelter is a value-laden decision on her part, it reflects widely held values in the larger community and the spirit of caring that already exists among students. Furthermore, the open-ended decision-making process that she subsequently encourages is important.

Encouraging Student Initiative

Students need encouragement and support to solve problems they bring up or see in the class, school, or community. As Berman (1990) noted in regard to the role that solving authentic problems can play in the lives of young people, "The most effective means of helping students develop a positive relationship with society is to give them the opportunity to enter and engage the real world around them" (p. 76).

The shelter work is a model experience students can apply to other issues and problems. Some examples of other projects, all initiated by students in Esther's class, are petitioning and writing to the town recreation department to have "No Dogs Allowed" signs posted on the school playground because they were tired of stepping in dog waste; canvassing the floor and meeting with the principal and custodian to get a heavily used bathroom stall repaired and to get soap in the bathrooms; holding a canned food drive for the local food pantry; and initiating a fund-raising campaign to help a kindergarten student and her family who were burnt out of their apartment. This sense of responsibility, compassion, empowerment, and action orientation is nourished by the shared commitment to the shelter project, as well as by the strong sense of a caring community it helps to form.

Consensus and Power Differences

Prior to having the students engage in work at the shelter, Esther makes sure that the students come to consensus about working at the shelter. However, since the issue was raised by the teacher, the process was weighted to favor arriving at a decision to serve the homeless. Esther describes the importance of the decision-making process and how she takes into account the power differential:

> I bring up the topic of my work at the shelter in class meeting. I tell the kids what some faculty, parents, and past students have done. I tell them that we do this work because we care about people less fortunate, and feel we can and do make a difference. I also tell them that if they are interested in participating in this project, they have to come to a consensus on the decision and commit to the project for the year. I tell them that if they are interested, they should continue to put the topic on the meeting agenda for discussion. After this initial introduction, I never bring up the topic again myself. One year, we had to assign a classroom to bake the brownies for two months because my class hadn't come to consensus yet.

In most cases, students almost immediately take over driving the process of making the decision. When students do continue to bring up the topic of working at the shelter, the discussion moves in the direction of specific questions and to committing as a class. Problems with the students' schedules are discussed, as well as other commitments they might have. As they move along in this decision-making process and get closer to coming to consensus on participating in the project, Esther always asks questions that encourage further reflection about undertaking the project.

> "Why help the homeless? It will take time and work." "What if the weather is bad, or the weather is great?" "What if soccer starts and we're busier outside of school?" Kids respond, "We'll know in advance, so we can plan for going." They say, "We can get a substitute to go to the shelter for us, or we can miss a practice or lesson once to go to the shelter." I know the decision is somewhat weighted by virtue of my position as teacher. I feel that my role is to facilitate the decision-making process by helping to raise issues, not to decide for the class. Not all topics or issues need to be value free for a free and open discussion to take place and for consensus to be reached.

Nilah stated, "Before Ms. Kattef introduced the idea, I hadn't thought about those people much. Now I think I will probably do a lot more than I would have." She adds, "Ms. Kattef first introduced us to the idea, but we didn't have to go along with it."

HOMELESSNESS: A THEMATIC CONTEXT, NOT A UNIT

The shelter project illustrates major themes of the classroom and the curriculum. In Esther's class, homelessness is not a unit to be studied, unless a student chooses to do so as an independent research topic. The project integrates major themes of care, community, responsibility, making a difference, and compassion. These are ongoing themes that are emphasized in curriculum areas as well as in the life of the classroom. These themes offer the students a lens through which to study animal life and the environment in the science curriculum; slavery, conflict, immigration, and the civil rights movement in the social studies curriculum; and independence, choice, and overcoming adversity in the reading and writing curriculum. The shelter project cuts across all these curriculum areas and embodies the major values and themes of the classroom in an ongoing fashion.

The shelter project also addresses specific skills. The various phases of the project integrate writing skills such as writing letters, newspaper articles, and advertisements, with math skills such as estimation, working with decimals, categorization and time, and the four basic operations of addition, subtraction, multiplication, and division. Communication skills and public speaking are also emphasized, as are reading and learning the different sections of the newspaper.

While some may wonder whether improving social skills and moral values elbows out academics, many observers don't see these areas as mutually exclusive. "Dealing with social issues is in some significant measure an intellectual thing," says Ted Sizer, chairman of the Education department at Brown University. "You think about the consequences of your actions and other people's actions. I don't separate the social and the intellectual sphere" (quoted in Kohn, 1988, p. 65). For Esther, it is important not to see the project as an "add-on," but to see how it can be integrated into the life of the curriculum and the classroom.

This service model at the Edward Devotion School harnesses the energy of the students, the faculty, and the community. As the project continues, more and more older students come back to participate. Esther hopes to have them explain their work and interest in the project, so it will not be initiated by her, as the teacher. In the meantime, the students are actively engaged in both a decision-making process and a project to help homeless people. Maybe most importantly, they know they can make a difference.

REFERENCES

Berman, Sheldon. (1990, November). "Educating for Social Responsibility." *Educational Leadership, 48*(3): 75–80.

Kohn, Alfie. (1988, November 6). "P is for Prosocial Teaching," *Boston Globe Magazine*, pp. 24–25, 61–71.

Kreisberg, Seth. (1992). *Transforming Power: Domination, Empowerment, and Education.* Albany: State University of New York Press.

Lickona, Thomas. (1988, February). "Four Strategies for Fostering Character Development." *Phi Delta Kappan, 69*(6): 419–423.

Noddings, Nel. (1987). "Caring as a Moral Orientation in Teaching." *Ethics in Education, 7*(2): 6–7.

Wood, George. (1990, November). "Teaching for Democracy." *Educational Leadership, 48*(3): 32–37.

▶ 18

The Letter That Never Arrived

The Evolution of a Social Concerns Program in a Middle School

ROBYN L. MORGAN   ROBERT W. MODERHAK

JACOB'S STORY

When Jacob's class wrote letters to develop one-on-one relationships with senior citizens at a local care center, he and other students anxiously awaited responses from their senior friends. Jacob, a seventh-grade Hispanic boy, seemed to be in turmoil with himself and his surroundings. Living with his mother and two brothers in a fairly humble environment, he had a number of disciplinary referrals to the office for fighting and various classroom disruptions, yet he managed to demonstrate a caring for others that belied his anger. His class had planned a service project that included each student corresponding with a senior resident at a local care center, followed by an actual visit with his or her new "pen pal." The students' visit would include the sharing of food, games, and conversation in hope of providing a much needed service to the people they recognized as being in need of companionship. However, the events that followed did not reflect what had been expected by the teacher or the students.

When all the students received their return letters from the care center residents, there was no letter for Jacob—just a note saying that his intended pen pal, Hannah, had died of a stroke. Not only did Jacob miss sharing the same excitement as the other students but he also received unexpected ridicule. When one student suggested that Jacob's photo, which he had included in his letter to Hannah, was the cause of her sudden death, other students laughed and playfully agreed. Jacob was crushed and disillusioned by the situation and his classmates' reaction.

Fortunately, Jacob's teacher was alerted to the dilemma and used the unforeseen set of circumstances to help the entire class learn more about aging, death, and how to treat each other. The "guilty" students gave sincere apologies to Jacob, but he still expressed feelings of emptiness. Finally, the day arrived for the visit to the care center, and Jacob reluctantly boarded the bus. However, when he was introduced to his new partner, Vern, who had been prearranged by Jacob's teacher, the emptiness dissipated quickly. Vern was a man in his early eighties whose memory and health were failing him, yet he had a twinkle in his eye that was engaging to Jacob. Vern and Jacob were inseparable that afternoon, and when Jacob placed a new baseball cap on Vern's head, as his prize for winning a board game, it was difficult to determine which of the unlikely partners was feeling more pride and fulfillment.

The wide range of emotions and experiences that engulfed Jacob during his introduction to service parallels those of the students, teachers, and other community service participants who will be highlighted in this chapter. The structure and process that led to such experiences will also be described in detail in order to allow other schools and organizations to understand the evolution that led to this currently successful program.

BACKGROUND

As a new school designated to serve students with diverse socioeconomic backgrounds, Westview Middle School (located in Longmont, Colorado) opened its doors in the fall of 1991 to a population of students who desperately needed better awareness and skills in the areas of social responsibility. Like so many students of this generation, these 10-to 14-year-olds had spent little time worrying about much else than their own needs and desires. For example, after her service project, Jenny, a bright eighth grade honor student, stated, "I didn't realize that these problems [of poverty and homelessness] were occurring in our community. I believe we can stop it or at least help it to not get any larger."

Based on the aforementioned needs, the bulk of Westview's advisor/advisee program (which we call Focus) was designed to help students acquire the knowledge necessary for working successfully with classmates and citizens in their community and world. All 750 students in grades 6, 7, and 8 participate in the Focus program on a daily basis. This program, developed by the school counselor, is a multifaceted, comprehensive attempt to help students and educators actively assault the apathy, insensitivity, and lack of tolerance that detracts from the middle school experience and society as a whole.

The Focus program consists of a sequence of structured days and activities that teach students a variety of social and interpersonal skills as well as provide an opportunity to practice those skills. Specifically, each week includes one day in recreational team building; one day in dialogue and communication; two days in personal-social skills development, such as decision making and fostering positive peer relationships; and one day of community service. For instance, students who have learned a specific communication skill, such as effective questioning techniques, are asked to design questions to be used when interviewing guest speakers who discussed growing up in poverty during the Depression. By enabling the middle-school students to ask open, affective-type questions instead of their typical closed, informational questions, students learned about how it felt for a person to go from being self-sufficient to poverty stricken almost overnight as a result of political and economic events at the national level. Moreover, by learning about the circumstances leading to the Depression, students gained an appreciation for the fact that history could repeat itself and that taking the relative affluence of our current time for granted would be a mistake.

In addition to the activities that occur in a traditional classroom setting, students are given opportunities in Focus to learn and practice their skills in a more relaxed setting. An example of this occurs one day a week when students exercise their teamwork and problem-solving skills, acquired in prior Focus sessions, by competing with other Focus classes in a nontraditional recreational activity.

An advantage of this sequence of training in social and interpersonal skills such as communications, decision making, problem solving, peer relations, and teamwork is that students can approach each new challenge in the Focus program, and the rest of their school experience, with a common set of skills and terminology. This advantage is evidenced as students move into the social issues and community service segment of the Focus program.

APPROACHING SOCIAL ISSUES

Middle school students typically respond with the greatest level of interest to those issues and events that are relevant to their world (which, for most adolescents, consists of a revolving series of events or issues of that day or week). In response, the topics and sequence for dealing with social issues through the Focus program are characterized by their timeliness. Focus exercises are designed to address "hot" topics as they unfold in the school and in the community. For example, as members of the Westview student body prepared to move into a new building that would become a showplace for visitors from many communities and nations, Focus activities were developed to address racial stereotyping and the study of international cultures (including acceptance of individual differences).

During such units, native speakers from a variety of cultures and countries are brought to school to speak and teach about their cultures as well as to learn from our students. As students were describing our middle school system to one such visitor, he repeatedly replied with a word that sounded much like the English word *hi*. So, after a few rounds of our students being confused and saying "hi" in return, the Japanese guest realized the problem and taught the students that the Japanese word he was using was a term of agreement rather than a greeting.

The students responded with humor, warmth, and a better understanding about possible unexpected communication differences between cultures. As a result of these and other such encounters, visitors from many countries and a variety of ethnic backgrounds have expressed their appreciation for the friendliness and acceptance shown by the students during their visit to Westview. A number of visitors inferred their that experience in other schools had not been as positive.

In another segment of the Focus program, students were educated about AIDS by an educator who has the disease and has committed himself to raising the awareness of students not only about causes and prevention but also about the broad range of people who contract the disease. This sequence of Focus activities was developed, in part, to address what was observed by adults in the building as a growing trend by students to tease each other with remarks about "having AIDS" and "being gay." Their flippant attitude about the disease and those who contract it was remarkably altered when, during this process many were moved to tears by the speaker's honesty, warmth, and courage. Rob, a former teacher, had been sent as a speaker from the local AIDS Project. He explained to students that he is not dying of AIDS, but instead *living* with AIDS. He told the students that they had a right to be afraid of AIDS but that they also had a responsibility to educate themselves so they would know what to fear.

During this segment, students learned that they, as a group, do not agree on their feelings regarding homosexuality. While many students came from families with strong convictions that homosexuality was immoral, others saw it more as an acceptable alternative lifestyle. Most students admitted that regardless of their views, they believed that nongays were basically safe from the threat of AIDS. After Rob and the students interacted about the clinical aspects of the disease, one bold student broke new ground by asking Rob how he had contracted HIV. While horrified, curious classmates held their breath, Rob very frankly explained, "I had participated in unprotected sex with a male partner who evidently was carrying the virus." Rob then proceeded to enlighten the students about the many possible ways that everyone in the population could be exposed to HIV. Students learned about the possible threat from blood sources, sharing needles, and all kinds of unprotected sex, including heterosexual. Students were amazed at the growing numbers of teenagers being infected with the virus and came to realize that their former beliefs had, in reality, given them and their families a false sense of security.

Rob's calm, honest answers paved the way for a flood of questions from students about Rob's feelings, treatment by others, and fears about death. The students were visibly moved when Rob explained the pain of not knowing whether he had infected anyone else before being diagnosed. He emphasized that exposing someone else to AIDS is like "holding a loaded gun to their head." However, he also taught students that AIDS could not be passed through sweat or tears, and that all human beings, even those with AIDS, need and deserve handshakes, hugs, and, most importantly, support and understanding. Rob thanked the students for inviting him to speak and said, "Your warmth and acceptance is a big part of what keeps me alive to help others."

During the reflection segment of the activity, students and their Focus teacher discussed how Rob seemed "just like them." One student noted that Rob was gay but he seemed like he would make a very good friend. The student was surprised because he thought he would "feel weird being around a gay guy." The shedding of such misconceptions through education demonstrates one of the major goals of dealing with relevant topics during the Focus program.

COMMUNITY SERVICE THROUGH ADVISOR/ADVISEE (FOCUS)

Philosophical Basis

In an article entitled "Preparing Citizens through Service," Clark (1993) suggested that educators consider carefully not only what service can do for society but what service can, will, and should do for American youth (p. 1). The purpose of a regularly scheduled time in the middle school curriculum for a service program provides such an opportunity. The benefits to the students who participate in the program are many and will be revealed throughout the chapter. But it should be pointed out that student feedback clearly states that the key qualities of developing a sense of self-worth, of accepting responsibility and intelligently addressing community, national, and world problems that many educators strive to instill in students, are being met through the service program. As seventh-grader Amy, a quiet student whose interests are basketball and soccer, reports, "doing service improves your *self-esteem* by knowing that someone has benefited from you." Her classmate, Whitney, a vivacious, popular student from a well-to-do family, concluded, "Some of the people really needed help. In fact, one lady was blind and I helped her eat. This gave me more *self-confidence* to know that I could help someone less fortunate than I am." Nick also experienced increased self-confidence because part of his service project helped him "with speaking in front of big audiences."

Another reason for including service in the curriculum is to help students recognize that their existence, which takes place largely in the school setting, is part of a larger community. George (1993) contended that "the goals of schools should be integrated with those of the surrounding community and society as a whole." (p. 3) The need for such an approach was evidenced in a situation where Brandy, an attractive sixth-grader whose fashionable appearance belied her lower economic status, mentioned that she and her mom needed to go to the OUR Center after school. The OUR Center is a local public assistance agency that collects food and clothing and then redistributes these items to needy families at either no cost or reduced cost. Her friend looked puzzled, and only after helping to donate canned food to the OUR. Center as part of her Focus service project did she realize that a food bank existed in town. The experience sensitized Brandy's friend to the fact that all types of families need help and support at times. Before participating in the service program, one parent said, "My son didn't think there were needy people in his own small town. He believed that such problems only existed in big U.S. cities and foreign countries. This has helped him realize how lucky our family is and the importance of helping others less fortunate."

Participating in service, therefore, keeps middle school students from being isolated and insulated from the concerns of the rest of the community and world. One especially caring eighth-grade teacher, Mrs. K., was pleased to report that Nate, usually seen as a care-free, happy-go-lucky boy, had really summed up her students' change of attitude when he wrote, "Even as kids, we can still make a difference in that we can help people far or near by just working on one project."

Format

The Westview Middle School service program is known to students as Service Day. Every week for 18 weeks, one day of the Focus program is devoted to developing and implementing a service project. In order to prevent local agencies from being inundated by well-intentioned adolescents, the onset of Service Day is staggered throughout the year. For example, the seventh grade might begin their series of Service Days at the beginning of the first quarter, whereas the eighth grade starts the second quarter, and the sixth grade starts the third quarter. Every Focus class, approximately 10 students per grade level, conducts a service project, so this staggered start ensures that not all classes are in the implementation stage at the same time.

Instructions to the Focus class are broadly stated to allow each class to decide on their own unique approach and project. Their guidelines merely state that they are to involve everyone in their class during the course of the project and use the skills they have learned in communications, decision making, and teamwork to reach consensus and proceed with their plan. Consequently, the resultant projects range from international service (helping preserve the rain forest), to national projects (providing aid to the victims of Hurricane Andrew), to local concerns (planting trees in parks, holding canned food drives, working at the Humane Society), and even providing service to schools (preparing elementary school students for middle school entrance, setting up recycling within the school, and providing grounds keeping and litter collection [necessitated by a districtwide cutback in custodial services]). By the end of the current school year, 80 separate projects will have been completed since the initiation of Service Day as a continuing, weekly activity into the middle school advisor/advisee curriculum.

Preparation

As Focus classes attempt to decide on suitable projects, students research ideas, draw from the expertise of guest speakers, and discuss the feasibility of each potential project. Effectively guided preparation is the cornerstone of success-ful community service. It is during this segment that the Focus teacher actively reinforces the positive use of key skills and provides reminders and additional practice for those individuals who need improvement.

For example, while attempting to reach consensus through class discus-sion, students incorporate skills previously learned in the Focus program such as effective communication, teamwork, and cooperation. Thus, while Betsy, a bright sixth-grader maintains that she learned to keep an open mind and listen to ideas during the process, Alyssa, a seventh-grade student who had been in-volved in community service with her family for a number of years and who often shows a maturity beyond her years, sums up the essence of the prepara-tion phase for her in the following way:

> It took a long time to decide what to do and even longer to decide how to do it. I learned so much about teamwork from the project. The project brought our class closer together. Each person had a part or a job to do to prepare the project. If that person did not do his or her job, the project wouldn't work. It's kind of like a jigsaw puzzle. Without all the pieces, the puzzle wouldn't go together.

Another student, who had struggled all year with overcoming shyness and mak-ing friends, said, "The positive part of working on the class service project was the opportunity to talk to each other more and have fun."

In one particular Focus classroom, sixth-grade students were discussing an activity in which they had been reading about the "letters to the editor" section of the local newspaper. The current topic in town that was drawing much atten-tion was the city council's decision to increase charges based on the volume of trash collected at each individual residence. The Focus teacher, Mr. O., saw an opportunity to get "hands-on experience for my students by taking them on a field trip to the local recycling center and then on a trip to the actual landfill, which was close to over capacity." Mr. O's tongue-in-cheek newsletter title "Let's Get Our Students' Hands in the Garbage" did increase the number of telephone calls to the principal's office the next day, and it was an eye-opening experience for his students. As Mr. O. said to the students' parents at the con-clusion of the Focus activity, "When students observed the effect of too much trash on our landfill and the positive effect that the recycling center could have on reducing that, they could see that the angry letters to the editor regarding the topic were more self-serving than an expression of real concern for the environment."

As the school year moved on, Mr. O. heard from parents that his handling of the topic had a continued effect on the way their children were conducting their own lives and, ultimately, the lives of their entire family. He was informed by a parent that the concern for the environment carried over beyond recycling of trash for one family: "I believe we do a better job of recycling newspapers and aluminum at home, but Lynn still looks through the trash every day to make sure that the family is not slipping." She continued, "And we know that it's a good thing to turn off the lights when we leave a room, but now Lynn lectures us on helping the environment by conserving the use of gasoline, although I'm not especially thrilled with walking to the store for small trips. I'll probably thank you later for that change to our lifestyle."

Helping students understand why the need exists for a particular service and what they can do to address the long-term problem that results in the need for the service is a goal of the Focus teacher during the preparatory period. Guest speakers have proven to have a strong influence on students when approaching this objective of true community service. Even though students were aware, for example, that the flood victims in the Midwest had to temporarily leave their homes during the height of the flood, it was not until they listened to a speaker from one town's Chamber of Commerce that they learned about the additional problems of disease, looting, and emotional trauma that accompany such a disaster. This newly acquired knowledge resulted in the students deciding to write letters of concern and support to middle school students whose lives were impacted by the flooding. The letters they received in return further emphasized the emotional devastation that can be understated during times of natural disaster. No longer did students see scenes in videos of the flooding as "cool or awesome"; they now knew that the floating houses and damaged belongings affected people forever.

Without an understanding of the various social and/or political issues affecting the situation, students are vulnerable to seeing the service itself as the only solution. A recent speaker from the Humane Society opened the eyes of a young girl who earlier believed it was cruel to prevent animals from "having babies," but stated, "Now I see that it is even more cruel to allow all those babies to starve or be mistreated." In another Focus class, students who adopted a highway learned from the county speaker that "in addition to keeping our environment clean, by picking up litter, you are saving tax dollars that can be used for other important needs." These students learned the connection between various public service projects. As one eighth-grade athlete stated, "When we save money from taxes in cleaning up the highway, the money can help the homeless shelter that we worked with last year."

Helping students to include other parts of the world in their approach to community has also been a goal of the preparation phase of the program. Students' previously mild interest in the problem of the diminishing rain forests of the world took on broader meaning when through their preparation activities they learned that their own town has and will be impacted in the future by the loss of rain forests on another continent. Not only did they learn that some species of birds and animals face extinction as the travesty continues but also that their own weather and climate would eventually be negatively affected by the results. The slides, videos, and discussions that helped raise their awareness proved to be essential in promoting the sense of urgency necessary in completing their service project.

Before implementation of the actual service segment, preparing students for some of the startling realities of working with people in need is essential. For instance, the sights and sounds of a senior care center can come as a shock and result in a frightening experience if students do not know what to expect. During one training session, the counselor and teacher shared the experiences of a previous class that had visited a nursing home. The report of one blonde-haired, sixth-grade boy whose mother had been active in politics helped. Kurt said, "Not all people in the nursing home are on life support and unable to get out of bed. They remind you of your grandparents, only more forgetful." During the training session, Anna, a straightforward girl advised, "So we should be prepared not to laugh, even though it does smell in there and the people are sometimes crazy. Everyone needs to be ready for unusual stuff but we should have fun!" Little did Anna know how important her words of wisdom would turn out to be.

As she and a friend, Gail, were reading to a bed-ridden elderly man during their class's visit to a nursing home, the spirited resident lifted his gown and exposed himself to the girls, much to their surprise. A nearby nurse verbally scolded him but he later repeated the unnerving action, resulting in the nurse lightly slapping his hand. Instead of being horrified or disgusted by the incident, as might have been the case for less highly trained students, the girls were more curious about how the old man cried after being reprimanded. Anna noted that when he cried, the man sounded and acted like her little brother when he receives a scolding. The other introspective student, Gail, deduced, "As people get older and sicker, they seem to need people to care for them like when we were little. They might also need to be reminded by someone like a mom that no *means* no!"

Equally important in the overall process is the preparation of the recipients of the service to greet the energetic, highly verbal middle school students. The staff at the home for preschoolers who are developmentally disabled, as well as the director of the homeless shelter, often need the help and encouragement of the Focus teacher to acquaint their residents with the characteristics of the whirling, twirling phenomenon they are about to encounter. Such forethought increases the potential for an optimum experience for all participants.

Participation

Once the preparation phase comes to a close, the Focus class embarks on the implementation of the service activity. One of the outstanding benefits of the participation phase is that it promotes equality and mutual respect among participants as the project that Tracey and Melissa collaborated on would demonstrate. In a purely academic setting, the discrepancy between Tracey and Melissa's performance and success would be quite noticeable due to Melissa's overwhelming academic ability and appropriate social/peer skills. But when it came to feeding and befriending a young woman with multiple disabilities, they were equally adept. This newly discovered appreciation for each other's talents led to a lasting friendship during the school year between the unlikely co-workers. The same equalizing influence was also evident when teachers and students alike got dirty from picking up the same "gooey" trash from the roadside their class had adopted in order to keep it litter free.

One seventh-grade class decided to assist some elderly citizens gift wrap presents at the senior center. The latter had purchased presents for friends or relatives but needed assistance in cutting paper, taping and tying bows and ribbons. One wide-eyed but normally outgoing 12-year-old girl named Sarah was assigned to work with an alert lady named Gussie, whose hands were so crippled with arthritis that they looked like lobster claws. Gussie saw that the student was frightened by her misshapen hands because Sarah avoided any physical contact when assisting her with gift wrapping. Our counselor watched as Gussie stopped wrapping and quietly talked to Sarah for an extended period of time. After this long discussion, Sarah was observed placing her hand on top of Gussie's hands and then continuing with the gift wrapping.

On the trip back to the school, Sarah explained that Gussie had said to her, "I know these old hands look terrible, but its just skin on these old bones and if you hold my hand for a minute, you'll see that you don't have to be afraid of them."

Flexibility is another key component during the participation phase. Without this attitude, many projects would meet disastrous results. An example took place when the local community agency that temporarily houses women and children of battered families sponsored a Christmas party that drew many more residents than expected, making the supply of food and gifts insufficient. A quick and discreet trip to the grocery store by a parent volunteer allowed the party to proceed without interruption or making anyone feel unwelcome and unexpected. In another service setting, an Alzheimer patient insisted on placing corn chips on the bingo card instead of the bingo markers that were provided. Her student partner did not know whether to snicker or run, until an alert teacher pulled her quietly aside and helped the student regain her composure. The student resumed the game with confidence and pride while using the salty, but equally effective, corn chips to help her senior partner finish the game.

One of the students in a class who cleaned and repaired old toys for underprivileged children summed up the feeling of many students about their participation in service when he fondly recalled, "Our class had a lot of fun and we got to know each other better by talking while we worked. Also, many of us have very good and funny memories that we will never forget."

Refocusing

The service component of the Focus program would not be complete without a period of refocusing. In this phase of the project, students use their remaining Service Days of the semester to reflect on their experiences and effectiveness, both as individuals and also as a group. This time is also used for students and teachers to express what they saw and felt during the semester of service.

The need for time to air their emotional responses to the community service sequence is apparent in the voices of the students and teachers. After a trip to the Humane Society, one student was outraged by the fact that a poodle was put up for adoption because the owner's new carpet and the color of the poodle did not match. Other students spoke about their sadness at seeing how many people there were in the homeless shelter. Additionally, students conveyed their confusion over the fact that while there seems to be such a surplus of food in the United States, people are still going hungry. Lindsay, a mature sixth-grader who lives in one of the loveliest homes in our area, had an especially moving experience: "Participating helped me to see that homeless people aren't just bums. They look and feel just like everyone else."

The teachers' concerns were, at times, echoed in the form of frustration. While one teacher, Mrs. B. swore she would "never again haul canned food to the shelter unless parents showed up to help," another teacher, Mrs. H., was covered with soap suds at the car wash project one Saturday morning and, in order to complete the project, she ended up working harder than any of her kids. However, those same teachers felt good, overall, about joining their students to help others and having their groups successfully use skills in brainstorming and teamwork.

The reflections of students after last year's community service program ring simple and true and are worthy of repeating in their original form. We expected student responses to differ based on their own social-economic backgrounds and on their maturity. But from several of the Focus classes that targeted senior citizens as the population they chose to serve, student observations did not reflect the diverse economic populations they represent in our school nor the significant difference in maturity levels that they demonstrate during the school day. For instance, Albert, an affluent boy who wants people to believe he is better than most, confessed that "old people are fun"; Danny, who would like to be thought of as much wealthier than he is, states that "the most important idea I gained was to not just let an elderly woman do hard things by herself. I will now help." The difference in student maturity levels showed in the statements of two sixth grade classmates: Matt shared, "I'm going to get old someday too, so I should not laugh at old people"; Kristi discovered, "Old people really like ice cream."

Another group of students, primarily eighth-graders, showed a more reflective side when reporting on their thoughts from a variety of Focus class activities. The counselor was pleased when she reported, "When you look at the responses from kids like A. J. and Tony, who are not able to afford much themselves, and compare their responses to the others such as Jenny, Erin, and Greg, who are not faced with those problems, it is comforting to see little difference in their heartfelt statements:

Every little thing you do to help people is helping one more person to survive.—A. J.

The world needs some help, and I can be the one to help.—Erin

If we can stop the problem [of the homeless] or help it to not get any larger, then our service is worth doing.—Jenny

Everybody needs food everyday, not only on holidays.—Aundie

It was more time and work than I expected, but it was still a ton of fun.—Greg

The only formal part of the refocusing period consists of the teacher filling out a sheet to record the details of the project, including useful contacts, phone numbers, and suggestions for improvement in the future. These sheets are repeatedly accessed as a source of ideas for future Focus classes.

Evolution

Jacob, who was mentioned at the beginning of the chapter, might have had a less positive experience were it not for classmates, teachers, counselors, and parent volunteers taking part in all three phases of the process. Because Jacob had learned about the problems of senior citizens in the preparation segment, he had some knowledge of the risk involved in entering a relationship with an elderly individual. The guidance he received during the participation process enabled him to bond with his "new" senior partner. And the refocusing that took place after the actual project allowed Jacob to appreciate his success and to make the decision to continue his relationship with his senior partner beyond the scope of the school year. However, this success story was the product of a continuing evolution that has taken place for the three years of Westview Middle School's service program.

During the first year, when not only the students but also the teachers and the counselor who coordinated the program were inexperienced in the area of community service, everyone was satisfied simply to pick out a service project and complete it. Many projects during the first year were no more than fund-raisers, with the donations being mailed to a distant, worthy cause. The results were evident in the feedback from many students who never really had a connection with the people or organization they were serving. When asked what he learned after his class's fund-raising service project, one student replied, "I now know I can charge 'em a dollar for a 50-cent blow pop." With additional in-service training, the second year brought with it teachers who had a better understanding and more confidence to make the move from a perfunctory project to one imbued with meaning. They were able to guide students into more meaningful choices for projects where their personal contact and understanding of the need became the focus of the service rather than a check from their parents designed to get them off the hook in Focus class.

The Focus teachers evolved in other ways as well. The same teacher who complained the first year about having to do most of the work on the service project was perceived by her class as "ramrodding" them into the project that she wanted and not letting them have choices. The following year, the same teacher, with more experience in group process, facilitated her Focus class in a project of "their" choice that resulted in a much higher level of participation and satisfaction on the part of students.

Other parts of the evolution led us to extend Service Day from one to two nine week quarters for the two younger grades. This was done because we have found that they need more time for the preparation phase. We have also found that it is worthwhile to supply the Focus classes with a list of known needs and projects in the community for them to consider as possible paths of interest. The latter revision took place after 5 of 10 Focus groups at one grade level chose the Humane Society as their project due to their lack of awareness about other possibilities. Clearly, the third year appears to be even more promising, as teachers and students have their past successes and setbacks from which to draw their enthusiasm and experience.

PRACTICAL CONSIDERATIONS FOR PROMOTING SUCCESS

Even the best-intentioned programs designed to expand the experiences of students have routinely been thwarted when practical considerations were not anticipated and effectively confronted. Therefore, the following review of essential components and examples of agony and ecstasy will assist those who are interested in initiating community service programs in the educational setting.

Personnel

In order to optimize the success of community service programs, one important factor to address is that of personnel. Having someone designated as an on-site coordinator to act as a valuable resource as well as a logistics person is an essential ingredient. The coordinator helps inspire, train, and encourage groups and individuals to pursue their service goals, as well as assists in providing contacts, strategies, and other materials that enhance these pursuits. In addition, the coordinator serves as a liaison between the school and the community agencies by fielding concerns and intervening when necessary to help keep these partnerships healthy.

Equally important to the success of a program is the commitment of the administrator to the concept. For example, an administrator's support is crucial in arranging coverage for teachers who need school time to implement projects and in assisting in the flexible scheduling of service activities that interact with the regular school day. Creative funding for supplies and transportation is also evident in those settings where the administrator has made community service and the study of social issues a priority.

Willingness to Risk

In keeping with the philosophy that the process as well as the actual product are both avenues for student learning, the attitude of the adults involved in community service must be characterized by a willingness to "risk." Allowing students to "crash" can be a valuable tool for student growth and discussion though quite uncomfortable for both the supervising teacher and the children. This was true in the case where the job of two students in one class was to set up a date for the class trip to a retirement village. The teacher made plans for the class to arrive at their destination based on the date given him by the two students only to find out, when they all arrived, that they were not expected until the following week. In retrospect, the teacher admits that he probably should have called to confirm the arrangements made by the student representatives, but he had not wanted to undermine their initiative and independence. Fortunately, the date for students to entertain and serve lunch was rescheduled. The students who "goofed" were forgiven after the teacher helped the stranded class deal with their own anger and disappointment, thereby using the whole experience as an opportunity for a worthwhile lesson.

Another teacher entered the unfamiliar territory of the kitchen to help his students make lollipops to sell as one part of their service program. But, in the subsequent evaluation, the majority of students shared the contention that their teacher made an error in mixing the recipe, causing the suckers to "taste like crud." Undaunted, the teacher survived the incident and has fearlessly and enthusiastically entered his second year of assisting his Focus class with community service projects.

Recognition

Student recognition for participation in service can be varied in type and content. When the recipients of the service write thank-you notes or express their appreciation verbally, students respond well, but less traditional forms of recognition should not be underestimated or overlooked. By planning ahead for someone to take photos or produce a video of the implementation stage of the community service project, the class can experience repeated enjoyment and encouragement each time they view the visual reminder. The school newsletter and local newspaper can also surprise students by featuring their community project as important news.

Many agencies have their own system for recognizing those who provide service to them. Students were thrilled when they dropped off their collection of canned goods at a safehouse shelter and were treated to a tour of the facility by the director. His description of the program and introduction of the students to other volunteers gave them a sense of importance and appreciation. The best recognition one class could imagine came in the form of a road sign signifying that their Focus class was responsible for "adopting" that particular stretch of highway. "It's a nice feeling to see the sign and be able to say I cleaned this road," boasted usually quiet and reserved Devin.

Parents and faculty members should not overlook the ever-increasing number of local and federal award programs designed to recognize students who provide community service. The city's local Compassion Award given to Melissa for her tireless one-on-one work with a student who is profoundly disabled provided a tremendous lift for a girl who is typically viewed by her classmates as being a "loner or wanna-be." Melissa privately shared her pleasure at receiving the award when she told her school counselor, "At least grown-ups don't think what I like to do is weird." On the other hand, sometimes extrinsic rewards can be a disappointment, as one class discovered when a staff member at one facility where they served said, "Oh, thanks" in a tone that signified that his words were only an afterthought.

The most precious kind of recognition seemed to come in less obvious ways for many students. After participating in litter pick-up around school grounds and being asked if he had received any thanks for his work, Matt, a mature honor student, sighed contentedly, "Just seeing a clean field is enough for me." Liz, a quiet sixth-grader who, with her Focus class, spent time entertaining residents at a care center, felt fulfilled when one woman told her that seeing the students perform made her smile for the first time in six months. Another student who participated in the same project felt appreciated because she remembered, "Most people clapped, grinned, and held us tight. It didn't just help them; it helped me too."

MAJOR STUDENT OUTCOMES

Information about student outcomes resulting from participation in the community service program at Westview Middle School was gathered via verbal and written surveys. All students, teachers, and parents were invited to provide input through one or both of these methods. Their responses were overwhelmingly positive and seemed to center around three distinct themes (which will be discussed shortly). In an attempt to preserve the purity of the feedback, many direct quotes will be used to illustrate the outcomes.

Fostering Continued Service Involvement

Many students responded to the survey by stating that the community service program they experienced in school led to their continued participation in service. A high percentage of these responses came from students who had direct contact with senior citizens during their projects. Their continuation of service has come in the form of visits, letters, and making "goodies" for their senior friends.

Other students have extended their service to other settings. Shanna, a stylish, high-achieving 12-year-old, has started collecting surplus clothing to give to the Salvation Army, while Britt, an enthusiastic red head, makes a point of picking up any litter that she sees because of what she learned during her project. One parent expressed delight that the recycling project her son conducted at school has made him more willing to help with recycling at home. A number of students said they discovered new ways to help others and expressed a new interest in pursuing careers that involve service.

As the school year was coming to an end, it was found that a number of students who had participated in community service projects had received so many intrinsic or extrinsic rewards that they were "hooked on service." Students were directed to the counselors when they told their teachers that with summer coming soon they didn't know who needed help the most, but wanted to continue to serve the community. These students who are self-proclaimed "service addicts" say that they now see so many needs that they have developed a commitment to serve whenever possible.

Breaking Harmful Stereotypes

When it came to dispelling stereotypes about the people they met during the community service program, students felt most mistaken about their former impressions of the homeless and seniors. Following their visit to the homeless shelter, three students, who were equally unaware of those less fortunate because their family status had insulated them, showed their eyes had been opened from the experience:

> Before, all I thought was that these people [the homeless] were old and poor. Now I know they are just like me.—Becky, a 12-year-old with the innocent look of a younger child

> Homeless people aren't always dirty and gross.—Caleb, a sheltered seventh-grade boy

> Homeless people are just like normal people and have normal feelings too. Now I can understand why some people are homeless.—Michelle, a pretty girl with dark hair and eyes

When referring to senior citizens, these students also saw the error in their former opinions:

> I learned that old persons are people too, and they need help from us, but they need love and respect from everybody.—Alicia, a smiling, pleasant seventh-grader

Old people aren't as mean and stubborn as they're made out to be.—
Barry, a wise cracking jock

Older people are not just crazy people with a bad memory. They have a
great sense of humor and know much more than you or me.—Liz, an
active vocalist and artist

Perhaps the most touching example of how breaking a harmful stereotype
can be a positive outcome of community service was one described by Melanie's
mother, who explained: "My mother is quickly approaching the stage when
she'll have to be moved into a care facility. This move is quite difficult for my
daughter to accept, but this service project helped her to understand that these
facilities are not bad and that change in perception has been very comforting for
her."

In addition to the harmful stereotypes that are dispelled relating to the recipients of the service, other progress toward open-mindedness can result among
those conducting the community service projects. Darby, who is a popular, aloof,
star athlete, was as disgusted as the rest of his class with their collective lack of
progress in organizing a celebration for local elementary school students. But
when Wendy, who he had viewed as a "nerd," started assigning people to tasks
and putting the entire class into motion, Darby started to see her in a different
light. "She might not be a lot like me, but when it comes to getting all of us
going, she was a hero. Without her, our project would not have been a great
success." Darby's words of respect translated into positive change evidenced
by his new willingness to treat Wendy in a friendly, open manner.

Enhancing Student Attitudes about Service

In addition to the negative stereotypes that changed for many students during
community service activities, there were also new perceptions formed about
service in general. Some of those perceptions dealt with the age, time, or resources needed to perform meaningful service. Four eighth-graders showing,
the optimism of their age, stated:

I learned that even as kids we can still make a difference.—Nate

When you are a young man or woman you get a lot of age discrimination by people who think we're too young to change something, but I
learned it's a bunch of hogwash.—Andie

You can take 10 minutes a day and it can change the whole day of a
needy person.—Megan

Now I know it's not as hard as you think to help someone. And the
reward is greater than any cash one.—Nick

Two seventh-graders—as different as the nervous, excitable Aaron who has few friends to Katrina, the totally involved student athlete who has many admirers—had similar feelings:

> It showed me I could help some people hundreds of miles away without leaving my own hometown.—Aaron

> Most of the time you think that the only way you can cheer people up is to buy them something they have always wanted, but all that the people at the nursing home need is a 15-minute visit.—Katrina

THE STORY CONTINUES . . .

Since each student and adult is a member of the world community, there will always be a need for social issues to be examined and addressed and for service to be provided. Helping students to realize the privilege they inherit by being an active participant in such a process is a goal that educators can cherish. Therefore, in no small sense, the future of the world community depends on the success of this pursuit. As Jacob, the young man mentioned at the outset of this chapter, said, "We, in our schools, can make a difference."

REFERENCES

Clark, Todd. (1993, Spring). "Preparing Citizens through Service." *Constitutional Rights Fund Network, 4*(2): 1–4.

George, Patricia (Ed.). (1993, September). "Community Service Promotes Student Awareness." *Schools in the Middle, 3*(1) : 24.